PRACTICAL BUSINESS LAW

John Jude Moran, J.D.

Assistant Professor of Business Law
Wagner College

Adjunct Professor of Business Law
Saint Peter's College

PRENTICE-HALL, INC., Englewood Cliffs, New Jersey 07632

Library of Congress Cataloging in Publication Data

MORAN, JOHN JUDE.
  Practical business law.

  Includes index.
  1. Commercial law—United States. I. Title.
KF889.M67 1985   346.73'07   84-26482
ISBN 0-13-689027-X   347.3067

Editorial/production supervision
  and interior design: Linda C. Mason
Cover design: Edsal Enterprises
Manufacturing buyer: Ed O'Dougherty

Printed in the United States of America
10 9 8 7 6 5 4 3 2 1

ISBN 0-13-689027-X 01

Prentice-Hall International, Inc., *London*
Prentice-Hall of Australia Pty. Limited, *Sydney*
Editora Prentice-Hall do Brasil, Ltda., *Rio de Janeiro*
Prentice-Hall Canada Inc., *Toronto*
Prentice-Hall Hispanoamericana, S.A., *Mexico*
Prentice-Hall of India Private Limited, *New Delhi*
Prentice-Hall of Japan, Inc., *Tokyo*
Prentice-Hall of Southeast Asia Pte. Ltd., *Singapore*
Whitehall Books Limited, *Wellington, New Zealand*

This book is dedicated to my mother and my grandmother.

CONTENTS

CONTRACT LAW

PREFACE

Successful teaching begets successful learning. To accomplish this, the text presents pinciples of law in a simple step-building approach; illustrates those principles with stimulating examples; and aids the student in remembering the many principles of law in an original way.

Practical Business Law is a simple approach to the law with a foundation of legal principles explained in layman's language. The principles are illustrated through the use of practical cases and examples. This provides the student with a book he or she can truly understand and appreciate. At the same time, the text affords the professor the opportunity to discuss the principles more fully by introducing his or her own examples and instances of practical experience.

The purpose of an example is to explain a principle of law by utilizing factual circumstances. Examples, if vivid and interesting, can help the student remember particular points of law. To capture the students' interest, each chapter contains examples using characters and factual settings which occur in our everyday lives. Some of these examples are humorous. The usual examples concerning transactions between *A* and *B*, or *XYZ* corporation, are monotonous and do not lend themselves to easy memorization.

The ultimate task in learning is to apply the principles of law to factual situations. This can be accomplished through the use of cases and chapter review questions to stimulate class discussions. Cases will be included in each chapter that focus on the important principles of law to be learned. These cases and the review questions at the end of each chapter will be extracted from actual cases to enhance class discussions while providing the student with a pragmatic view of the reasoning behind court discussions.

This book contains forty chapters divided into five categories: introduction to the law, contract law, commercial law, property law, and business law. This is designed to accommodate schools offering basic and advanced law courses, as well as those offering individual courses in contracts, property, corporations and partnerships, and the Uniform Commercial Code.

J.J. Moran, J.D.

1

THE HISTORY OF LAW

INTRODUCTION

There are two basic systems of law in the free world. One system is based on a code; the other system is based on case law. The code system was founded on Roman law, conceived during the Roman Republic and the Roman Empire. Roman law was codified in the sixth century by Justinian I, and was called the Justinian Code. After the fall of the Roman Empire, Roman law lay dormant for over six hundred years, until it was revived in the twelfth century in Italian universities. Students studied the Justinian Code, and the popularity of Roman law soon spread throughout the European continent. After the French Revolution, Napoleon codified Roman law into the Napoleonic Code, which has become known as the French Civil Code. This code has served as the model and the foundation for the law of many countries throughout the world, including those in continental Europe, Central and South America, South Africa, as well as in the Province of Quebec and the state of Louisiana.

The case law system has evolved out of the English common law, which had its birth in the Middle Ages. English common law relies on the written opinions of judges and the principle of precedent; the latter being commonly referred to by its Latin meaning, *stare decisis*. For example, if a case has been decided one way in the past, English common law dictates that all similiar cases thereafter should be decided in the same way for purposes of uniformity, unless such a decision would be clearly against the weight of the evidence or in violation of one's conscience. The common law came into its own in the seventeenth, eighteenth, and nineteenth centuries. The common use of the printing press played a large part in its development, because the judges' opinions could then be reproduced in volume for reference and study.

The importance of case law can best be appreciated through its role in interpreting the endless stream of statutes, some of them vague, which come from the legislatures.

The laws of the United States, Great Britain, and in most of Canada are based on the case law method. The origin of the legal systems of these countries can be traced back to the common law of England. The development of both of these legal systems is interrelated with religion, philosophy, history, politics, and sociology. The discussion that follows is a brief description of the historical origins of the two systems of law that prevail today.

THE ORIGIN OF LAW

When people lived in caves, the parents, as head of the family, had the primary responsibility of insuring that family customs were passed on to their children, who in turn passed them on to their children, and so on.

Conformity was often imposed upon the young through severe physical tests or even torture. It was believed that torture insured conformity. As families grew, tribes developed. The customs of the family then became the customs of the tribe. When tribes fought with one another, the victors imposed their customs upon the conquered, who usually became enslaved or melded into the victorious tribe. Property rights were an outgrowth of this consequence. Children were taught that what was given to them, what they found or hunted, and what they conquered in battle, was theirs. The right of personal property ownership extended to tools, hunting and fishing equipment, food, and slaves. If one member of the tribe stole from another, the punishment imposed might include exile or death. The right to own real property was the most highly regarded of all rights. With ownership of land came power. Greater territorial rights meant a greater hunting and fishing area, and perhaps the choice of a safer location for shelter. Tribal battles were fought over land and personal property. Many battles began because of a violation of territorial rights. As societies became more developed, central governments were established and laws were enacted to govern the people.

Laws are only as successful as the willingness of people to abide by them. There is a need for uniformity of laws among people. Alexander the Great conquered the world, but his empire fell apart because he had no uniform laws with which to govern the people. The Roman Empire endured for such a long time because, after their conquests, the Romans governed the conquered people with an established set of laws and regulations.

ROMAN LAW

The Romans worshipped many gods and believed that the will of the gods controlled human conduct. The Romans' early system of government was controlled by individual clans independent of one another. They were self-governing, implementing the customs of the clan. The elders held executive, legislative, and judicial power. The clans increased and eventually formed the city of Rome. Roman law developed from the customs of the clans. The priests were considered the custodians of the law because they were usually very powerful and among the most highly educated. People sought them out for advice and requested them to settle disputes.

Property had great importance to the Roman family, because power to govern usually went with it. It was out of property law that contract law developed. The law of contracts gave people the right to trade their property with one another. The making of a contract was considered sacred; it required a ritual performed by a priest before whom promises were made. A promise was binding, as long as the proper formalities were carried out. Contracts were used for the following purposes: transfer of property; making of loans; employment; sale of goods; and formation of syndicates, joint ventures, agencies, and partnerships. A monetary system was created as a substitute for bartering; and contracts for buying and selling became prevalent with the use of coin money. The system of banking was predicated on the lending of money in return for the payment of interest. Loans were granted based on a pledge of collateral as security, or based on the general credit of the borrower; but if payment could not be made, the borrower would be taken as a slave until the loan was repaid. Usury laws were established to set a maximum rate of interest that could be charged on a loan. As commerce grew, partnerships originated involving two or more individuals who decided to administer their businesses jointly by sharing in the profits and by being liable for the partnership's debts. Joint ventures were also established for a single common goal, usually a trading voyage. The joint venture was dissolved upon the completion of the voyage. Syndicates, consisting of many members and managed by a board of directors, similiar to our corporations, were formed to develop and finance various businesses and projects. Guilds and unions of craftsmen were also formed.

The law of wills was created to determine the disposition of a person's real and personal property upon death. The father, as patriarch, had a duty to support and protect his family. On his death, his property passed down his bloodline. This meant that children could inherit only from their fathers.

Tort law grew in response to the right of the people to be secure in their person and in their property. Tort laws concerning fraud, duress, and negligence developed with restitution being the remedy for the redress of private offenses, along with the imposition of a penalty to deter future wrongdoing. People were also responsible for the acts of agents or servants who were in their employ. Personal injuries including mutilations were also torts, but the remedy at that time was retribution: "an eye for an eye."

The Roman Republic

Rome's republican form of government was composed of an upper and a lower assembly. The upper assembly, called the senate, was composed of 600 members appointed for life, all of whom were ex-magistrates. Magistrates were local leaders, similar to our town mayors, usually the heads of powerful upper-class families. The senate proposed legislation at the request of a magistrate. The lower assembly was chosen from among the people (plebeians). The assembly initiated legislation at the direction of the tribunes, who were magistrates appointed to protect the rights of the people against the patricians. The highest authority, the consuls, were elected by the people in the assembly, however only the chief priests could nominate the candidates. The tribune's authority permitted a certain number of plebeians to rise to power. These individuals, together with the patricians, controlled the senate and formed a new class of nobles that dominated the republican form of government. The mass of the people had no voice because a sufficient number of upper-class citizens frustrated the people's attempts at equality in representation and decision making.

The plebeians resented the way the senate controlled and manipulated the government, and constant clashes were the result. With such widespread discontent, the time was ripe for someone to take advantage of the situation. That someone was Julius Caesar. He and Pompey held the position of consul. Caesar had long identified himself with the common people who opposed senate rule. He worked his way up through the governmental ranks and, after his term as consul, he served as governor in Gaul (which now encompasses France). Caesar's military exploits in the west only seemed to infuriate the senate and create jealousy in the heart of Pompey. The senate ordered Caesar to give up his command and return to Rome as a private citizen. Instead, Caesar marched on Rome and sent Pompey and the senators fleeing for their lives. He pursued them and defeated their forces in Egypt, North Africa, and Spain in 45 B.C. This left Caesar as the military leader of the Roman world, throughout which Roman law was imposed.

The Roman Empire

Caesar envisioned the expansion of the Roman Empire with himself as monarch. He had begun the process of dismantling the republican form of government and building the monarchy when a group of hostile nobles, led by Brutus and Cassius, assassinated him in the senate chambers. But what Caesar had begun could not be suppressed. Augustus, Caesar's adopted heir, succeeded him and became the first emperor of Rome. After two and a half centuries of dictatorial rule, the Roman Empire, early in the third century A.D., began to show signs of economic and military weakness. This weakness can be attributed to widespread moral decadence and a general demoralization of the people. In the meantime, the Germanic tribes were being pushed west by Slavic invasions, to the boarder of the West Roman Empire. The Romans had become languid and could not muster sufficient forces to stop the constant invasions. The fall of the Roman Empire began early in the fifth century when the Visigoths, a Germanic tribe, invaded Rome. The Roman emperor was ousted in A.D. 476. The title was reclaimed by Justinian I in A.D. 535, but the resurgence of the Roman Empire was short-lived. In A.D. 565, Justinian died and the empire was to rise no more. In spite of this, during his rule, Justinian completed the most influential civil code ever written.

The Justinian Code, better known as the Roman Civil Code, is the final compilation of the laws of ancient Rome. It contains over 4,600 separate laws and is comprised of fifty Digests which capsulize the decisions of the classical jurists from 25 B.C. to A.D. 225 and twelve Codes which include legislation adopted from A.D. 275 to the sixth century, when Justinian had the Code prepared. There were also Institutes, which were educational textbooks having statutory authority, and Novels which were actually additions to the Code that contained the legislation propounded during Justinian's reign.

REVIVAL OF ROMAN LAW

The revival of Roman Law began in the twelfth century in the Italian universities where students began to study the Roman Civil Code. This practice spread throughout continental Europe over the centuries that followed. In 1795, after the French Revolution, the French drafted a constitution creating a conservative republic held by five directors. The constitution also provided for separation of church and state, abolition of slavery, implementation of the metric system, and the scientific codification of French law.

Napoleon Bonaparte established a coup d'état under the guise of parliamentary and democratic reform, and set up a Consulate with himself as the First Consul. This form of government and the term *consul* was derived from the Roman Republic. Napoleon also created the Bank of France, but his greatest achievement came in 1804 when the first of five codes, known originally as the Code Napoléon, was finally completed. The codes were based on the Roman Civil Code. The first code was the Civil Code, containing 2,281 articles. Four more codes were drafted in the years 1807, 1808, and 1811. These four codes were the Code of Commerce, the Penal Code, the Administrative Code, and the Acts of Chambers of Deputees. These five codes of law and procedure captured the revolutionary ideals of liberty and equality. The five codes of Napoleon, as modified and supplemented by other laws, case decisions, and treatises, became known as the French Civil Code. This code has been adopted around the free world, except in those countries where English common law has been adopted.

ENGLISH LAW

Britain was originally inhabited by the Celts. Julius Caesar made two conquering expeditions to Britain, and as a result, Rome was in control until the early fifth century, when they were forced to relinquish control as a result of a series of barbarian invasions. In the seventh century, three Germanic tribes, the Angles, the Saxons, and the Jutes, took control of Britain and drove the Celts westward to Ireland. The name *England* means the land of the Angles.

Each of these three tribes ruled a portion of England, and an attempt was made to establish a democratic system of government. The township was a unit of their government, which advocated independence for individuals and freedom of election. Courts of the town were administered by the elders. The representatives of each town would meet at designated intervals as a court of appeals, known at that time as *Hundred Moot*, to decide appeals from individuals and to arbitrate disputes among towns. The highest court of the land was known as the Folk Moot.

In the latter part of the ninth century, the Danes, a Scandinavian tribe, attempted to conquer and settle England, but were defeated through the leadership of Alfred the Great. Alfred the Great paved the way for a united kingdom, which came about in the middle of the tenth century.

In 1066, William the Conqueror led the Normans in the conquest of England. William confiscated the land for himself and his Norman followers, and established feudalism. His followers became barons, lords of the fief. In return, they had to promise to serve the king in the military and judiciary, in addition to making payments of money. The barons rebelled, unsuccessfully at first, in opposition to this tyranny, but their perserverance paid off. The kings were soon forced to recognize their power and the barons kept the kings in check. The government became more efficient in administration by developing its own councils and courts.

Conflicts between the barons and the successive kings arose again. In 1215, the barons drew up a schedule of reforms which they forced King John to sign. This became known as the Magna Carta. It provided that no freeman could be deprived of life, liberty, or property without due process of law. The provision can be found in the Fifth and Fourteenth Amendments to the United States Constitution. The effect of this provision was of monumental importance because it made the king and his government subject to the law. Whenever the people felt the king had infringed upon their rights, they could turn to the Magna Carta for redress. The Magna Carta contained sixty-three chapters, dealing with freedom of religion, right of inheritance, freedom of trade, and right to trial by jury.

In the thirteenth century, the foundation for a representative form of government was laid. On several occasions, discussions were held between the king, the assembly of his vassals, and middle-class freemen; and by the close of the reign of Edward I, the tradition had been established. The people had a representative assembly, but with only advisory status; it lacked power. The barons consulted the Magna Carta and discovered one of its provisions prohibited the king from assessing and collecting nonfeudal taxes without the consent of a representative assembly. Since the king was heavily dependent upon the revenues from these taxes, the assembly used its consent as leverage to get more of a voice in the affairs of the country. The Magna Carta was confirmed and laws were passed regarding separation of church and state, limited jurisdiction of the church and the courts, abolition of arbitrary taxes, abolition of the king's right to interfere in private disputes, freedom of election, right to hold property, administration of justice and criminal law, and legal procedure through the use of writs. A writ is a legal document calling for the prohibition of certain actions by the party against whom it is sworn. The correct writ had to be chosen or the aggrieved individual would forfeit his or her right to a remedy.

This representative form of government became the foundation for the present-day English Parliament. During the thirteenth century, the population of many towns grew greatly in number. These towns were granted royal charters, which earmarked the birth of self-government. During the next century, Parliament strengthened its power over taxation and with that, its power to negotiate with the king. The representatives of the rural districts combined with the representatives of the towns to form a collective group which was to become the House of Commons. The barons, who were politically influential at the time, became the House of Lords.

In the fourteenth century, Inns of Court originated. Learned men of the law congregated in the Inns to discuss legal matters. Students voluntarily gathered to hear lectures and to study law. They read the law and observed court proceedings, and eventually were called to the bar and admitted to practice.

The invention of the printing press by Gutenberg in 1438 was a great aid in the development of the law and democracy. The printing press reproduced the law which then became available to all citizens who could read. In prior centuries, the law was restricted to the select few who had access to the limited number of transcripts.

In the 1600s, two important statutes were enacted. The Statute of Frauds required certain contracts to be made in writing, in order to prevent fraud. The Habeas Corpus Act gave people the right to know on what grounds they were being detained, or if they were being deprived of their liberty.

COMMON LAW

In England, the common law originated in the kings' courts during the Middle Ages. Laws were made by the judges with the decision dependent on their common sense. This was a vast improvement over the previous methods, such as trial by ordeal and trial by battle. Nevertheless, harsh decisions resulted either from the judges' temperament or by their adherence to a strict construction of the law. The necessity to curtail this problem led to the birth of the King's Court of Chancery, which dealt with matters equitably, based on fairness. The Chancellors now using principles of equity would hear cases when a common law remedy was not satisfactory. At times, Chancellors would advocate strict construction of the law, and the differentiation between the law of equity and the common law would be slim; but equity would soon prevail. Our present system of law permits courts to administer both legal and equitable remedies.

The common law provided the parties with the right to a jury trial. The basic remedy under the common law was money damages, as opposed to the many possible equitable remedies. Modern case law encompasses both common law and the law of equity. In our legal system, statutory or code law is promulgated by the legislature. Statutory law preempts case law where it is applicable. In all areas not preempted, case law has precedence.

The common law differed from the Roman law in that the common law was centered around the decisions made by the judges, whereas Roman law was centered around a code promulgated by the legislature. The Roman Civil code covered all areas of the law. The judge need only look to the code for the resolution. In the Anglo-American system founded on common law, the jury must interpret the facts and the judge must apply the appropriate law. The common law (or case law) system is centered on the judge and the jury. Under this system, the law changes with society's norms because judges have the discretion to fashion their decisions to each case's particular set of facts. In a code system, on the other hand, change can only come about through legislative amendments to the code.

LAW OF THE MERCHANT

The age of commerce reigned supreme from 1350 to 1650, starting with the birth of the Hanseatic League. This was a compact formed by various cities for the purpose of trading with one another without the imposition of tariffs. The league adopted a federal constitution, and an assembly met once a year to discuss issues of foreign policy and internal management, and to legislate regulations. Cities that did not observe the regulations were expelled from membership in the league. As nations gained internal strength, the cities no longer had use for the league.

The law of the merchant had its birth in the league, and continued to grow thereafter. The law of the merchant developed along with the growth of commerce.

There was a need for a uniform set of laws for national and international commerce. Promissory notes were invented to obviate pirates and robbers while traveling. Bills of exchange were also used; and these became promissory notes upon endorsement. The merchants' law of trade and commerce was recognized as early as 1600 by Lord Coke, the chief justice of England. He permitted the law to be used as evidence of a custom. In 1750, the law of the merchant was adapted into the English common law and enforced by the courts; then in the late 1800s, it was codified, and thus given statutory authority. In the same century, the French codified it into their Civil Code. The law of the merchant was finally codified by the United States into what is now called the Uniform Commercial Code (UCC). The law of the merchant provided the foundation for the development of the following areas of the law:

Contracts for the sale of goods, simply known as Sales
Commercial Paper, also known as Negotiable Instruments
Agency
Partnerships including Joint Ventures
Insurance
Trademarks

2

THE AMERICAN LEGAL SYSTEM

HISTORY OF THE AMERICAN LEGAL SYSTEM

In 1607, Jamestown became the first permanent English settlement in America. It was funded by a group of merchants known as the London Company. The first local council was assembled in 1608, with John Smith as its president. The House of Burgesses was the first representative assembly in America. It was convened in 1619, just eleven years after that first council was called together. The House of Burgesses was composed of two representatives from each settlement.

In 1620, a group of Pilgrims landed at Plymouth Rock in Massachusetts. They were funded by the Plymouth Rock Company, a group of stockholders. Upon arriving in America, forty-one Pilgrims signed the Mayflower Compact, the first constitution in America, thereby forming a "civill Body politick . . . to enacte, constitute, and frame such juste and equall laws, ordinances, acts, constitutions, and offices, from time to time, as shall be thought most meete and convenient for the generall good of the Colonie unto which we promise all due submission and obedience." The right to vote was based on the ownership of property; citizenship was restricted to the religious orthodox; trial by jury was guaranteed for criminal matters, trespass, and the nonpayment of debts; while estates of decedents had to be administered one month after death.

Though there were local interpretations, the English common law became the basis for law in America where the English colonized and conquered. It soon spread throughout America as this nation expanded.

In 1700, the Supreme Judicial Court of Massachusetts was founded as the highest court in the state, which it remains today. The practice of law was recognized as a profession in 1701. A lawyer's oath was formulated and required upon admission to the bar.

The heavy taxes imposed on the colonists by Great Britain, along with the lack of representation, led to the revolutionary war. The Sugar Act of 1764, the Stamp Act in 1765, and the tax on tea which, in 1773, led to the Boston Tea Party, all provided the reason for the constant cry "No taxation without representation." The colonists were actually not looking for complete independence; they merely wanted a more conciliatory attitude from Great Britain, but that was not the result. As punishment for the Boston Tea Party, Parliament passed, in 1774, the so-called Intolerable Acts, which were designed to crush the revolutionary tendencies of the colonists. The Intolerable Acts were actually the culmination of the oppressive acts by Great Britain that would lead the way toward the revolutionary war. The American Revolution began the following year.

The First Continental Congress was established following a resolution proposed by the Virginia House of Burgesses, which recommended that representatives of all colonies meet "to deliberate on those general measures which the united interests of America may from time to time require." Fifty-five members from twelve colonies met in Philadelphia on September 5, 1774. They met for seven weeks, and as a result declared thirteen acts of Parliament as infringing upon their rights as colonists; petitioned the king of England; addressed the people of Great Britain; solicited the French government for support; and advised all the colonists to terminate trade with Great Britain.

The Second Continental Congress met on May 10, 1775. A month later, it declared war on Great Britain and resolved that a Continental army should be raised. The Second Continental Congress served as a quasi-national government until the outcome of the revolutionary war, in 1781.

After the Declaration of Independence was signed on July 4, 1776, the Articles of Confederation were drafted and submitted to the Second Continental Congress, which in turn offered the articles to the states for ratification.

There was no executive or judicial branch of government authorized by the Articles of Confederation. As a result, there was no president or federal court system. All legal matters were left to the individual state courts, including the regulation of interstate commerce. The Second Continental Congress had no power to assess and collect taxes. The congress could determine only what was needed and suggest that cost be apportioned among the states according to the value of the real estate in each state. General Washington, while commanding the colonial forces, repeatedly asked for money and men, but the Second Continental Congress had a difficult time meeting his demands because of their lack of power.

The inherent weakness in the Articles of Confederation was that the governing power was reserved to the states. Since the states were not equal in such things as population and commerce, the more powerful states would be able to exercise greater control over the weaker states, with the Second Continental Congress being relegated to the position of a figurehead. There was a need for the uniting of the states under a strong central government which would have the power to deal directly with the people rather than through the states.

An assembly of state delegates met for a constitutional convention during the summer of 1787 to draft a national constitution which would supersede the Articles of Confederation. Various state delegates made conflicting proposals, and finally a compromise was adopted on July 16, 1787. It provided for equal representation in the House of Representatives based on state population. The Senate represented the states and the House of Representatives represented the people. Congress was given the power to regulate interstate and foreign commerce, an important change from the Articles of Confederation. The only irreconcilable dispute was between the northern and southern states over the issue of slavery. The resolution of this issue was put off to a later date. There was broad newspaper coverage and discussion on the proposed Constitution. "The Federalist Papers" provided essays and commentaries on the proposals. It took three years for all thirteen states to ratify the Constitution. But on September 13, 1788, the Second Continental Congress proclaimed the ratification by nine states and directed the new government to convene on March 4, 1789 with George Washington as the first elected president.

UNITED STATES CONSTITUTION

The United States Constitution was adopted on September 17, 1787 and ratified thereafter by the original thirteen states. There are seven articles in the Constitution. The first article speaks to the legislative powers of the Congress consisting of a Senate and a House of Representatives. The Senate is representative of the states with each state having two senators. The House is representative of the people with the number of representatives apportioned among the states according to population. Congress can exercise its legislative power to create laws through the origin of a bill, and its passage in both the House and the Senate. The bill is then presented to the president for confirmation. If he signs the bill, it becomes law. If he chooses to veto the bill, it returns to the House with his objections. After reconsidering the bill, the House and the Senate can override the president's veto by a two-thirds majority vote.

Congress has the power to collect taxes and duties; pay the debts of the United States; provide for the common defense and general welfare of the people; borrow money; regulate interstate and foreign commerce; establish uniform bankruptcy laws throughout the United States; coin money; establish courts inferior to the Supreme Court; declare war; and make all laws necessary and proper for executing its congressional powers. Congress' two most effective ways of regulating individuals and businesses are the taxing power and the power to regulate interstate and foreign commerce.

The taxing power has a strong effect on the activity of businesses and individuals who are subject to the particular taxes enacted. The main thrust of the tax must be to raise money, not to regulate. This must be accomplished through a method which is uniform throughout the states. A determination must be made as to the purpose of the tax. The provisions of the tax must be examined and a projection of the effect of the tax must be made. The fact that the main purpose of the tax must be to raise revenue does not, in practice, curtail Congress' power to regulate, since raising revenue is relatively easy to justify. Even if the main purpose of a tax is regulatory in nature, it may still be upheld if it is necessary and proper. To be necessary and proper, the regulatory effect must be to collect or enforce the tax; or must be within the realm of one of the other enumerated congressional powers; and must not be in violation of any of the constitutional protections afforded by the first ten amendments, the Bill of Rights.

In regard to commerce, Congress has the power to regulate anything which directly or indirectly has a substantial effect on commerce. Congress has exclusive power with regard to foreign commerce. In regard to interstate commerce, Congress' power is concurrent with the states except where there exists a conflict between Congress and a state legislature. In such cases, Congress can preempt the state legislature. Interstate commerce extends to all commercial activities that affect more than one state, including crime, labor disputes, wage and price controls, and racial discrimination. Even intrastate activities which have an effect on interstate commerce are within the purview of regulation under the commerce clause. The only criteria that must be satisfied are that a rational basis exists for finding that goods, services, or people's conduct affect commerce; and that the means selected by Congress to regulate be reasonable, appropriate, and not in violation of any fundamental rights protected by the Bill of Rights. The spending power is another important power which must be considered. Under its spending power, Congress can create federally funded programs, such as social security and welfare, which have a profound effect on the lives of individuals.

The second article of the Constitution describes the executive branch of government, which is invested in a president and a vice-president for a four-year term. The power of the president includes the authority to act as commander-in-chief of the armed forces; to make treaties; and to appoint ambassadors, judges of the Supreme Court, cabinet members, and other executive officials with the advise and consent of the Senate. The president takes an oath of office to execute faithfully all laws of the United States.

The third article of the Constitution creates the judicial branch of the government. The power of judicial review is given to one Supreme Court and to other inferior courts created by Congress. The power to exercise judicial review encompasses cases where a legal remedy is sought, as well as cases where an equitable remedy is requested. The jurisdiction of the Supreme Court and the other inferior courts is restricted to cases arising under the Constitution and the federal statutes; controversies in which the United States is a party; and disputes between two or more states, or between citizens of different states.

The fourth article of the Constitution delineates the full faith and credit laws: Each state shall give full faith and credit to the laws of every other state. The priviledges and immunities clause prohibits arbitrary discrimination against citizens of other states. The individual states are guaranteed a republican form of government and protection against both invasion from without, as well as domestic violence from within.

The fifth article provides the method for making amendments. A two-thirds vote of both the House and the Senate is required to propose an amendment to the Constitution. The amendment must be ratified by three-fourths of the state legislatures.

The sixth article declares the Constitution shall be the supreme law of the land, and the courts in every state shall be bound by it. The officers in each of the three branches of government must take an oath binding them to support the Constitution.

The seventh article conditioned the establishment of this Constitution on the ratification of the conventions of nine states.

BILL OF RIGHTS

On December 15, 1791, the fifth article of the Constitution was invoked and the first ten amendments were adopted and immediately ratified. These amendments were in response to the widespread feeling in several state conventions that the Constitution did not adequately safeguard individual liberties. These ten amendments are known as the Bill of Rights because they define individuals' rights with respect to liberty, and because they are analogous to the Bill of Rights adopted by England in 1689 that proclaimed political liberties for all Englishmen.

Many of our individual rights and freedoms are protected by the First Amendment: freedom of religion, freedom of speech, and freedom of the press; the right of the people to assemble in a peaceful manner; and the right of the people to petition the government for a redress of grievances. The establishment clause of the First Amendment prohibits the government from establishing a national regligion, thus insuring freedom of religion. The Second Amendment protects the rights of the people to keep and bear arms in order to secure and maintain a free state. There have been many attempts, some successful and some not, to restrict this amendment through the regulation of arms by gun-control laws. The Third Amendment protects the rights of homeowners to be secure in their homes by providing that soldiers shall not be allowed to take shelter there without the owner's permission.

The Fourth, Fifth, and Sixth Amendments have a profound impact on criminal proceedings. The Fourth Amendment protects people, their homes, and their effects against unreasonable searches and seizures by the state or federal government.

The Fifth Amendment guarantees the protection of life, liberty, and property by means of the due process clause; the right to an indictment by a grand jury for a capital offense; the right to be tried only once for a crime, thus prohibiting double jeopardy; the right to just compensation for property condemned for public use. The Fifth Amendment also guarantees the right to remain silent inherent in the privilege against self-incrimination. This is used most often in criminal investigations and is known as "taking the Fifth."

The Sixth Amendment insures the right to a speedy and public trial by an impartial jury of one's peers in the state where the crime was committed; the right to counsel in the preparation of a defense; the right, if indigent, to be provided with counsel without charge; and the right to be confronted by opposing witnesses.

The Seventh Amendment insures the right to a trial by jury in civil cases. The use of cruel and inhuman punishment is prohibited by the Eighth Amendment. The Ninth Amendment states that the rights set forth in the Constitution do not restrict or discredit other rights held by the people. The reserve clause of the Tenth Amendment states that all powers not delegated to the United States by the Constitution are reserved to the states or to the people. Initially, the Bill of Rights guaranteed protection of individual freedoms solely in relation to the federal government. It was not until 1868 that the Bill of Rights was applied to the states through the due process clause of the Fourteenth Amendment. There have been only sixteen additional amendments to the Constitution since the Bill of Rights was ratified in 1791.

FEDERAL COURT SYSTEM

The power of the federal courts to hear and decide legal issues is limited to causes of action involving $10,000 or more, based on violations of the Constitution or federal statutes, and to cases where there is diversity of citizenship. Diversity arises when plaintiff and defendant are citizens of different states. In cases involving multiple parties, diversity arises when there is no plaintiff or defendant from the same state. These cases may be started either in federal or state court. Federal courts will apply the law of the state which has the controlling interest in the lawsuit. If a plaintiff chooses to proceed in state court, the defendant may make a motion to move the case to federal court. The purpose of hearing diversity cases in federal court is to provide the out-of-state party with an impartial forum. This is designed to overcome potential bias of a state court in favor of the party who is domiciled there. Domicile is the state in which a person has his or her principal place of residence and in which he or she votes and pays taxes. The domicile of a corporation is the state in which it was incorporated and in which it has its principal place of business.

A plaintiff who brings a cause of action based upon a violation of a constitutional right, must prove that the violation directly inflicts an injury on the interest the plaintiff is seeking to protect. This interest must be within the zone of interests that the Constitution or federal statute is seeking to protect. In other words, the plaintiff must have a personal stake in the outcome of the case. This gives the plaintiff sufficient standing to sue in federal court.

The federal court system is composed of the following trial courts: Court of Claims, bankruptcy courts, Tax Court, Customs Court, and district courts; and the following appellate courts: circuit courts, Court of Customs and Patent Appeals, and the Supreme Court. See Figure 2-1.

United States Supreme Court is the highest court of the United States and is the only court directly created by the Constitution. There are nine justices, who sit on the Court with a lifetime term. They hear appeals from the following: the highest courts of each of the fifty states, the eleven circuit courts of appeals, the Court of Claims, and the Court of Customs and Patent Appeals. The Supreme Court reviews cases brought by right of appeal or writ of certiorari. Right of appeal is an appeal taken by a losing party from a decision made by any of the previously mentioned courts. Although a person has a right to bring an appeal, the Supreme Court may affirm the lower court's decision without an opinion, or summarily dismiss the appeal without a hearing. The Supreme Court will hear a case on a writ of certiorari when the dispute is timely, of great importance, and where conflicting decisions have been made regarding the case. When the Supreme Court hears a case, a majority of votes is required for a decision. An opinion is usually written by one of the justices in the majority; those agreeing for a different reason may write concurring opinions; and those disagreeing may write dissenting opinions espousing their belief.

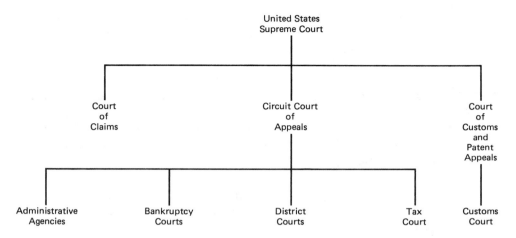

FIGURE 2-1 The Federal Court System

Circuit Court of Appeals is the first appellate court to which federal appeals are taken. The country is divided into ten circuits, with the courts being located in the major city in each circuit. The eleventh circuit is the District of Columbia, which requires its own circuit because of the large number of appeals involving the federal government. Appeals are heard from the bankruptcy courts, the Tax Court, the district courts, and administrative agencies such as the ICC, FTC, and FCC.

Court of Customs and Patent Appeals hears appeals from both the Customs Court and the United States Patent Office concerning patents and trademarks.

Court of Claims is a court of original jurisdiction with the authority to hear all claims made against the United States government except tort claims, which are heard by the district courts.

Customs Court is a trial court with limited jurisdiction to hear matters involving the classification of imported goods and the duties imposed on them.

Bankruptcy courts are located in each area where there is a district court. They have original jurisdiction in all matters involving bankruptcy.

Tax Court is located in Washington, D.C. It hears all matters regarding the Internal Revenue Code.

District courts are located in geographical districts throughout the United States. Each state has at least one district with some states, such as New York, California, and Texas, having upwards to four. District courts are trial courts which have unlimited general jurisdiction over all diversity cases and federal matters except those special matters which are covered by the trial courts with limited jurisdiction.

Administrative agencies are not courts, but each agency holds hearings regarding issues under the jurisdiction of the agency. The rulings made as a result of these hearings are appealable to the circuit courts of appeals. However, because of the technical nature of the subject matter, the decisions made by the respective agencies will generally not be overturned unless they are clearly arbitrary and capricious. Some of the more well known agencies are the Environmental Protection

Agency (EPA), Federal Communications Commission (FCC), Federal Trade Commission (FTC), Interstate Commerce Commission (ICC), Internal Revenue Service (IRS), and Securities and Exchange Commission (SEC).

REVIEW QUESTIONS

1. What are the three branches of government provided by the Constitution?
2. How is the United States Constitution, as adopted, preferable to the Articles of Confederation?
3. What are the Bill of Rights?
4. When and how were the Bill of Rights applied to the states?
5. In what situations will the federal courts hear and decide cases?
6. Describe the structure of the federal court system.

3

COURT PRACTICE AND PROCEDURE

INTRODUCTION

To begin a journey through the legal system, individuals must have a legal cause for action. A *cause of action* gives a person the legal right to sue another for damages suffered. It is their ticket of admission to the American legal system. A person initiating a lawsuit based on his or her legal right to sue, is known as the plaintiff. The person against whom the suit is brought is called the defendant. Damages are awarded for the harm suffered by the plaintiff. The defendant is the person who allegedly caused the harm or who is allegedly accountable for it. The person is held to be "allegedly" responsible until the outcome of the case is decided, under the theory that a person is innocent until proven guilty. The determination of actual liability is the reason the suit is brought: to see whether or not the defendent is responsible. Once a lawsuit is initiated, there are many rules of practice and procedure that must be followed to establish and prove a case. These include jurisdictional and evidentiary guidelines.

JURISDICTION

Jurisdiction is the authority the court must possess to hear and decide particular legal issues and to bind the parties involved to the court's decisions. Keeping in mind that rules of jurisdiction vary from state to state, the following discussion is predicated on those rules which are most representative.

Subject matter jurisdiction is the authority the court must possess to hear and decide particular legal issues. The requirement of subject matter jurisdiction may not be waived either by the court or the parties to the action. Personal jurisdiction is the court's authority over the parties involved in the lawsuit. The plaintiff must follow a procedure to obtain jurisdiction over the defendant's person and/or property in a civil case. Once jurisdiction is obtained, the court having subject matter jurisdiction may hear the case and render a decision which will bind both the plaintiff and the defendant.

Subject Matter Jurisdiction

The structure of a typical state court system is outlined in Figure 3-1. This structure is representative of most states, if not more complex, because some states do not have intermediate courts of appeals. There are two types of courts: trial courts and appellate courts. A lawsuit must begin in a trial court. The purpose of a trial is to resolve questions of fact. In most states, the supreme court is the highest court of the state, but in New York, the highest court is referred to as the court of appeals.

Appellate courts handle appeals from the trial courts. When a party is not pleased with a decision, that is, he or she feels that the law has been incorrectly applied, a "motion for an appeal" may be made and a notice of appeal must be served on the opposing party and filed with the trial court. The county courts and the courts below that level are the trial courts where most decisions are tried and determined.

An appeal is a review by a higher court as to the appropriateness of a lower court's application of law to the facts of the case. An appellate court may not review questions of fact unless they are against the weight of the evidence. A "question of fact" is an actual event which is disputed by the parties and which must be resolved in order for the principle of law to be applied. Where a jury trial is requested, the jury will determine questions of fact; otherwise, the judge will make the resolution. "Questions of law" are the application of principles of law to an agreed upon or resolved factual determination and are reserved to the judge.

The Court System of a Typical State

The *state supreme court* is the highest court in all states except New York. The supreme court decides appeals from the intermediate appellate courts, or from trial courts in the states which do not have intermediate courts. The supreme court's decisions bind all of the courts in the state as well as its citizens, unless preempted by the United States Supreme Court.

Appellate courts are intermediaries which act as a buffer between the trial courts and the supreme court. They are the first courts of appellate review. They hear appeals from all of the trial courts: county courts, family courts, probate courts, and courts of claims. In those states heavily congested with court cases, the appellate courts relieve the supreme court of the burden of deciding all appeals. They act as a filter that allows only the most important cases to flow to the supreme court.

County courts, also known as district courts, circuit courts, superior courts, courts of common pleas, and, in New York, as supreme courts, are courts of unlimited general jurisdiction. This means that they may hear any legal matters, with the following general exceptions: federal suits (federal courts); family altercation suits (family court); monetary suits against the state (court of claims); and matters relating to decedent's estates (probate court). Furthermore, the county courts' jurisdiction may be monetarily limited: for example, to suits involving $10,000 or more. If this is the case, there is another trial court of unlimited general jurisdiction to hear

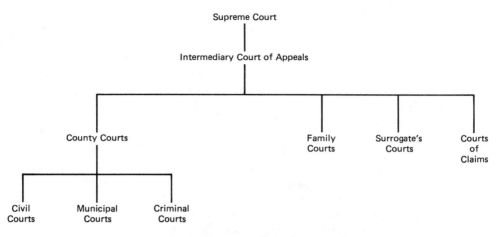

FIGURE 3-1 The Court System of a Typical State

matters involving less than $10,000. This court is usually referred to as the civil court or municipal court. Appeals from the county courts are made to the appellate court having jurisdiction over that particular county.

Courts of claims have exclusive jurisdiction concerning monetary suits against the state. Appeals are made to the appellate court in the respective district.

Family courts hear matrimonial actions and family altercation proceedings such as support, neglect, juvenile delinquency, and paternity suits. Family courts are located in each county and appeals are made to the respective appellate court.

Probate courts, located in each county, administer decedent's estates. Appeals are made to the appellate court in the respective district.

Civil courts are generally located in each major city. There is usually a monetary ceiling, such as $10,000. Cases requesting damages in excess of the monetary ceiling would be heard in the county courts. There may be a separate part for landlord and tenant altercations, and for traffic violations. Appeals are made either to the county court or to the appellate court in the respective district.

Criminal courts are located in major cities. Appeals are made to the appellate courts.

Municipal courts and justice of the peace courts are generally located in smaller cities and towns, and have a much lower monetary limitation. They usually have both civil and criminal jurisdiction and may be looked upon as a combination of the civil and criminal courts on a smaller scale. Appeals are made to the county courts in the county in which they are located.

There are also small claims courts which have monetary ceilings ranging from $500 to $2,000. These courts provide individuals with the opportunity to resolve small cases without the need for retaining a lawyer. Small claims courts open the legal system to individuals who would otherwise be prevented from commencing a lawsuit because of the expensive legal costs involved. Many small claims courts have evening sessions to accommodate working people. Formal procedural and evidentiary rules are relaxed with the judge acting more like a mediator.

Personal Jurisdiction

To acquire personal jurisdiction, three constitutional requirements of due process must be satisfied: The defendant must have contact with that state, must have an opportunity to be heard, and must be given notice by proper service of a summons.

A court's exercise of jurisdiction over a defendant must be done with justice and in fairness to the defendant. To avoid the arbitrary exercising of jurisdiction by all courts, it is necessary that the defendant have some relationship (contact) with that particular state.

Notice must be given to defendants to apprise them of the claim against them. This may be accomplished by proper service of a summons, with or without a complaint. The summons is a one-page document delineating the parties' names, the venue (the county in which the action is to be commenced), and notice that failure to appear will result in a default judgment. The complaint sets forth the nature of the action and details of the relief requested. When the summons is served without a complaint, it must concisely state the charges against the defendant and the relief requested by the plaintiff.

The summons may be served by any adult who is not a party in the action within the state. Service may be made any day of the week except Sunday. After service is made, a full description of the person served along with a copy of the summons and complaint must be filed with the clerk of the court. The description entails: sex, age, height, weight, and color of eyes and hair.

Defendants must be provided with an opportunity to be heard in court to contest the claim against them. The defendant must be given sufficient time to appear in the action—generally thirty days from receipt of the summons. A shorter period may be prescribed if the defendant was personally served in the state.

Effect of Jurisdiction

Obtaining personal jurisdiction over a defendant allows the plaintiff to commence an action against the defendant in a court of law. Jurisdiction and a cause of action against the defendant give the plaintiff the right to sue that particular defendant. Jurisdiction is important to the plaintiff in that if he or she can obtain it in his or her state over an out-of-state defendant, he or she may have the convenience of suing in familiar courts with a familiar attorney.

Jurisdiction, together with a cause of action, gives a person the right to sue another for a legal remedy. It is important to note that although an individual may be able to obtain jurisdiction over a person, this does not mean he or she has a cause of action. Even if there is a cause of action, it does not guarantee the case is won. The plaintiff must still prove the facts set forth in the cause of action which he or she is alleging has caused the injury.

PLEADINGS

The pleadings are the written declarations of the plaintiff and the defendant. They consist of the plaintiff's complaint which is served upon the defendant and the defendant's answer to the complaint. In a civil case, the plaintiff is the party who is commencing the lawsuit based on a cause of action with the hope of being granted a remedy. A cause of action gives the plaintiff a legal right to sue. The defendant is the party against whom the action is brought and against whom the plaintiff is seeking a remedy. To commence a lawsuit, the plaintiff must serve the defendant a summons and complaint. The summons gives the defendant his or her constitutional notice of the commencement of the action. The complaint explains why the plaintiff is suing the defendant and describes the relief requested. It sets forth the factual allegations upon which the plaintiff is claiming the relief requested, and the reasons why the defendant should be responsible for this relief. If the complaint is not served with the summons, then it may be served later on the defendant's demand.

The defendant's response to the plaintiff's complaint is called an answer. An answer must admit or deny the plaintiff's allegations. A general denial indicates that all the plaintiff's allegations are believed to be untrue. A special denial is used when the defendant denies particular allegations and admits the rest. All allegations that are not denied are deemed admitted.

The defendant may also raise an affirmative defense or a counterclaim in his or her answer. An affirmative defense is raised in situations where the defendant admits that the plaintiff's allegations are true, but argues that his or her actions are justified under the circumstances. Many of these affirmative defenses, such as bankruptcy discharge, nonpayment, release, and incapacity are described in Chapter 14, Contractual Defenses.

A counterclaim is a cause of action the defendant has against the plaintiff. The counterclaim need not arise out of the palintiff's claim. It may pertain to a totally different matter. If a counterclaim is raised by the defendant, the plaintiff must respond to it. This response is known as a reply. It is similiar to a defendant's answer in that the plaintiff must deny all of the allegations set forth in the counterclaim, otherwise the allegations will be deemed admitted.

To summarize, an answer is defendant's response to plaintiff's complaint; and a reply is plaintiff's response to a defendant's counterclaim, if one is raised in the defendant's answer. After serving the answer, the defendant may implead a third person who is, or may be, liable to him or her for all or part of the plaintiff's claim. The defendant must serve a separate complaint upon the third party in order to bring that person into the action. It is then up to the court's descretion to admit the third party into the lawsuit.

The pleadings are liberally construed, and immaterial defects are ignored. The pleadings should be sufficiently particular to apprise the other party of the material elements giving rise to the cause of action or defense. Parties may amend pleadings to correct errors or to add a cause of action. Generally this may be done once without the court's permission. After that, the court's permission is necessary, and will be granted as justice requires.

DISCOVERY

Discovery is the next step before trial. Discovery allows both parties to examine each other's witnesses, property, documents, and records prior to trial in order to get a clear picture of the evidence which will support the factual allegations and denials set forth in the complaint and answer, respectively. It prevents surprise and helps to even out discrepancies in the parties' resources. Full disclosure of all material and necessary evidence is required except for the following: privileged information, the attorney's trial strategy, and evidence prepared for litigation. However, the latter must be disclosed to the other party upon his or her request in cases where the evidence is material and necessary, cannot be duplicated, and would cause undue hardship to the party if he or she would have to proceed without it. An example of this would be opinion evidence or evidence of tests regarding personal property which has subsequently been destroyed. The evidence requested must have a significant relationship to an issue in the case. Substantial or irrelevant requests that are intended to burden or harass the other party need not be acknowledged. The main types of discovery devices are depositions, inspections, and examinations.

Depositions can be either oral or written. Oral depositions are often referred to as examinations before trial (EBT). Depositions give each party the opportunity to ask questions of the opposing party, and that party's witnesses, before trial. This is the most popular discovery device. A written transcript of the testimony is usually made with the aid of a legal stenographer. Testimony of individuals who will not be able to appear at trial may be preserved by deposition, and the written transcript of the deposition may be introduced at trial. Written depositions are called interrogatories. They are questions submitted to the opposing party in writing to which the opposing party must respond if the questions are reasonable.

Inspections of certain premises, personal property, documents, and records under the control of the opposing party may be requested through discovery upon sufficient notice where they relate to the issues in the lawsuit.

Examinations of the physical or mental condition of an opposing party may be had, by court order, when that party's condition is at issue in the action. The need for the information must be great; it must outweigh the right to privacy of the party to be examined.

PRETRIAL CONFERENCE

A pretrial hearing is often held between the judge and the attorneys of the opposing parties after discovery. The judge may encourage them to settle out of court if the circumstances warrant. If not, the triable issues of fact are discussed and the itinerary of the trial is planned.

TRIAL

The trial may be by judge or jury. The right to a trial by jury is guaranteed under the Seventh Amendment to the United States Constitution, and under the constitutions of the individual states, but one party must exercise the right to a jury trial by requesting it.

At the onset of the trial, opening statements are made by the attorneys of both parties. In the opening statement, the plaintiff's attorney presents to the jury the allegations of fact set forth in the complaint and the relief requested. The jury, at this point, has not had the opportunity to learn of the complaint. The plaintiff's attorney then proceeds to inform the jury as to how he or she will prove the allegations through the production of real evidence and the testimony of witnesses. The opening statement by the defendants' attorney will usually be in the form of a rebuttal to the statements made by the plaintiff's attorney. The attorney for the defendant will deny the factual allegations made by the plaintiff and will inform the jury of how he or she intends to disprove them.

The plaintiff has the burden of proving the cause of action set forth in the complaint. The plaintiff's attorney begins the trial by calling witnesses to testify to the truth of the allegations listed in the plaintiff's complaint. After direct examination of each witness by the plaintiff's attorney, the attorney for the defendant is given the opportunity to cross-examine that witness. The defendant's attorney will attempt to discredit the plaintiff's witness by trying to show prior inconsistent statements, bias, unjustifiable hostility toward defendant, or a bad reputation for truth and veracity. The attorneys have the option to reexamine the same witness. The attorney who called the witness may elect to reexamine that witness on redirect examination in order to clear up any inconsistencies brought out in that witness's testimony on cross-examination.

The same procedure for examination that was followed regarding the plaintiff's witnesses applies to defendant's witnesses, as well.

The plaintiff and defendant may present further evidence, in a rebuttal, to negate each other's position. After the attorneys for both sides have rested their cases, they will make their closing statements to the jury. The closing statement consists of an attorney's plea to the jury to return a verdict for his or her client, including the reason why the attorney believes they should. The plaintiff's attorney will usually explain how the evidence presented proves the factual allegations recorded in the complaint. The defendant's attorney will argue that the evidence presented on the defendant's behalf disproves the allegations set forth in the complaint.

After the closing statements, the judge will instruct the jury with regard to the particular law that applies to this case. The jury, triers of fact, must make a decision based upon the factual evidence presented. Then the jury will apply the law, as the judge instructed them, to their factual determination and pronounce a verdict for either the plaintiff or the defendant. If their verdict is for the plaintiff, the jury may be requested to resolve the issue concerning the amount of money damages to be awarded.

EVIDENCE

Evidence is the medium for proving disputed facts. Each party presents evidence on his or her own behalf. The evidence presented may be in the form of testimony, writings, or documents. Courts may also take judicial notice of matters of common knowledge without requiring the party to prove their existence. Examples of facts courts will take judicial notice of include: the metric system, the calendar, the law of gravity, the population of each state, etc. Real evidence, which is the actual production of the object that is in issue or related to the issues may also be introduced.

To be admissible, evidence must be material, relevant, and competent. Evidence is material and relevant when it is probative of (tends to prove) a fact in issue. Evidence is competent when the person testifying is capable of understanding the oath and is able to perceive, remember, and recall the facts. A competent witness can testify to the facts, but may not interpret or draw conclusions from them unless the evidence is related to the senses, and involves speed, color, emotion, taste, sound or smell; or the person testifying is an expert witness. Expert witnesses may be qualified by proof of their skill, knowledge, or experience. They may give their opinions based on the evidence presented, but not based on hearsay evidence.

Hearsay is an out-of-court statement offered as proof of the truth of the matter asserted. Generally, when a person is testifying as to what another person said, that is considered hearsay evidence. Hearsay is not admissible as evidence in a court of law to prove the issue in dispute, but may be admitted to show a person's state of mind at a particular time related to the issue.

The burden of proof rests with the plaintiff in a civil case, and with the state in a criminal case. In a civil trial, the plaintiff must prove his or her case by a preponderance of the evidence, which means over 50 percent. The plaintiff has the burden of producing evidence which will prove his or her cause of action. If the evidence presented by the plaintiff is not sufficient, the judge will direct the verdict for the defendant, because the plaintiff has not met the burden of proof. If the evidence presented by the plaintiff is sufficient to prove the cause of action, then the defendant must rebut this evidence or justify his or her actions by presenting a valid defense. If the defendant succeeds, he or she will win the case; if not, the judgment will be entered for the plaintiff.

In a criminal trial, the state must prove its case beyond a reasonable doubt, which is a much more difficult requirement than that demanded in a civil case. The burden of going forward with proof rests on the state and the outcome depends on whether the state can meet that burden; and if so, whether the defendant can rebut the state's evidence or present a justifiable defense to acquit himself or herself of the alleged crime.

ARBITRATION

Arbitration is an alternative to the use of the court system. Arbitration is a means for the settlement of a dispute, expeditiously and inexpensively, pursuant to a written arbitration agreement. The agreement will provide for the selection of an arbitrator. An arbitrator is a mediator, who is free to examine the facts and grant a judgment based on a factual determination. An arbitrator has a duty not to be biased. The arbitrator makes the award in writing, and this then is served upon the losing party. Upon confirmation of the award, a judgment is entered in the court records. It is binding on both parties and generally not appealable unless the arbitrator acted in an arbitrary and capricious manner or had an interest in the outcome.

Many states now require mandatory arbitration of all civil cases below $10,000 because the courts have become so inundated with lawsuits that they are unable to handle the caseload. Many states have instituted arbitration panels consisting of local attorneys who sit once a month and hear all cases within their jurisdiction. It is an extremely fast, efficient, and inexpensive means for disposing of minor civil cases. It appears to be the trend of the future.

JUDGMENTS

A judgment from a court action or an award from an arbitrated case is the final determination of the rights of the parties. After the court enters a judgment in favor of one of the parties, that party may attempt to collect it from the other. The person who is awarded the judgment is known as the judgment creditor, and the person against whom it is directed is known as the judgment debtor. The enforcement of a judgment is another matter. Most people erroneously believe that once the judgment is pronounced in their favor, their opponent will expeditiously pay the award granted them. While most people abide by the judgment rendered by the court, many do not.

There are various methods of collecting judgments. Judgments concerning the title to real or personal property may be enforced by having the county sheriff seize the property, pursuant to an execution order, and transfer it to the judgment creditor. Money judgments may be derived from any property legally transferable or assignable by the judgment debtor with certain exceptions designated by statute for subsistence. Property may be seized by the county sheriff pursuant to an execution order and sold at public auction. The proceeds of the sale may be applied to the judgment. The judgment creditor may also obtain a lien against property owned by the judgment debtor. A judgment lien against property means that the propety cannot be sold until the amount of the lien is satisfied by payment. An income execution order may also be issued against the judgment debtor, but the amount garnished may not exceed 10 percent of the salary or wages earned. In spite of these methods of collection, a judgment is often worthless. The judgment debtor may be judgment proof. He or she may have filed voluntary bankruptcy, or othe creditors may have forced the judgment debtor into involuntary bankruptcy. The judgment debtor may not be working and may have no other assets from which to collect the judgment; or the judgment debtor may have disappeared and cannot be located. Judgments usually can be enforced anywhere from ten to twenty years, but rarely do individuals pursue the matter for that length of time.

APPEAL

The party against whom the judgment is made has a right to appeal the case to a higher court, which is referred to as an appellate court. An appeal may be made only in regard to the law applied in the trial, not the facts. No evidence will be heard by the appellate court. A notice of appeal must be filed with the clerk of the trial court within the prescribed time limits after the judgment is entered in the court records. The person making the appeal is the appellant, and the person against whom the appeal is made is known as the appellee. The appellant's attorney must file the record of the trial with the appellate court together with a brief presenting the appellant's argument. The appellee must also submit a brief, refuting the appellant's arguments. The appellant may, at his or her option, file a reply to the appellee's brief. Both parties, through their attorneys, may supplement their briefs by presenting an oral argument before the court.

The appellate court then makes its determination and either affirms the decision of the trial court for the appellee, or reverses it in favor of the appellant. If this appellate court is an intermediary appellate court, then an appeal may be made to the state supreme court by submitting a petition within the allotted time frame. The trial record, along with the intermediary appellate court's opinion, will be filed with the state supreme court for review. New briefs must be filed and new arguments presented.

The decision of this court will be final unless a federal issue is involved, which would mean an appeal to the United States Supreme Court. The state supreme court will either affirm the decision of the lower court for the appellee, or reverse it with instructions to enter a judgment for the appellant. There are times when the appellate court's instructions call for a new trial to be granted by the trial court. This means the entire trial process must be started over. Only a very small percentage of the cases appealed from the trial court's decisions are changed by the appellate courts. In fact, many cases do not even go to trial, but rather are settled out of court because of the time and expense involved.

The cost of commencing an appeal presents financial problems for many individuals who feel that there are questions of law which have been unjustly resolved. Many appeals are lost or abandoned as a result, with the victorious party being the one willing to spend the most and tie up the case the longest. This is clearly evident where the amount in dispute is relatively small and where the individual's opponent is a large corporation such as an insurance company.

NEED FOR LAWYERS

When you read this book, you will acquire a certain degree of knowledge concerning the law. It is important to understand the danger inherent in trying to be your own lawyer. There is an old saying, "A person who acts as his own lawyer, has a fool for a client."

REVIEW QUESTIONS _____

1. Define jurisdiction, summons, complaint, answer, counterclaim, reply, discovery, deposition, pretrial hearing, appeal, arbitration, judgment, evidence, and hearsay.
2. What is the structure of a typical state court system?
3. What is the jurisdiction or function of each court in the state court system?
4. What is the difference between a trial court and an appellate court?
5. What is the difference between a question of fact and a question of law?
6. What are the documents which comprise the pleadings?
7. What is the difference in the burden of proof between a civil case and a criminal case?
8. Who are the plaintiff and the defendant?
9. Describe the various stages of a trial.
10. What is the function of the jury?

4
CRIMINAL LAW AND PROCEDURE

INTRODUCTION

Criminal law is an entire and separate branch of law unto itself. It concerns itself with identifying criminal conduct and providing the appropriate penalty to punish criminals and to deter them from committing future offenses. All of the other areas of law, including those discussed in this book, come under the heading of civil law. The impact of criminal law on business is evidenced by the amount of money and property lost through theft on the part of employees and customers, as well as outright criminals. Businesses spend large sums of money for crime detection and security protection in the form of cameras, televisions, alarms, guards, watchdogs, fencing, and lights.

BUSINESS CRIMES

The crimes that have the most profound effects on businesses are discussed next:

Burglary
Arson
Fraud or embezzlement
Forgery
Larceny
Extortion, bribery, and blackmail

Burglary

Although the term *burglary* had been restricted to the breaking and entering of a dwelling place at night, it now encompasses all unlawful entries into a building or structure belonging to another with the intent to commit a crime therein. Some states have even expanded the term to include those who unlawfully remain in a building with the intent to commit a crime after gaining legal entry.

Arson

Arson is the intentional burning of a building or structure belonging to another, by means of fire or explosive devices. A person who burns down his or her own building or structure to collect the insurance is also guilty of arson and will be denied the proceeds from the insurance policy.

Embezzlement

Embezzlement is the fraudulent taking of the property of another by someone who already has lawful possession of it. The embezzler either has been entrusted with property, as in the case of a stockbroker with an individual's securities; or has been given access to the property because of the nature of his or her job, as in the case of a bank teller. The act of embezzlement occurs when the embezzler interferes with the owner's rights to his or her property by converting the property to the embezzler's own use.

Criminal Fraud

A person who uses the mails to further a scheme to defraud individuals or to obtain money from them under false pretense is guilty of the crime of criminal fraud. The intentional use of inaccurate weights and measurements and the use of false labeling for the purpose of misleading the general public are also criminal actions.

Forgery

Forgery is the fraudulent imitation or alteration of a signature or document in order to deceive. This crime has been committed the moment the signature or document is forged. It is not necessary for the forged document to be transferred to an innocent party.

Larceny

Larceny is the taking away of someone else's personal property without consent and with the intent to steal. A person who finds property or who mistakenly takes it is not guilty of larceny because there is no criminal intent to steal. A person committing larceny may obtain possession of the property by means of trickery, false pretenses, or embezzlement.

Extortion, Blackmail, and Bribery

Extortion involves the threat of future physical or economic harm unless the demands imposed upon the victim are satisfied. Blackmail entails the threat to accuse the victim of a crime or to expose personal and confidential information which would cause the victim social, political, or economic disgrace. Bribery is the offering of money or other property or advantages to a public official to influence decisions made by him or her in the course of official duties.

OBJECTIVES OF CRIMINAL PROCEDURE

The main objective behind criminal procedure is to realize fast and accurate investigations of crimes while protecting the individual freedoms of citizens. The procedure for a criminal case differs from that of a civil case (discussed in the previous chapter). When a crime has been committed or is about to be committed, an arrest may be made, the accused and his or her property may be searched, and any incriminating evidence found may be seized.

CONSTITUTIONAL RIGHTS
WHEN ARRESTED

The test to determine whether a lawful arrest was made and whether the search and seizure were proper is found in the Fourth Amendment to the Constitution. The Fourth Amendment protects people, their homes, and their effects against unreasonable searches and seizures by the state or federal government. A search and seizure must be carried out pursuant to a warrant based on probable cause. Probable cause is the reasonable belief that a person committed a crime or that a certain person or item incident to a crime may be found at a particular place. A search warrant issued on probable cause must be supported by an oath and affirmation describing the place to be searched or the person or property to be seized. A deliberate falsification of any of this information by the maker of the warrant is grounds for suppression of the evidence seized or release of the person. A search may be made without a warrant only under special circumstances.

The Fifth and Sixth Amendments also have an important impact on the rights of the accused when he or she is arrested. These rights have resulted in the *Miranda* warning. In 1966, the United States Supreme Court in *Miranda* v. *State of Arizona*, 384 U.S. 436, promulgated these rights when it held,

> At the outset, if a person in custody is to be subjected to interrogation, he must first be informed in clear and unequivocal terms that he has a right to remain silent . . . The warning of the right to remain silent must be accompanied by the explanation that anything said can and will be used against the individual in court. This warning is needed in order to make him aware not only of the privilege, but also of the consequences of foregoing it . . .
> . . . an individual held for interrogation must be clearly informed that he has the right to consult with a lawyer and to have the lawyer with him during interrogation under the system for protecting the privilege we delineate to-day . . . it is necessary to warn him not only that he has the right to consult with an attorney, but also if he is indigent, a lawyer will be appointed to represent him.

Since, these warning were not given to Miranda, the Supreme Court reversed the decision of the Arizona Supreme Court and awarded judgment for Miranda.

PROCEDURE AFTER ARREST

The accused is taken to the police station after an arrest to be booked; that is, charged with a specific crime. The accused will then be questioned by the police for the purpose of obtaining more information about the crime or a voluntary confession. Often a suspect will be requested to stand in a lineup for the purpose of verifying the identity of the perpetrator of the crime. The accused then will be brought before a judge who will advise the accused of his or her rights and set bail. Then formal proceedings begin.

In felony cases, about half the states provide for an indictment by a grand jury. The other states allow the prosecutor to use his or her discretion in a proceeding based on either a grand jury *indictment* or on *information* which is similiar to a plaintiff's complaint in a civil case. A preliminary hearing is granted by the court where the prosecutor has brought forward the proceedings on information without a grand jury indictment.

After the indictment or information is filed, the accused is arraigned. An arraignment takes place when the accused is brought into court for the purpose of being informed of the charges against him or her. The accused is once again advised of his or her constitutional rights and the indictment or information is recited. The accused is then afforded an opportunity to respond to the charge. It is here that plea bargaining takes place. Oftentimes, the accused will plead guilty to a lesser crime. This avoids the need for a time-consuming and expensive trial. It also helps clear the congested trial calendar. If the accused does not plead guilty to a charge, then a trial will begin. The Sixth Amendment guarantees the accused a trial by jury in cases involving serious offenses such as felonies.

TRIAL

The trial begins with a reading of the indictment or information by the clerk of the court. The accused's plea is also given. The prosecution and defense counsel will make their opening statements. Since the burden of proof is on the prosecution, it will proceed with the introduction of real evidence and the testimony of witnesses to prove beyond a reasonable doubt the allegations set forth in the indictment or information. This burden of proof is much greater than required in a civil trial. The defense counsel may cross-examine each witness introduced by the prosecution. The right to confront or cross-examine opposing witnesses can be found in the Sixth Amendment. After the prosecution concludes, the defense counsel may introduce real evidence and the testimony of witnesses to disprove the prosecution's evidence, and thus try to create a reasonable doubt in the minds of the jury. The prosecution will cross-examine the witnesses introduced by the defense in an attempt to discredit or minimize their impact on the outcome of the trial.

After the defense rests its case, the judge will charge the jury with principles of law pertinent to the issues raised by the evidence. The jury is instructed to deliberate and arrive at a verdict based on the judge's charges. If the accused is found guilty, a judgment convicting him or her will not be entered until a sentence is imposed.

SENTENCING

Sentencing is administered through a separate hearing in which additional arguments and evidence are presented to determine the appropriate punishment. During the gap in time between the jury's verdict and the sentencing, the judge may authorize either that bail be continued or that the defendant be taken into custody. After a sentence is imposed, the judge will inform the defendant of his or her right to appeal the conviction or the sentence.

REVIEW QUESTIONS

1. What is criminal law?
2. What are the various business crimes?
3. What constitutional rights does a person have when arrested?
4. A prosecutor may proceed against a person accused of a crime based on an indictment or on information. What is the difference between the two?
5. What is the procedure after a person is arrested?
6. What is the burden of proof in a criminal trial?
7. What was the significance of the United States Supreme Court's decision in *Miranda* v. *State of Arizona?*

5

TORTS

INTRODUCTION

Torts are private civil wrongs committed by people against people, their privacy, or their property as distinguished from crimes, which are public wrongs committed against the state. However, many crimes are also torts, thus giving the victim the legal right to sue for money damages to redress the wrongs committed.

EXAMPLE Robert Suskind is walking crosstown to his eastside apartment after seeing a Broadway show. He is mugged by Wilfred Malone, who slashes Suskind's arm with a switchblade and steals his wallet. Malone is apprehended two days later. Is Malone's actions a crime or a tort? Both! The state may criminally prosecute Malone for robbery. The crimes of larceny and criminal assault are included in robbery. Suskind may sue Malone in a lawsuit for civil assault and battery to recover for the injuries he sustained. He may also sue Malone for conversion of his wallet to regain the lost money and credit cards.

There are two types of torts: intentional and unintentional. Intentional torts include assault, battery, conversion, defamation, fraud, false imprisonment, invasion of privacy, interference with business relations, malicious prosecution, nuisance, strict liability, and trespass. Unintentional torts include negligence, products liability, and misrepresentation.

INTENTIONAL TORTS

Assault and Battery

An assault is the apprehension of a harmful or offensive contact, as distinguished from the contact itself, which is a battery. An assault is an attempt, with force, to injure another. There must be some act denoting apparent present ability and the intention to assault, and the person against whom it is directed must be aware of this act.

A battery is an intentional unpermitted contact made by one person with another. The contact may be made with any part of the body or anything connected with it, such as a hat, necklace, or pocketbook. A battery includes contacts which do actual physical harm as well as less serious ones which are nonetheless offensive and insulting, such as kissing or pinching a stranger in public. The relationship of the parties and the circumstances under which the act is committed will necessarily affect the unpermitted character of the contact.

The difference between an assault and a battery is the difference between physical contact and the apprehension of it; the first is a battery and the second is an assault. It is an assault when a person swings a fist to strike another, and a battery when the fist hits the victim's nose.

Infants are liable for their torts; however, an infant under the age of four is generally thought to be incapable of formulating the necessary intent to commit a tort.

EXAMPLE Ron Andrews and Art Westfield are having a few beers at the Tip Top Tavern when they get into a heated argument over a televised ball game they are watching. Ron swings his big fist at Art but misses as Art cringes, falling backward off the stool. Art sustains severe head injuries. Meanwhile, Ron's fist strikes Joe, the bartender, who was busy nursing a Bloody Mary. Have Art and Joe any recourse against Ron Andrews? Yes! Art Westfield may sue Ron Andrews in tort for assault because of his apprehension of being punched. There was no battery because Ron's fist never touched Art. Joe may sue Ron Andrews in tort for battery because he was struck by Ron's punch. There was no assault because Joe never saw Ron's fist.

Conversion

Conversion is the unlawful taking of personal property from the possession of another. It is the converting of another's property for one's own use. Conversion may be made by mistake, but if it is done intentionally it amounts to criminal theft, which is considered under the headings of larceny, embezzlement, and robbery.

EXAMPLE Mary Rogers works as a cashier in Macy's Department store. She takes a break one afternoon to go to the powder room. She mistakenly leaves her pocketbook at the register. When she returns, her pocketbook is there, but her wallet has been removed. The store detective apprehends Debbie Wilson, a stock clerk, with Mary's wallet in her hand. Has Mary Rogers any civil recourse for Debbie Wilson's theft? Yes! Mary may sue Debbie in tort for conversion—the wrongful taking of property. Debbie Wilson may also be criminally prosecuted for the crime of larceny or theft.

Defamation

Defamation is a false statement communicated to at least one other person orally or in a permanent form such as a writing, which causes harm to a third person's reputation. Libel is written defamation, while slander is oral defamation. Libel is actionable without proof of special damages because a writing remains in existence and could be distributed widely, whereas oral defamation is usually temporary and limited to the range of a person's voice, except when the oral statement is recorded and continuously broadcast on television, radio, or sound tracks.

The requirements for libel are: a false statement which is published and read by someone other than the one about whom it is written. The true intention of the writer is that which is apparent from the natural and ordinary interpretation of the written words, and when applied to individuals, the interpretation placed upon those words by people acquainted with the plaintiff and the circumstances. General damages are automatically awarded for harm to reputation in the community or in business, and for personal embarrassment and mental anguish. Special damages may be awarded if the victim can prove he or she suffered an actual pecuniary loss from the harm to his or her reputation.

EXAMPLE The *Star Gazette* publishes an article that accuses Lawrence Binghamton, president of the town's savings bank, of pilfering depositors' money through the authorization of several large personal loans to himself. These statements are proven untrue. Nonetheless, Binghamton's bank loses numerous depositors. Has Binghamton any recourse? Yes! He may sue for libel by claiming the statement was false and proving that it led to a decline in his business.

Slander requires a defamatory statement which is heard by someone other than the person against whom it is directed. Special damages must be proved except in four situations where general damages are recoverable without proof. These situations include: derogating some characteristic important to a person in that person's trade or business, such as honesty or integrity; accusing a person of committing a crime of moral turpitude; denouncing someone by stating he or she has contracted a loathesome disease; or imputing that a woman is unchaste.

EXAMPLE Peter J. Roberts is a local attorney who has ambitions of running for city council. He is speaking at a town hall meeting when Matt Brady, his opponent's promoter, yells out that Peter J. Roberts is a swindler and a liar, and that he would cheat his constituents just as he has cheated his clients. Even though Brady's statements are false, Roberts is not endorsed by his party and his business suffers a severe decline as a result. Does Peter J. Roberts have any recourse? Yes! Roberts may recover general damages for the harm suffered to his business and political reputation.

Truth is an absolute defense when the statement made is fully true. But the truth must be proved. There is a special rule pertaining to defamatory statements made by the media concerning public figures. Even if the statement cannot be proven to be true, the media will not be liable unless malicious intent can be substantiated. Malice is the making of a false statement with the intent to injure another.

EXAMPLE In the previous example, assume Matt Brady's allegations concerning Peter J. Roberts were the truest words ever spoken, but that he has no way of proving them. What result? The result will be the same. Roberts will recover general damages. Although truth is an absolute defense, the burden of proof is on the person who made the statement.

This lawsuit involves a libel action brought by a police commissioner against the *New York Times* because of an advertisement which had purportedly defamed him.

The *New York Times* published an advertisement, signed and paid for by several individuals, that complained about the conduct of the police in dealing with a racial disturbance in Montgomery, Alabama. The police commissioner claimed that statements in the advertisement defamed him personally because he was in charge of the police during the racial disturbance. Under Alabama law, the published opinion of the press is accorded only the privilege of "fair comment." The argument presented here was that the *New York Times* overstepped their privilege. Based on this reasoning, the jury awarded Sullivan $500,000. This award was affirmed in the Alabama Supreme Court.

The issue is whether the First Amendment confers a privilege concerning false statements made by the press.

The United States Supreme Court held the First Amendment does grant a qualified privilege to the press concerning false statements provided they are not made with malice. The press must not be limited merely to fair comment or opinion. The reasoning behind the First Amendment is that the freedom to discuss issues of public concern will aid individuals in drawing more truthful conclusions. Judgment for the *New York Times*.

Fraud and Misrepresentation

Fraud involves the intentional misrepresentation of a material fact which induces another person to act in reliance on that fact to his or her detriment. When the false statement of a material fact is made unintentionally, then the tort of misrepresentation applies, and not fraud. Fraud and misrepresentation are contractual defenses as well as torts. A lawsuit involving them may be brought based on tort law or contract law. A further discussion of fraud and misrepresentation appears in Chapter 14, Contractual Defenses.

EXAMPLE | One day while strolling through Richmond Hill Mall, Bill Comisky decides to browse around Peter's Jewelry Store. He spots what appears to be a gold necklace on sale for $49. He figures this would be perfect for his fiancée's upcoming birthday. Bill goes in and asks the clerk, Marjorie Travers, whether the necklace is made of gold. She excuses herself and goes into a back room where she questions Bernard Peters, the store owner. He replies that the necklace is 14K gold, knowing this to be false. Marjorie conveys the message to Bill, ignorant of its falsehood. Bill, relying on the statement, makes the purchase. On his fiancée's birthday, they discover that the necklace is not 14K gold. What recourse is available to Bill Comisky? Bill may sue Marjorie Travers for misrepresentation and Bernard Peters for fraud. Marjorie Travers made a material misrepresentation of fact that Bill justifiably relied on to his detriment. She made this statement innocently, without an intent to defraud. Bernard Peters is guilty of fraud because his misrepresentation was intentional.

False Imprisonment

False imprisonment and false arrest are the confinement of a person to an area against his or her will, with no opportunity to escape. The restraint may be accomplished by means of physical barriers or threats of force. Most states have enacted new laws which allow merchants to detain a customer when they have a reasonable suspicion that the person has engaged in shoplifting and where the confinement is reasonable. Confinement that is not reasonable and not consented to will result in false imprisonment. The same may be said for false arrest. General damages are normally awarded for the embarrassment and mental distress suffered.

EXAMPLE Christopher Daniels works as a security guard in Hutton's Department Store. One day, he notices a customer take off her jacket, lay it aside, and put on one from the racks. He follows her at a distance, but loses her in the crowd. He figures he will catch her as she leaves the store. Mistakenly, he apprehends Gloria Henn, who is wearing a similiar jacket that she purchased a few weeks before. Daniels requests Gloria Henn to accompany him to the manager's office where both he and the manager intimidate her as they attempt to elicit a confession. Gloria, in tears, asks if she may call her husband. They refuse permission until the police arrive. Later, Gloria's husband appears, producing the receipt for her jacket. The store manager and detective apologize, but Gloria sues them for false imprisonment. What result? Most states have enacted laws which give merchants the right to detain a customer when they have a reasonable suspicion that the person has engaged in shoplifting and where the confinement is reasonable. Here, the intimidation used to secure a confession, coupled with a refusal to permit Gloria the opportunity to extricate herself by calling her husband who could produce the receipt, amounts to unreasonable confinement. Gloria may be awarded general damages for the embarrassment and mental distress she has suffered.

Invasion of Privacy

Personal privacy is protected against invasions causing economic loss or mental suffering. There are four distinct invasions: intrusion on a person's physical solitude; publication of private matters violating ordinary decencies; putting a person in a false position in the public eye by connecting him or her with views he or she does not hold; appropriating some element of a person's personality for commercial use such as photographs.

EXAMPLE Statler Beer is introducing a new beer called Sparkling Lite. To market the product, Statler is featuring an unauthorized poster of the Reverend Luther Winthrop advocating the purchase of Sparkling Lite. The Reverend Winthrop is a well-known fundamentalist minister who openly decries the consumption of alcohol. Has Rev. Winthrop any recourse? Yes! He may sue Statler Beer asserting that the poster was not consented to and that it puts him in a false position in the public eye by connecting him with a view which he does not hold and a product that he does not deem appropriate.

Publication of private matters that are newsworthy is privileged as long as it does not violate ordinary decencies. A false report by the media of a matter of public interest is protected by the First Amendment right of free press, in the absence of proof that it was published with malice.

Interference with Business Relations

A person who intentionally interferes in a business relationship through the use of fraudulent inducement or other unethical means which result in an unfavorable contract, or in the loss or breach of a favorable contract, is liable for damages. The victim must prove damages, such as the specific loss of a customer, except where the nature of the falsehood is likely to bring about a general decline in business.

EXAMPLE | Phil Murray owns a service station in Mobile, Alabama. The On-The-Spot Car Service Company approaches Phil about maintaining their twelve-car fleet. This would greatly enhance Phil's business. While they are still negotiating, Michael Dean, owner of a rival service station, circulates a false rumor that Phil Murray is incompetent and unreliable when it comes to servicing cars. As a result, Phil loses the contract with On-The-Spot Car Service. Thereafter, he discovers that Michael Dean originated the false rumor and sues him for damages. Will Phil be successful? Yes! Michael Dean's intentional interference with the contractual negotiations between Phil Murray and On-The-Spot Car Service caused Phil to lose the contract. Phil is entitled to the profits he lost because of Michael Dean's interference.

Abuse of Process

An individual who abuses the judicial process by bringing unjustifiable litigation against an innocent person will be liable for the actual damages suffered by that person. The innocent party must prove that the person commencing the suit acted maliciously and without probable cause. Malicious prosecutions include bringing a groundless insanity, insolvency or criminal proceeding against another individual.

EXAMPLE | In Springfield, Illinois, Charles Montgomery is running for state senator. His chief opponent, Bob Carlton, has Louise Thompson start a false paternity proceeding against Charles Montgomery, who already has a reputation for being a ladies' man. Charles Montgomery is able to overcome the adversity and win the election by employing a highly expensive and personally financed advertising campaign geared to restoring his reputation. The cost of the campaign amounts to $75,000. Charles Montgomery sues Bob Carlton and Louise Thompson for abuse of process. Will he be successful? Yes! Montgomery will be able to recoup the $75,000 if the full amount is determined as being necessary to overcome the abuse of process. Both Carlton and Thompson are liable for commencing the unjustifiable litigation against Montgomery, an innocent person.

Nuisance

A nuisance is the unreasonable, negligent, or unlawful use of property. People may not use their property in such a way as to deprive others, in turn, of the reasonable use and enjoyment of their property. Zoning laws have been developed as a result of nuisances. Zoning segregates designated areas for certain purposes; it protects the reasonable use and enjoyment of property.

EXAMPLE | Dr. Frankel and Dr. Draco are interns at the South Bronx Morgue and Psychiatric Center. Dr. Draco does much of the embalming at the morgue, while Dr. Frankel handles the lobotomies at the psychiatric center. They live in Coney Island. Every Saturday night they have an all-night monster mash with their friends. The noise is very disturbing to their neighbors. Do the neighbors have any recourse? Yes! They can sue Dr. Frankel and Dr. Draco in tort for nuisance because they are impairing the neighbors' rights to the use and enjoyment of their homes. The neighbors may ask the court to grant an injunction prohibiting the interns from playing loud music and carrying on past a certain hour.

The attractive nuisance doctrine was formulated to protect children from hazardous conditions. An attractive nuisance is anything which attracts unsupervised children and could prove dangerous to their safety, such as an unfenced swimming pool. The attractive nuisance doctrine is invoked when the owner knows or should know that children might be trespassing and when the condition caused by the owner imposes a danger to children who, because of immaturity, do not appreciate the danger involved. Owners are held liable under this doctrine for any injury to children caused by the attractive nuisance. The risk of injuring children far outweighs the presence of the attractive nuisance.

EXAMPLE Jake Smith owns an estate in Reno, Nevada. He constructs an above-ground swimming pool, but neglects to enclose it with a fence. One day, a neighbor's five-year-old child wanders onto the unfenced deck area and falls into the pool. Unable to swim, the little boy drowns. His parents sue Jake Smith for the wrongful death of their son. What result? The parents will win because the unfenced swimming pool created an attractive nuisance which led to the boy's death.

Strict Liability

Strict liability in tort imposes a responsibility on a person who increases the risk of harm to other individuals in the community by lawfully bringing something onto his or her land which is or could be dangerous, such as wild animals, explosive devices, and the like. If other individuals are harmed as a result, the person who brought about the danger will be absolutely liable even though he or she was not negligent in any manner. One party must bear the loss. The party who brought about the danger is the logical choice even where he or she acted without fault by taking every possible precaution. There is no liability for merely increasing the risk of harm to others. Liability occurs only when damage results.

EXAMPLE Rita Mullins is the owner of Babette, Muffin, and Scruffy, three poodles who are colored grey, black, and champagne. Phil Fogarty lives next door to Rita. On one sunny afternoon in July, he is preparing a barbecue for his family and friends. He lays out twelve porterhouse steaks on a picnic table. He goes inside to look for the grill and charcoal. In the meantime, Babette, Muffin, and Scruffy have wandered into his yard to sniff around. By the time Phil returns, the dogs have devoured three of the steaks and licked the rest a few times. Phil sues Rita for the value of the twelve steaks. Will he be able to collect? Yes! Rita is absolutely liable for the damages done by the dogs under the theory of strict liability.

There is no liability for anything which exists naturally on the surface of the land, unless a person interferes with it and this results in injury to the property or the person of another. There is liability if anything that is brought onto the land, or under the land, escapes and causes damage. This is true regardless of what precautions are taken except if the event causing the damage occurred through an act of God.

EXAMPLE In the example concerning Jake Smith's pool, assume that after twelve years the walls of the pool gave way, spilling fifteen thousand gallons of water. In a neighboring yard, Dolores Galvin was holding an outdoor reception for her daughter's wedding. Most of the water came pouring into Dolores's yard, overturning the elaborate buffet and soaking tablecloths, guests' feet, the wedding gown and veil, and ruining the entire occasion. Have Dolores, her daughter, and their guests any recourse? Yes! They may sue Jake Smith for damages, under the theory of strict liability in tort. Jake Smith is absolutely liable, even though he was not negligent. He must assume direct responsibility for the damage caused by the collapse of the pool's walls, regardless of the precautions he took.

Trespass

Trespass is the unlawful entry onto the land of another. An owner owes no duty to a trespasser except to refrain from willful conduct in disregard of human safety, such as the setting of bear traps or a spring gun.

EXAMPLE Two youngsters, Pat and Mike, climbed a twelve-foot-high fence on the perimeter of a junkyard. Once inside, they began to jump on all of the wrecked vehicles. Pat landed on the windshield of a 1966 Plymouth and fell through, causing him to suffer a broken leg. Mike ran to the office to telephone for help. When he opened the door, he was confronted with a full-size Doberman Pinscher. There was no posted warning, and the dog could not bark because its vocal cords had been removed. Mike ran as fast as he could, but was caught from behind. Pat and Mike sued the junkyard dealer for their injuries. Have they any recourse? Both Pat and Mike were trespassing. The owner owes them no duty except to refrain from willfully causing them harm. Pat has no recourse, because the junkyard owner is not responsible for the safety and condition of the vehicles. The presence of a watchdog is permissible. But, where no warnings are posted and the dog's bark cannot be heard, the willful intent to cause harm may be inferred. Mike will be able to collect for the injuries he sustained from the silent Doberman.

Wrongful Death

When a person commits a tort which results in the death of another, an executor or personal representative of the decedent may bring a wrongful death action on behalf of the estate. The lawsuit may be brought for any wrongful act or any neglect which causes death. Some states allow the victim's beneficiaries, usually consisting of the immediate family, to bring a wrongful death action against the defendant. Recovery may include damages for the decedent's pain and suffering, loss of earnings, medical expenses, and, most importantly, the survivors' loss of the decedent's support and services. There is no compensation given to the family for their grief, mental suffering, or loss of the loved one.

The actual amount awarded for future loss of support and services is measured according to guidelines which take into account the decedent's life expectancy, current and projected income, health, and past contributions to his or her family. The jury is generally given wide latitude in making an award, rather than being restricted to compliance with a definite formula. Juries have awarded high verdicts to parents, even in cases involving minors where the parents would actually have received no pecuniary benefit had the child lived because children generally cost more to rear than they contribute.

EXAMPLE

David Sands was a lifeguard at Malibu Beach. On a hot afternoon, he was preoccupied in a social conversation with a bikini-clad beauty and failed to observe Walter Roberts drowning. By the time he responded, Roberts had died. Roberts' estate sued Sands for Roberts' wrongful death. Is this a good cause of action? Yes! Wrongful death may result from neglect. Here, Sands had a duty to observe and act, and since he failed to do so, he is responsible. Suppose Walter Roberts' drowning was caused by a friend who playfully held him under water, without intending to drown him. Could a wrongful death action be brought against the friend? Certainly! The fact that Roberts' death was accidental does not affect the cause of action. What matters is that Roberts is deceased.

UNINTENTIONAL TORTS

Negligence

Negligence is the failure to perceive a risk which results in an injury that was foreseeable. Negligence is caused by conduct which falls below the standard established by law for the protection of others against risks of harm. The negligent party must have had a duty to perceive the risk of harm which he or she fails to meet. The key to negligence is that the defendant failed to act as a reasonable person would in light of the risk. The plaintiff has the burden of proving this. The elements that give rise to negligence are:

Negligent act	Foreseeable injury
Duty owed	Resulting loss or damage
Proximate cause	

There must be a negligent act caused by the defendant, where there was a duty owed to exercise reasonable care. The negligent act must be the proximate cause of a foreseeable injury that results in loss or damage to the injured party.

Negligence is an act performed in a careless manner, or an ommision to act, which proximately causes injury to another. Liability for the negligence does not arise until it is established that the person who was careless owed a duty toward the person bringing suit. A duty to exercise reasonable care arises whenever there is a danger of one person's causing injury to another. The injury to the plaintiff must have been proximately caused by the negligent act of the defendant. Proximate cause means the negligent act must have been reasonably connected to the plaintiff's injury. The injury to the plaintiff must be foreseeable. A foreseeable injury is that which would be reasonably anticipated as a consequence of the defendant's negligence. In most states, the defendant is responsible for damages resulting from only foreseeable injuries.

The plaintiff must sustain a definable loss or damage and prove that this loss or damage resulted from the injury caused by the defendant's negligence. The plaintiff's loss is recompensed with money damages.

Palsgraf v. Long Island Railroad Company
248 N.Y. 339, 162 N.E. 99 (1928)

Palsgraf sued the Long Island Railroad for injuries sustained as a result of the alleged negligence of its employees.

Mrs. Palsgraf was standing on a platform waiting for a train. A man carrying a package was running to catch a train that was already moving. As the man jumped aboard, two guards attempted to assist him for fear he might fall. One guard grabbed his arm, while the other pushed from behind. The package in the man's arms was dislodged in the process. It fell on the tracks and exploded because it contained fireworks. The explosion caused a set of scales several feet away on the platform to overturn and fall upon Mrs. Palsgraf.

The Long Island Railroad contended that they owed no duty of care to her because the injuries she received were not the result of any foreseeable harm.

The court agreed with the Railroad's contention and established the doctrine of foreseeability which states, "Negligence is not actionable unless it involves the invasion of a legally protected interest, the violation of a right." In this case, the Railroad did not violate Mrs. Palsgraf's rights because she was not within the zone of danger. They owed her no duty of care because the risk of harm to her was not foreseeable. "One who jostles one's neighbor in a crowd does not invade the rights of others standing at the outer fringe when the unintended contact casts a bomb upon the ground. The wrongdoer as to them is the man who carries the bomb not the one who explodes it without suspicion of danger . . ." Judgment for Long Island Railroad.

This is the most famous of all tort cases. Of the seven judges sitting on the New York Court of Appeals, the highest court in the state of New York, four judges limited recovery to foreseeable risk of harm and decided in favor of the Long Island Railroad. The three remaining judges dissented from the majority opinion and held that a person who is negligent must take the existing circumstances as he or she finds them, and may be liable for consequences brought about by his or her negligent acts even though the consequences were not foreseeable.

The doctrine of foreseeability may also be applied to situations where one party's negligence has injured a person and caused others to attempt to rescue. Under the doctrine of "danger invites rescue," the negligent party is responsible for injury to the rescuers, where they act reasonably, and where it is foreseeable that people might go to the rescue of the injured person.

EXAMPLE | The Laurens, a French family-owned corporation, are building a trestle bridge across Niagara Falls. They employ Sweeney Todd, known to be good with a saw, as their chief carpenter and general contractor. One day Sweeney, who is rushing to finish work in order to leave for his home on Fleet Street, omits three of the four nails securing one of the tracks. Two months later, the bridge opens and the first train rolls across. Morris Goldberg and his cousin Ira Stein are among the last to board the train. They have a big date in Toronto with Apple Annie and her sister Orange Blossom. They are forced to stand between the cars because the train is overcrowded. Casey Jones, the train's engineer, misjudges the correct speed needed to make a smooth transition around a curve and sends Goldberg flying out the door. The train stops 100 feet down the tracks. Ira Stein bolts off the train to look for his cousin. When he steps on the track that is not properly secured, it gives way and he joins his cousin in the Falls. Their estates sue the Laurens for wrongful death. The Laurens acknowledge their responsibility for Goldberg only. What result? Ira Stein's estate may also recover under the doctrine that danger invites rescue, because it was foreseeable that Ira Stein might go to the rescue of his cousin.

Joint Responsibility

When the negligence of two or more defendants is responsible for a person's injuries, the negligent parties will be jointly and severally liable. This means the injured party may collect the full amount from either or both of them. If one defendant pays more than his or her apportioned share, then that defendant will have the right to contribution from the other. Contribution is a defendant's right to reimbursement for money paid out in excess of his or her apportioned fault.

EXAMPLE In the previous example, if the Laurens and Sweeney Todd were each adjudged 50 percent at fault for Stein's death, but Ira Stein's estate recovers the total award from the Laurens, do the Laurens have any recourse against Sweeney Todd? Yes! They may exercise their right of contribution and sue him for his percentage of the fault: 50 percent.

Infant's Negligence

Infants are held to a special standard regarding negligence. An infant under the age of four is held to be incapable of committing a negligent act. An infant between the ages of four and fourteen is presumed to be incapable of negligence, but this presumption may be rebutted by the introduction of evidence regarding the infant's maturity, experience, and intelligence. Infants between the age of fourteen and the age of majority, which in most states is now eighteen, are presumed to be capable of negligence, but this presumption may be negated by showing the infant's lack of maturity, experience, and intelligence.

If an infant commits a tort at the direction of his or her parent, the parent may also be liable. In situations where an infant engages in activities which are usually restricted to adults, such as flying an airplane or driving a car, the infant will be held to the standard of care required of an adult. This is for the protection of innocent victims.

Contributory Negligence

People must exercise reasonable care in looking out for themselves. To recover damages for a defendant's negligent conduct, a plaintiff must not have been negligent in any way which might have contributed to the resulting injury. When a plaintiff is contributorily negligent, some states have enacted comparative negligence statutes which apportion the fault between the plaintiff and the defendant according to their degrees of negligence. If the plaintiff is 25 percent negligent, that person may recover only 75 percent of the damages for the injury received. The purpose of comparative negligence statutes is to protect those who were slightly negligent from being barred from recovery. If the plaintiff's own negligence was the proximate cause of the injury, many states will bar any form of recovery. Contributory negligence consists of the plaintiff's failure to discover or appreciate a risk that would be apparent to a reasonable person. Even when this is the case, the plaintiff may still recover if the defendant had the last clear chance to avoid injury to the plaintiff.

EXAMPLE Lucrezia Borgia owns a diner in the Bensonhurst section of Brooklyn. One day, she is applying, around the perimeter of the room, a new poison that she developed to kill ants and roaches. She leaves the bottle on one of the tables in the far corner of the diner, near where she is working. The bottle is properly labeled with the word "poison" and with the skull and crossbones. Tony Ciperino is sitting at the next booth waiting for his pepper steak. When it arrives, he reaches back to the table behind him and grabs the poison, thinking it is Worcestershire sauce. Tony Ciperino applies it generously to the pepper steak. When he takes a bite, it has a very spicy taste to it. He likes it. Suddenly he falls over. Ciperino is rushed to the emergency room of a nearby hospital. Dr. Crippin, whose motto is "We either cure or kill," pumps Tony's stomach and saves his life. Assume that Lucrezia is assessed 90 percent of the fault, and Tony Ciperino is considered to be 10 percent contributorily negligent. What result? Under comparative negligence statutes, Tony would be able to recover 90 percent of his damages. Under a contributory negligence statute, he may be barred from any recovery unless it is determined that Lucrezia had the last clear chance to avoid Tony's injury.

Assumption of Risk

Assumption of risk is the intentional exposure by the plaintiff to a danger or risk, which the plaintiff is aware of, such as riding in a car with a drunken driver. The reasonableness of the injured party's conduct is determined by balancing the risk against the value of the action taken. The risk of an accident while riding with a drunken driver will be compared with the value or importance of getting a ride home.

Assumption of risk is a matter of knowledge of the danger and an intelligent acquiescence to that danger. A plaintiff must know and appreciate the risk involved. The choice to incur the risk must be made voluntarily. The effect of an assumption of risk is to relieve the defendant of all legal duty toward the plaintiff. This happens in situations where the plaintiff voluntarily enters into a relationship with the defendant with the knowledge that the defendant will not protect him or her against the risk. One example of such a case would be a person who is hit by a baseball while watching the game at the ballpark.

However, assumption of risk does not apply where the plaintiff acted in a reasonable manner during an emergency. Under these circumstances, the defendant is not relieved from his or her legal duty to the plaintiff.

EXAMPLE Papillon is a free-lance travel writer on a guided tour of the caves of Devil's Island. The entrance to one cave is blocked by huge signs reading "Do not Enter—Haven of the

Bats." Papillon figures a few snapshots would enhance his story. He sneaks into the cave and snaps a few pictures. When the flash goes off, he is attacked by the bats and sustains severe injuries. Does he have any recourse against the proprietors of Devil's Island? No! Once he has disregarded their conspicuous warnings, Papillon assumed the risk of injury.

REVIEW QUESTIONS

1. Define torts, assault, battery, conversion, defamation, fraud, false imprisonment, invasion of privacy, interference with business relations, malicious prosecution, nuisance, attractive nuisance doctrine, strict liability, trespass, misrepresentation, and negligence.

2. Tuttle owned a barbershop in a small town in Minnesota. Buck, a town banker, financed the operation of a competing barbershop for the sole purpose of putting Tuttle out of business. Buck spread false and malicious lies about Tuttle, threatened his customers, and continued to finance the competing barbershop even though it was losing money. Tuttle sued Buck for loss of profits resulting from the loss of many of his customers. Buck asserts that he was lawfully diverting customers to make his barbershop profitable. What result? Tuttle v. Buck, 107 Minn. 145, 119 N.W. 946 (1909).

3. Fletcher owned a mill that required a large reservoir of water in order to operate. Fletcher dug up a sizable area of ground and filled it with water. Subsequently the water leaked into an abandoned coal shaft, through underground passages, and finally into a mine operated by Rylands. Rylands sued Fletcher for the damage the water caused to his mining operation. Fletcher argued that he did not act negligently in the construction of the reservoir and Rylands admitted this to be true. Can Rylands still recover for the damage done to his mining operations? Rylands v. Fletcher, L.R. 3 H.L. 330 (1868).

4. The Hambergers rented an apartment from Eastman. They later discovered that Eastman had installed a wiretap in their bedroom that was connected to Eastman's residence. The wiretap was capable of transmitting and recording any sounds made in the Hambergers' bedroom. The Hambergers sued Eastman for invasion of privacy and alleged at the time of the suit that they were still unable to perform the normal and ordinary duties of a husband and a wife because of the invasion of privacy. What result? Hamberger v. Eastman, 106 N.H. 107, 206 A.2d 239 (1964).

5. Thomas worked as a security manager for E.J. Korvette in its store located in King of Prussia, Pennsylvania. Thomas was about to purchase a game for his child's birthday when he was diverted by a suspected shoplifter, whom he followed out of the store with the game still in hand. He put the game in the trunk of his car and paid for it later. The assistant manager had observed what Thomas did and asked him to produce the sales receipt. Thomas could not produce the receipt because he had misplaced it, and he resigned because of the accusation. Later Thomas was arrested on the grounds of larceny. Subsequently, he found the sales receipt, but it did not match the price of the game. Thomas said the cashier had

erred. The store then circulated a notice to all employees that Thomas had been arrested. When Thomas attempted to get employment in the same field, a prospective employer who was checking references was told by Korvettes not to hire Thomas unless they wanted a thief working for them. After the criminal charge was dismissed, Thomas sued Korvettes for false arrest, malicious prosecution, and defamation of character. What result? Thomas v. E.J. Korvette, Inc., 329 F. Supp. 1163 (E.D. Pa. 1971).

6. Mrs. Maddux was a passenger in her husband's pickup truck when a car, driven by Donaldson, crossed the dividing line after coming around a curve and skidded into Maddux's pickup truck. Immediately thereafter, a car driven by Bryie plowed into the rear end of Maddux's truck. Mrs. Maddux sued both Donaldson and Bryie, but Donaldson's insurance company was insolvent. Bryie claims that he should not be responsible for the total amount of damages for Mrs. Maddux's injuries because she could not prove which defendant caused her injuries. What result? Maddux v. Donaldson, 362 Mich. 425, 108 N.W.2d 33 (1961).

7. Mrs. Briney owned a boarded-up farmhouse that she inherited from her parents. The farmhouse was several miles from her home. There were frequent trespassers who broke into the farmhouse to vandalize it. "No Trespassing" signs posted by the Brineys were of no use. The Brineys secured a shotgun to a bedpost in the farmhouse with the barrel pointed at the bedroom door. A wire was run from the trigger to the door knob, so that it would act as a spring device when someone opened the door. The gun was originally pointed at the stomach area, but then lowered to the leg area because, as Mr. Briney admitted, he did not want to injure anyone. Katko and his friend broke into the house about a month later. Katko opened the bedroom door and the shotgun went off blowing apart much of his right leg. He sued the Brineys for damages to his leg. The Brineys argued that they were protecting their property and owed no duty to a trespasser. What result? Katko v. Briney, 183 N.W.2d 657 (Iowa 1971).

6

CONTRACTS: AN INTRODUCTION

INTRODUCTION

ELEMENTS OF A CONTRACT

A contract is a legally enforceable agreement. For an agreement to be legally enforceable, the following elements must be present: a mutual agreement, executed in proper form, voluntarily made by two or more capable parties wherein each party promises to perform or not to perform a specific legal act for valuable consideration. Each element in this definition must be satisfied by each party for the contract to be valid. The validity of the contract is what gives it legal effect.

Following are the elements of a contract in summary form:

Purpose (*lawful*)
Agreement
Legal capacity
Act (promise to perform)
Consideration
Execution in proper form

Individual chapters will be allocated for each element. A simple explanation of each term at this juncture will provide you with sufficient insight to help you understand the correlation of the elements as each chapter is studied.

Purpose (lawful)

The purpose for which the contract was consummated and the acts undertaken to accomplish that purpose must be lawful. Lawful means that the purpose and the acts must not contravene any federal statute or any statute of the state which has subject matter jurisdiction over the contract. When both the means employed and the end result are consistent with the law, then the contract will be valid. If the agreement contemplates the performance of an illegal act or the achievement of an illegal purpose, the contract is invalid.

Agreement

An agreement is arrived at through an offer on one party's part which is accepted voluntarily by another party. An agreement, in and of itself, is not binding because it has no legal obligation without the other five contractual elements. Often the terms *contract* and *agreement* are used interchangeably. Keep in mind that for the two terms to be synonymous, the other five elements giving rise to a legal obligation must be present.

Legal Capacity

For a contract to be valid and enforceable, the parties involved must have the legal capacity to enter into a contract. Since the parties are binding themselves to a legal obligation, each one must be competent to contract. They must be responsible for their actions to assure that the performance of their promises will be completed in accordance with the terms of the contract. The fulfillment of the requirements of legal age and sanity give the presumption that a party is capable of entering into a contractual relationship.

Act (promise to perform)

A promise is a commitment to perform or not perform a specific act, in the present or in the future. The act must be one that is possible to perform, not something illusory. The parties become legally obligated to perform the act when they make their promise to perform. The performance of the act is the reason why each party entered into the contract.

Consideration

Consideration is something valuable given in exchange for something valuable received. The promise to perform a certain act or acts is the consideration given by each party. Generally, what is given need not be identical in value to what is received. It is sufficient that the performance of the act has some intrinsic value.

Execution in Proper Form

Certain contracts are required to be executed in writing in order that they be valid. This is referred to as the statute of frauds requirement, the main purpose of which is to prevent fraud. Whenever possible, all contracts, except those of nominal value, should be reduced to writing in order to evidence the existence of a contract. This is to avoid ambiguity and to protect the parties involved.

VALIDITY OF A CONTRACT

A valid contract, which is created by the presence of the six elements, can be enforced in a court of law should a breach arise. If one or more of the contractual elements is lacking, then the contract is void. A void contract can be carried out by the parties, but it is not a legal contract, and cannot be enforced in a court of law. A contract may also be voidable. A voidable contract is valid unless one party who has a special right to disaffirm the contract decides to do so, thus rendering the contract void. Generally, at the time a party possesses a contractual defense, the contract becomes voidable. When the party exercises his or her right to disaffirm the contract by presenting a defense, the contract becomes void. Chapter 14, Contractual Defenses, covers this matter in detail.

CONTRACTUAL RIGHTS AND DUTIES

A contract is a legal relationship comprised of certain rights and duties. A duty arises to perform specifically what is promised. This duty is a legal one which, if breached, gives the aggrieved party a legal cause of action. A cause of action is a right to sue for a legal remedy. The remedy most often awarded is money damages; however, under certain circumstances, the court may grant the equitable remedies of specific performance or rescission. A more thorough discussion of remedies is provided in Chapter 13. In certain instances, the individual committing the breach may have had just cause for doing so. This just cause will be raised as a contractual defense which, if proven, will relieve the individual from liability for the breach of contract.

FREEDOM TO CONTRACT

The parties to a contract have the freedom to set up their own rights and duties concerning such things as payment, and time and place of delivery. This facilitates the smooth and efficient operation of business and individual transactions. However, this freedom to contract is not absolute. Contracts that involve price fixing, discrimination, or that are unconscionable are invalid because they are unduly harsh or one-sided. Except for certain limitations such as the ones just mentioned, freedom to contract is protected by Article I, Section 10 of the Constitution and by the laws of the individual states. The states set up laws for the interpretation of contractual terms and for the enforcement of promises. These form the laws of contracts.

IMPORTANCE OF CONTRACTS

The law of contracts is the basic foundation of business law. Our economy operates through contracts as the following example illustrates.

EXAMPLE | There are many interrelated contracts that enable the *Daily Planet* to publish its newspaper and that enable people to buy it. The following paragraphs give a list of the contracts involving the *Daily Planet* organization, its employees, and the people who buy the newspaper.

The *Daily Planet* is published in Sun Valley, Idaho, with a daily circulation approaching 55,000. The *Daily Planet* has individual contracts, for a set salary, with each member of its editorial staff, including its editor in chief, Mars Hanley. The reporters also have contracts with the *Planet*, particularly Jupiter Jones, its star reporter. Jupiter's contract is negotiated by his agent, Sun Spots, Inc. Jupiter has an agency contract with Sun Spots to represent him in contractual matters. The terms are a 10 percent commission of any salary paid above the *Planet's* original offering. Haley's Comics has a contract with the *Planet* for the weekly inclusion of *Pluto* in the Sunday comic strip. Venus, a syndicated columnist, is paid a royalty stipulated by contract for each beauty aid column that the *Planet* publishes. There is also a contract with Global Weather Forecasting Services allowing the *Planet* to reprint its forecast.

The advertising which appears in the paper is placed with the Asteroid Advertising Agency, which works on a commission basis. The local television commercials which are responsible for the *Daily Planet's* skyrocketing rise in circulation are also devised by Asteroid Advertising in return for a fee. The paper on which the *Daily Planet* is printed is supplied by Universal Paper Corporation in Crater Lake, Oregon. The trees and the paper mills are located in the Petrified Forest in Arizona. This weekly delivery of pulp is crucial to the publication of the *Daily Planet*. Failure to deliver would result in a loss of profits.

The actual printing of the newspaper is handled by employees belonging to the Mercury Printers Union. The union contracts with the *Planet* on behalf of all employees engaged in printing operations. The *Daily Planet* engages the law firm of Galaxy and Globe to represent them in contract negotiations with the union. The Solar System Underwriting Syndicate underwrites the insurance needs of the *Planet*, including insurance protection for fire; liability, including personal injury and libel; and life and health insurance for employees.

Neptune Newsstands, Inc., provides a forum in which the newspapers are sold. Neptune contracts with the *Daily Planet* for delivery of a certain amount of newspapers to each stand, on consignment, with a commission paid based on the number of papers sold. The unsold newspapers are returned.

The actual delivery of the newspapers from the *Daily Planet* to the Neptune newsstands is handled by the Star Delivery Corporation. The *Planet* gives them a delivery location sheet and pays a fixed fee per truck and driver on a weekly basis. This contract is renewable on a yearly basis, with the standard weekly fee being set at the beginning of the renewal period. If negotiations concerning the fee break down, the paper is not delivered. The contract between Star Delivery and the *Planet* provides for an arbitrator to be brought in to settle the disputes, with the arbitrator's fee to be apportioned between both parties. This is done to avoid lengthy contract disputes and to resolve the matter expediently. Finally, when a conflict is reconciled and the papers are delivered to the newsstands, individuals may purchase them. The purchase of a newspaper is a contract.

This scenario presents the law of contracts in only one instance. It is typical of the situations involving contracts and yet it is unique. You will understand this as you read further into the book. The factual circumstances surrounding the contract will be the guiding principle. The parties to a contract may be individuals, corporations, partnerships, or governments. The *Daily Planet*, Sun Spots, Universal Paper, Neptune Newsstands, and Star Delivery are corporations. Galaxy and Globe, Asteroid Advertising Agency, and Solar System Underwriting Syndicate are partnerships. Individuals include Jupiter Jones, Venus, Haley, and Mars Hanley. The parties may act for themselves or through an agent. Jupiter Jones hired Sun Spots as his agent. The *Daily Planet* used the law firm of Galaxy and Globe as their agent. There may be two or more parties involved in a particular contract. The *Daily Planet's* contract with the printers' union involves three parties: the *Daily Planet*, Mercury Printers Union, and the individual employees. Certain individuals are employees, such as Mars Hanley, Jupiter Jones, and the printers. The others, such as Star Delivery, Neptune Newsstands, and Asteroid Advertising Agency, are independent contractors. Independent contractors are not employees, but rather act independently in the means they employ to achieve the agreed-upon result, such as delivery of newspapers to newsstands each morning.

Most of the contracts referred to here will be expressed in writing to avoid ambiguity and to protect the parties involved, by evidencing the existence of the transaction. The aforementioned contracts do not include every possible type of contract. They serve as a sample of the contracts having a direct effect on the *Daily Planet*, its employees, the independent contractors involved, and the individuals buying the newspaper. Contracts are interwoven throughout the *Planet's* operations. Without contracts, this business would not be in agreement on how to operate. Although the *Daily Planet* is only one business out of thousands, it illustrates the dependence of a business on contracts, and the dependence of those connected with the business. Contracts truly provide the basis for business operations.

HOW CONTRACTS RELATE TO US

In the previous section we saw how important contracts are to the people involved at all levels of a business. We must now turn our attention to the manner in which contracts relate to us, especially when we are adversely affected.

EXAMPLE | Tommy Moon walks to his local Neptune newsstand, flips the proprietor a quarter, and returns home with the morning edition of the *Daily Planet*. Did Tommy Moon make a contract with Neptune newsstands? Yes! He made a contract to purchase the newspaper. Although there was no written or oral agreement to that effect, there is a contract implied from the actions of the parties. The factual circumstances give rise to the contractual obligation.

Let us check to see if all the contractual elements are present: there is lawful purpose, agreement, legal capacity, promise to perform a specific act, consideration, and execution in a proper form. There is an **agreement** to buy and sell a newspaper. Both Tommy Moon and the representative of the Neptune newsstand are presumed to have the requisite **legal capacity** to contract. There is the **promise** to exchange a newspaper for a quarter. This **act** is legal. The newspaper and the quarter furnish the required **consideration.** And since the contract does not have to be in writing, it is **executed** in proper form, implied from the actions of the parties. A valid contract has been made.

Although the contract is simple, all of the required elements must be present for it to be valid. The example illustrates the contractual significance of a transaction that we make every day in our lives. Why must we be aware of this? Because certain legally enforceable rights and duties have been created. Suppose Tommy Moon moved to a new house that was not within walking distance of a Neptune newsstand. Being an avid reader of the *Daily Planet,* Tommy Moon buys a three-year subscription to the newspaper for $300. After six months, the paper is no longer delivered. Tommy figures, "No big deal." Upon calling the *Planet* to register his complaint, he is advised that all subscriptions are handled exclusively by Saturn Subscription Services, as stated in the subscription contract. Saturn informs Tommy that the primary responsibilty lies with the *Planet*.

Tommy Moon is now concerned about the existence of his contractual rights and the contractual duties of the *Daily Planet* and Saturn Subscription Services to deliver the newspaper. He checks to see if all the contractual elements have been met. Then Tommy Moon wants to know what legal remedies are available to him and whether the defenses raised by the *Planet* and Saturn are viable. How can Tommy learn more about his contractual rights? He can begin by reading this book, with special attention to the chapters dealing with contracts.

The ensuing discussion points out other areas where contracts touch our lives and the lives of our families. Perhaps contract law, along with income tax law, are the two types of law which most directly affect you. Think of how many contracts you and your family enter into each month. Mortgage or rent payments are paid pursuant to the respective mortgage contract or lease. Mortgages are contracts between the homeowner and the mortgage holder, generally a bank or the previous owner. Leases are contracts between landlord and tenant. Contracts are entered into with the following companies for which a monthly service charge is imposed: electric, gas, telephone, fuel, credit card, insurance (life, health, automobile, and homeowner coverage). Furthermore, when home repairs are made, contracts are entered into with electricians, carpenters, roofers, plumbers, and television repairmen, to name a few. Daily or weekly purchases of food, gas, and newspapers are also contracts. So are school tuition payments. Contracts run the gamut from the simple to the highly complex. Often we do not realize we are entering into simple contracts. We seem to do it unconsciously. However, our realization quickly develops when something goes wrong, such as: the milk purchased is sour, the plumber does not adequately fix the bathtub leak, or the landlord sues for nonpayment of the rent.

We realize we have certain rights and defenses and we intend to take full advantage of them. The chapters devoted to contracts will explain what these rights and defenses are and how businesses and individuals can make use of them. It is important to develop an understanding of, and an appreciation for contracts. Thus, when we enter into them, we can view them from the proper perspective, whether the contracts are simple or complex.

SIGNIFICANCE OF A WRITTEN CONTRACT

Generally, there is no problem with the validity of an oral contract; the difficulty arises in trying to prove its existence. Many valid contracts are dismissed by the courts because their terms cannot be proved. In an oral contract, if one party does not fulfill his or her obligation, the other party, without witnesses, will have an arduous task trying to prove the existence of the contract. The old saying "It's my word against yours" is very true and applicable to oral contracts. Even with witnesses, there are still problems. Over a period of time, witnesses tend to forget; their testimony is often conflicting and may even be perjured. For convenience, simple contracts, particularly those of nominal value, tend to be oral; but valuable and important contracts should be in writing to evidence their existence. All states have recognized this principle by adopting a statute of frauds requiring certain contracts to be in writing. The main purpose behind the statute is to prevent fraud by requiring evidence of the contract's existence. This protects the parties involved by avoiding misunderstandings. A more detailed discussion of the statute of frauds is presented in Chapter 11.

A contract expressed in oral or written form is referred to as an express contract. Contracts may also be implied from the actions of the parties. These contracts are referred to as implied contracts. They come about when no words are spoken by the parties and no writing is made, but where the actions of the parties dictate agreement to the terms of the contract. Implied contracts arise in situations involving a simple transaction, such as the buying of food, gasoline, or a newspaper. When a person boards a bus or a train and deposits a token or hands the driver or conductor a receipt of payment, there is an implied promise to transport the individual to any of the various scheduled stops.

TYPES OF CONTRACTS

There are basically four categories of contracts:

Real property contracts
Sales contracts
Personal service contracts
Special contracts

Real property contracts are contracts for the sale of land.

Sales contracts cover the broad range of contracts for the sale of personal property. The Uniform Commercial Code (UCC) is the controlling authority in those states which have adopted and incorporated it into state law.

Personal service contracts are contracts where one person promises to perform a service for an individual in return for that individual's promise to provide compensation for the services rendered. Personal service contracts include employment contracts, where an individual is employed on a salary basis, as well as contracts with professionals or independent contractors, where performance is on an hourly or per case basis.

Special contracts are contracts which are of such an important and specialized nature that a separate body of law is devoted entirely to those subjects. The following areas of law are based on contract law: Bailments, Insurance, Agency, Partnership, Commercial Paper, and Suretyship. There is a chapter devoted to each of these legal subjects in this book.

Basic contract law is still applicable and often serves as the foundation and supplement for the law regarding these special contracts.

PROPER APPLICATION OF STATE LAWS

Each state has its own law of contracts. State laws are enacted to interpret and enforce contracts. When terms or phrases are ambiguous, a conflict may develop. The courts interpret the contract to determine the intention of the parties. The language of the contract is construed according to its fair and reasonable meaning. This determination is made by considering the language within the context of the entire transaction. There must be some substantial connection between the state and the contract or the parties to the contract for the state to have jurisdiction. The state must have sufficient interest to interpret the contract and legally enforce the rights and duties of the parties involved. To determine the proper application of state laws, the following rules apply: When a contract is made between two parties of a state and the contract is to be performed in that state, the law of that state will govern.

An example of this is the *Daily Planet's* contract with Galaxy and Globe, a local law firm, to represent them in contract negotiations with the Mercury Printer's Union. When a contract will be performed in a state other than the one where the parties are located, there is a presumption that the law of the state where performance will take place will govern. The *Planet* has a separate contract with Star Delivery to deliver newspapers across the Idaho border into Montana. The presumption is that Montana law will govern. The parties may override this presumption by stipulating in the contract that the law of the state where the contract is made, Idaho, will govern. Contracts involving real estate are governed by the law of the state in which the property is located. Personal service contracts are generally governed by the state in which substantial performance is to be rendered; however, as stated before, the parties may stipulate otherwise.

UNIFORM COMMERCIAL CODE

The Uniform Commercial Code (UCC) was created for the purpose of establishing a uniform set of laws among the individual states which would be compatible with the growth of commerce. A uniform set of laws was needed because of the numerous contracts between parties of different states and the need to resolve the conflicts which arise out of those contracts in a consistent manner. The UCC has been adopted in the District of Columbia and all fifty states except Louisiana, which has adopted it only in part. The Code has ten articles, with each article devoted to a different aspect of a commercial transaction.

Article 1 General Provisions
Article 2 Sales
Article 3 Commercial Paper
Article 4 Bank Deposits and Collections
Article 5 Letters of Credit
Article 6 Bulk Transfers
Article 7 Documents of Title
Article 8 Investment Securities
Article 9 Secured Transactions
Article 10 Effective Date and Repealer

This book will deal with all of the articles to some degree; however, separate chapters are devoted to the more important topics, such as sales (contracts for the sale of goods), commercial paper, and secured transactions.

The purpose of the UCC is threefold. First, it simplifies the laws governing commercial transactions. Second, it allows for the growth of commercial practices through the incorporation of customs and terms used in particular trades. Third, it makes the law of commercial transactions uniform throughout the United States. Article 2 of the Code—Sales—applies to contracts for the sale of goods. Its main purpose is to make the law of contracts simple and clear; to make the law uniform throughout the states; and to make it flexible enough to give the parties freedom to determine their respective rights and duties. When each state adopted the UCC, it became part of that state's contract law. The UCC is controlling in respect to contracts for the sale of goods. Basic contract law supplements the UCC and fills in the gaps. However, the elements of a contract must still be present in all commercial transactions. The Code has expanded contract law and made important modifications.

In a commercial transaction involving the sale of goods, the buyer, the seller, and the property contracted for are often in different states. The *Daily Planet's* contract with Universal Paper Corporation typifies this. The *Daily Planet* is located in Sun Valley, Idaho; Universal Paper Corporation is in Crater Lake, Oregon; and the paper to be delivered is from the Petrified Forest in Arizona. Since performance—delivery of the newspapers—is to be made in Idaho, and since one of the parties is domiciled in Idaho, Idaho law would govern unless otherwise stipulated by contract. To avoid conflicts wherein the parties would each want the law of the state most favorable to them to govern, the UCC has simplified this problem by making the law of contracts for the sale of goods uniform in all states.

However, when the UCC became a part of each state's contract law, it also became open to judicial interpretation by the individual courts in each state. In time, this may lead to varying interpretations of the provisions of the UCC. This means that it will be important to the parties to have the case decided in the court giving them the most favorable interpretation of the Code, whether it be a liberal or a strict construction.

1. Define a contract.
2. What are the elements of a contract?
3. How does an agreement become legally enforceable?
4. What is the importance of contracts?
5. How do contracts relate to us?
6. What are the various types of contracts?
7. Universal Paper Corporation (Oregon) contracts to sell the land it owns in the Petrified Forest (Arizona) to the *Daily Planet* (Idaho). Which state law governs?
8. The *Daily Planet* buys the *Morning Star* newspaper, which is based in Jupiter, Florida. Meteor Mike signs a contract with the *Planet* in Sun Valley, Idaho, to be editor-in-chief of the *Morning Star*. After six months, the *Planet* is suing Meteor Mike for nonperformance of his duties. Which state law governs? Could this have been altered by contract?
9. What is the significance of the UCC?
10. In the example in the text, Tommy Moon wants to know what his rights are in respect to the cancellation of his subscription. Can you advise him?

7

AGREEMENT

INTRODUCTION

An agreement is a definite understanding between two or more parties wherein each party promises to perform or forbear from performing a specific act. An agreement is made by an offer on one party's part which is voluntarily accepted by another party. An offer communicates the offeror's intention to be bound by the terms of the offer, which must be set forth, and requests the offeree to accept those terms. When we speak of an offer, we mean an enforceable offer, where acceptance of the terms results in a contract. This presupposes the presence of the other contractual elements: lawful purpose, legal capacity, promise to perform a specific act, consideration, and execution in proper form.

An offeror is the person making the offer. This individual has the freedom to set the terms of the offer. This freedom is unrestricted to a large extent because the offeree is protected by the right to refuse the offer. The offer may be modified or revoked by the offeror at any point prior to acceptance. Upon acceptance, the offeror is bound to the terms of the offer. An offeree is the person to whom the offer is made. This person is under no obligation to accept the offer. The offeree may accept, make a counteroffer, reject, or allow the offer to lapse. An acceptance indicates the offeree's willingness to be bound by the terms of the offer. An acceptance of the offer binds both parties to each other by contract.

EXAMPLE | John Smith arrived in Plymouth, Massachusetts on a boat from England. He was on a sightseeing tour with the Pilgrims when he first saw Plymouth Rock. Smith told the tour guide, Pocahontas, that he wanted to speak with the owner of Plymouth Rock. Pocahontas took Smith to Jamestown, Virginia, to speak with her father, Powhatan, who was the owner of Plymouth Rock. The great Indian chief did not fancy John Smith.

Pocahontas interceded on Smith's behalf and was able to convince her father to offer him Plymouth Rock. The wise old chief acquiesced in his favorite daughter's request, but he asked for $48 in trinkets, double the price for Manhattan Island, and made Smith promise not to marry Pocahontas. Smith gladly accepted. Is there an agreement between the parties? Yes! An agreement was made when Smith accepted Powhatan's offer. So, Smith lost Pocahontas, but ended up with a piece of the rock!

CHARACTERISTICS OF AN OFFER

There are three essential characteristics of an offer:

Definite terms

Communication to offeree

Valid for a reasonable time

Definite Terms

An offer generally must be clear and definite in its terms, especially in regard to quantity, price, time, place of delivery, identification of the parties, and description of the goods being offered.

Subject matter description

Time

Identification of the parties

Price

Number, quantity

Delivery place

An offer must be clear and definite in order that the offeree will be able to recognize that the offeror wishes to make a valid contract based on acceptance of the terms indicated. Both should know the exact terms to which they are agreeing. Specifically, the offeree wishes to know what is required of him or her, and what the offeror intends to do in return. It is rare that someone purchases something without asking what the price is, where and when the item can be delivered, and the quantity that is needed. These are basic facts you should agree upon before buying. If the offeror makes a mistake that is not reasonably evident in one of the material terms, then he or she is bound if the offeree accepts before receiving notification of the error.

EXAMPLE

Powhatan's offer to John Smith must include the description of the property, the price which he is asking, and the time and place he intends to deliver the deed. The quantity term is not significant except as it relates to the amount of acreage of land sold, which is part of the legal description of the property. If Powhatan tells Smith he intends to sell him the northern section of Plymouth Rock, but mistakenly includes part of the eastern section and Smith accepts the offer as stated, is Powhatan bound by his mistake? Yes! There is an agreement as long as Smith is not aware of Powhatan's mistake.

The terms of an offer must be clear and definite in order for the court to interpret the rights and duties of the respective parties in case of a dispute. Terms which are ambiguous or indefinite cannot be enforced. The court does not have the power to create terms because that would restrict the parties' freedom to bargain with each other. The UCC looks to the actions of the parties to determine what their course of performance or course of dealing has been. This will help to resolve ambiguities, because the parties themselves know best what they meant by the phrases they used in the contract, and their actions are the best source for finding out what that meaning is. The court will also ascertain the meaning attributed to a disputed term in the particular trade or business.

EXAMPLE In the previous example, the northern section of Plymouth Rock was the description of the property agreed upon by Smith and Powhatan. Suppose this is the fifth tract of land purchased from Powhatan. In each case, the parties have made it their practice to mark the trees at the perimeter of the property with war paint when each tract of land is sold. The trees at the perimeter of the northern property are so marked. Is the description "northern property" of Plymouth Rock sufficiently clear to allow the court to enforce the contract? Yes! The parties' practice of painting the peripheral trees with war paint is their course of performance. This course will be followed unless the contract expressly provides otherwise.

Certain contracts are permitted to be indefinite when particular terms cannot be defined in advance.

Contingency Contracts Contingency contracts are established between lawyers and their clients where the fee will depend upon the outcome of the suit. The outcome will be decided at a future time, but the attorney's fee is a percentage of the court's award, and that percentage is fixed from the beginning, when the attorney and client make the contract. Contractors incorporate a cost-contingency clause in their contracts in case of unforeseen or inflationary rises in their basic costs.

EXAMPLE Marion Blackburn is hurrying to the Rolling Hills Country Club in the suburbs of Philadelphia for her final match in the club's bridge championship. In her haste, she runs through a red light and totally smashes a 1966 Plymouth driven by William Jackson. Jackson, recognizing her from her pictures in the society section of the newspaper, figures this is his lucky day. He races down to the law office of an "ambulance chasing" attorney who specializes in accident cases. The lawyer asks Jackson, "You've suffered severe whiplash, haven't you?" Jackson replies in the affirmative. The lawyer offers to take Jackson's case on the contingency that if the suit against Marion Blackburn is won or settled, he will get one-third of the award. Is this offer enforceable? Yes! The offer is enforceable although the actual fee will not be determined until the result of the suit.

Output Contracts and Requirement Contracts Output contracts require the seller to deliver its total output of a certain product to a particular purchaser. Requirement contracts obligate the purchaser to buy all of its supplies from the same seller. The seller's output and the purchaser's requirements must be made in good faith. They must be comparable to a preconceived estimate, if one was made; or, if not, they must be consistent with outputs or requirements made in prior years. A seller's output or a purchaser's requirements may not increase or decrease drastically in order for them to take unfair advantage of a fluctuation in the price of the item manufactured or ordered.

EXAMPLE | George Cornwallis, an English merchant, operates a tea processing plant in Concord. Clifford Bannister owns a small farm in Lexington where he grows tea leaves. Bannister, an elderly man, is tired of loading and delivering the tea leaves to different tea plants. Cornwallis offers to pick up the tea leaves if Bannister will sell him his entire crop each year.

Is this offer enforceable? Yes! This is an output contract. The terms will be settled at the end of the harvest.

Martha Washington is the proprietor of a posh catering hall in Boston where she regularly runs Singles Tea Parties. Cornwallis, knowing that tea is hard to come by, offers to sell it to Martha if she agrees to purchase all she requires from him. Is this offer enforceable? Yes! This is a requirement contract, where the terms will be settled at the end of the tea season.

The UCC does not require contracts for the sale of goods to be definite in all respects. It liberalizes rules pertaining to the formation of a contract. Contracts exist even where certain material terms have been left out, if the intentions of the parties to make a contract are clear and there is a reasonable basis for fixing the omitted term and giving an appropriate remedy should a breach occur. The gap-filler provisions of the Code will supplement the contract and it will not fail because of its indefiniteness. "Reasonable price" and "reasonable time" will be substituted where a contract does not provide for these terms. Place of delivery will be at the seller's place of business in cases where this term is not mentioned. The three other key terms: quantity, identification of the parties, and description of the goods must be stipulated or the contract will fail for indefiniteness.

EXAMPLE | Newark Airport's North Terminal has reopened for passenger flights. Willie Hearst obtains the newspaper concession at the terminal. He is approached by a representative of Dow Jones, Inc., the publisher of the *Wall Street Journal,* who offers to deliver 150 copies to Hearst on a daily basis. Is this an enforceable offer? Yes! Dow Jones' offer to Hearst is enforceable under the UCC even though certain terms were omitted. The price must be a reasonable price for wholesale delivery of newspapers. The delivery time must be reasonable for Hearst to be able to sell the newspapers. If Hearst wanted to receive the papers at his newsstand at 4 A.M. for sale to early morning flyers, he should have requested this term before the contract was made.

Communication to Offeree

An offer must be communicated through the method selected by the offeror. An offer becomes effective when the offeree receives it. If the offeree learns of the offer through another source, it is not enforceable. An offer is not assignable, because the offeree has no contractual rights to what is offered. Only upon acceptance, when a contract is made, are legal rights and duties created. At that time, a contract may be assigned subject to certain restrictions. Assignments and their applicable restrictions will be discussed in Chapter 12.

Martha and Henry Jameson own fifteen acres on Beaver Creek in Arkansas. After living there for thirty-five years, Henry dies, leaving Martha alone. She realizes she must sell the property, but she refuses to sell it to the Willotson Lead and Sulfur Mining Company when they inquire about it. A few days later, Erma, the town gossip, overhears Martha offering to sell her property for $75,000 to Betty and Jimmy Rodgers, newlyweds, who grew up in the community. Erma rushes to the telephone to inform Sam Willotson, the owner of the mining company. The Willotson Mine notifies Martha Jameson that they heard the property is offered for sale for $75,000 and they accept the offer here and now. Martha refuses by saying Willotson's acceptance is not valid. Is Martha correct? Yes! Martha is correct because the offer can only be accepted by the Rodgers, the young newlyweds to whom it was made.

Valid for a Reasonable Time

An offer is valid only for a "reasonable time" unless a definite time is stated. What is reasonable depends on what is being offered and on the terms of the offer. Offers for perishable goods would logically be open for a shorter period than offers for durable goods, as would offers for the sale of securities at a fixed price as compared with offers for the sale of real estate.

How the offer is made also affects its duration. An offer that arises during a conversation in person or on the phone must be accepted during the conversation or it lapses unless a definite time for acceptance is stated.

EXAMPLE Jack Stafford, a golf course architect, is discussing plans for designing a golf course in the community of Whispering Willows with the community's developer, Thomas Courtney. During dinner, Courtney offers Stafford $5 million to design the golf course. Stafford replies "Five million dollars sounds interesting. Let me think it over." Nothing more is said of the offer during their dinner conversation. The following week Courtney receives a call from Stafford accepting the offer. Courtney claims Stafford's acceptance was not timely made. Is he correct? Yes! Courtney is correct because an offer that arises during a conversation must be accepted before the conversation ends or it lapses. Stafford's purported acceptance merely operates as a counteroffer.

PRELIMINARY NEGOTIATIONS

Preliminary negotiations include all communications between parties that do not constitute an enforceable offer. Its purpose is to lead to an offer by providing buyers with information concerning products, services, or real estate. Buyers may be negotiating with several businesses at the same time to determine the most advantageous deal. If each negotiation were said to be an offer, the buyer might become involved in several contracts that he or she would not be able to perform. This would inhibit parties from negotiating. Preliminary negotiations may go through several stages, especially in complicated contracts. Each discussion might involve a different contractual provision or even an aspect of a provision.

The following is a list of those statements which do not qualify as offers because they are generally considered to be preliminary negotiations:

Invitations
Circulars
Emotional statements
Catalogs
Advertisements
Price quotes
Social invitations

Invitations

A statement that leaves terms open for negotiation is not an enforceable offer, but an invitation to negotiate. An invitation to negotiate is a communication requesting people to make offers. It cannot be accepted because its terms are not definite. A key to determining whether a statement is an offer or an invitation is the class of people to whom the offer is directed. A statement made to the general public must be construed as an invitation, otherwise an offeror would be reluctant to deal with the general public for fear of breaching the contract if the general public's needs could not be met. If the statement is restricted to a certain few, the odds are greater, though not conclusive, that the statement is an offer.

Lefkowitz v. Great Minneapolis Surplus Store, Inc.
251 Minn. 188, 86 N.W.2d 689 (1957)

Lefkowitz sued the Minneapolis Surplus Store for breach of contract. Lefkowitz alleges that on two occasions he accepted an offer made by the defendant through a newspaper advertisement by being the first to respond.

The first newspaper advertisement was published by the store on April 6, 1956. It states:

> Saturday 9 A.M. Sharp
> 3 Brand New
> Fur
> Coats
> Worth to $100.00
> First Come
> First Served
> $1
> Each

On April 13, the store published a second advertisement which read:

> Saturday 9 A.M.
> 2 Brand New Pastel

Mink 3-Skin Scarfs
Selling for $89.50
Out they go
Saturday, Each $1.00
1 Black Lapin Stole
Beautiful,
Worth $139.50 . . . . $1.00
First Come
First Served

On the respective Saturdays, Lefkowitz was the first to present himself at the appropriate counter in the store and he indicated his willingness to pay the price of $1.00. The store refused to sell Lefkowitz the merchandise on both occasions because, according to their house rule, the offer was open only to women. The Great Minneapolis Surplus Store contends that a newspaper advertisement is not an offer, but rather an invitation to the reader to make an offer which can be accepted only by the store.

The issue is whether the newspaper advertisement constituted an offer by being so clear and definite that it left no terms open for negotiation.

The court decided the advertisement was an offer and awarded the plaintiff damages. Performance was promised in return for compliance with the store's request. The house rule has no validity because the restriction was not placed in the advertisement. Judgment for Lefkowitz.

A reward, although made to the general public, is an offer because its request for performance can be made by only one, or at most a few individuals. Acceptance of the reward requires some knowledge of the reward coupled with actual performance.

EXAMPLE | Timothy Baldwin lives in an apartment complex in Hillcrest. One day while visiting his local post office to mail a package to his sister in Alabama, he notices a description of a man wanted for robbery in the famous Brink's case. The description matches a man who moved into the apartment across the hall from Timothy. He immediately notifies the police and the culprit is apprehended. At the police station, Timothy is asked what he plans to do with the reward money. Timothy responds he did not know of any reward, but will gladly accept it. The Brink's Company refuses to pay Timothy the reward. Are they right? Yes! Timothy acted without knowledge of the reward; therefore, he is not legally entitled to it.

Circulars, Catalogs, Advertisements, and Price Quotes

Circulars, catalogs, advertisements, and price quotes are all forms of invitations intended to acquaint the prospective purchaser with certain items, property, or the services the seller provides. In doing so, the seller hopes that prospective customers will discuss terms that will eventually lead to enforceable offers. These forms of invitations are not enforceable unless they are so clear and definite, as in the Lefkowitz case, that no terms are left open for negotiation. However, laws have been enacted to protect consumers from false advertising by imposing criminal penalties on an advertiser who deliberately attempts to mislead the public.

When the recipient of the invitation or advertisement offers to buy something, then the seller may accept or reject the offer depending on whether the particular size, color, and style requested is available. As you know, all sellers do not carry every color, size, and style of every product that is made. They are free to carry what they feel are the most popular items. It would restrict their freedom if they were requested to act otherwise.

EXAMPLE | Abe Lincoln is spending a quiet day at home, leafing through a Sears catalogue when suddenly an advertisement catches his eye, "Sears Paints Great American Homes." Lincoln concludes that he is a great American and that Sears should paint his home. Abe hurries down to accept the offer. The store manager, John Wilkes Booth, informs Lincoln that although Sears acknowledges that he is a great American, it is their belief that his log cabin is not a great American home. Has Lincoln any recourse? No! The advertisement was an invitation for Lincoln to make a request. Its terms were not definite enough to constitute an offer. Lincoln splits and makes tracks for Washington.

Emotional Statements

Emotional statements made in anger, excitement, or jest do not constitute an offer. Whether or not a statement was made in anger, excitement, or jest depends on the objective actions of the parties, not on their subjective state of mind. The key is what the person said and the context in which it was said, not what may have been in that person's mind at the time. The person seeking to enforce the agreement must reasonably believe the other party seriously intended to enter into a contract. The surrounding circumstances are helpful in arriving at this determination.

Lucy v. Zehmer
196 Va. 493, 84 S.E.2d 516 (1954)

Lucy brought suit against Zehmer for specific performance of a contract. Lucy alleges that Zehmer sold land known as the Ferguson Farm to him for $50,000.

The contract states "We hereby agree to sell to W. O. Lucy the Ferguson Farm complete for $50,000.00, title satisfactory to buyer," and signed by the defendants, A. H. Zehmer and Ida S. Zehmer.

The underlying facts hold the key. Lucy and Zehmer had several drinks at a local tavern. Lucy asked Zehmer if he had sold the Ferguson Farm. When Zehmer replied "No," Lucy offered him $50,000. Zehmer intimated that Lucy did not have the money, to which Lucy replied that Zehmer should put the agreement in writing and sign it, which both he and his wife did. Zehmer asserts that the contract was made in jest; whereas Lucy contends it was a valid contract that became binding when he delivered the money which was refused. The capacity of the parties would seem to be in issue, however, Zehmer's attorney conceded that Zehmer was not too drunk to make a valid contract.

The issue is whether the agreement was valid or made in jest.

The court declared that if a person's actions manifest a reasonable intention to agree, then it is immaterial what his or her state of mind was at the time. This case is a prime example of this rule. Judgment for Lucy.

Social Invitations

Social invitations, such as dates or invitations to parties or weddings, are not legally enforceable offers, although they can be accepted. As a matter of public policy, it has been decided that people should not be subject to breach of contract suits for breaking a date or changing their mind about going to a party. People can have agreements concerning social affairs and these agreements may have moral and social implications if they are broken, but they have no legal consequences.

EXAMPLE | Miles Standish has admired Priscilla for a long time and finally gets enough courage to ask her for a date. She accepts and invites Miles to meet her family. Miles is too shy to meet her family, so he asks his friend John Alden to call for Priscilla in his stead. Alden, being a good friend, does as Miles requests. He meets the family, but after one look at Priscilla, decides to take her out himself. Has Miles any recourse against Priscilla or Alden for the broken date or his broken heart? No! Dates are not offers; they are social invitations which have no legal consequences.

SPECIAL OFFERS

Invitations requesting bids are called soliciting offers. At an auction, an auctioneer is inviting the audience to bid on particular items. When someone from the audience bids, that person is making an offer. A higher bid has the effect of cancelling all the lower ones. Acceptance rests with the auctioneer when he pounds the gavel and thus creates a contract of sale to the highest bidder. Bidders who have second thoughts may retract their offers, but must do so before the auctioneer has banged the gavel. The auctioneer may refuse the highest bidder and withdraw the item if a fair price has not been bid. However, if the auction is being held "without reserve," then the auctioneer must accept the highest bid. The words "without reserve" must be specifically stated. These words signify that the owner is agreeing not to withdraw the property regardless of how low the highest bid might be.

An auctioneer is the agent for the seller. Auctioneers are generally professional salespeople who act on the seller's behalf to get the highest possible bid for each item that is offered for sale. An auctioneer may represent an individual seller or many sellers in a general auction; he may conduct a sale of public property or an estate auction in which a deceased's personal effects are sold off to settle an estate.

EXAMPLE | James Madison has come to the conclusion that the federal deficit must be narrowed. He decides the government should auction off some of its national treasures. He appoints Ben Franklin, an auctioneer, to hold the auction at Independence Hall in South Philadelphia. When Franklin asks, "What am I offered for the Liberty Bell?", the highest bid is $50,000 by Patrick Henry. Madison believes the Liberty Bell is worth at least

$100,000 and instructs Franklin to refuse the offer. Patrick Henry shouts, "Give me the Liberty Bell or give me death." Has he any recourse? Unless the auction is held without reserve, Madison is not bound to accept the highest bid.

The sale of stocks, bonds, and commodities are transacted on a bid-asked basis. Sellers will be trying to get the highest bid for their securities and commodities, just as buyers will be trying to purchase at the lowest possible bid. The prices bid and asked generally have some relationship to the price of the previous sale. When a bid is accepted, a contract is made. Auction sales and the sale of securities on the stock exchange floor are contracts, implied from the actions of the parties through recognized sign language.

Construction bids that a landowner requests from general contractors are not offers. The bids submitted by the general contractors are offers. The owner has the opportunity at that point to accept or refuse the lowest bid. To arrive at their bid, general contractors will request bids from subcontractors in specialized fields such as electricity, masonry, plumbing, and carpentry. The bids submitted by subcontractors are offers. A general contractor's use of a subcontractor's bid does not constitute an acceptance of that bid even if the general contractor is subsequently awarded the contract. When the contract is awarded, the general contractor is free to accept or reject the subcontractor's bid. A subcontractor has the freedom to retract the bid at any point prior to the general contractor's acceptance.

OPTION CONTRACTS

An option gives the offeree the exclusive right for a specified period of time to accept or reject the stipulated offer. An option is a contract because the offeree must give some form of consideration in return. The offeree is paying for time. The time may be used to attempt to negotiate a better deal either with the offeror or with another party. People will often be in a better position to make a decision three or even six months down the road. They may foresee an improvement in their financial state or an economic recovery which might make the option more valuable to them. Even if the offeree rejects the offer at first, he or she may later accept it as long as the option has not expired. The offeror is restricted from selling to another party for the duration of the option.

EXAMPLE Michael and Vivian Stone are a young couple starting out in life. They plan to build their future in the Sun Belt. While vacationing in Galveston, they discover their dream house on Galveston Island. The price is $125,000, which is more than they can afford at the moment, but in six months they should receive $50,000 from the estate of Vivian's uncle. They approach the Adams family, owners of the property, and ask if they will hold their $125,000 offer open for six months in return for a payment of $500. The Adams family agree. Two months later, after separating from her husband, Vivian informs the Adams family that she and her husband no longer intend to purchase the house. The Adams family immediately sell the house to another couple. Three months later, Michael and Vivian Stone are back together and the bequest from the estate comes through. The Stones notify the Adams family of their intent to exercise the option. Are they better late than never? Yes! Michael and Vivian Stone may still accept the offer to purchase the property for $125,000 because the option has not expired. Upon the exercise of the option, the contract between the Adams family and the other couple will be voided.

TERMINATION OF AN OFFER

An offer may be terminated by:

Revocation
Operation of law
Lapse of time
Destruction of subject matter
Death
Incompetency
Counteroffer
Express rejection

Revocation

The offeror may cancel by revoking the offer for any reason at any time prior to the offeree's acceptance. The revocation must be communicated to the offeree and does not become effective until the offeree receives notice of it. The revocation is still effective even though the offeree learns of it through another source. If the offeree accepts prior to receiving notice of revocation, a valid contract is made.

EXAMPLE Glen Murrow, a collector of rare memorabilia, offers to sell the original White House tapes to Elliot Hart, a record producer, if Hart accepts within ten days. One week later, while vacationing with historian Jacob Simpson at his favorite hotel, the Watergate, Hart tells Simpson of Murrow's offer. Simpson informs Hart that Murrow has now decided to donate the original tapes to the government for auction along with the government's other national treasures at Independence Hall in Philadelphia. Hart asserts the ten days have not expired. Is Murrow bound by the time limit? No! Glen Murrow is not bound by the time limit because no consideration was given in return by Elliot Hart. Murrow can revoke at any time and Hart's learning of the revocation from Jacob Simpson fulfills the requirement of proper notice.

The UCC provides that if the offeror makes an offer to the offeree, and then sells to a third person in the ordinary course of business without notifying the offeree who then accepts the original offer, the third person may retain the goods and the offeree's remedy will be limited to loss of profits. This rule was enacted to protect the buyer in the ordinary course of business who would otherwise be reluctant to enter into a contract for fear an offer may have been made to another. A buyer in the ordinary course of business is a person who buys in good faith and for valuable consideration without knowledge that someone else may have superior rights to the goods purchased. An offeror may reserve the right to sell to another without notice to the offeree, as long as this right is stipulated in the offer. Revocation of an offer to the general public may be made through the medium used to convey the offer. Individual notification is not necessary, because it would be costly and practically impossible.

A promise by the offeror not to revoke for a stated period is not enforceable unless the offeree provides consideration in return, which would make it an option contract. There are certain situations where an offeror may not revoke an offer:

Changing position in reliance on the offer

Acceptance of the offer

Partial performance

Changing Position in Reliance on the Offer   Where the offeree changes his or her position in reliance on the offer with the intent to accept, the offeror will be stopped from revoking the offer as long as the offeree acted reasonably. The change in position must be significant. The reasoning is based on the doctrine of promissory estoppel. It will be discussed to a greater extent in Chapter 8.

EXAMPLE   The Mets, who would do anything to get out of last place in the National League's Eastern Division, decide to resort to advertising to get new talent. Jack E. Robinson responds to the ad and gets a preliminary tryout in New York. He is then offered a tryout with the team at its St. Petersburg training camp. The team representative advises Robinson that the team will provide room and board for a guaranteed five-week tryout, but he must furnish his own transportation to Florida. Robinson resigns from his position in New York and arrives in Florida on the appointed day. But after the first day of tryouts, he is cut from the team and refused further accommodations. Has Robinson any recourse? Yes! Although revocation of an offer can generally be made at any time prior to acceptance, the Mets will be prevented from revoking their offer because Robinson changed his position in reliance on their promise. He left his job in New York, paid for the transportation costs to Florida, and is trying to accept their offer to try out for the team. He is prevented from doing so by the team itself. Robinson must be given the opportunity to accept the offer by being allowed to try out.

Acceptance of the Offer   Acceptance of the offer without knowledge or receipt of revocation will bar any attempt by the offeror to revoke.

EXAMPLE   Dolly Madison was fond of little George Washington. She told him that she would pay him $5 if he would chop down her cherry tree. Dolly told her husband, James Madison, of her benevolence toward George. James told Dolly to withdraw the offer, because the cherry tree was his favorite. While they were away at the Presidential Ball, the cherry tree was cut down. Upon their return Dolly questioned young George who responded, "I cannot tell a lie, it was I who chopped down the cherry tree, and I want the five bucks." Must Dolly acquiesce to George's demand? Yes! Dolly must pay because George accepted the offer without knowledge of revocation.

Partial performance   When the offeree performs or begins to perform a substantial part of the offer, then any revocation by the offeror will result in a breach of contract. The UCC provides an additional exception for sales contracts, called a firm offer. A firm offer, signed by a merchant, is irrevocable for a period of up to three months.

Operation of Law

An enactment of a new law which makes the offer illegal, cancels the offer. If the offer has been accepted prior to the change in law, the validity of the contract depends upon whether or not the law is retroactive.

EXAMPLE | Dexter Bradshaw III takes matters into his own hands in arranging for his twentieth birthday party at his parent's home. They are, fortunately for Dexter, in Europe. He engages a small but deafening rock group to entertain, and invites the coolest of his preppie friends for the weekend. On the afternoon of his birthday, he drives down into town to pick up a supply of gin, vodka, and scotch to get the party off the ground. Dexter offers to buy five bottles of each for $150. Before the salesman accepts, he asks Dexter for proof of his age. Dexter produces his driver's license and proudly states that he is twenty years of age today. The salesman reluctantly informs Dexter that the governor of the state has raised the drinking age from eighteen to twenty-one, and that he cannot accept Dexter's offer. Dexter turns away from the liquor store painfully envisioning himself with a houseful of guests, trying to get things going with soft drinks. Has Dexter any recourse? No! Dexter has no recourse because the enactment of the new law has effectively cancelled the offer.

Lapse of Time

An offer is enforceable for the length of time stated in the offer. When the time expires, the offer is cancelled. If the offeror fails to restrict the duration of the offer, it is enforceable for a reasonable time. What is reasonable depends upon what is being offered and the surrounding circumstances. An offer for securities or commodities at a fixed price on an exchange may be enforceable for only a matter of minutes or seconds because of the volatility of price fluctuations. Real estate offers and offers to render a personal service are generally of a longer duration because the price does not fluctuate as rapidly. Once an offer lapses, a party wishing to accept may only make a new offer. In situations where no time is fixed and the offeror receives the offer after what is believed to be a reasonable time, the offeror must notify the offeree immediately that the acceptance is not valid or run the risk that his silent conduct will operate as an acceptance. If it is important for the offeror to restrict the duration of the offer, it is always best to state the length of time that the offer is open. Otherwise, a lawsuit may result to determine whether acceptance was made within a reasonable time.

EXAMPLE | William Penn owned a large oat farm. In June, Penn contacted the Quakers, a food-processing concern, and offered to sell them his oats. The Quakers finally accepted Penn's offer in September, long after the oats had been harvested. By this time, Penn had made other arrangements. Penn refused to ship the oats to the Quakers, claiming an unreasonable amount of time had passed. Do the Quakers have any recourse? No! Since contracts are generally made before harvest, Penn is right, a reasonable time to accept the offer has lapsed.

Destruction of Land or Personal Property

Destruction of the subject matter will nullify the offer if the subject matter was unique or had been specifically designated for the purchaser in a sales contract. This is because it would be impossible to replace the destroyed subject matter. Each parcel of real estate is unique; so are certain goods that are handcrafted or are one of a kind. An offer for goods which can easily be replaced does not terminate unless the seller had separated certain goods from the rest and designated them for the purchaser, or the contract specified that the goods would come from a particular crop or shipment and these goods subsequently were destroyed.

EXAMPLE | While strolling through South Philadelphia, George Washington came upon an upholsterer's shop with a star-spangled banner in the window. Washington approached the proprietor, Betsy Ross, and offered to buy the flag; he told her he would return the next day with the money. That night a fire consumed the shop and destroyed the flag. Did George's offer go up in smoke? Yes! The offer to purchase the star-spangled banner has been nullified by its destruction.

Death or Incompetency

Death or incompetency of either the offeror or the offeree terminates the offer unless there is a firm offer or part performance by the offeree that can be completed by the offeror's personal representative. An offer is personal and if the offeror dies, the offer dies with that person. This is generally true whether or not the other party has been notified. An offer is enforceable only by the person to whom it is made; if the offeree dies, no one else has the power to accept it. A contract is not terminated by incompetency or death, because certain legal obligations have been created that must be carried through. Otherwise physicians and hospitals would hesitate to make contracts with terminal patients for fear of not getting reimbursed. An exception to this rule would be personal service contracts. An individual's services are unique; there is no way to enforce the contract or provide a remedy. An offer has no legal obligations. This is generally why offers do not survive the people who make them or the people to whom they are made.

EXAMPLE | Joseph Fredericks was a vice-president at the Bank of America. One spring evening while eating dinner at the home of his friend Stephen Pearson, talk drifted around to Patricia Pearson, who was about to receive her M.B.A. degree. Fredericks, who had always been fond of her, told her parents he would like to offer her a job in the bank's mortgage service department at a starting salary of $20,000, to begin two weeks after she got her degree. Patricia was ecstatic on hearing the news of Frederick's offer and on returning home from the university, hurried down to the bank to thank her benefactor, only to learn that he had been killed the night before in an automobile crash. Patricia and her family were in shock. A few days after the funeral services, she informed the bank of Mr. Fredericks' offer to hire her, but she was refused employment. Did Mr. Fredericks' offer die with him? Yes! Patricia's acceptance of the offer was precluded by his death.

Counteroffer

Counteroffers are a reply to the original offer where at least one of the key terms has been altered. The addition or alteration of material terms impliedly amounts to a rejection of the original offer with the substitution of a new offer. Once a counteroffer is made, the offeree cannot have a subsequent change of heart and accept the original offer. It is important to distinguish between a counteroffer altering a material term and an inquiry asking if a material term may be changed. The latter is not a counteroffer.

An inquiry may be merely a suggestion or a request. The way an inquiry is worded does not amount to a rejection of the original offer and a proposal of a new offer. "Is this your highest offer?" or "Is it possible for you to make delivery at my place of business?" are inquiries; whereas, "In reply to your offer of $4,000, my price is $5,000" or "I accept your offer only if delivery is made at my place of business" are counteroffers.

An inquiry may also be expressed in the following way: "I am considering your offer, but I would like to inquire whether you are flexible in regard to the price." The words "I accept your offer to buy 100 Polaroid cameras for $5,000, and I hope you will sell me an additional 100 for $4,550" amount to a valid acceptance of the first 100 cameras. This contract is not affected by the buyer's subsequent offer to purchase an additional 100 cameras.

In contracts between merchants for the sale of goods, the UCC provides that additional terms contained in the acceptance become part of the contract unless they alter the material terms of the offer; acceptance is restricted to the terms set forth in the offer; or the offeror gives notice of objection within a reasonable time.

Express Rejection

Rejection by the offeree may be made by communicating his or her refusal to the offeror. If the offeree does not reply, the lapse of time will signify a rejection. Once the offeree communicates notice of rejection to the offeror, the offeree cannot have a change of mind later and accept the offer. When offers are requested from the general public, an offer may not be rejected solely because of the offeree's race, religion, nationality, or sex. This rule applies to public service companies providing electric, gas, telephone, fuel, medical care, and insurance, and to hotels, restaurants, employers, landlords, and other sellers.

EXAMPLE Slick Rick, a local con artist, observes Thompson L. Worthington III, whom he takes to be a typical tourist in his floppy hat, sunglasses, Hawaiian shirt, Bermuda shorts, sandals with knee-high socks, and a camera hanging around his neck. Worthington is flashing a roll of bills. Slick Rick sidles up to him and offers to take Worthington on a boat tour around Manhattan Island, but Worthington replies that he has already made the tour on the Circle Line. What is the effect of Worthington's reply? His reply is a rejection of Slick Rick's offer. Slick Rick then tries a different angle and offers to sell Worthington what he represents to be a Cartier watch for $110 in cash. Worthington answers, "I will accept, if I can pay with this credit card." Slick Rick laughs and walks away saying, "Not without a credit reference." What is the status of Worthington's answer? It is a counteroffer changing the method of payment, which was a material term in Slick Rick's offer.

METHODS OF ACCEPTANCE

An offeree has the legal power to consummate a contract by accepting the offer in the manner requested. Acceptance of an offer must be made by the party to whom the offer was made. Offers cannot be assigned to a third party unless they are option contracts. There must be an unconditional acceptance of the material terms of the offer. Incidental additions do not operate as a rejection. An acceptance or the adding or altering of material terms is a counteroffer, and a contract will not result except for those situations allowed by the UCC. Where similar acceptances will be made repeatedly or at a certain interval, those acceptances already made are contracts; however, the rest can be rejected if notice is given to the offeror.

Acceptance must be communicated to the offeror in the manner requested in the offer. Acceptance of an offer by mail is effective when it is mailed, even if the mail is delayed or lost.

EXAMPLE Clark in St. Joseph, Missouri, writes to his friend Lewis in Sacramento inviting him to sail up the Missouri and Columbia rivers and explore the Oregon Territory. Clark mails his offer on April 3, stating acceptance must be made within one week. Delivery by mail takes five days. Later he realizes that Lewis is no fun and decides to revoke his offer, mailing the notice on April 7. Lewis receives the offer on April 8 and does not send his acceptance until April 11. The next day, Clark's notice of revocation arrives. Lewis's acceptance does not reach Clark until two weeks later, because of a delay in the mail. Will Lewis join Clark in their search for the Oregon Territory? Yes! Lewis's acceptance on April 11 is well within the one-week time limit which expires on April 15. The fact that there was a delay in the delivery of the mail does not affect Lewis's acceptance. Clark's notice of revocation is not effective because it was received on the day after Lewis accepted.

If the offeree responds in a manner different from the one that is stipulated, then acceptance is effective upon receipt. The offeror may change the general rule by providing that acceptance is only effective upon receipt. The parties may agree that the contract will be valid only when a written document is prepared that contains all the key terms, is drafted in a clear and definite manner, and is signed by both parties.

The UCC provides that acceptance in response to offers for the sale of goods may be made in any reasonable manner unless the offeror specifies otherwise. Acceptances in contracts which are implied by the actions of the parties may be made by certain expressions of assent, such as the nodding of a head or the exchange of goods in return for money. There must be some affirmative movement on the offeree's part to signify acceptance.

EXAMPLE Olaf Anderson is in the United States on a student exchange program. He is studying music at a school in Kentucky. Although Olaf has a rudimentary command of the English language, he had difficulty communicating with Kentuckians because of their Southern accents. At a country fair in Cabin Creek, he stops to look around and decides to have something to eat. When he is given the menu, he does not understand the meaning of many of the words. Rather than appear ignorant, he points to the plate of the person next to him. He is served a delicious meal of grits, fatback, black-eyed peas, Kentucky fried chicken, and shoofly pie. Is his gesture a valid acceptance? Yes! The parties understood the nature of the transaction although neither speaks the other's dialect. The contract created through the offer by Olaf and the acceptance by the country fair restaurateur is implied from the actions of the parties.

Acceptance may be made by performance or forbearance of an act such as the prompt shipment of goods in a sales contract. The offeror must be given notice of acceptance. Immediate performance or forbearance by the offeree will usually be sufficient to apprise the offeror of acceptance. If not, the offeror must be informed by other means within a reasonable time.

Silence will generally not constitute acceptance even if the offeree states that it will, because one person cannot be forced to reply to an offer. If this were not true, some unscrupulous individuals could offer to buy other people's houses or personal effects, or even hire their services by informing them that unless the offer was expressly rejected, their silence would constitute an acceptance. Innocent people would be besieged by offers of this type and would be forced to go to great lengths to inform the offerors of their refusal. This was the case with such items as books that were sent through the mail along with a letter stating that acceptance will be implied if the item is not returned within a certain allotted time period, which was usually on the short side. Most states have adopted the Postal Reorganization Act of 1970, which provided that unordered merchandise need not be paid for or returned.

In certain situations, silence will operate as an acceptance. These exceptions to the general rule are:

Contract stipulation

Conduct of the offeree

Benefit of services received with knowledge

Actions of the parties

Prior dealings

Contract Stipulation

The parties have the freedom to stipulate in the contract that, for their convenience, silence will operate as an acceptance. This stipulation must be made freely by the parties. It often arises in contracts which are repetitive.

EXAMPLE | Peggy March signs a contract to join the Record of the Month Club. The contract provides that Peggy will receive five albums of her choice for the unbelievably low price of $1.00. Thereafter, Peggy must buy three albums each month at the price of $7.98 each. There is a stipulation allowing Peggy to cancel the contract by giving two weeks' notice before the next choice of selection is due. If Peggy is continually silent, will this operate as an acceptance of three new albums each month? Yes! Each delivery of record albums is a contract made by offer and acceptance. The parties have stipulated that Peggy's silence will constitute an acceptance; therefore, Peggy's continued silence signifies acceptance in these repetitive contracts.

Conduct of the Offeree

If the offeree's conduct leads the offeror into reasonably believing that silence will constitute an acceptance, and if delay through silence causes the subject matter to become unmarketable or if other damages are sustained, then acceptance through silence may be inferred. The offeree has a duty to speak and inform the offeror of his refusal.

EXAMPLE Samuel Adams informed John Hancock that he would like to purchase fire insurance on property he owned on Bunker Hill near Boston. John Hancock accepted by issuing the policy. Every year on July 4, the policy was automatically renewed, and a bill was mailed to Samuel Adams two weeks later. Subsequently, on July 11, a fire totally destroyed the property and John Hancock refused to pay the face value of the policy on the grounds that silence does not constitute acceptance. Does Samuel Adams have any recourse? Yes! John Hancock's conduct has reasonably led Samuel Adams to believe that the insurance has been granted for another year. If John Hancock wishes to cancel the policy, Adams must be informed in advance, thereby giving him a reasonable time to find insurance elsewhere.

Benefit of Services Received with Knowledge

An offeree who receives the benefit of services performed with knowledge and who has reason to know they were offered in the expectation of profit, has impliedly accepted the benefit and he or she is responsible for the reasonable value of the services performed.

Actions of the Parties

Contracts implied by the actions of the parties may be accepted in silence although an affirmative act on the offeree's part is required. Depositing a token in a turnstile is such an action. So is the banging of the auctioneer's gavel.

Prior Dealings

When a transaction is based on prior dealings where the offeree has given the offeror reason to believe that silence will be the method of acceptance, silence will be effective in the present case as well.

EXAMPLE The Adler sisters, Mabel and Harriet, lived in a small town in a dry county in Utah. Their good friend Mildred would visit them each month and, as a favor, bring a basket of cheer filled with three bottles of scotch; two bottles each of rye, gin, and vodka; and one bottle of vermouth for those lovely dry martinis. Mabel and Harriet gladly accepted and paid Mildred for the liquor. On her last visit, Mildred brought the usual basket of cheer, but this time Mabel and Harriet, having finally joined Alcoholics Anonymous, refused to accept it. Mildred, who was a teetotaler, had no use for the liquor. Must she suffer the loss? No! Although silence is generally not effective as an acceptance, Mildred relied upon Mabel and Harriet's silence based upon prior dealings. A contract will be implied from the actions of the parties, to prevent Mabel and Harriet from becoming unjustly enriched at Mildred's expense.

REVIEW QUESTIONS

1. Define the following terms: agreement, offer, acceptance, offeror, offeree, requirement contract, output contract, contingency contract, and option.

2. List and explain the ways an offer may be terminated.

3. In what situations may silence be effective as an acceptance?

4. Brewer had a contract to buy McAfee's house and to move in on June 12. Brewer asked McAfee if he would sell certain pieces of furniture in the house in a separate transaction. McAfee sent a letter to Brewer on April 30 listing each piece of furniture, the price, and schedule of payment. A copy of the letter was to be signed and returned by mail, if satisfactory. Brewer misplaced the letter, but wrote to McAfee on June 3 enclosing a check for $3,000 and asking him to send another list including the "Mahogany secretary desk" in the deal. McAfee replied as requested on June 8; left the furniture in the house; and purchased another set of furnishings for his new home. The contract for the sale of the original house was closed in the middle of June. Brewer moved into the house, but refused to make further payments for the furniture. He claimed there was a misunderstanding of the pieces to be purchased and that the letters, as written, were not sufficient to form an agreement. What results? McAfee v. Brewer, 214 Va. 579, 203 S.E.2d 129 (1974).

5. John Deere Company advertised that an auction sale would be conducted with property sold to the highest bidder. Drew bid $1,500 for a tractor, but the auctioneer did not accept the bid. He announced that the Deere Company itself had bid $1,600. Drew insists that Deere's action constitutes a breach of contract. What result? Drew v. John Deere Company of Syracuse, Inc., 19 A.D.2d 234, 241 N.Y.S.2d 267 (1963).

6. Thoelke owned real estate in Florida. Morrison, who wished to purchase the property, drafted a contract, signed it, and sent it to Thoelke. Thoelke signed it and returned it by mail. Before Morrison received it in the mail, Thoelke telephoned him cancelling the contract. Is there a valid contract? Morrison v. Thoelke, 155 So.2d 889 (Fla.) 1963.

7. Holder, a general contractor, was preparing a bid on a public construction project. Acoustical tile work was needed. Southern California Acoustics submitted a bid which Holder relied on in making its own bid. The contract was awarded to Holder, who then substituted another subcontractor for the tile work. Southern California had refrained from bidding on other work to insure that they could perform this task. Do they have any recourse against Holder for not using them? Southern California Acoustics v. C. V. Holder, Inc., 79 Cal. Rptr. 319 (1969).

8. Shuford made an offer to sell machinery to a certain company. Nutmeg heard about the offer and attempted to cut in and accept the offer. Shuford refused Nutmeg's acceptance. What result? Nutmeg State Machinery Corp. v. Shuford, 129 Conn. 659, 30 A.2d 911 (1943).

9. Hunkin-Conkey Construction Company entered into a contract with Brooks Towers to erect a building for them by December 1967. There were major alterations made by the architect in the plans. Upon receiving notice of the changes, Hunkin-Conkey determined the extra time needed to complete the work and filled out a form offering to do the work. The architect approved a few of the offers, but did not respond to the others. Hunkin-Conkey relied upon the architect's inaction as an implied approval. The owner sued for damages caused by the delay in construction. Hunkin-Conkey contended that silence on the part of the owner and architect constituted an acceptance of the time extensions. What result? Brooks Towers Corp. v. Hunkin-Conkey Construction Co., 454 F.2d 1203 (10th Cir. 1972).

10. Ryder had an option until September 1 to purchase Wescoat's farm for a stated price. He paid valuable consideration for this right. On August 20, Ryder told Wescoat that he would not exercise the option. On August 30, Ryder changed his mind and accepted the terms of the option, but Wescoat refused to honor Ryder's acceptance because of his earlier refusal. What result? Ryder v. Wescoat, 535 S.W.2d 269 (Mo. Ct. App. 1976).

11. A&P sent a letter to Geary offering to renew a lease on a building for one year. Geary mailed a reply, accepting A&P's offer. On the same day, A&P mailed a revocation of its offer. What result? Geary v. Great Atlantic & Pacific Tea Co., 366 Ill. 625, 10 N.E.2d 350 (1937).

8

CONSIDERATION

INTRODUCTION

Consideration is something valuable given in exchange for something valuable received. Parties enter into a contract for a reason; they want to receive something they think is valuable. That something is the consideration given by the other party. In return, they too, must be willing to give something. What they give constitutes their consideration, given in exchange for what they receive. The consideration given by each party may take the form of performance, forbearance, or the promise to perform, or to forbear from performing, a specific act.

Performance is valuable consideration because the act performed establishes the existence of a contract and the rights and duties of the parties to the contract.

EXAMPLE | James West informed Artemus Gordon, a rare antique dealer, that he would pay $1,250 for a mahogany desk if one could be located. Two weeks later, Gordon procured the desk, but West refused to pay for it. Is West bound by Gordon's performance? Yes! West's promise to pay was made in return for Gordon's performance. Gordon's performance is valuable because he complied with West's request.

Forbearance constitutes a valuable consideration because one party is forfeiting a legal right or freedom to act, within prescribed limits. There must be no impairment of constitutional rights in return for a promise. Once the forbearance is undertaken, a contract is created. It does not matter whether the person making the promise in return for the forbearance receives a benefit.

William E. Story II brought an action to recover money promised to him by his uncle.

At a family reception, Uncle Bill promised William II $5,000 if he would forbear from drinking, smoking, swearing, and gambling at cards or billiards until the age of twenty-one. The promise was witnessed by many family members. The nephew agreed and adhered to his part of the bargain. After reaching twenty-one, he wrote to his uncle asking for the $5,000 stating he had kept his part of the bargain. The uncle wrote back saying, "I have no doubt but you have, for which you shall have five thousand dollars, as I promised you. I had the money in the bank the day you was twenty-one years old that I intend for you, and you shall have the money certain." He went on to describe how hard he worked for the money and how he hoped William II would not squander it. He also said in the letter that he purchased fifteen sheep when the nephew was born. After putting them out to pasture repeatedly they multiplied to a number approaching six hundred. The sheep he promised to young Bill, as well.

After an exchange of correspondence, it was agreed that the uncle should retain the sheep and the money in trust for his nephew. Two years later, Uncle Bill died. The executor refused to deliver the money or the sheep because young Bill gave no valuable consideration in return for the uncle's promise.

The court held that the nephew had a legal right to drink and smoke before twenty-one. Forbearance from this legal right is valuable consideration to support a promise of payment. Judgment for William II.

A promise to perform or forbear is valuable because people are bound by those promises they make which have legal value. Most contracts involve performance or forbearance in the future but are made beforehand. Since parties cannot be bound by a performance or forbearance that has not occurred, they are bound by their promise to perform or forbear. This enables the contract to become viable immediately, fixing the rights and duties of the parties in regard to future performance or forbearance.

EXAMPLE Eddie and Dolly Vardon owned a small frame house in Butte, Montana. The winters were frigid there, but they were kept warm by an old oil burner which was maintained by the Winkler Fuel Company pursuant to a service contract. On February 2, a brutally cold afternoon, the electrodes in the oil burner shorted out, preventing it from operating. The Vardons notified Winkler and requested emergency service. The Winkler representative promised to send a repairman within the hour, but the repairman did not appear until the following morning. Dolly Vardon suffered a case of pneumonia as a result, which required her to be hospitalized for several weeks. The Vardons sued Winkler for breach of contract in failing to repair the burner. Will they be successful? Yes! Winkler's consideration in the contract was a promise to perform a service, which it failed to do.

Both parties must be bound by a legal duty. There must be a mutual obligation. Consideration satisfies this mutual obligation by creating in each party a legal right in return for giving the consideration and a duty in return for receiving it. This is why consideration is probably the most important element of a contract.

EXISTENCE OF CONSIDERATION

Consideration must exist for a contract to be valid. The requirement that consideration be valuable refers to legal value. This determination was made to resolve conflicts over which agreements ought to be enforced. Each party must give something of legal value in order for a contract to be valid. Social agreements, gifts, and agreements backed by a family seal are not elevated to the status of a contract because considerations of this sort have no legal value. Years ago, in the case of a family seal, a person's good name was sufficient consideration to uphold a contract because people knew and trusted each other. The development of commerce has led people to contract with individuals throughout the country whom they have never met. This form of progress diminished the significance of the family seal.

As a general rule, the law will not look into the adequacy of consideration unless it is grossly one-sided. This is because people attach different values to different things, depending upon such things as their taste, interests, desires, and needs. Personal values are subjective. Whether a person has benefited from a contract depends upon subjective values, how the person feels. The law acknowledges people's freedom to contract and it respects their judgment as to the legal value of the consideration they receive. Individuals making imprudent contracts with unfavorable results are not given recourse (unless they have entered into the contract as a result of fraud, duress, or an unconscionable act) because they have exercised their freedom to contract. Only in certain circumstances will people's freedom be restricted and their judgments overruled.

EXAMPLE Years ago, a man owned a vineyard. Early one morning he saw some men standing idly by; he offered to employ them for the day in return for a silver piece. They agreed. Later in the day, he came upon some other men standing idle. He asked them why they were idle and they replied that no one had hired them. He instructed them to go to his vineyard to work and he would give them just compensation. At the end of the day, he gave each man a silver piece. The men who had begun work in the morning argued that they received inadequate consideration because those who worked for only one hour received as much as they themselves did. Are these men correct? No! The law is concerned with the existence of consideration, not its adequacy. The silver piece is valuable consideration and these men exercised their freedom to contract, by agreeing to accept it for a day's work. The fact that someone else worked less and received the same is of no significance because an employer may be as generous as he pleases with his own money.

When money is exchanged, the amount given must be equal to the amount received, otherwise the discrepancy constitutes a gift. Allowances are made for accrued interest and other compensating factors, such as advance payment in return for a reduction in interest. People and institutions do not lend money with the expectation of receiving less, except when the loan is actually a gift in whole or part, or when some other consideration, such as services or property, is given to supplement the reduced payment.

Illusory contracts fail because of extreme inadequacy of consideration where one party is bound by a promise and the other party is not. Illusory promises are unreasonably disproportionate in allowing one party the privilege of acting at will. The power to cancel with notice, or for cause, is not illusory as long as the parties act in good faith.

EXAMPLE | Joel Sandman, a distributor of soft drinks, enters into a contract to deliver Lem & Lime. The contract contains a clause which permits Lem & Lime the option of cancelling the contract at will, though Sandman is obliged to honor the contract as long as Lem & Lime wishes. Two months later, Sandman cancelled the contract with Lem & Lime in favor of a better contract with Creamy Cola. If Lem & Lime sued Sandman, could he raise the defense that the contract was illusory? Yes! This contract was harsh and one-sided.

A promise subject to a future condition, known as an aleatory promise, is valuable consideration and not illusory even though the contract may never materialize.

EXAMPLE | Mr. and Mrs. Brady contracted to sell their Cameron Ridge home to Rita Hall for $400,000. A week later, an offer for $425,000 was made by another prospective purchaser, but it was refused because a contract with Rita Hall had been signed. The contract contained a clause conditioning the sale of the house on Rita's obtaining a mortgage. This is a form of an aleatory promise. Two months later, Rita was turned down for a mortgage, by which time the other prospective purchaser had bought another house. The Bradys intend to keep Rita's $40,000 down payment for the time lost in selling the house and the damages suffered in their not being able to accept the $425,000 offer. Are they entitled to the down payment? No! Rita's promise to purchase the house was valuable consideration even though it was conditioned on her being able to procure a mortgage. Since this condition was not satisfied, the contract is cancelled and the down payment must be returned. If the contract had contained another clause giving Rita the right to cancel the contract at will, her promise would have been illusory.

PRIOR LEGAL OBLIGATION

A promise to pay more than the agreed price for the performance of an existing contract, or a promise to accept less than the amount owed, has no valuable consideration unless something additional is given to serve as consideration. When a person promises to perform an act which he or she is legally obligated to perform, this does not constitute valuable consideration. A contract based on a promise of this sort is not valid and cannot be enforced. This rule concerning preexisting legal obligations applies to people's duty to observe the law; to individuals who have responsibilities through public service and public administrative positions; and to parties bound by contract.

EXAMPLE Jack Mullins owned a number of apartment houses in the South Bronx. He was concerned about the number of fires attributed to arson in the area. He contacted the local fire department and spoke to the captain. Mullins was advised that the huge number of false alarms in the area prevented the fire department from responding to all alarms. The captain reassured Mullins that a call concerning one of his apartment houses would be given prompt attention if Mullins would contribute $500 at the end of the year to the Fireman's Benevolent Association. Mullins agreed, but refused to make the contribution. Can the captain hold Mullins to his promise? No! The captain is a public official under a preexisting legal obligation to respond to fire alarms. He gave no legal consideration to support Mullins's promise to contribute the $500.

A party who requests more money or time to complete a contract is not giving any consideration in return for the other party's consent, because the first party is already legally obligated to complete the contract under the original conditions. If the other party acquiesces, that promise is not enforceable. This situation often presents itself in a form of economic duress exerted by a contractor at a point where the owner has no alternative but to allow the contractor to proceed at a price greater than the price agreed upon.

There are two exceptions to the rule that preexisting legal obligations are not sufficient as consideration. First, where a significant change is made in the contract, that change will be valuable consideration if it supports a return promise to pay more money or grant more time. The change may include additional work to be performed, alteration in the nature of the work, or performance in a shorter period of time.

EXAMPLE The 1988 Winter Olympic Games are scheduled to be held in Poland, but because of internal conflict, the Games must be rescheduled elsewhere. The International Olympic Committee asked the city of Denver, the site of the 1992 Winter Olympics, if they would host the 1988 Games instead. Denver agreed. The construction firm, which was building the ice hockey arena and the ski jumping platform, was offered an additional sum of money by the city of Denver if the construction could be finished in time for the 1988 Games. The firm agreed and completed the work on time, but was paid only the original contract price. Is the firm entitled to the additional sum? Yes! Although the construction firm was under a preexisting legal obligation to build the ice hockey arena and the ski jumping platform, it gave valuable consideration by performing something which it was not legally obligated to do—build the arena and platform four years earlier.

The second exception to the rule involves unforeseen situations which arise and make performance more difficult. Unforeseen situations also provide sufficient consideration to support a promise to pay more or to grant additional time. The unforeseen event must not have been reasonably apparent to the parties at the time the contract was made. The parties must be taken by surprise. Unforeseen circumstances generally do not include weather, shortages, price changes, or strikes, because these problems are readily foreseeable by the parties.

EXAMPLE It's Old Timer's Day at Fenway Park in Boston. To publicize this special event, the Boston Red Sox decide to give a free team-autographed baseball to every fan in attendance. Spaulding agrees to supply all the baseballs needed at a set price of $20,000, based on average attendance figures for the last five years. A week before the game, word leaks out that the greatest Red Sox player of all, Ted Williams, for the first time since his retirement will make a surprise guest appearance. The attendance on Old Timer's Day exceeds 50,000 fans. Spaulding agrees to distribute 50,000 autographed baseballs, but only at a much greater cost because of the unexpected increase in the number of people. The Red Sox acquiesce at the moment, but then pay Spaulding only $20,000. Is Spaulding entitled to the extra cost? Yes! Although Spaulding is under a preexisting legal obligation to perform for $20,000, an unforeseen event has occurred— the arrival of Ted Williams—which takes both parties by surprise. It would be unjust to require Spaulding to perform without adequate compensation.

A person who makes part payment and asks to be relieved from paying in full, after services have been performed, is not giving any consideration for the reduction in price. Even if the part payment is accepted, the balance may still be collected unless the party has been released from his or her legal obligation. Otherwise, the reduction in price is valid only when some other form of consideration is given as a substitute for the remainder or when the amount is validly disputed and a settlement known as an accord and satisfaction is made. Accord and satisfaction will be discussed later in this chapter.

Parties may release each other from their duties to perform by mutual agreement. One party may release the other party from the obligation to continue performance after that performance has been partially or substantially completed: A party's right to release another is part of the freedom to contract. The release must be in writing, supported by consideration, and signed by the releasing party. In the writing, the releasing party must express the intent to discharge the other party from his or her legal obligation. No particular set of words is required to make a release effective, as long as the releasing party's intent is evident. Where the party's intent is clearly conveyed in the writing, the requirement of consideration is not always necessary. For example, the UCC requires delivery of a signed writing, but no consideration is necesssary.

EXAMPLE   A wealthy man was departing on a journey that was to last seven years. Before he left, he entered into contracts with three of his employees. He gave $500,000 to the first, with $1,000,000 due upon his return; $200,000 to the second, with $400,000 due; and $100,000 to the third, with $200,000 due. After seven years, the wealthy man returned to settle his accounts. The first and second employees fulfilled their promises, but the third man did not. He had buried the money for fear of losing it. He asked the wealthy man to accept less than what was owed to him. The wealthy man accepted the small sum, but then decided to collect the rest. Once he accepted the small sum, has he any recourse? Yes! The wealthy man's promise to accept less than what was owed to him is not binding because the third individual gave no consideration to support the request and promise. If the third individual had obtained a written release from the wealthy man when the $100,000 was returned, he would have protected himself against a lawsuit brought by the wealthy man to recover the remainder owed.

PAST CONSIDERATION

Valuable consideration must be given by each party, either in the present or in the future. Past consideration is legally insufficient to support a present promise, because it is no longer valuable. A party wishing to reciprocate at a later date may do so; however, the promise to reciprocate is not enforceable because it is not supported by valuable consideration. The promise is merely gratuitous or it is one made through a sense of moral obligation. An agreement to return what was given by another in the past, based upon a moral obligation, is admirable, but not binding because the necesssary legal consideration is not present. There are exceptions to this rule which will be discussed later.

EXAMPLE A multimillionaire was riding through Death Valley in his limousine when he ran out of gas. He was on his way to Las Vegas to close a deal on the sale of one of his hotels located on "the Strip." A few minutes later, a pickup truck approached from the opposite direction and the millionaire told the driver of his plight. Although the driver of the pickup was headed to Los Angeles, he turned his pickup around and drove all the way back to Las Vegas. In his rush, the millionaire forgot to get the man's name. Years later, they met again by chance. This time the aging millionaire promised to leave the "good Samaritan" $10,000 in his will, but he never did. After the millionaire's death, the good Samaritan sued the estate to enforce the promise. Will the good Samaritan win? No! The millionaire is not bound by his promise. The good Samaritan's action was past consideration that revived in the millionaire a sense of moral obligation to reward his benefactor. This moral obligation is sufficient to support the millionaire's promise only if he freely chooses to remember the good Samaritan in his will, but it is not sufficient to legally bind him to do so.

LOVE AND AFFECTION

Love and affection are not sufficient consideration to enforce a return promise because they have no legal value. There is no legal value because there is no way to measure the value of love and affection.

Love and affection are an important reason why people give gifts. Gifts are a transfer of title to property which passes when one party expresses a present intention to transfer property. This is done by delivering the property or some form of ownership to another, who then accepts it. Property may be transferred via a gift because of love and affection. However, a gift is not a contract, and a mere promise to give a gift is not enforceable because there is no consideration to support it.

The Story of the Texas Gentleman

There was a man living in Texas who was known throughout the state as the Texas Gentleman. Now the Texas Gentleman was not an ordinary individual. He was an exceptionally tall man, standing six feet, six inches tall, and seemed even taller when he wore his huge ten-gallon hat. One Friday morning, on the spur of the moment, the Texas Gentleman decided to visit the Big Apple. He took the weekly special to JFK Airport and the express train to Grand Central Station. The Texas Gentleman stepped out onto Forty-second Street at noon, where he was unknown to everyone. He wandered aimlessly for a while, but finally, by chance, he met a beautiful young woman who offered to show him the sights of Manhattan. They visited the Empire State Building, the Statue of Liberty, and Rockefeller Center. After their excursion, they stopped on a street corner for a momentary rest. It was here that the Texas Gentleman exclaimed, "Darlin', for bein' so kind to me and showin' me all the gorgeous sights, I'd like to express my appreciation to you by buyin' you a few li'l trinkets in this here five-and-dime." The "five-and-dime" he referred to was Tiffany's. Upon entering, the young woman proceeded to select $35,000 worth of trinkets. The Texas Gentleman did not bat an eye. He opened his checkbook and began to write a check for the full amount. The cashier beckoned to the manager, who then informed the stranger that his credit must be verified before the check could be accepted. At this time it was after 4 P.M. in New York, which meant it was after 3 P.M. in Texas and the Texas banks were closed.

The manager anxiously explained his position because he did not wish to lose the sale. The Texas Gentleman interrupted the manager with this reply, "Sir, I understand your position. You don't know me and here I'm gonna write out a check to you for $35,000. I tell you what we'll do. Give me that little box over there and we'll stuff these trinkets in it. I'll mark my name in big red letters on the box. Bright and early Monday morning, we'll be by, and by then you could have checked my credit balance." The manager was happy, the young woman was happy, everybody was happy. The young woman pranced away with the Texas Gentleman, holding tightly to his arm. Bright and early Monday morning, the Texas gentleman came sauntering through the door wearing his big ten-gallon hat, with the young woman at his side. The manager hastened to greet them. "Sir," he exclaimed, "we checked with your bank and you do have an account, but no where near $35,000!" With that, the young woman began to scream and yell as she stormed out the door. The Texas Gentleman was unmoved by all of this. The manager began to apologize, but he was quickly interrupted by the Texas Gentleman who said, "Sir, never you mind, cause thanks to you I just had one helluva weekend."

Does the young woman have any recourse against the Texas Gentlemen? No, because his promise to buy the trinkets was merely gratuitous. Consideration was lacking on her part, since love and affection are not deemed legally sufficient.

Even though this is true, if a gift is given and title has passed, the party receiving it does not have to give the gift back nor return any other form of consideration upon request.

In a social agreement, there is no intention by the parties to make their promises legally binding. They intend to carry them through and usually they do. The moral and social obligations inherent in a social promise are often sufficient to carry through the promise. Society has agreed, as a matter of public policy, that no legal right or duty arises from a social agreement. This permits social engagements to be more free and less restricted than business arrangements—a fundamental distinction between the two.

EXAMPLE Bob is an eligible bachelor in his forties. While out of town, he met a stunning nineteen-year-old blonde named Carol. She agreed to accompany him on a two-week Caribbean Cruise. Bob thereupon purchased the tickets and arranged to take two weeks off from the office at his own expense. He also purchased a more youthful and up-to-date wardrobe, at Carol's suggestion. Two days before departure, he received a mailgram stating that she had changed her mind. Stunned and angered as well, Bob's first reaction was to sue Carol for the cost of the tickets—$4,500—and for the $2,000 wardrobe as well. Would he be well advised to follow this course of action? Decidedly not! A social invitation is not binding on either party. Although social pressure is usually sufficient to enforce the invitation, it may be terminated at a whim, without recourse for the damages suffered.

EXCEPTIONS TO CONSIDERATION

Even though consideration is one of the requirements of a valid contract, there are some exceptions to this requirement:

Moral obligation

Estoppel (promissory)

Commercial Code exceptions

Composition of creditors

Accord and satisfaction

Moral Obligation

Moral obligation, that sense of fairness and responsibility toward others, may cause people to revive a past debt discharged by the statute of limitations or because of infancy. The moral obligation, by itself, is not legally binding. To be legally enforceable, the promise to repay must be in writing.

A statute of limitations is a time limit within which a lawsuit must be brought by the aggrieved party. The time limitation varies depending upon the area of the law involved. A debt avoided through the defense of infancy may be ratified by the infant upon reaching the age of majority. The statute of limitations and the defense of infancy safeguard individuals from a lawsuit resulting in a possible judgment against them. This safeguard is a legal one which may be waived in writing by the party after the statute of limitations has run, or by the infant after reaching majority.

The moral obligation to repay the debt always exists, but it is not legally enforceable until the new promise is made in writing. A writing is required in most states to evidence the intention of the debtor. The writing may be informal and may be explained by other evidence. When the new promise is made in writing, the past consideration supported by the moral obligation will revive the original debt. Part performance will also revive an old debt and create an implied promise to repay the balance. It is within the debtor's purview to dispense with the legal protection afforded, in whole or in part. The debtor, although under no legal obligation, may choose to repay part of the debt or condition repayment on the happening of an event such as the attaining of financial stability. This condition must be satisfied first, before the creditor has a right to repayment of the debt.

EXAMPLE | Marge Hudson was a neighborly widow who lived next door to the Hutchinsons. The Hutchinsons had twin daughters, aged seventeen, who wanted to attend Vassar College, but lacked the money to pay for the tuition plus room and board. Marge loaned Jane and Joan Hutchinson $10,000 each to help cover their expenses for the first year of study. Before reaching eighteen, but after the tuition and room and board had been paid, both girls repudiated the contract. Marge was brokenhearted, but took no legal action. After Jane and Joan were graduated, their parents advised them to repay the loans. Jane told Marge personally, while Joan sent her a letter. Marge was delighted; her faith in them restored. But neither Jane nor Joan ever repaid the loan. Has Marge any recourse? Yes, but only against Joan because her ratification was made in writing. A promise to repay a past debt that was excused can only be revived if it is made in writing. Jane's oral promise to repay the past debt is not enforceable.

Estoppel (Promissory)

When a person changes his or her position in reliance on a promise, and that change in position is foreseeable, the person making the promise will be stopped from asserting that there is no consideration to enforce the contract. This is the doctrine of promissory estoppel. It is equitable in that enforcement of a promise may be upheld for reasons of fairness and justice even though the recipient of the promise gave no consideration in return. To invoke the doctrine of promissory estoppel, the person making the promise must reasonably expect it to motivate the other person to change his or her position by taking some substantial and justifiable action in reliance on the promise. The person taking the action must be going to suffer a detriment for his or her reliance on that promise if it is not carried out. This is the reason for enforcing the promise—to prevent the person relying on the promise from suffering a loss.

EXAMPLE
It was the middle of a scorching hot summer. Timothy Woodwirth, who worked on the night shift for the Brooklyn D.A.'s office, was out pounding the pavement during the day in his three-piece suit looking for a higher paying position. He entered the reception area of the law firm of Collins, Egbert, and Phillips. He informed the receptionist of his request for an interview and she notified Mr. Phillips. Mr. Phillips spoke to Timothy and then introduced him to Mr. Egbert. After the interviews, Timothy was offered a position with a salary of $25,000. He was to begin work in two weeks. In the interim, Mr. Collins returned from an extended vacation. He strenuously objected to the hiring of Timothy because of his lack of experience in civil litigation. As senior partner in the firm, he won out. Meanwhile, Timothy had resigned from the D.A.'s office and was ready to begin work when he was advised of Mr. Collins's decision. Has Timothy any recourse? Yes! Although Timothy gave no consideration in return for the promise made by Mr. Egbert and Mr. Phillips to hire him, he relied on their promise by resigning from the D.A.'s office to work for their firm and thus suffered a real detriment, loss of a job. Under the doctrine of promissory estoppel, the law firm must compensate Timothy for lost wages until he finds another suitable legal position.

Hoffman v. Red Owl Stores, Inc.
26 Wis.2d 683, 113 N.W.2d 267 (1965)

The Hoffmans brought a suit against Red Owl Stores to recover losses they suffered when they relied upon Red Owl's representations concerning the purchase of a franchise.

Red Owl promised the Hoffmans a franchise store for $18,000. Hoffman sold his grocery store and bought a lot where the new franchise was to be built. Subsequently, the figure was raised to $24,000, and then to $26,000. Then Hoffman was induced to sell his bakery building as the last step required before the franchise was issued. Finally, the deal fell through, leaving the Hoffmans without any dough, so to speak. The defendants contend there was no agreement as to specific terms regarding the new store building.

The issue concerns whether the doctrine of promissory estoppel can be invoked where the specific terms of the agreement have not been finalized.

The court ruled that promissory estoppel will be granted where the person making representations should reasonably expect the other party to rely on those representations. The reliance by the aggrieved party must be justifiable. Here, the Hoffmans were repeatedly assured a franchise by Red Owl if they followed instructions. The Hoffmans justifiably relied on the representations and followed the instructions to sell their business because they thought they would get the franchise. Judgment for the Hoffmans.

The doctrine of promissory estoppel extends to charitable, religious, and educational organizations who ask people to pledge money for a particular cause. The charitable organizations rely upon the subscriptions made by donors in order to fill a need. This reliance is justifiable. Although the charitable organization is giving no consideration in return, people will be bound by their promises under the promissory estoppel exception.

Commercial Code Exceptions

The UCC has provided certain exceptions where the need for consideration may be dispensed with to allow for the smooth operation of contracts for the sale of goods.

Modifications   Modifications of contracts for the sale of goods require no new consideration if they are made in good faith. The good-faith requirement protects each party against any unconscionable modification of the contract attempted by the other party. The modification may be oral unless the contract is required to be in writing by the Statute of Frauds. Also in the case where a contract provides that all changes must be in writing, then a party to the contract who is a consumer must be advised in the written contract that oral modifications are not binding. This rule protects the consumer against oral misrepresentations.

Modifications of contractual provisions occur too often to require parties to draft a new contract each time an alteration is made. The UCC has simplified the consideration requirement by providing that the original consideration given to create the contract will support any future modification made in good faith. This enables the parties to make adjustments, as needed, at any point during the contract. By making it compulsory for all alterations to be made in good faith, the UCC has developed a built-in guard to protect the freedom to contract.

Firm Offers   Firm offers are similar to option contracts, except that no consideration is given to support them. A firm offer must be made in a signed writing and may be irrevocable for up to three months at the offeror's discretion.

Discharge of Debts   A claim for breach of contract for a debt that is due and certain may be discharged in whole or in part when a release is signed and delivered by the party against whom the breach was committed. Under the UCC, the release is binding upon the party who made it even though there is no consideration to support it.

Composition of Creditors

A composition of creditors is a procedure where two or more creditors may agree to accept less than the amount the debtor owes to avoid the debtor's filing for bankruptcy. The percentage received under an agreement of this nature is generally greater than that received under the bankruptcy settlement because of fees and expenses. Although the debtor is giving no valuable consideration for the creditor's agreement, the agreement is enforceable because of the debtor's forbearance from filing for bankruptcy.

EXAMPLE | Jim Walters, who worked as a machinist, had tried to provide his family with all the comforts of life. In doing so, he had accumulated a sizable amount of debt. He was able to make ends meet until he was laid off from his job because of a slowdown in factory orders. Jim informed his creditors that he would have to declare bankruptcy. All of his creditors gathered together and mutually agreed to accept half of what was owed. Jim paid the creditors according to this agreement. Are the creditors bound by this agreement or can they sue for the balance? The composition of creditors is bound by their agreement to accept less than the amount owed to them. Jim's consideration for this agreement is his forbearance from filing for bankruptcy.

Accord and Satisfaction

An accord and satisfaction occurs when one party substitutes some other form of consideration for that which was originally promised, and the substituted consideration is accepted by the other party as full satisfaction of the legal duty owed. An accord is a promise to release a claim in return for substituted performance. Satisfaction results when the substituted performance is rendered. When there is a valid dispute over the amount owed, the cashing of a check marked "paid in full" operates as an accord and satisfaction. The party sending the check is offering substituted performance in return for a release from claim, and the receiving party is accepting the accord as full satisfaction of the debt owed. The receiving party must be notified of the other party's intent to reach an accord. This gives the receiving party the opportunity to reject the accord.

EXAMPLE | Charlie Russo was complaining of a severe toothache. He visited Dr. Malone, his regular dentist, who advised him that three of his wisdom teeth needed to be extracted. Dr. Malone referred Charlie to an oral surgeon named Dr. Winthrop and advised him that each extraction would cost $55. Charlie made an appointment with Dr. Winthrop and had the three teeth extracted. One week later, Charlie was feeling well again until he received the bill. Dr. Winthrop charged $75 for each extraction. Charlie sent Dr. Winthrop a check for $165 marked "paid in full" along with a note explaining that Dr. Malone had advised him the cost would be $55 for each extraction. Dr. Winthrop cashed the check, but then sued Charlie for the balance. Is he entitled to collect it? No! There was a valid dispute in regard to the amount owed. The dispute arose because of Charlie's reliance on Dr. Malone's assurance of the price. When the check marked "paid in full" was cashed, an accord was reached, which was satisfied when the check cleared and Dr. Winthrop's account was credited for $165.

REVIEW QUESTIONS

1. Define consideration, promissory estoppel, and accord and satisfaction.
2. List and explain the exceptions to consideration.
3. Boettger promised in writing to donate $5,000 to a charitable organization that was concerned with the conservation of game birds. He paid half of the donation, but then refused to pay the rest, asserting that he received no return consideration. The charity sued him to collect the balance pledged. What result? More Game Birds in America, Inc. v. Boettger, 125 N.J.L. 97, 14 A.2d 778 (1940).
4. Jewelry owned by Martino was stolen during a burglary of her home. She offered a reward for its return. Gray, a police officer, recovered the jewelry. Martino refused to pay the reward to Gray. What result? Gray v. Martino, 91 N.J.L. 462, 103 A. 24 (1918).
5. August Schultz agreed to leave certain real estate to his grandson in his will, if the child was named after him. The parents named the child as requested. When Schultz died, there was no mention of the grandson in the will. The child, through his parents, is seeking to have the real estate transferred to him. What result? Lanfier v. Lanfier, 227 Iowa 258, 288 N.W. 104 (1939).
6. Jaffray owed Davis and other creditors the sum of $7,700. An agreement was made by the creditors to accept Jaffray's promissory notes (IOUs) for $3,500, which were secured by collateral, in full satisfaction of the debt. Jaffray paid the notes, but the creditors were still looking to collect the balance owed on the original debt. Does the creditors' agreement to accept a lesser sum than owed fully release Jaffray from being required to pay the balance? Jaffray v. Davis, 124 N.Y. 164, 26 N.E. 351 (1891).
7. Boston Redevelopment Authority condemned a building used by Graphic Arts under its power of eminent domain. Eminent domain is the right of the state to take over private land for public use where the public welfare will be served best. Boston Redevelopment wanted Graphic Arts to remain in business. Graphic Arts agreed to relocate its business and not liquidate, if Boston Redevelopment would pay for the moving expenses. The expenses totaled $130,000, but Boston Redevelopment paid only $75,000. They contended that Graphic Arts' promise was inadequate and illusory. May Graphic Arts recover the balance due for the moving expenses? Graphic Arts Finish, Inc. v. Boston Redevelopment Authority, 327 Mass. 40, 255 N.E.2d 793 (1970).
8. Drennan, a general contractor, was preparing a bid on a school project. He asked Star Paving Company to submit a bid for certain masonry work. Drennan used the subcontractor's offer of $7,000 in making his own bid. The contract for the school project was awarded to Drennan, and he informed Star Paving that he accepted their offer. Star Paving refused to perform, citing an error in their

calculations. Drennan was able to get someone else to do the work for $4,000 more. Is Drennan entitled to reimbursement from Star Paving? Drennan v. Star Paving Company, 51 Cal.2d 409, 333 P.2d 757 (1958).

9. Vinson, a building contractor, entered into a contract with Leggett to build a house for him for $4,000. After working for seven weeks, Vinson discovered he could not complete the contract as agreed and informed Leggett. Leggett instructed Vinson to finish the job and that the extra costs would be paid. When the building was completed, the contract price was paid in full. Leggett refused to pay for the additional labor and materials, which amounted to $2,200. What result? Leggett et al. v. Vinson, 155 Miss. 411, 124 So. 472 (1929).

10. Hornbuckle signed two promissory notes totaling $6,000. When payment on the notes became due, there was a dispute over the actual amount owed. Hornbuckle sent two checks to Continental Gin marked "on note account" and "settlement of note account in full." Continental Gin deposited the first check and attempted to deposit the second after crossing out the clause "settlement of note account in full." The bank refused to accept the second check. Continental Gin sued Hornbuckle for $4,000, the balance remaining on the note. What result? Hornbuckle v. Continental Gin Company, 116 Ga. 449, 157 S.E.2d 829 (1967).

9

LEGAL CAPACITY

INTRODUCTION

Legal capacity refers to the ability of the parties to enter into a valid contract. It is one of the elements of a contract. The ability to enter into a contract refers to the mental state of the parties. When people enter into contracts, legal obligations arise, and the parties must possess the requisite legal capacity to be bound by these obligations. To be competent to contract, the parties must intend to enter into a contract fully aware that certain rights and duties will be created by their promises. They must be responsible for their promises and the actions which result from them. This will insure that the performance of their promises will be completed in accordance with the terms of the contract. All parties are presumed to be competent. The fulfillment of the requirements of legal age and sanity give added strength to the presumption that the parties are capable of entering into a contractual relationship. This presumption is rebuttable and may be disproved by raising the appropriate contractual defenses.

If a person enters into a contract without the requisite capacity, the contract will be voidable. A voidable contract is legally enforceable unless one party has a special right to rescind the contract and decides to exercise that right. Rescission has the effect of cancelling the contract and returning the parties to status quo—the position they were in before the contract was made. The special right to rescind is held by those parties who have a viable contractual defense. We are specifically concerned with contractual defenses pertaining to lack of capacity. Those parties who lack the legal capacity to make a valid contract, such as infants and insane individuals, can invoke their special right to rescind—infants by their own discretion, and the insane by their guardians.

SPECIAL RIGHTS OF AN INFANT

In most states, any individual under the age eighteen is legally termed an infant, or a minor. Infants do not have the legal capacity to contract because they lack the experience to understand the ramifications of contracts and to make sound judgments about them. Actually, they do not have the necessary business sense to deal with adults. This does not apply to minors who are in business for themselves. The defense of infancy gives an infant the right to rescind a contract at any time during minority or within a reasonable time after reaching majority. The purpose behind the defense is actually to discourage adults from entering into contracts with minors except for necessities such as food, clothing, and shelter. The minor may set forth his or her infant status by exercising the special right to rescind, or by raising it as a defense in a lawsuit for damages resulting from breach of contract. This is to protect infants against adults who might take advantage of them. The special right to rescind assures the infant of a fair deal. The infant is given the opportunity to decide if the contract is really for his or her betterment; otherwise it can be abrogated. Only an infant can abrogate a contract; the infant's parents or guardian may not raise the defense on behalf of the infant, nor can people who employ infants to act for them. However, a personal representative of an infant's estate may exercise the special right to rescind or raise the defense of infancy in any situation where the minor would have had that right.

When a minor decides to rescind a contract, the whole contract must be rescinded, not part of it. The decision may be made at any point, whether the contract is fully or partially completed. Upon rescinding the contract, the infant is entitled to a return of the consideration given.

EXAMPLE | Little Johnny Bradon is auditioning for the lead role in a high-school musical entitled "Come Blow Your Horn." He purchases a horn at the Pied Piper's musical instrument store, figuring he will get the part. When the director realizes Little Johnny cannot play a note, he gives the part to someone else. Little Johnny returns the horn, but the Pied Piper refuses to give him his money back. Can Little Johnny blow the whistle on the Pied Piper? Yes! He may rescind the contract because of his special status of infancy and he is entitled to a return of his consideration.

RESTITUTION

In most states, adults are entitled to a return of the consideration belonging to them only when it is still in the infant's possession. When it is not, the adult does not get the item back and has no recourse against the infant for its loss. The rationale is that the importance of protecting an infant overrides the potential financial loss to an adult. Adults contract with infants at their own risk. They must run this risk or there would be nothing to discourage them since they would be assured of getting their consideration back. This prevails even though infants may take advantage of their special status. As a matter of public policy, an adult's rights are subordinate to an infant's rights. Adults may protect themselves by requiring proof of legal age or, where they decide to contract with an infant, by requiring the infant's parents to act as sureties guaranteeing payment of the debt. The infant may still abrogate the contract, but his or her parents will be responsible.

Hogue v. Wilkinson
291 S.W.2d 750 (Tex. App.) 1956

Wilkinson brought an action for rescission of a contract to buy chinchillas. Wilkinson asserted his defense of infancy and offered to return the chinchillas that were still alive.

In 1953, Wilkinson, eighteen years of age, purchased a pair of chinchillas from Hogue and McCoy for $1,150. A month later, he bought another pair for $700. Upon delivery, Wilkinson paid the full amount owed. The next year, the number of chinchillas had doubled to eight. In 1955, while still a minor (the age of majority was twenty-one) Wilkinson disaffirmed both contracts and offered to return the six remaining chinchillas. Hogue and McCoy would not accept the chinchillas in return and refused to return the contract price to Wilkinson.

Hogue and McCoy assert that restitution of all eight chinchillas would have been required to effectuate rescission. Furthermore, they assert that the two deaths were attributed to the negligence of Wilkinson.

The issue is whether Wilkinson can excercise his special right as an infant to rescind the contract without making complete restitution.

The court allowed Wilkinson to disaffirm the contract and regain the purchase price. They asserted that the law in the state requires infants to make restitution only if they are able. They also held that negligence on the part of a minor does not result in a forfeiture of the special right of rescission. Judgment for Wilkinson.

Increasingly, though, courts have been looking to the circumstances surrounding the contract to see if the minor actually received a benefit and was treated fairly. If this is the case, the minor is required to forego part of his or her consideration. This is to pay for the reasonable benefit to the infant or loss the adult sustains.

EXAMPLE | Jack and Jill were sweethearts. They were both sixteen. As a surprise for Easter, Jack bought Jill a large ceramic Easter egg from a gift shop. In Jill's apartment, there was a beautiful terrace overlooking Cameron Lake. Jill sat the egg on the terrace wall. A blustery wind developed and blew the egg off the wall. It crashed into a thousand pieces. Jack and Jill fetched a pail and picked up all the pieces. They tried to put the egg back together again, but their attempt was unsuccessful. So Jack returned the pieces to the gift shop, but they refused to reimburse him. Has Jack any recourse? Yes! In most states, Jack would be entitled to a return of his consideration because he is an infant. The fact that the gift shop's consideration is returned all in pieces is part of the risk they must accept in dealing with infants. In those states which follow the modern trend and take into account the depreciation of the consideration while in the infant's possession, Jack would not receive much in return because the egg was cracked.

NECESSITIES

Necessities are the things which are needed for an infant's sustenance. The definition of a necessity varies according to the infant's life style, particularly his or her financial and social status. Minors are liable for the reasonable value of the necessities furnished to them by merchants. The reasonable value of the necessities may be no higher than the contract price. Clothing, food, shelter, education, and medical expenses are categories generally included under the title of necessities. Not everything included in these categories is a necessity. A raincoat would be considered a necessity, but not a mink coat. A hamburger and a coke would be necessities, too, but not caviar and champagne. Most states do not view cars as necessities where minors are concerned; however, some states make an exception when the car is used in a trade or as transportation to and from work. The reason a minor may not assert the defense of infancy against a request for payment for necessities is to encourage adults to provide infants with the things they need.

EXAMPLE Cindy Meyers, while hiking through the backwoods of Vermont, decides to stop at the Three Bears Inn. She enjoys a nice dish of cereal and a warm bed. The next morning, she refuses to pay for the room and board, asserting infancy as a defense. Is the defense applicable? No! Food and shelter are necessities, and an infant is liable for the reasonable value of necessities.

Parents have a duty to support an infant until the infant reaches majority. Adults supplying necessities to minors have a legal right (a cause of action) to demand payment from the parent of the minor. Parents, in turn, do not have the right to raise the defense of infancy on the minor's behalf, or to exercise the minor's special right to rescind. This is especially true when the parent guarantees payment for the infant's contract.

EXAMPLE Henry and Gretchen were both seventeen when they married. They purchased a split-level house from an Englishman, who required that their parents sign a guarantee of payment on the infants' contract. When Henry and Gretchen defaulted, their parents refused to pay, raising the defense of infancy. Are the parents still liable? Yes! The parents are liable for payment because the defense of infancy is not available to them.

EXCEPTIONS TO THE DEFENSE OF INFANCY

There are special contracts which are designated by some states as being exempt from the special rights of an infant. There are two rationales for the denial of the defense of infancy. The first applies to those contracts which benefit minors. Where the benefit to a minor outweighs the protection afforded by the defense, the defense will not be granted. This is to encourage adults to make these contracts readily available to minors. The contracts to which this rationale applies include: life and health insurance contracts; loans; employment agency contracts; contracts with common carriers, such as airlines and railway and bus companies; and court-approved athletic and entertainment contracts. Court-approved contracts for child entertainers and athletes are enforceable and can only be rescinded by the infant with the court's permission. The court is a party to the contract.

Gastonia Personnel Corporation v. Rogers
276 N.C. 279, 172 S.E.2d 19 (1970)

Gastonia sued to recover its fee for aiding Rogers, an infant, in obtaining a position of employment. The personnel agency alleges that the contract for services was a necessity that cannot be rescinded by Rogers.

Rogers was under twenty-one, the age of majority, when he sought out Gastonia's services. He was married and his wife was expecting a baby shortly. This caused him to quit school and search for a job. Rogers signed a contract with Gastonia employment agency that included the following statement: "If I AC-CEPT employment offered me by an employer as a result of a lead (verbal or otherwise) from you within twelve months (12) of such lead, even though it may not be the position originally discussed with you, I will be obligated to pay you as per the terms of the contract."

After making several telephone calls on his behalf, the employment agency was able to set up an interview with Spratt-Seaver, Inc. As a result of the interview, Rogers was hired as a draftsman with a starting salary of $4,784. He refused to pay the agency's fee of $295, claiming he was an infant.

The issue is whether services rendered by an employment agency are a necessity.

The court held that the view of necessities should be enlarged to encompass services which are necessary to enable the infant to earn sufficient compensation to provide for the necessities of living. To hold otherwise would handicap minors by restricting employment agencies from entering into contracts with them. This would make it more difficult for minors to obtain employment, and, in Rogers' case, would cause a serious hardship for his family. Judgment for Gastonia Personnel Corporation.

The second rationale for the denial of the defense of infancy refers to institutions and business arrangements and the maintenance of certain standards through the enforcement of commitments. This group of exceptions encompasses the institutions of marriage and the armed forces. It also applies to business contracts involving partnerships, good-faith purchasers, and to the buying and selling of corporate stock.

Marriage is the commitment of two individuals to a lifetime of devotion toward one another. The commitment must be honored for the institution to be sound. A minor who enters into a marriage cannot annul that marriage on the basis of age alone. In cases where the parents did not consent, the marriage may be annulled by either the infant or the parents. The need to protect the institution of marriage outweighs the need to protect the infant. The same rationale applies to minors who enlist in the army.

As we saw in the example about Henry and Gretchen, they are having financial problems with their split-level house. Gretchen, unhappy with the situation, decides to annul the marriage because of her age. Can she do this? No! Once a minor freely consents to enter into marriage, the marriage cannot be annulled by the infant solely on the basis of age.

Minors who enter into partnerships will not be able to rescind contracts made by the partnership with third parties. Although the partnership agreement may be rescinded by a minor, the minor is personally liable for all claims made while still a partner.

EXAMPLE Peter Dawson and his friend Kevin Schmidt enter into a partnership to sell choice cuts of meat to restaurants. Peter is a minor. One night, a blackout occurs that causes the meat in their freezer to spoil. When the partnership is sued by the restaurants for nondelivery of the meat, Peter immediately terminates the partnership and refuses to be liable for any debts on the grounds of infancy. Do all the debts fall on Kevin's shoulders? No! An infant who enters into a partnership is presumed to have sufficient business sense to be treated as an adult. Peter may terminate the partnership, but he will not be relieved of his responsibility for debts of the partnership previous to the date of termination. To place the total burden on Kevin's shoulders would be unjust.

The UCC provides that a good-faith purchaser who buys goods from a third party, and is unaware that they came from a minor, may retain them. The purchase must be made in good faith in order to nullify the minor's right of rescission. This encourages people to buy without worrying that their contracts can be voided by a third-party infant. This UCC rule applies only to the sale of goods by a minor, not to the sale of real estate.

EXAMPLE Billy Wilson, who is thirteen, has amassed a large collection of comic books including Spiderman and the Hulk. Billy has been accepted to play in the local Peewee Hockey League. The hockey equipment is very expensive, so Billy decides to sell his comic collection, without knowing its real value. Joe Hamilton, proprietor of the local second-hand bookstore, offers Billy a nickel for each comic book. Billy accepts, but later, after learning the real value of the comic books, demands that they be returned to him. Joe has already sold Billy's collection to Frank Warner, a good-faith purchaser. Can Billy recover the comic books from Frank? No! The UCC gives a good-faith purchaser precedence over an infant who is seeking to reclaim the goods. Billy's only recourse would be to sue Joe for the actual value of the comic books.

A contract for the purchase or sale of corporate stock cannot be abrogated by a minor on the basis of infancy. Minors have the right to own stock and to buy and sell it. In return for this right, the minor must be bound, otherwise the minor may be unjustly enriched by rescinding the contract. This could happen in cases where the stock has decreased in value.

EXAMPLE Michele Lange, who is seventeen, gets a hot tip from her boyfriend about the stock of the Seven Dwarfs' Corporation. They manufacture apparel for little people. Michele calls a brokerage company and asks them to purchase 1,000 shares of the stock at $7 per share. The stock is purchased by the brokerage company and Michele sends them the money. Two weeks later, the stock drops to $2 per share. Michele decides to get rid of her boyfriend and sues the brokerage company for return of her consideration. Will she be able to recover the money? No! The purchase of stock by an infant is an exception to the general rule permitting an infant to rescind a contract. It would be unfair to make the brokerage company bear the loss.

MISREPRESENTATION OF AGE

In most states, the defense of infancy is still available to a minor if there has been a misrepresentation of age made to an adult. This occurs where the minor claims to be an adult and the adult is justified in believing this to be true. However, some states have enacted statutes to prevent this because the intentional misrepresentation of age on the minor's part constitutes fraud. The purpose behind the defense is to discourage contracts between infants and adults. If an infant fraudulently induces the adult to enter a contract, the courts in these states will deny the infant protection. A minor will not be allowed to defraud adults and reap the benefits. In fact, a few states hold the minor liable in tort for the fraud committed. Generally, though, the court's determination will depend on whether the adult has suffered any loss, including the loss of profits. The infant's fraud gives the adult a special right to rescind the contract. This right is discretionary and the adult may exercise it if the contract is not beneficial. Proving fraud, however, is an arduous task, particularly if there is no writing to evidence the fraudulent intent on the infant's part.

EXAMPLE Jenifer Presley was hired as a model to do television commercials for a well-known mattress company. She signed a contract stating that she was eighteen. The company later discovered she was only sixteen and cancelled the contract. Has Jenifer any recourse? No! An adult or company who is fraudulently induced into entering a contract by an infant who has misrepresented his or her age, has the special right to rescind the contract.

RATIFICATION

Ratification is the infant's intention to be bound by the contract; it is manifested through the objective actions of the infant. Upon reaching majority or within a reasonable time thereafter, infants may ratify all contracts made during their minority. Ratification may be made through words; through acts, such as making payments; or through inaction, such as receiving benefits. Some courts hold that receiving benefits alone is not sufficient to establish ratification without some positive action or statement on the infant's part. It depends on whether the contract was completed during the infant's minority. If the contract was completed and the infant retained benefits, ratification will be implied. If the contract had not been completed, then some overt act or statement is usually necessary on the infant's part. The rule applies to cases involving payments that a minor makes on an installment contract after reaching majority. If the minor wishes to preserve the right to rescind, the actions taken by the minor should support the intention to rescind and not be inconsistent with that intent. Otherwise, ratification may result. Ratification is absolutely binding on the infant once it is made, and it is retroactive to the date when the contract was made. A special rule applies to real property contracts. It requires that a minor must wait until majority either to ratify or rescind the contract. The contract cannot be rescinded during the infant's minority.

<table>
<tr><td>EXAMPLE</td><td>Jack, a seventeen-year-old boy, spotted a tall candlestick while browsing through a gift shop at Christmas time. The shop owner asked Jack why he wanted such a tall candlestick. Jack replied that he was going to try out for the college track team as a hurdler and needed something to practice with. The candlestick cost $100 and Jack paid for it in full. Jack turned eighteen in January, but it was not until spring that he first used the candlestick. Jack was nimble and Jack was quick, but Jack could not clear the candlestick. In fact, he fell on it and broke it in half. Jack brought the candlestick back, but the owner refused to return Jack's money. Has Jack any recourse? No! The contract was completed during Jack's minority and impliedly ratified in January when he reached eighteen. Suppose Jack had agreed to pay off the candlestick in ten monthly installments and made payments up to April. Would the result be different? No! The installments paid after January, when he reached eighteen, would be a positive act on his part constituting ratification.</td></tr>
</table>

SPECIAL RIGHTS OF THE INSANE

A special right to rescind is given to insane persons in order to protect them from being taken advantage of during their incapacity. There are two types of insane persons. The first, a judicially declared incompetent, is pronounced insane by the court. All contracts made by a judicially declared incompetent are void. A void contract is unenforceable in a court of law.

<table>
<tr><td>EXAMPLE</td><td>The Mad Hatter, a judicially declared incompetent, entered Wonderland Fashion Store and asked Alice, the owner, to pick out a half dozen of the most expensive hats in the store. The Mad Hatter paid by check. His court-appointed guardian stopped payment on the check and returned the hats. Does Alice in Wonderland have any recourse? No! All contracts entered into by a judicially declared incompetent are unenforceable.</td></tr>
</table>

The second type of insane person—a non-judicially declared incompetent—has not been reviewed by a court; however, the incompetent nature of the person is evident to a reasonable observer. Temporary insanity is another example of non-judicially declared incompetence. A person may be temporarily insane while intoxicated or under the influence of narcotics or hallucinogenic drugs. Contracts made by non-judicially declared incompetents, including the temporarily insane, are voidable and may be rescinded by the person lacking capacity.

<table>
<tr><td>EXAMPLE</td><td>Ruby Keaton, a poor unfortunate housemaid, has a few too many one night. She races out to a department store and buys a whole new outfit, including a pair of glass slippers, spending most of her savings in the process. Her condition is quite apparent. She gets into the taxi and tells the driver she is in a hurry to meet Prince Charming at the Debutante Ball. After having a great time at the ball, she realizes it is almost midnight. She hurries home, and in her excitement loses one of the glass slippers. The next day she receives the bill from the department store, which sobers her up very quickly. Is</td></tr>
</table>

The non-judicially declared incompetent may make a binding contract during a lucid interval and the defense of insanity would not apply. There are some people suffering from psychological disorders who do understand the nature of a transaction. Their contracts are binding. So, not all contracts made by insane persons are voidable.

EXAMPLE Mrs. Hubbard was a senile old woman who was known to be tight with a buck. One day she went to Shoetown and purchased five pair of rather expensive shoes, for $250. When she received the bill, she refused to pay. She appeared quite normal when she bought the shoes. Is Mrs. Hubbard responsible for payment? Yes! Mrs. Hubbard is responsible for payment because the contract was entered into during a lucid interval, when she was capable of understanding the contract. Her objective actions govern at the time the contract was made, including her appearance, demeanor, emotional behavior together with what she said when making the purchase.

When exercising the right to rescind, an incompetent person must make restitution. If the incompetent person is unable to return the consideration, the defense of insanity may be disallowed. This occurs where the other party made the contract in good faith, without knowledge of the incompetent person's state of mind. Knowledge of the incompetency is measured by objective actions, not the state of mind of the alleged incompetent. The incompetent person, like an infant, is liable for the reasonable value of necessities furnished.

The person alleging incompetency has the burden of proving it. To establish incompetency, it must be shown that either the person did not have sufficient mental capacity to understand the nature of the transaction, or that the person entered into the contract because of an uncontrollable reaction brought on by some mental illness and that this was known to the other party. Even if a person is successful in proving his or her incompetency, he or she may not be able to disaffirm the contract. This is because the person's incompetency may not have been reasonably evident to the other party. This is an objective test. The decision will turn on whether the person dealing with the alleged incompetent is reasonable in his or her belief that the alleged incompetent possessed sufficient mental capacity to appreciate the nature of the transaction and whether the contract was fair and reasonable. Contracts of the insane may be ratified or disaffirmed by the insane person upon regaining sanity, or by a legally appointed guardian or a personal representative.

EXAMPLE Little Linda Ryan was mildly retarded. She lived with her grandmother, who was her legally appointed guardian. July 11 was Grandma's birthday, so Linda went to a flea market to find a present for her. She purchased a set of crystal glasses by writing a check in the amount of $150. The check bounced. Grandma was about to advise Linda to disaffirm the contract when she discovered the set of glasses was Waterford crystal. Grandma anxiously paid the $150. Does this constitute ratification? Yes! This act by Grandma, Linda Ryan's legal guardian, amounted to ratification.

1. Define legal capacity, infancy, necessities, and insanity.

2. What are the different types of necessities?

3. Wesley, owner of a funeral home, had Marilyn, age thirteen, sign a promissory note for the payment of funeral services for her father. A judgment was obtained against Marilyn for nonpayment of the note. A year after reaching majority, Marilyn discovered that her credit rating was tarnished by the judgment against her. She brought an action immediately to disaffirm the promissory note because of her infancy. What result? If Marilyn is allowed to rescind, must she return the casket? Terrace Company v. Calhoun, 37 Ill. App.3d 757, 347 N.E.2d 315 (1976).

4. Lee, an infant, purchased a car from Haydocy Pontiac for $2,500 with a $100 down payment. She signed a statement certifying that she was twenty-one years of age. The car was stolen a few months later. Lee refuses to pay the balance of the contract. What result? Haydocy Pontiac, Inc. v. Lee, 19 Ohio App. 2d 217 (1969).

5. In 1954, Robertson, an infant, bought a pickup truck from Julian Pontiac. At this time, he was three weeks away from reaching majority. Over a month later, electrical difficulties caused a fire which destroyed the truck. Robertson wishes to rescind the contract and recover his down payment. Pontiac asserts that Robertson is bound by the contract because the truck is a necessity. Robertson did not use the truck for work. What result? Robertson v. King, 225 Ark. 276, 280 S.W.2d 402 (1955).

6. In 1965, Sheehan Buick sold a Riviera to Rose for $5,000. Rose was a minor at the time. At the time of the sale, Rose handled all negotiations. His parents advanced part of the cash. He used the car for school, business, and social purposes. Buick claimed the car was a necessity and that the contract could not be rescinded. What result? If disaffirmation was allowed, should Buick be entitled to the value of depreciation while the car was in Rose's possession? Rose v. Sheehan Buick, Inc., 204 So.2d 903 (Fla. D. Ct. App. 1967).

7. Hanks owned farmland in Nebraska, a portion of which he used for a coal business. Hanks sold one-fourth of the coal lands to McNeil Coal Corporation in 1937. In 1940, Hanks was judicially declared insane and his son was appointed conservator of the estate. The son contended that his father was insane at the time the contract was made. He sought to have the sale of the coal lands rescinded. The father was involved with religious cults at the time and his behavior was often erratic. However, those who had business dealings with him testified that Hanks acted rationally. What result? Hanks v. McNeil Coal Corporation, 114 Colo. 578, 168 P.2d. 256 (1946).

8. Paolino, an infant, agreed to guarantee payment of a debt owed by Branda to Mechanics Finance. Paolino represented that he was twenty-one. Branda defaulted on the debt after making two payments. An action was commenced by Mechanics Finance against Paolino, three months after he attained majority. They assert that he misrepresented his age and that he impliedly ratified the

contract by remaining silent after reaching majority. What result? Mechanics Finance Co. v. Paolino, 29 N.J. Super. 449, 102 A.2d 784 (1954).

9. Strandberg, a minor, agreed to purchase several lots, owned by the Rubins, for $6,000. The payment was to be in monthly installments. After reaching majority, Strandberg made payments in November and December, and then disaffirmed the contract in February. He refused to pay the balance owed, claiming infancy as a defense. The contract had been recorded by the Rubins in January. What result? Rubin et al. v. Strandberg, 288 Ill. 64, 122 N.E. 808 (1919).

10. On a number of occasions, Stuhl, age seventeen, traveled on Eastern Airlines and paid them with checks that subsequently bounced. The trips were taken by Stuhl for business purposes. When Eastern sued Stuhl for nonpayment, he raised the defense of infancy. What result? Eastern Airlines v. Stuhl, 65 Misc. 2d 901, 318 N.Y.S.2d 966 (Civ. Ct. N.Y. 1970).

10

LAWFUL PURPOSE

INTRODUCTION

The purpose for which a contract is made, and the acts being undertaken to accomplish this purpose, must be lawful. Lawful means there must not be any contravention of any federal statute, or any state statute having jurisdiction over the subject matter of the contract. When both the means employed and the end result are consistent with the law, the contract will be valid. There is a presumption the parties intended to form a legal contract unless the opposite is shown. If the contract contemplates the performance of an illegal act, or the achievement of an illegal purpose, the contract is void. A void contract is unenforceable in a court of law. When the contract is void because of illegality, generally no remedies will be granted. A valid contract which subsequently becomes illegal through the enactment of a new law or a change in public policy, will be unenforceable because the public welfare is paramount to the contractual freedom of individuals. In a contract where one party has reason to believe that the other party will use the subject matter of the contract, which is legal, for an illegal purpose, the contract may be valid and the innocent party may enforce it. The illegal activity must not be criminal and the innocent party must not participate in the activity.

EXAMPLE | Billy the Kid, a card shark, purchases a deck of marked cards from a novelty shop. The shop owner knows that the Kid is going to use the cards in a showdown with Pat Garett at the Crystal Palace saloon in Virginia City; but does not participate in that event. Is the contract to purchase the cards valid? Yes! This contract is valid because the Kid is making a legal purchase and because the shop owner's affiliation with the Kid is restricted to the sale of the deck of cards. By the way, Pat Garett, with an ace up his sleeve, shoots the Kid down.

There are two types of illegal contracts: contracts in violation of either a federal or state statute, and contracts against public policy.

CONTRACTS IN VIOLATION OF A STATUTE

Laws are promulgated by federal and state legislatures through statutes. All citizens of the United States must obey federal statutes, and citizens are also bound by the statutes of the state in which they live. Our discussion in this chapter concerning statutes is restricted to state statutes. Government regulation of business through federal statutes is discussed in Chapter 40. Those agreements which contravene state statutes predominantly fall under one of the following categories:

Contracts to commit crimes and torts
Violations of licensing requirements
Usury
Gambling
Sunday laws

Contracts to Commit Crimes and Torts

Contracts to commit crimes and torts are illegal and definitely not legally enforceable. It is an accepted fact that these contracts are made and carried out. It might be said that these contracts are illegally enforceable. Criminal laws are designed to punish individuals for the wrongs they have committed. Tort laws are enacted to reimburse aggrieved parties for the damages they sustained as a result of the wrongs committed against them. Contract law discourages agreements made to commit crimes and torts by providing no forum for their enforcement. The courts will leave the parties where they lie, so to speak.

EXAMPLE Al Capone puts a $10,000 contract out on the Bugsy Moran Gang, to be executed by Machine Gun Kelly on St. Valentine's Day. The massacre is carried out, but Capone refuses to pay Kelly the $10,000. Kelly sues Capone, but Capone hires the Great Mouthpiece, a defense counsel who has never lost a case. The Mouthpiece argues that contracts to commit crimes are not enforceable in a court of law. Has the Mouthpiece won another case? Yes! The Mouthpiece is correct and the courts leave the parties where they lie.

Violations of Licensing Requirements

Licenses are required of persons who intend to practice in certain professions, trades, and recreational activities. Licenses are a prerequisite to admission into the following professional fields: law, accounting, medicine, nursing, and teaching. Trades and businesses requiring a license include: carpentry, plumbing, masonry, contracting, meat and food processing, hairstyling, and bar and restaurant establishments. Hunting, fishing, and boating are recreational activities for which a license is generally needed. There are two types of licensing: regulatory and revenue raising.

Regulatory statutes protect the public from individuals who are unscrupulous and incompetent by requiring in the first case, proof of integrity, and in the second, proof of skill. Integrity is judged through personal interviews with the regulatory association, references, and examinations testing the knowledge of professional ethics. Skill is measured either through an examination of knowledge or demonstration of workmanship, or it can be based on years of service as an apprentice. A contract made by a party who is in violation of a regulatory statute is void. The party in violation will not be able to enforce the contract to receive the agreed-upon compensation even if the work is of the highest quality. Generally, the quality of the work makes no difference because there is a strong public interest to protect people against those not licensed. However, some courts will allow recovery where the person in violation is honest, competent, and made no claim to having a license. The reason for the recovery is to prevent unjust enrichment by the person receiving the services or goods. The court may also allow an innocent party to enforce the contract if that party lacked knowledge of the violation.

EXAMPLE Richard Harrington is an attorney licensed to practice in the state of Wisconsin. He is asked by his sister, who lives in Pontiac, Michigan, to represent her and her husband in a matter involving a breach of contract to purchase real estate. Harrington is not licensed to practice in Michigan and does not get the court's permission to appear for this isolated case. His defense is successful, but his sister refuses to pay the fee after a falling out. Is Harrington entitled to the fee? No! Without a license to practice, most states will refuse an attorney compensation for his services.

Revenue-raising statutes are those which allow anyone to obtain a license or permit upon payment of a fee. This is to raise funds both to support the licensed activity and to maintain other government programs. Examples of revenue-raising statutes include tennis and campground permits, automobile registration, incorporation fees, transfer taxes, and other general registration fees. Courts are more lenient in enforcing contracts which involve a violation of a statute intended for revenue raising. The justification of protecting the public interest from unskilled or dishonest individuals is lacking. Infringement of statutes of this type generally result in fines meant to encourage future compliance.

EXAMPLE Dennis Hansen is licensed to practice law and has registered with the State Board of Law Examiners. Five years later, he forgets to pay his yearly $50 registration fee due January 1. On January 3, Hansen agrees to represent Charles Darrow in a landlord and tenant dispute. The trial is completed on January 30. On February 1, Hansen is notified by the state board that he is delinquent in his payment of dues, which he promptly rectifies. Upon learning of this, Darrow refuses to pay Hansen for his services, alleging that Hansen was in violation of a licensing requirement at the time he rendered the services. Is Darrow's assumption correct? Darrow is correct in theory, but not in practice. Hansen will be able to collect his fee because the statute he violated was not designed to protect the public from the unqualified, but only to raise revenue. A person who has passed the bar exam is licensed to practice law. If he or she fails to register, this can be remedied by paying the annual fee. It has no effect on the lawyer's qualifications for practicing law.

Usury

State statutes limit rates of interest charged on borrowed money. Usury contracts involve the charging of interest in excess of the maximum rate allowed by statute. When money is loaned, certain additional charges are permitted for the recording of the loan and for the investigation into the financial background of the borrower. These are considered as separate service charges, and are not included as part of the interest rate. However, "points" may be tacked on to the interest charged by prorating the points over the life of a loan. Points are an assessment charged by a lending institution for making the loan. The reason for prorating points over the life of the policy is to avoid usury in the first year when the points are charged. Courts differ on the status of late-payment penalties. Some provide that the penalty becomes part of the total interest charged, while others do not.

The effect usury has on a contract for the loan of money depends upon the state where the contract is made. Among the states, there are three prevalent attitudes toward usury, running from the most lenient to the most severe. First, lenders may recover the principal loaned together with the maximum interest allowed, thus forfeiting only the excessive interest charged. Second, lenders must suffer the loss of all interest charged. Third, lenders must relinquish both principal and interest.

EXAMPLE Bonny and her husband Clyde are looking to buy a house in Bay Ridge, Brooklyn. They need $2,000 more for the down payment. They have been turned down by all the banks because of their bad credit rating. They get a tip to see a man named Dutch Schultz, who agrees to lend them the money at a rate of 2 percent per week. They purchase their dream house only to find they are having great difficulty repaying the interest on the loan. Schultz insists they must pay the interest. Is Schultz correct? No! The loan is illegal because the interest charged is usurious.

There are three instances where the usual limitations of usury do not apply:

Corporations
Small loan companies
Sales of goods on credit

Corporations are not endowed with the defense of usury because it is designed to protect people from unscrupulous lenders.

Small loan companies were introduced in order to provide loans in small amounts to deter debtors from bargaining with loan sharks. Some states impose a limit on the amount of money that can be borrowed, and a restriction on the interest that can be charged on a monthly basis. Many states allow small loan companies the right to charge a higher rate of interest. This is because of the greater risk involved in giving credit to high-risk individuals. Typically, these loans are the ones that larger institutions would not grant because of the imbalance between profit and risk.

Sale of goods on credit requires payments to be made on an installment basis. An installment sale is a contract which requires a promise to pay a certain amount at a stated time for the consideration received until full payment is made. An interest charge is assessed each month on the unpaid balance. There is a sharp difference between sale of goods for cash and for credit. Credit sales are not subject to usury statutes because they are not loans. A maximum monthly rate of interest is permitted under the truth-in-lending laws of each state. These laws generally impose a duty upon the lender to provide the borrower with a statement listing the cash price, the original payment made, the unpaid balance, and the monthly finance charge. If the borrower is obligated to make the installment payments to a bank, then the installment contract is actually a loan and would be regulated by the usury laws.

EXAMPLE Ma Barker runs the Bullet Hole Donut Shop in Hell's Kitchen. She buys donuts from a supplier. Terms of the sale are thirty days for payment. An interest rate of $1^1/_2$ percent is charged on the unpaid balance after the thirty days. Is Ma getting a fair shake on the interest charged? Yes! The rate is within the standard set by the truth-in-lending laws for contracts involving the sale of goods on credit.

Gambling

Individuals who engage in gambling are making wagering agreements. Most states except Nevada and New Jersey's Atlantic City prohibit gambling. People who gamble forfeit their right to the other party's consideration or to a return of their own consideration. Courts will neither enforce a bettor's right to winnings nor will they enforce a bettor's duty to pay up for money owed. Loan sharks, bookies, and other illegal betting establishments do not rely on the courts to enforce bets.

Many states allow exceptions to gambling laws for charitable and religious organizations to engage in bingo, bazaars, nights at the races, Las Vegas nights, and the selling of chance books. Lotteries are sanctioned by some states for revenue-raising purposes. Sweepstakes are generally permissible as long as there is no request for money and no purchase necessary.

Speculative agreements involving the buying and selling of securities and commodities are legitimate because the securities and commodities represent ownership in corporations. This is true even though most investors are betting on price fluctuations to make profits. Option contracts on securities and commodities (puts and calls), which give the holder the right to buy or sell a specific security or commodity at a fixed price before the expiration of a certain date, are tolerated. This is because there is a possibility of ownership through the right to exercise the option. This theory prevails, although most option contracts expire unexercised, which indicates that in many cases, the reason behind investing in options is purely speculative, if not outright gambling.

Individuals are allowed to relieve themselves of the possible financial burden resulting from property damage, medical expenses, or loss of life, by allocating the risk to an insurance company. The person contracting for the insurance must possess a substantial interest in the property or person to be insured.

EXAMPLE Paul Nelson owns a catering hall on the Lower East Side. He contracts with an insurance company to provide him with fire and liability coverage. Nelson often rents out his main hall to the local chapter of the Knights of Columbus for bingo games and Las Vegas Nights. He lets out the basement to Johnny Ringo, who runs his own Las Vegas Nights and employs the East Side Kids to supervise the games. Are any of these contracts legal? The insurance contract is legal because risks involving insurable interests can be allocated. Paul Nelson's contract with Ringo is illegal, but the contract with the K of C is valid because they, as a religious organization, are allowed to operate games of chance to raise money for their cause. Ringo's employment contract with the East Side Kids is illegal and unenforceable.

Sunday Laws

Sunday-law statutes prohibit the performance of certain work, especially work that involves manual labor and the operation of establishments selling or serving liquor, on Sundays. Sunday laws are formulated by individual states and vary greatly. There are exceptions to this rule dictated by necessity, convenience, recreation, and charity. Service stations, restaurants, hotels, and common carriers such as airlines, private bus and train companies must be allowed to operate on Sundays. Technicians and repairmen needed to operate city services must be authorized to work on Sunday. Places of recreation that may be open on Sundays comprise: amusement parks, theaters, sports arenas, beaches, golf courses, campgrounds, and county or state fairs. In many states, supermarkets are permitted to open on Sunday because they are considered necessary to the public good. To find out the various contracts that are prohibited, state statutes and local ordinances should be consulted.

CONTRACTS AGAINST PUBLIC POLICY

Contracts which have a detrimental effect on the general public are considered to be against public policy. The meaning of the term has changed with time and according to society's norms and values. Examples of contracts against public policy are:

Contracts that endanger public welfare

Contracts that restrict competition

Unconscionable contracts

Discriminatory contracts

Contracts that contain exculpatory clauses

Contracts that Endanger Public Welfare

Contracts that endanger the public health, safety, morals, and general welfare are against public policy. Parties who attempt to impede justice by refusing to testify, suppressing evidence, or intentionally hindering court procedure, in return for some form of compensation, are engaging in contracts which have a harmful effect on the general public.

EXAMPLE Jesse James and his brother Frank are under contract to do a demolition job in downtown Manhattan on St. Patrick's Day. They are transporting nitroglycerin in a truck down the Avenue of the Americas when they are caught. A block away, over two million people are gathered to watch the St. Patrick's Day Parade. Could this blow up? Definitely! This contract endangers the welfare of over two million people, many of whom are already bombed. Since it is against public policy, the James Brothers will not be allowed to continue on their preplanned route.

Individuals, who exert undue influence over public officials and fiduciaries through contracts involving bribery, are acting against public policy. Contracts which create a conflict between the personal interests and the duties of a public official or fiduciary must be avoided unless complete disclosure is made. Lobbying is legal if information is presented to further the position of one side. However, if the contract for lobbying entails the use of undue influence or is based on a contingency fee, it is void because it is against public policy.

EXAMPLE   The FDA is considering passing a regulation to prohibit the use of red dye in meat. The Meat Packers Association feels this will have a detrimental effect on the sale of meat because the red dye makes the meat look more attractive and nutritious. The Meat Packers Association hires Michael Richards, former head of the FDA, to lobby for their cause. They offer Richards $250,000 if he is successful in having the legislation defeated. Richards threatens to expose certain documents which will cause great embarrassment to a number of key administrators in the FDA. They squash the proposed legislation as a result. Are the tactics employed by Richards legal? No! The use of undue influence in lobbying is not lawful, and neither is the contingency fee arrangement. Richards will forfeit the $250,000.

Contracts that Restrict Competition

Contracts used by individuals or corporations to restrict free trade via monopolies, price fixing, or other forms of unfair competition, are illegal because they violate the Sherman Antitrust Act. Attempts made to discriminate in favor of certain purchasers by charging them a preferred rate, or by granting them exclusive dealing contracts, are in restraint of trade, and thus are violations of the Clayton Act. Our system of capitalism is predicated on the theory of competition. Contracts in restraint of trade will be discussed in more detail in Chapter 40, Corporate Antitrust Legislation.

EXAMPLE   At the intersection of Clove Road and Ridge Boulevard, Sylvester Oates operates a gas station and David Maxwell operates an automobile repair shop. Their businesses are on opposite corners. On one of the other corners, Luke Browning opens a gas and service station. Oates and Maxwell have been doing quite well over the years by referring business to one another, but now Browning is cutting into their profits. They enter into a contract to reduce prices to whatever extent is necessary to drive Browning out of business. Is this a valid contract? No! It restricts free competition and is replete with violations of the Sherman Antitrust Act.

Contracts not to compete are generally found to be not in the best interest of the public. However, contracts containing a covenant not to compete may be lawful where the contract is for the sale of a business or where it involves employment. A provision restricting the seller of a business from competing in the area where the business is located for a period of up to five years is generally granted for the protection of the purchaser. These are general guidelines. The court will look to see whether the area and time restrictions are reasonable and sufficient to protect the purchaser from unfair competition by the seller. In most cases, the contract will not fail if the area or duration is excessive, but the clause will be stricken. Some states will determine reasonable limitations and apply them. A close watch is undertaken by the courts to preserve free competition.

EXAMPLE Bill Mart sells his gun and rifle shop in Dodge City to Bob Masterson. The contract contains a clause restricting Bill Mart from opening another gun and rifle shop within the city limits for a period of five years. Will this clause be enforced? Yes! The clause is designed to protect Bob Masterson from unfair competition by Bill Mart because the town is not big enough for both of them. Its time limitation is reasonable in that it gives Bob sufficient time to establish himself in the community.

A clause in an employment contract may prevent an employee from working in the same field for a certain length of time. The courts do not look with favor upon such clauses, and enforce them only where the employee's knowledge of trade secrets or the future of the business is at issue. The enforcement of employment restrictions usually applies to management.

Karpinski v. Ingrasci
28 N.Y.2d 48, 320 N.Y.S. 2d 1, 268 N.E.2d 751 (1971)

Karpinski sued Ingrasci for breach of contract caused by Ingrasci's violation of a restrictive covenant. Karpinski asked that the restrictive covenant be enforced through the use of an injunction, and that he receive damages for lost profits as well.

Karpinski was an oral surgeon with a successful dental practice in upstate New York, drawing clients from five counties. In 1962, he opened a second office in centrally located Ithaca. At that time he hired Ingrasci, an oral surgeon, as his assistant for three years. The employment contract provided that Ingrasci

promises and covenants that while this agreement is in effect and forever thereafter, he will never practice dentistry and/or Oral Surgery in Cayuga, Cortland, Seneca, Tompkins, or Ontario counties except: (a) in association with the (office of Karpinski) or (b) If the (office of Karpinski) terminates the agreement and employs another oral surgeon.

Ingrasci also signed a $40,000 promissory note for Karpinski which would become due if Ingrasci violated the restrictive covenant.

The week after the three-year period expired, Ingrasci opened an office in Ithaca. Kapinski lost many of his clients to Ingrasci.

The issues are whether an injunction should be granted restricting Ingrasci from practicing dentistry and oral surgery in the five counties specified, and whether Karpinski is entitled to enforcement of the stipulated damage clause in the amount of $40,000 for the breach.

The court decided that Karpinski had a right to enforce the restrictive covenant to protect his practice of oral surgery, which he had developed over many years in the five counties. The injunction was granted to provide this protection, but it extended only to the practice of oral surgery, not dentistry. The damages stipulated in the contract were not allowed because the injunction would prevent a permanent breach. Karpinski was awarded damages for only the period during the breach when Ingrasci opened his practice. Judgment for Karpinski.

The limitations set forth in the contract must be reasonable. The courts will not enforce restrictions upon employees which are unduly harsh and permit employers to derive more protection than that necessary to guard their secrets or to protect their business interests.

EXAMPLE Earl Williams bought a liquor store on the South Side of Chicago. He hired Tyrone Jackson, a kid fresh out of the school of hard knocks, to manage it for him. A provision in the contract prohibited Tyrone from opening a liquor store within the city limits for the rest of his natural life. After learning the trade, Tyrone quit and opened his own place in the downtown section of Chicago known as the Loop. Can Earl enforce the provision? No! The provision is too broad in its geographical area and much too unreasonable in its time restraints.

Unconscionable Contracts

Unconscionable contracts are unduly harsh and one-sided, usually involving parties of unequal bargaining power. The harshness of the contract must be so severe as to shock the moral conscience of the community. These contracts are against public policy because freedom to contract is impaired by one party's taking unfair advantage through greater bargaining strength. Unconscionability especially pervades those contracts which are entered into by employees and by consumers. The enactment of minimum wage and minimum hour laws, workman's compensation, and occupational safety and health standards, assists in guarding against unconscionability in employment contracts. Consumer contracts are aided by the Uniform Consumer Credit Code and truth-in-lending laws, which defend against oppressive and harsh contracts imposed upon consumers. Standardized contracts containing terms and conditions which must be adhered to, if the consumer wishes to contract, are strictly construed by the courts against the party who drafted the contract.

EXAMPLE The Dalton brothers are in the demolition business. They employ Roger Milton to handle their explosive devices for a period of one year. Milton has to work under conditions that are continually unsafe. The devices could blow up at any time. The Dalton brothers do not provide Milton with any protective equipment or take any safety precautions in his behalf. Milton decides he wants out of the contract. Is Milton bound? No! The contract is unconscionable in that it exposes Milton to danger by making him work without proper safety equipment.

Discriminatory Contracts

Contracts discriminating against a person because of religion, race, national origin, or gender, are illegal because they violate both public policy and the Constitution of the United States. Their main purpose is to discriminate against people and exclude them based on the classifications just mentioned.

The Civil Rights Act of 1964 was enacted to insure that all individuals would be guaranteed equal employment opportunity. The act prohibits the use of discriminatory tactics in hiring, firing, determining compensation or other terms or conditions of employment. This prohibition encompasses not only those discriminatory acts which are overt, but it also extends to those acts which are subtle. The Equal Employment Opportunity Commission (EEOC) is entrusted with policing employment tactics which may be discriminatory.

EXAMPLE The Black Hand is a national organization of funeral directors. Their membership is restricted. A pair of funeral directors, named Jack O'Brien and Abdul Mohammed applied for membership. Jack was refused because of his national origin, and Abdul because of his religion. Jack and Abdul claimed discrimination. Are they correct? Yes! When a national organization of a particular occupation limits membership to people of a certain religion or national origin, that is discriminatory and unconstitutional.

Contracts that Contain Exculpatory Clauses

Parties attempting to disclaim liability through the use of an exculpatory clause in the contract may not do so when the liability is caused by their own negligence. This is especially true in contracts affecting the public where parties attempting to escape responsibility have superior bargaining power due to the nature of their position, such as utilities. This is to insure that the party with greater negotiating strength does not downgrade its service or produce an inferior product by becoming lax in its workmanship; otherwise the party will be allowed to act in a manner harmful to the public with little fear of accountability.

Smith v. Kennedy
43 Ala. App. 538, 195 So.2d 820 (1966)

Kennedy sued the Birmingham Beauty College and one of its students for injuries caused by the negligent application of a chemical solution to her hair.

Mrs. Kennedy went to the beauty college to get a permanent wave. She was asked to sign the following agreement:

HOLD HARMLESS AGREEMENT
(Student Operator Beauty School)

July 23, 1962

I, Mrs. W. O. Kennedy, residing at Trussville, Alabama, Route I, Box 735 do hereby acknowledge that I am fully aware that Birmingham Beauty College is a school for beauty culture and cosmetology, that the operators in this school are not being held out as skilled and trained operators, that for this reason, a reduction in the prices customarily charged is being made for this work. Therefore, in consideration of the reduction in price given in this work, it is agreed and understood that I will in no wise hold the above named school, its proprietors, officers or agents, or any of its operators liable or accountable for any injury or damages that may occur to me as a result of work performed on me in this school.

The student who attended Mrs. Kennedy used a liquid solution on her hair that ran down onto her face and neck. She felt a burning sensation, but the student assured her there would be no harmful effect. Later that day she was treated at a hospital for chemical burns on the neck.

The issue is whether the agreement signed by Mrs. Kennedy exculpates the beauty college and the student from liability due to negligence.

The court held that "Under Alabama law a party may not by contract absolve himself from liability for the negligence of himself or his servants." Judgment for Kennedy.

In bailment contracts, parties attempt to exonerate themselves from all blame through inconspicuous notification on a sign, for instance, or on the back of a ticket. A bailment is a contract whereby one party agrees to be responsible for the property of another in return for a fee. The party making the promise must exercise reasonable care in respect to the property. Tickets given as an indication of ownership do not effectively excuse parties from liability growing out of their own negligence. Some common carriers, parking lots, restaurant coat-check concessions, tailors, and ski lifts, for example, give tickets in an attempt to shift the risk of liability to the customer. In their dealings with the public, these businesses have a nontransferable duty to exercise due care regarding the property in their possession. Although liability cannot be disclaimed, it may be limited in certain instances. A discussion of these limitations appears in Chapter 25, Bailments.

In private contracts, risks may be assigned by one party to another if the contract is entered into freely. The relative bargaining strength of the parties will be examined to determine whether the assignments of risk are made freely.

EXAMPLE | Referring to the example before last, suppose Roger Milton continues to handle explosive devices for the Dalton brothers. Milton is usually competent, but this time it blows up in his face because of a faulty detonation device installed by the brothers. Milton sues the Daltons, but the contract provides that Roger assumes all risk of injury. Has he any recourse? Yes! The Daltons cannot exculpate themselves from liability for injury caused to Milton through their own negligence.

REVIEW QUESTIONS

1. Define lawful purpose, usury, Sunday laws, unconscionability.
2. Define exculpatory clauses, and contracts in restraint of trade.
3. Wilson contracted with Kealakekua Ranch to perform architectural services amounting to over $33,000. The ranch refused to pay for the services when it discovered that Wilson, who was licensed, had failed to pay a $15 registration fee. What result? Wilson v. Kealakekua Ranch, Ltd., 551 P.2d 525 (Hawaii) 1976.
4. Tovar, in seeking employment as a resident physician with Paxton Hospital in Illinois, fully described his qualifications to the hospital. The hospital hired Tovar with the assurance that the position would be for life. Tovar gave up a position

in Kansas and moved to Illinois in reliance on this. Two weeks later, Tovar was fired because he did not have a license to practice medicine in Illinois. Based on Tovar's representation, the hospital assumed he had his license. Tovar sued the hospital for breach of contract. What result? Manuel Tovar v. Paxton Community Memorial Hospital, 29 Ill. App. 3rd 218, 330 NE.2d 247 (1975).

5. D'Orio sold checkerboards and checkers to the Startup Candy Company. Startup used the items in a game it devised. Players paid a certain sum to select a paper with a checker problem on it. If they could solve the problem, they received a prize. There were ten problems and all were solvable if players possessed a certain skill. D'Orio brought an action to recover the reasonable value of the items sold to Startup contending that they were used for gambling purposes to conduct a lottery. Lotteries were prohibited by statute in Utah. What result? D'Orio v. Startup Candy Co., 71 Utah 410, 266 P. 1037 (1928).

6. Fein was thinking of purchasing a Budget Rent-A-Car franchise. Budget required all prospective purchasers to sign an agreement containing a restrictive covenant not to compete in the automotive business for two years in the Western Hemisphere. After signing the agreement, Budget divulged secret information to Fein regarding the way they developed local businesses. Subsequently, Fein discontinued negotiations and bought a franchise from one of Budget's competitors. Budget sued Fein to enforce the restrictive covenant. What result? Budget Rent-A-Car Corporation v. Fein, 342 F.2d 509 (5th Cir. 1965).

7. McConnell agreed to represent Commonwealth in trying to obtain the distribution rights to pictures produced by Universal. In return, he was paid $10,000 and was promised a commission. McConnell obtained the distribution rights by bribing an agent of Universal. Commonwealth did not sanction the bribe and refused to pay the commission to McConnell. What result? McConnell v. Commonwealth Picture Corp., 7 N.Y.2d 465, 199 N.Y.S.2d 483, 166 N.E.2d 494 (1960).

8. Hy-Grade Oil Co. maintained an account with New Jersey Bank. A night depository agreement was signed by Hy-Grade. The agreement contained a clause exculpating the bank from all responsibility regarding the use of the night depository facilities. By using the night depository, Hy-Grade made a deposit which was never credited to its account. The bank refused to acknowledge the deposit, citing the exculpatory clause in the agreement. What result? Hy-Grade Oil v. New Jersey Bank, 138 N.J. Super. 112, 350 A.2d 279 (1975).

9. Overbeck was a holder of a Sears credit card. Sears charged $1\frac{1}{2}$ percent per month on all balances unpaid after a thirty-day period. This rate was in excess of the maximum legal rate of interest allowable in the state. Is Sears guilty of usury? Overbeck v. Sears, 169 Ind. App. 501, 349 N.E.2d 286 (1976).

10. Williams bought a stereo for $500, on an installment basis, from Walker-Thomas Furniture Company. The contract provided that title to the goods remained with the seller until the last payment was made. After paying over $500 she defaulted, asserting that she had paid the price of the stereo. Walker-Thomas argued that they still had title to the stereo under the provision in the contract and they wanted to reclaim it. Williams contended that Walker-Thomas sold the

stereo to her knowing that she already had over a $150 balance due on her account with them, and that she had two children to feed on $200 a week. Furthermore, she asserted that Walker-Thomas used their superior bargaining strength in requiring her to sign this contract. Is this an unconscionable contract? What effect would her personal problems have on the outcome? Williams v. Walker-Thomas Furniture Co., 198 A.2d 914 (D.C.) 1964.

11
FORM
AND
INTERPRETATION

FORMATION

There are a number of ways for contracts to be formed. They may be expressed either orally or in writing, or they may be implied from the action of the parties. Contracts formed by any of these methods are equally valid. Generally, there is no problem with the validity of an oral contract; the difficulty arises in trying to prove its existence. Many valid contracts are dismissed by the courts because their terms cannot be proved. If, in an oral contract, one party does not fulfill his or her obligation, the other party without witnesses will have an arduous task trying to prove the existence of the contract. The old saying "It's my word against yours" is very true and applicable to oral contracts. Even with witnesses, there are still problems. Over a period of time, witnesses tend to forget; their testimony is often conflicting and may even be perjured. However, for the sake of convenience, simple contracts, particularly those of nominal value, tend to be oral.

All valuable and important contracts should be in writing so there is evidence of the existence of a contract. All states have recognized this principle by adopting a statute of frauds that requires certain contracts to be in writing. The main purpose behind the statute is to prevent fraud by requiring evidence of the contract's existence. This avoids misunderstandings which lead to misrepresentations. Additionally, without the statute of frauds, those oral contracts which would otherwise not be enforceable could be enforced. This would dramatically increase the caseload with the courts guessing as to the final verdict because of the conflicting oral evidence.

The idea for a statute of frauds originated in England, in the latter part of the seventeenth century. Prior to that time, all oral contracts were enforceable based on the principle that a contract is as good as a person's word. However, the parties themselves were not allowed to testify because many were willing to commit perjury in order to win the case. Only witnesses could testify on the party's behalf, but many witnesses were bribed to give false testimony. Innocent parties who lacked witnesses of their own could not rebuke the false testimony of the other party's witnesses because of the rule forbidding parties to testify. As a result, fraud became commonplace. In an attempt to protect the innocent, the British Parliament enacted the Statute of Frauds, which required certain contracts to be in writing.

In the United States, each state has its own statute requiring certain contracts to be in writing. If the statute's requirements are not met, enforcement of the contract is denied. This bars honest individuals from being able to enforce contracts that are not in writing. The need to prevent fraud is greater than the hardship imposed upon those honest people. If, however, the denial of enforcement perpetrates a fraud upon an innocent party, the statute will be abandoned. The courts will not allow the statute to cause the fraud it is seeking to prevent.

The contracts which are generally required to be in writing are:

Land
&
Miscellaneous
Sale of securities
$500 or more sale of goods
One year of performance (in excess of)
Other than goods, personal property, exceeding $5000
Suretyship contracts

LAND

Real estate or real property is defined as land and everything that is permanently attached to it. This includes buildings, vegetation, crops, timber, and minerals. However, a contract for the sale of crops or lumber is a contract for the sale of goods regardless of whether the buyer or seller severs the crops or timber from the land. Timber refers to trees; lumber refers to trees after cutting.

EXAMPLE | Cyrus McCormick orally contracts to sell five hundred bushels of wheat and corn and to sell and deliver an acre's worth of lumber to International Harvester for a total price of $400. He uses his newly manufactured reaper to harvest the crops. When he delivers the lumber and crops, International Harvester refuses to accept, claiming the sale of timber and crops is a contract for real estate that must be in writing. Are they correct? No! Once crops and timber are severed from the land they become goods. A contract for the sale of goods priced under $500 does not have to be in writing.

The Uniform Commercial Code has a special rule for contracts involving the sale of minerals. If the minerals are to be removed by the seller, the contract is for the sale of goods; but if the removal is to be made by the buyer, it is a contract for an interest in the land and must be in writing.

Contracts for the sale of real estate or an interest in real estate must be in writing. An easement is the legal right to use the land of another for a specific purpose. An assignment of a mortgage does not have to be in writing because the assignment itself is not an interest in land, but rather a transfer of a debt. An assignment is a transfer of rights and duties from one person to another. A further discussion of mortgages, easements, and leases is presented in Chapter 28, Real Estate Transactions; and Chapter 30, Landlord and Tenant.

Ancillary agreements such as title searches, repairs, improvements, or additions to real property are not required to be in writing. They do not qualify as interests in real property because they are personal service contracts. However, some states provide that brokerage contracts must be in writing. To satisfy the requirement, many states require that the full legal description of the land be set forth in the contract. This includes lot and block numbers, metes and bounds, in addition to the normal address.

EXAMPLE | The U.S. Air Force is looking to purchase a large tract of property to test their new B-52 bombers. The Air Force enters into a contract to purchase land in a town called Kitty Hawk. The contract and mortgage are in writing, but the only legal description of the property is in metes and bounds. The Air Force inquires about whether the contract and mortgage must be in writing and about the legal sufficiency of the property description. All contracts for the sale of land must be in writing, as well as mortgages, because they are interests in land. The metes and bounds description is sufficient because it adequately describes the boundaries of the property. Many rural areas do not have addresses or lot and block numbers.

MISCELLANEOUS CONTRACTS

Contracts in which collateral is pledged as security by a debtor must be in writing in accordance with Article 9, Secured Transactions, of the UCC. The writing must set forth a description of the collateral. The writing requirement may be dispensed with only if the collateral is in the possession of the creditor.

EXAMPLE | In addition to the mortgage, the Air Force takes out a loan to clear a landing strip. Their bombers serve as collateral. This security agreement is made orally. If the Air Force defaults on the loan, can the lender take possession of their bombers? No! A security agreement must be in written form setting forth the description of the collateral pledged.

Contracts made in consideration of marriage must be in writing to bind the person making the promise. This does not apply to the vows made by the bride and groom, but it does apply to prenuptial agreements made by the couple regarding their respective rights to each other's property. This written requirement does not conflict with the ban in most states on a suit for breach of promise to marry.

EXAMPLE | Peter Cobb, chairman of the Mountain States University Physics Department, promises to appoint his fiancée, Marie, to the faculty if she will marry him. Can she enforce this promise? The promise will become enforceable only when the wedding takes place. If he changes his mind and breaks the engagement, does she have any recourse? No!

There no longer exists a remedy for breach of promise to marry. Many years ago, a woman could sue for damages for loss of support caused by a broken engagement. This is no longer possible.

An executor's promise to pay personally the unpaid claims against an estate incurred by the decedent or arising because of the decedent's death must comply with the written requirement. This is because these claims were not incurred or authorized by the executor. An executor's promise to be personally responsible for claims he or she authorized arising after the decedent's death does not have to be in writing. The estate will be responsible for these contracts. The reasoning behind this rule is that the executor's promise may be made in a state of emotion, because of the closeness in the relationship. Executors are frequently family members or close friends. Also, creditors may try to coerce the executor into becoming liable.

EXAMPLE Matthew Carson is the proprietor of an investment brokerage company. He introduces a new money market account. His regular customers invest $5 million in the new account. Carson invests a large percentage of the funds in Brazilian and Mexican bonds, which are low-grade investments. In time, Brazil and Mexico declare a moratorium on the bonds—a period during which no interest will be paid—and Carson's customers sue him for negligent investing of their funds. Carson built his business on a foundation of integrity. The shock of the moratorium and the resulting lawsuits cause him to have a fatal heart attack. His customers try to influence Carson's son, the executor of his estate, to repay the debts owed in order to clear his father's name. In a moment of weakness, the son, who is independently wealthy, promises to be responsible, but later refuses to pay. Can his father's customers hold him to his oral promise? No! An executor's promise to be liable for the unpaid claims against the estate must be in writing.

Promises to leave money or property to someone in a will must be in writing to be valid. Some states require a writing to name or change a beneficiary in a life insurance policy. Contracts between a principal and an agent, such as a corporation and one of its officers, are often required to be in writing if the contract an agent enters into on behalf of a principal is required to be in writing by the statute of frauds.

SALE OF SECURITIES

For the purchase or sale of securities, the UCC, under Article 8, Investment Securities, requires a writing signed by either the client or the broker who is acting as agent. The agency contract between broker and client must also be in writing. An agency contract allows the broker to act on the client's behalf, usually upon verbal instructions. The signed writing must state the quantity and price of the securities to be bought or sold. There must be delivery of the securities bought. Delivery may be made to the client's account if this is previously agreed in writing, and it usually is. A writing must be sent, within a reasonable time, to confirm the sale of securities. The person receiving it has ten days to send written objection to the sale.

EXAMPLE | Henry Post opens an account with his local broker. He signs a statement giving the broker the authority to buy and sell for him. Post telephones his broker, telling him to purchase 5,000 shares of Ford Motor Company stock at $30 per share. The stock drops to $20 per share and Post refuses to pay, alleging that there was no written contract. Is he correct? No! The broker need only send a written confirmation slip to evidence the transaction within a reasonable time. Although his signature does not appear on the confirmation slip, Post is bound by the agreement he signed when he opened the account.

$500 OR MORE FOR THE SALE OF GOODS

Under Article 2, Sales, the UCC provides that contracts for the sale of goods for $500 or more must be in writing. The $500 minimum requirement applies to a sale of a single item in excess of $500, as well as a sale of a number of items totaling more than $500. This applies when the parties intend the sale of a number of items to constitute a single contract. If they intended the sale of each item to be a separate contract, the writing requirement of the statute of frauds would not apply.

The writing required need only be a note or memorandum to evidence the existence of a contract. There may be an omission or mistake in one or more of the material terms as long as the parties and the goods can be identified. The quantity term must be specified; but, if misstated, it will be enforceable only up to the misstated amount. The other terms: price, time and place of delivery will be supplemented by the gap-filler provisions of the UCC if they are not mentioned in the writing as outlined in Chapter 7, Agreement. The court will assume the parties intended a reasonable price, a reasonable time for delivery, and delivery at the seller's place of business. The courts will be looking to the intention of the parties for making the contract. This is a progressive step in liberalizing the writing requirement.

EXAMPLE | Alexander Graham Bell III, in working on his new telecommunications invention, uses a tremendous amount of number 18 wire. He calls his local supplier and asks him to deliver twenty rolls of the thin wire. The supplier agrees, but never delivers. His defense to a suit for nondelivery is that the contract is not in writing. Is the supplier correct? It depends on whether the value of the contract is over $500. In accordance with the UCC gap-filler provisions, the court will assume the parties intended a reasonable price. If the court decides a reasonable price for the wire exceeds $500, then the contract will fail because it is not in writing. If a reasonable price is less than $500, the oral contract will be enforceable.

Exceptions

The UCC provides certain exceptions to the requirement of a writing for contracts involving the sale of goods priced at $500 or more. This liberalization is furthered through the exceptions made by the UCC to the requirement itself.

Merchants contracting with each other

Admission that the writing was a mere formality

Payment made or performance rendered

Specially manufactured goods

Merchants   Merchants contracting with each other can satisfy the statute of frauds requirement under the Code by sending a written confirmation within a reasonable time. This is sufficient to bind the merchant who sends it. It is also binding upon the merchant receiving it, even though that party's signature does not appear on it, unless written notification of objection is sent in return within 10 days.

EXAMPLE | The Mayor telephoned a light bulb distributor to request delivery of 5,000 bulbs, which he wanted to use to illuminate the town of Menlo Park for their hundredth anniversary celebration of the opening of Edison's laboratory. The contract was valued at $1,000. The mayor received written confirmation of the contract a week later. The terms provide for 10,000 bulbs at a cost of $2,000. Can the mayor object? Yes! His objection must be in writing and must be sent within ten days from his receipt of the distributor's confirmation.

Admission   An admission in court, by one of the parties, that a contract for the sale of goods was made is sufficient to require enforcement of the contract.

EXAMPLE | Singer verbally agrees to deliver ten sewing machines to its local sewing center by November 17. The company forgets to make delivery and is sued for breach of contract. In court, Singer admits there was a verbal agreement, but states it was not in writing as required by the statute of frauds. Has Singer sewn up the case for his opponent? Yes! The contract is enforceable because of Singer's admission. The purpose behind the statute of frauds is to evidence the existence of a contract and to prevent fraud. Here Singer's admission is evidence of the contract's existence. To refuse enforcement would perpetrate a fraud on the sewing center.

Payment or Performance   An oral contract for the sale of goods will be enforceable where the goods have been received and accepted, or where payment has been made and accepted. A party's receipt and acceptance of goods or acceptance of payment, in effect, stops that party from denying the existence of a contract. The contract will be enforceable against that party based on the doctrine of promissory estoppel, up to the quantity of the goods received or the payment made, even though there is no writing.

EXAMPLE | Issac Newton made a telephone call to Gravity Fruits, Inc., to place an order for 100 bushels of apples. The purchase price was $3,000. Newton received and accepted 50 bushels of apples, but refused to pay, asserting the contract was not in writing. Is Newton required to pay? Yes! Issac must pay because his receipt and acceptance of goods constituted an admission of a valid contract under the UCC. The contract is valid, but only up to the amount he received and accepted, 50 bushels.

Specially Manufactured Goods   An oral contract to manufacture special goods may be enforceable against the buyer. The seller must incur a substantial loss in acquiring or manufacturing the goods, and the goods must not be readily saleable in the seller's business.

EXAMPLE | Robert Fulton, president of a shipbuilding company, verbally agrees to build a steamboat for the State of Mississippi, which plans to sell tickets for excursions along the river that bears its name. After the steamboat is completed, the State of Mississippi repudiates the contract because of a lack of funds. Since there is no longer a market for steamboats, can Fulton enforce the contract even though it is not in writing? Yes! The steamboats are specially manufactured goods not suitable for sale elsewhere. The UCC permits an oral contract in this situation in order to prevent an unjust loss from falling upon the manufacturer.

ONE YEAR OF PERFORMANCE (IN EXCESS OF)

Contracts with a duration of performance in excess of one year are required to be in writing. This includes contracts where the duration is either fixed or indefinite. The majority of states also require contracts requiring forbearance for more than one year to be in writing. However, if there is a possibility, no matter how remote, that a contract may be completed within one year, no writing is required.

Most states require that the duration of performance for both parties exceed one year in order for a writing to be required. In many of these states, loans need not be in writing because the lender's performance, the actual loaning of the money, takes place within one year. Some states require stricter compliance by stipulating that only one party's performance in excess of one year is needed to invoke the writing requirement. This avoids future problems in long-term contracts difficult to resolve because of witnesses who relocate, lose their memory, or die.

The measurement of time generally commences on the day after the contract is entered into—not the day that performance begins—and runs until performance is completed. This assures the parties that the time limitation will expire on the anniversary of the day the contract is made.

EXAMPLE
AT&T hires Alexander Bell and Robert Morse to perfect their telephone and telegraph systems by an oral agreement made on January 1. Bell is to begin work on April 1 and to complete the work on January 31, ten months later. Morse, who is eighty-seven years of age, has a lifetime contract. Neither is in writing. Are the contracts enforceable? Bell's contract is not enforceable. To be enforceable it must be in writing because its duration is thirteen months, commencing at the time the contract is made—January 1. This is true even though Bell does not begin to work until April 1. Morse's contract is enforceable. A lifetime contract does not have to be in writing because it is possible that he may die within one year of the making of the contract.

Co-op Dairy, Inc. v. Dean
102 Ariz. 573, 435 P.2d 470 (1968)

Dean sued Co-op Dairy for breach of an oral employment contract and asked for the balance of the year's salary agreed upon, plus moving expenses. Dean alleges that the one-year employment contract was to commence the day after the parties agreed upon the contract. If this is correct, the oral contract will be upheld because it is not in excess of one year. Contracts in excess of one year must be in writing.

Dean was hired by Co-op Dairy's general manager on February 12, 1962. Co-op Dairy agreed to pay for Dean's moving expenses from Oklahoma to Arizona. Dean did not begin work until February 26, 1962. After he began, all the delivery and supervisory personnel resigned. They threatened not to return until Dean was fired. The company acquiesced to the demand. The company concedes that Dean's work was satisfactory. Co-op Dairy argues that contracts for employment which will commence in the future must be in writing.

The issue is whether the contract could have been completed within one year from the date it was made.

The court decided that since no commencement date was agreed upon, Dean could have begun work on the day after the contract was made. The fact that he began later does not cause the contract to violate the statute of frauds because it was possible for the contract to be performed within one year. Judgment for Dean.

PERSONAL PROPERTY CONTRACTS OTHER THAN GOODS IN EXCESS OF $5,000

The UCC provides that contracts for the sale of personal property other than goods, such as royalty and patent rights, where the price exceeds $5,000, must be in writing.

EXAMPLE | Johann Gutenberg patents his new invention, the printing press. He orally contracts to sell the patent rights to a local manufacturer for $10,000. He subsequently realizes that the printing press has unimaginable worth because it can mass-produce books such as this one for all the world to read. Gutenberg repudiates the contract. Who gets the patent? Gutenberg retains the patent because contracts involving the sale of patents where the price exceeds $5,000 must be in writing.

SURETYSHIP CONTRACTS

A promise to be liable for the debt of another must be in writing in order to evidence the existence of the promise. The reasoning behind this requirement is that it is unusual for people to pay the debts of others. A surety is a person who guarantees payment to a creditor for the debt of another person, who is known as a debtor. The surety's liability must be secondary. Primary responsibility for payment of the debt must rest with the debtor. Only in the event that the debtor does not pay does the surety become liable. The surety's promise must be made to the creditor.

A person's statement that he or she will be responsible for payment or that the debt should be charged to his or her account is one of primary accountability. This does not have to be in writing. Written evidence is required only where the surety's responsibility is secondary.

Peterson v. Rowe
63 N.M. 135, 314 P.2d 892 (1957)

Peterson brought an action against the Rowe brothers to recover for professional services he rendered for their father. The plaintiff, a physician, alleges that both brothers assumed primary responsibility for the payment of his services.

The Rowe brothers brought their father in for emergency treatment for a hemorrhage. Later, the father underwent surgery. The Rowe brothers told the plaintiff, "Well, we want you to do everything you can to save his life and we don't want you to spare any expense because whatever he needs, doctor, you go ahead and get it and I will pay you." Two days later, one of the brothers reiterated his promise: "Do not spare any expense on my father and I will pay you for it . . . We will pay you $200 now and then we will pay you $200 every month." Peterson's services amounted to $3,000. The brothers paid the first $200 and then refused to pay thereafter. They contended that they were under no legal obligation to pay for their father's expenses, because their agreement was not in writing. Peterson argued that they were not guaranteeing their father's promise to pay, but rather they were agreeing to be primarily accountable for the services rendered on their father's behalf. A primary promise to pay the debt of another is not required to be in writing under the statute of frauds.

The issue is whether the statements made by the Rowe brothers constitute a primary promise for which they would be liable, or a secondary promise to guarantee payment, for which they would not be liable without a writing.

The court decided that it was at the brothers' request that the services were performed, and that they received a benefit from these services. This request was a primary promise for which they are liable even though the promise was made orally. Judgment for Peterson.

Many times there is a question as to whether the writing is a guarantee of payment or merely a recommendation of the debtor's ability to pay. To make a proper interpretation, the court will look to the relationship of the parties, the circumstances under which the writing is made, and the motivation of the potential surety for making the statement. The statute of frauds encompasses those contracts which are voidable, such as an infant's contract, but, not those that are void or illegal. A surety who guarantees payment of an infant's debts in writing is liable, even though the infant has the legal right to abrogate the contract.

To be positive that a surety's promise is secondary and therefore required to be in writing, certain criteria must be present. A surety's guarantee of payment must be made to a creditor for the benefit of a debtor. The performance of a surety must be conditioned upon the debtor's nonperformance. The duty owed by the debtor will be forgiven upon payment by the surety. A duty then arises in the debtor to indemnify the surety, but not in excess of what the surety paid.

EXAMPLE | George Thompson borrowed money from the local bank in Naples, Florida, to build a condominium development. His friend David Griffen orally guaranteed payment of the debt. Thompson was starry-eyed with enthusiasm for the prospects of the condo market. The following year, prospective buyers' interest in the condo market, which had become saturated with new developments, suddenly dried up. Thompson was forced to default on the loan. Is Griffen's statement a primary or a secondary promise? This is a secondary promise because Griffen's statement was made to benefit Thompson, not himself. Is Griffen accountable for the loan? No! An oral contract to be liable for the debt of another is not enforceable; it must be in writing.

THE WRITING

To satisfy the statute of frauds, the writing must be sufficiently clear and understandable, that it is capable of being enforced on its face without an oral explanation. This is not to say that certain oral modifications or explanations are not admissible, but to evidence the existence of a contract, the writing must stand alone. The writing must include the following material terms: subject matter, time, identification of the parties, price, number (quantity), and delivery place. The UCC is much more lenient in its writing requirement for a sales contract by the use of its gap-filler provisions for time, price, and place of delivery.

The writing itself may be a formal written contract, or a note or memorandum. The writing may make reference to other writings or letters as long as there is some continuity between them. The party against whom enforcement is sought, or an agent of that party, must sign the writing. It need not, however, be written and signed at the time the parties exchange promises as long as this requirement is taken care of prior to a lawsuit by one of the parties. Until the promises are put in writing and signed, they are not legally enforceable. Some states require that a party's contract with his or her agent be in writing where the contracts the agent will be entering into are required to be in writing by the statute of frauds. A signature written in pencil, stamped, or typewritten, will usually be as valid as one written in ink. Oral contracts may be substantiated when the material terms are set forth by a writing such as a check, invoice, sales slip, or receipt.

Courts try to determine the parties' principal objective and look at everything else in light of that. Words are given their usual meaning except if they have special significance when used in a trade or business. In such cases, the special meaning will be given precedence. The court will assume that the common practices and procedures of the trade or business will be followed unless the parties specifically state otherwise. Contracts are strictly construed against the party who drafted them and in favor of the other party as long as his or her interpretation is reasonable. Written additions to standard form contracts will take precedence over the printed matter in these types of contracts.

EXAMPLE | William Packard purchases a Chrysler from Alfred DeSoto, a used car dealer. The contract is a printed form which provides Packard with one day for inspection; but at the end of the contract, there is a written clause that provides three days for inspection. Packard and DeSoto quarrel about the inspection time and about whether the term *inspection* includes a test drive. Will Packard get three days for inspection and a test drive? Packard will get the three days for inspection because a written clause takes precedence over a printed form. The term *inspection* is ambiguous. The courts will look to its usual meaning in the trade to see if it includes a test drive. If the term has no definitive meaning in the trade, the court will probably decide in favor of Packard because DeSoto, in drafting the contract, had the opportunity to resolve the matter by defining the term.

VIOLATION OF THE STATUTE OF FRAUDS

If a person is sued for breach of an oral contract which is required to be in writing, this person must raise the violation of the statute of frauds as a defense in his or her answer to the plaintiff's complaint in order to nullify the lawsuit. Contracts which fall into more than one category of the statute of frauds must satisfy each of those categories in order to be valid. Most states hold that a contract which does not satisfy the writing requirement is void, but some states declare it to be voidable. Voidable means that whoever did not sign the writing can raise the statute of frauds as a defense and can void the contract at any time before completion. If performance is completed by both parties, the statute of frauds defense is no longer available because performance by both parties evidences the existence of the contract.

In situations where enforcement will not be granted, the contract will be rescinded and the consideration given by each party must be returned. In the case where services have been rendered, the courts will require the receiving party to pay for the reasonable value of those services, to prevent the unjust enrichment of the party receiving the benefit. Some states prevent real estate brokers from recovering the reasonable value of their services under oral contracts. This protects the public from claims of dishonest brokers.

The writing requirement will be abandoned only where its enforcement would perpetrate a fraud upon an innocent party. The statute of frauds must not defeat its own purpose. These situations arise where part performance has been rendered, where restitution is not adequate, and where an unconscionable result will follow if the contract is not enforced. The part performance must establish the existence of the alleged oral contract. This means all doubt as to the contract's existence must be eliminated. The part performance rendered must be substantial, and made in reliance on an oral contract for the court to enforce it without a writing.

EXAMPLE Thomas Ford rented from Sam Buick a warehouse in Pontiac, Michigan, for three years, under an oral lease. He made a down payment and took possession. After Ford converted the warehouse into a factory for assembly of "Model T" replicas, Buick cancelled the lease, claiming it was not in writing. What result? Ford may enforce the contract. To require compliance with the statute of frauds in this situation would be to perpetrate a fraud the statute is seeking to prevent.

An agreement executed in proper form, in compliance with the statute of frauds, is one element of a valid contract. This does not mean the contract will be enforced. The party seeking to enforce the contract must prove his or her case. Evidence of a writing will be important proof, but the decision as to whether a valid contract exists and should be enforced, rests with the judge or jury based on their interpretation of the evidence.

PAROL EVIDENCE RULE

Parol evidence means oral evidence. The Parol Evidence Rule forbids the introduction of all prior oral or written agreements and simultaneous oral agreements to contradict a written contract.

When the court determines from the face of a writing that it is intended to be the final expression of the parties' agreement, then the parol evidence rule applies. The rule reflects the parties' intentions to be bound by a written contract incorporating the important terms of all prior oral or written agreements. The parties protect themselves from exposure to the uncertainties connected with oral testimony including perjury, fraud, or the death of witnesses or their loss of memory. The parol evidence rule applies to all contracts, not only those required to be in writing. But it has special significance to those contracts required to be in writing in that it insures the effectiveness of the Statute of Frauds requirement. That is why parties should make sure all important promises, terms, and conditions agreed upon orally or in writing, prior to the writing of the contract, are incorporated in the final written contract. This guarantees enforcement of those terms which otherwise might be barred by the parol evidence rule.

The main drawback of the parol evidence rule is the fact that there are many situations where the court will allow an exception to the rule. These exceptions minimize the effectiveness of the rule. Some states have even allowed parol evidence to show the parties' intentions in making the contract.

EXAMPLE Benjamin Franklin enters into a written contract on July 11 to supply Thomas Edison with keys and kites to be used in his experiments on electricity. The contract provides that 50 keys and 100 kites will be shipped to Edison's headquarters in Menlo Park for a total price of $1,000. Franklin sends 65 keys, fifteen more than were ordered, and 75 kites, twenty five less than were ordered, and bills Edison for $1,500. Franklin attempts to introduce a prior written agreement made on July 4 that states the contract was for 65 keys. At the time the July 4 writing was made, he asserts that by verbal agreement the number of kites was changed to 75. Finally, Franklin argues that when the July 11 contract was signed, he asked Edison for $1,500 upon delivery and Edison agreed. Can these statements be introduced into evidence? No! The July 4 oral and written statements are precluded by the parol evidence rule because they were made prior to the written contract. The parol evidence rule also bars the July 11 simultaneous oral statement. The July 11 contract is the final expression of the parties' agreement. These changes would only be valid if they were incorporated into the July 11 contract.

Exceptions to the Parol Evidence Rule

The courts have allowed the many exceptions to the parol evidence rule because they feel that unfair judgments will result if the rule is strictly enforced. Parol evidence will be admitted when it provides evidence of the following:

Fraud
Ancillary agreements
Failure of condition precedent
Contract ambiguities

Fraud   Parol evidence in contradiction of a written contract may be admissible where it shows evidence of fraud, duress, illegality, or mistake. The circumstances surrounding the contract and the conduct of the person making the promise are important items that the court must ascertain.

EXAMPLE Michael Amato successfully developed a printing business with the help of a loan from Richard Furst, a distributor of playbills. Amato contracts to print 500,000 copies of *Playbill* which Furst will distribute to the various Broadway theatres in return for $70,000. In a plot to take over Amato's business, Furst asks Amato, at the signing of the contract, to print 50,000 additional copies. Amato agrees. Furst later refuses to deliver the additional copies claiming there was no contract for their distribution. Knowing that Amato will not be able to pay off the loan unless those additional 50,000 playbills are distributed and paid for, Furst calls for repayment. May Amato introduce the oral statement made simultaneously to the making of the contract? Yes! The simultaneous oral statement may be introduced as evidence of the fraud Furst was attempting to perpetrate.

Ancillary agreements   Parol evidence may also be introduced to show ancillary agreements which are not contradictory to the written contract, and which are of a type not ordinarily expected to be part of the writing.

EXAMPLE | Sean O'Rourke agreed to buy 1,000 bushels of cotton from Eli Whitney. At the time of the writing, O'Rourke asked Whitney to throw in a case of gin. Eli agreed. When the cotton was delivered there was no gin. May O'Rourke introduce the oral statement into evidence regarding the gin? Yes! The oral statement may be introduced—not to contradict the writing, but to show an ancillary agreement had been made.

Failure of Condition Precedent   The failure of a condition precedent or the failure by the other party to provide consideration may be shown in court by parol evidence in an attempt to rescind a written contract. A condition precedent is a contingency which must be satisfied before the parties are bound to perform the contract.

EXAMPLE | A large engineering firm asked Albert Edwards to conduct experiments for them on his process of converting uranium into plutonium. The terms of the contract include a payment of $75,000 plus a $25,000 bonus. They told him the bonus would be given only if he proved his theory by February 2 of the following year. Later, the two parties signed a written contract which did not mention the February 2 deadline for the bonus. Due to an unexpected setback, Edwards did not prove his theory until March 29. The firm paid him $75,000 and Edwards sued for the bonus. May the engineering firm introduce the oral statement made concerning the bonus? Yes! Prior oral statements are admissible to show failure of a condition. Edwards is not entitled to the bonus.

Contract Ambiguities   Finally, parol evidence is permissible to explain ambiguities in the language of a written contract. This exception poses the strongest threat to the viability of the parol evidence rule because of the possibility of a large number of claims based on ambiguous terms. Under this exception, the UCC permits the introduction into evidence of the usual course of performance in the trade or business, as well as the meaning attributed to any ambiguous term in the particular trade or business.

EXAMPLE | Jack Pulaski is opening a new health spa in Columbia, South Carolina. He telephones Atlas Barbell Company ordering 5,000 pounds of free metal weights for the exercise and weight room. Jack then sends Atlas a letter confirming the order of 5,000 pounds of free weights by telephone. The letter omitted his oral request for metal weights. Atlas sends a return letter confirming Jack's written request. When the weights are delivered, to Jack's amazement, they are the plastic weights filled with sand. The cost for these weights is $3,200. Jack expected all-metal weights, which would have cost $2,000. Jack telephones Atlas and informs them of the mistake. Atlas replies that these weights are the latest thing and are used more widely than the metal weights. Can Jack introduce the telephone conversation into evidence? Yes! Prior oral testimony, as well as the meaning attributed to the term *free weights* in the trade, may be admitted into evidence to explain the ambiguity confronting the parties as to whether the term means metal or plastic weights.

Subsequent oral or written agreements are always admissible to prove that a material term has been changed or that the contract has been rescinded. However, if the original written contract was required to be in writing, and the change made to that contract also falls within one of the statute of frauds categories, then that change must be in writing. This does not apply to modifications which remove the original contract from the purview of the statute of frauds.

EXAMPLE | Kodak hires George Roblard to develop its camera business east of the Mississippi. The employment contract is made in writing for a term of three years. Subsequently, a written modification is made that puts Roblard in charge of all operations west of the Missisippi, as well. The duration of the contract is orally modified to a period of ten months because of Roblard's ill health. Are these modifications admissible? Yes! A written modification is always admissible. The oral modification is admissible under the parol evidence rule because it takes a three-year contract out of the grips of the statute of frauds by making it into a contract for less than one year, which does not have to be in writing. On the other hand, if a contract for ten months is modified to a period of three years, the modification must be in writing to satisfy the statute of frauds.

REVIEW QUESTIONS

1. Define formation of a contract, statute of frauds, and parol evidence rule.
2. List the contracts that must be in writing and explain them.
3. Presti alleges that he made an oral contract with Wilson to buy a thoroughbred horse called "Goal Line Stand" for $60,000. Wilson denies that he agreed to sell the horse or that he received the check. Presti supports his claim by producing the check stub. His secretary asserts that the check was prepared and mailed. Is there a valid contract for the sale of goods? Does this agreement fall under any of the UCC exceptions for contracts required to be in writing? Presti v. Wilson, 348 F. Supp. 543 (N.D. N.Y. 1972).
4. Hanan entered into an oral contract with Corning Glass in February to serve as a management consultant for one year commencing May 1. Corning Glass later refused to honor the contract, setting up the statute of frauds as a defense. What result? Hanan v. Corning Glass Works, 63 Misc. 2d 863, 314 N.Y.S. 2d 804 (1970).
5. Merrill Lynch alleges that it entered into a contract with Shpilberg to sell him $1,000,000 worth of TVA bonds. Shpilberg asserts that the parties were in the process of negotiating, but there was no contract. The only evidence offered by Merrill Lynch to prove the existence of the contract is the confirmation slip mailed to Shpilberg. It stated all the salient terms and Shpilberg did not promptly object to it. Is there a valid contract? Shpilberg v. Merrill Lynch, Pierce, Fenner & Smith, Inc., 535 S.W. 2d 227 (Ky.) 1976.
6. Pittsburgh-Des Moines Steel Company, a general contractor, was to construct a wind tunnel for Boeing. Pittsburgh subcontracted part of the work to York.

York contracted with Freitag, a supplier, to purchase materials for the job on credit. Boeing and Pittsburgh orally agreed to be responsible for York's debts to insure that York received the materials needed for continued performance. Subsequently, Freitag was not paid by York, so Freitag sued Boeing and Pittsburgh. What result? R.H. Freitag Mfg. Co. v. Boeing Airplane Co., 55 Wash.2d 334, 347 P.2d 1074.(1959).

7. The Blanchards were friends of Calderwood. They attended to his needs for over seven years. In return for their services, he promised to leave them the real estate he owned. Calderwood died without a will. The Blanchards are seeking to enforce his oral promise to transfer the real estate to them. What result? Blanchard v. Calderwood 110 N.H. 29, 260 A.2d 118 (1969).

8. Darling-Crose Machine Company employed Estrada as a sales engineer pursuant to a written contract. The contract provided that Estrada would get a 35 percent commission on all sales made. Subsequently, Estrada quit. Darling-Crose payed only half of what Estrada was entitled to under the contract for orders solicited before delivery was made. They said this was the custom of the trade because important functions were to be performed after the orders were solicited. Is Darling-Crose allowed to introduce into evidence this custom of the machine tool trade? Estrada v. Darling-Crose Machine Company, Inc., 80 Cal. Rptr. 266, (Cal.Ct.App. 1966).

9. Abercrombie maintained an account with a brokerage firm. The firm charged Abercrombie's account for a debt incurred by Waters. On occasions in the past, Abercrombie had orally agreed to be charged for Waters's debts. This time Abercrombie refused to accept responsibility. What result? Howard, Weil, Labonisse, et al v. Abercrombie, 140 Ga. 436, 231 S.E.2d. 451 (1976).

10. Butler Brothers subcontracted certain highway construction work to the Ganley Brothers. The Ganleys were fraudulently induced into signing a contract drafted by the Butlers. A clause in the contract stated that the Ganleys entered into the contract based upon their examination of the construction plan, without reliance upon any representations made by the Butlers. The Ganleys brought an action for damages based on fraud. May the Ganleys introduce oral testimony to prove fraudulent inducement or does the clause in the contract prevent such oral testimony? Ganley Bros., Inc. v. Butler Bros. Building Co., 170 Minn. 373, 212 N.W. 602 (1927).

12

RIGHTS OF THIRD PARTIES

INTRODUCTION

Third-party contracts are entered into with the intention of benefiting a third party, or of assigning rights and duties to a third party. The former is called a third-party beneficiary contract and the latter is known as an assignment. In a third-party beneficiary contact, rights of the third party are created by the original contract. In an assignment, third-party rights are created after the contract is made through a transfer of rights to a third party.

THIRD-PARTY BENEFICIARIES

Third-party beneficiary contracts are contracts entered into by two parties for the purposes of benefiting a third person. The purpose or intention to benefit a third party can be established through oral testimony in accordance with the parol evidence rule. The third person possesses a legal right to enforce the contract once he or she is notified of the benefit and either accepts or relies upon it. Cancellation of the contract or subsequent alterations cannot be made without the third-party beneficiary's consent, unless the right to cancel or alter has been reserved through a stipulation in the contract.

There are three types of third-party beneficiaries, here referred to as:

Creditor beneficiary
Incidental beneficiary
Donee beneficiary

Creditor Beneficiary

Where consideration has been furnished to one of the two contracting parties by a third person, that third person is known as a creditor beneficiary. Third-party beneficiary contracts occur where a debtor furnishes another person with consideration in return for that party's promise to repay a debt owed to a creditor. The creditor beneficiary may recover the debt from either party upon nonperformance.

EXAMPLE | Jim Rose agrees to sell his seafood restaurant, The Crab House, to Joe Page. The contract provides that Page will assume the mortgage on The Crab House, which is held by Scorpion Enterprises. After taking possession, Page fails to make the monthly mortgage payments. Can Scorpion sue Rose for nonpayment? Yes! Scorpian is a creditor beneficiary to the contract between Rose and Page.

Incidental Beneficiary

A third person who will receive an incidental benefit arising from a contract that was made without that purpose in mind, is an incidental beneficiary. If the benefit is not realized, the incidental beneficiary cannot enforce the contract because he or she is not legally entitled to it. People who are not parties to a contract and who are not intended beneficiaries of the contract have no right to enforce the contract. Enforcement is predicated upon being able to show an interest in the benefit that is sufficiently substantial as to qualify the third person as a donee beneficiary.

The difference between an incidental beneficiary and an intended beneficiary can be made by determining whether performance of the benefit is made directly to the third person; whether the third person has any right to oversee the performance; or whether the third person's right to the benefit is set forth in the contract.

EXAMPLE | The City of San Francisco employs the Philips Construction Company to reconstruct part of the roadway on the Golden Gate Bridge by November 9. The work is not completed until January 8. Sy Gold, a justice on the California Supreme Court, must drive fifty extra miles because of the bridge construction. Can he sue Philips Construction for lost time and expenses? No! The contract was not made directly for Gold's benefit. He is an incidental beneficiary to the contract between San Francisco and the Philips Construction Company.

Donee Beneficiary

A donee beneficiary is a third person who has not given any consideration in return for a benefit. The party designating the third person donee beneficiary has supplied the necessary consideration to the other contracting party. That other contracting party, in turn, must promise to confer a benefit upon the third person. Either the donee beneficiary or the party making that designation has the right to sue the other party for breach of contract if the benefit is not performed.

If the party making the contract for the benefit of the third party does not perform his or her obligation, the third-party beneficiary, whether creditor or donee, will not be able to enforce the contract.

Virginia's Uncle Pat names her as beneficiary to his life insurance policy. After a falling-out, Uncle Pat wants to know if he can change the beneficiary without her consent. The policy does not speak to this issue. Since Uncle Pat did not reserve the right to change beneficiaries, Virginia's consent is required. The right to change beneficiaries is a standard part of most insurance policies. However, when that right is not stated, as occurred in this example, the right to change beneficiaries must be specifically written into the policy when it is drafted. Without it, the beneficiary's consent is required. If the insurance company refuses to pay Virginia after Pat dies, on the basis that she has given no consideration, what will her argument be? Virginia will assert that the consideration paid by Uncle Pat in the form of premiums supports the promise by the insurance company to pay her as beneficiary. However, if Uncle Pat allowed the policy to lapse by failing to make timely premium payments, Virginia would have no recourse.

Saylor v. Saylor
389 S.W.2d 904 (Ky.) 1965

This suit involves a contest between the estate of Adrian Saylor and his widow as to the ownership of a joint bank account. The widow claims that she is the donee beneficiary of a joint account Mr. Saylor maintained with the bank.

The bank issued a passbook to Mr. Saylor in the names of "Mr. or Mrs. Adrian M. Saylor" when he made a $6,500 deposit of his own money. Subsequently, he deposited over $2,100 of his own money into the account. A year later he died. The estate contends that the money should go into the estate because Mrs. Saylor never signed the signature cards nor even knew the account had been opened.

The issues are (1) whether Mrs. Saylor is a donee beneficiary, and (2) whether she, as a donee beneficiary, can enforce a contract made for her benefit.

The court recognized the view that a person may create a joint tenancy by depositing his or her own money into an account bearing his or her name and another's. It is not necessary that the other party furnish consideration or be aware that he or she is a beneficiary. The fact that Mrs. Saylor did not sign a signature card is of no consequence because perhaps Mr. Saylor did not want her to withdraw funds while he was alive. However, he intended to make her a beneficiary entitled to whatever funds remained in the account upon his death; otherwise there would have been no reason to open a joint account. Mrs. Saylor, as a donee beneficiary, has the right to enforce the contract made for her benefit. Judgment for Mrs. Saylor.

ASSIGNMENT

An assignment is the transfer of a party's rights in a contract to a third person. Parties transfer their contractual rights to a third person: (1) as payment of a debt; (2) in exchange for payment or performance; or (3) as a gift. The party making the assignment is known as an assignor. An assignor is one of the original contracting parties, who is seeking to transfer his or her contractual rights, and possibly his or her contractual duties, to a third person. The third person, to whom the assignment is made, is called an assignee. The other original contracting party is referred to as an obligor. An obligor is one who owes a duty to perform for an assignee because of an assignment. It is also possible that an assignor or an assignee owes a duty to perform for the obligor.

An assignment must be differentiated from a novation. A novation is an agreement made by three persons wherein one of the two original contracting parties is released from all contractual liability through the substitution of a third person. A novation is actually a new contract with the third person assuming all the rights and duties of the party who has been relieved. In an assignment, an assignor is still accountable under the contract even though the assignor's rights and duties have been transferred to a third person. An assignment is not a new contract because there is no agreement to release the assignor from liability.

EXAMPLE Bob Hill owns a cattle ranch in Texas. An irrigation system is needed to maintain fertile grazing areas. Claude Eastman is hired to construct an irrigation system. A short time later, Bob Hill sells the ranch to John Long, a retired justice, who wants to raise cattle for investment purposes. Eastman agrees to release Hill and render performance for John Long, who has assumed the duty to pay. Subsequently, Eastman is offered a much larger irrigation project in the prairie lands. He assigns his rights and duties under the contract to Timothy Scott, who is equally competent. What is the relationship of the parties in the two situations? The first is a novation. Bob Hill, an original contracting party, is released from all responsibility, while John Long steps into his shoes. The second is an assignment. Eastman, the assignor, assigns his rights and duties under the contract to Tim Scott, the assignee. Scott thereby becomes primarily liable for performance; however, Eastman can also be held accountable, if Scott does not perform.

Consideration is not a prerequisite to the making of an assignment; therefore, gifts created through assignments are permissible. However, these gratuitous assignments may be revoked by an assignor by death, by bankruptcy, by a subsequent assignment of the same rights in return for consideration, or through notice, unless the assignment has become irrevocable. In many states, assignments become irrevocable: (1) if they are made in writing and signed by the assignor; (2) if the assignee has received payment or performance from the obligor; or (3) if the assignor has delivered to the assignee a document, which is necessary to evidence the existence of a contract, such as a deed, mortgage, stock certificate, or bankbook.

EXAMPLE Alan Jacobs assigns his interest in the Los Angeles Rams to his nephew Clarence by transferring all the stock certificates he owns. After a falling out, Alan revokes his gift, but Clarence refuses to return the stock. Is this assignment revocable. No! The stock certificates have been transferred to Clarence, making the assignment complete. Ownership of the stock now resides with Clarence.

The UCC under Article 9, Secured Transactions, requires that all assignments of contract rights be made in writing. For this discussion, contract rights include the assignor's right to payment or to return performance by the obligor either before or after performance. (The UCC defines these rights as "accounts.") The right to sue for damages based on a cause of action for breach of contract may also be assigned from a party to a third person. Under a general provision of Article 1, the UCC requires assignments of causes of action to be in writing where the assigned right is over $5,000.

The writing requirement under Article 9 does not apply to a gratuitous assignment or an assignment of contractual rights where the assignee agrees to be responsible for the duties under the contract. A writing is required for these assignments only when they fall within one of the statute of frauds provisions.

EXAMPLE The Lobster Trap agreed to buy 100 pounds of crabmeat from The Crab House for $200. The Crab House delivered the crabmeat, but then assigned its right to payment to Pisces Emporium. Must the assignment be in writing? Yes! The UCC requires all assignments of contract rights to be in writing. If the Crab House had assigned its duty to deliver the crabmeat as well, then no writing would be required unless the value of the contract exceeded $500.

CONTRACT RIGHTS NOT ASSIGNABLE

Assignments of contract rights may be made with the following exceptions:

Clause in contract forbids assignments
Alteration of obligor's duties
Risk increased to obligor
Statutes which prohibit assignments

Clause in Contract Forbids Assignments

A contract containing a clause stating that assignments cannot be made without the consent of the obligor is generally not favored. However, a person may be restricted from assigning a contract where his or her duties involve special skill, knowledge, expertise, judgment, character, trust, or confidence. In these instances, clauses prohibiting assignments will be enforced as long as consent is not unreasonably withheld. Assignments of certain rights may not be curtailed. These include ownership rights in real estate, commercial paper, checks, and securities—except for closely held corporations. This also includes accounts receivable which arise through the completion of performance by one party, and contract rights which require no return performance by the assignee.

EXAMPLE The circus has come to town! The world-renowned trapeze artists, the Gemini Twins, are the main attraction. There is a covenant in the contract restricting the Gemini Twins from assigning their rights and duties under the contract. Is this covenant enforceable? Partially! The Gemini Twins' duty to perform is properly restricted because it involves special skills and experience. Their right to payment may not be limited. Would the restrictive clause be valid if it applied to the sellers of popcorn and peanuts? No! Their task is routine and can be performed by almost anyone.

Alteration of Obligor's Duties

An assignment may not be made which will materially alter the obligor's duties either by placing a greater burden on the obligor to perform, or by changing the performance altogether.

Beefcake Bob makes weekly deliveries of beef to Bill Taurus, who operates a Steak and Bake Restaurant in Tulsa. This week Taurus is full of bull, so he assigns his contract with Beefcake Bob to a Steak and Bake Restaurant in Oklahoma City. Must Beefcake Bob perform according to the assignment? No! The assignment has substantially altered his duties under the contract by requesting him to perform in another city, a great distance away.

Risk Increased to Obligor

Assignments which increase the risk an obligor must endure under a contract, will not be allowed.

EXAMPLE Bongo was a clown in the Sells Floto Circus. Subsequently the circus was sold and the performer's contracts were assigned to the new owner, who requested Bongo to perform in the Lion's den. Must Bongo accede? No! Bongo's contract may not be assigned in this case because it increases the risk of physical harm.

Statutes which Prohibit Assignments

Statutes may expressly forbid assignments involving benefits derived from alimony and workman's compensation; causes of action for personal injury; and right to wages. Wage assignments are generally not prohibited, but some states restrict them to a limited amount.

EXAMPLE Lucy Osborn, who works in the Fulton Fish Market, was injured after slipping on a mackerel. Lucy received workman's compensation, but attempted to assign the entire award to a gentlemen who made her an offer she could not refuse. The gentleman told Lucy she would be sleeping with the fish unless the assignment was made. Can a workman's compensation award be assigned? No! It is a personal right that can only be received by the injured party.

DELEGATION OF DUTIES

Delegation of duties occurs when the assignor transfers his or her obligations under a contract to a third person (assignee). A contractual obligation cannot be excused by delegating one's duties to a third party unless a novation is made. An assignor remains liable to an obligor for completion of the performance agreed upon, although the actual performance may be rendered by an assignee. This is because the obligor contracted with the assignor, not the assignee. The contract between the parties is still binding on both of them even though the assignee may perform the assignor's duties. If the assignee fails to perform the delegated duties in accordance with the contract, the assignor must perform them or be liable for breach of contract.

There is a difference between an obligor's performing for a third person instead of an assignor, and having a third person perform for an obligor instead of the party with whom the obligor contracted. In the first instance, the assignee is aware of the performance that will be rendered by the obligor before accepting the assignment. If the assignee is not satisfied with the terms of the assignment, he or she may reject them. Also, an obligor should not care whether performance is to be made to the original contracting party or a third person, as long as performance and the risks attached are substantially the same. However, in receiving performance an obligor exercises his or her freedom in choosing to contract with the assignor. If substitutions can be made at the assignor's whim which would relieve the assignor of liability, the obligor would lose the freedom to contract with whom he or she chooses. This is why an assignor's delegation of duties under a personal service contract may be restricted through incorporating a clause in the contract which prohibits any duties from being delegated without the consent of the obligor.

Contracts that require a unique performance that can only be rendered by the assignor cannot be assigned to third parties. This means that the assignor, as an original contracting party, cannot delegate his or her unique performance, regardless of whether a restrictive clause exists. However, contracts which are routine and impersonal may be freely delegated and the obligor may not unreasonably withhold consent. In situations where a delegation of duties has been made, the original contracting party who delegates the performance of his or her duties is responsible until performance has been completed.

An assignment of rights to an assignee may be made either alone or in conjunction with a delegation of duties. There is a trend to interpret the assignment of a contract as impliedly including a delegation of duties unless it is stipulated that only contractual rights are being transferred. That is why the designations of "assignor" and "assignee" are still used to describe the parties. This implication is best illustrated in construction contracts where it is customary for general contractors to delegate their duties to subcontractors while remaining liable for the completion of the contract.

EXAMPLE Lefty O'Toole was a famous baseball pitcher until he lost three games in the World Series and was nicknamed "The Goat." He retired from baseball and became involved in sports field maintenance. The volume of business was so great that he ended up with two contracts for April 10. Lefty assigned the contract with the Minnesota Twins to Frank Helms. He handled the Masters Golf Tournament at Augusta himself. There was a rainstorm before the Twins' home opener and Helms did a poor job of maintaining the field. As a result, the Twins were forced to cancel their home opener. Who is liable for the damages? Richard Brand, owner of the Twins, may sue both Lefty and Helms. If Lefty is required to pay damages to the Twins, he can sue Helms for indemnification because Helms breached the duties delegated to him under the assigned contract.

RIGHTS AND DUTIES OF AN ASSIGNEE

An assignee's rights are no greater than the rights of the assignor. If the obligor has any real or personal defenses against the assignor, these defenses will be effective against the assignee. This is true even when an assignee gives valuable consideration to the assignor. If a real or personal defense is raised by the obligor, the assignee has a cause of action against the assignor for breach of contract, but not against the obligor. Personal defenses may be waived by an obligor, but not real defenses. The specific real and personal defenses will be discussed in Chapter 14, Contractual Defenses.

Joseph Feller, a representative of Scorpion Enterprises, sells Janet Perez a twelve-volume set of astrology encyclopedias for $120. Feller fraudulently represented that the set of encyclopedias contained a daily listing of horoscopes for the next five years. Scorpio Enterprises assigns its right to payment to the Universal Collection Agency. Janet discovers the false representation and refuses to pay, setting up fraud as a defense. Can Universal recover the $120? No! The personal defense of fraudulent inducement is effective against the collection agency, because the defense would be good against Feller and Scorpion Enterprises. Universal's only recourse is to sue Scorpion Enterprises for breach of its assignment contract. Then Scorpion can dismiss Feller for his fraudulent actions.

An assignment is effective immediately, without notice to the obligor, unless the contract provides that notice must be given. However, an assignee should notify the obligor of the assignment in an expeditious manner once the assignment is made. This is for the assignee's protection, as well as for the obligor's information. If the obligor does not receive notice of the assignment before he or she renders performance for the assignor, the obligor will not be liable to the assignee. This is based on the reasoning that as between two innocent parties, the party with the opportunity to prevent the mistake of injustice (assignee) is the one who must bear the loss.

The assignee has the power to prevent the problem through prompt notification; otherwise, the assignee will be relegated to recovering the loss from the assignor. If the obligor has notice of the assignment, but performs for the assignor anyway, the obligor will be liable to the assignee for not fulfilling his or her duty under the assigned contract. If the assignor does not turn over the consideration received from the obligor, the assignee has a cause of action against the assignor as well as the obligor.

EXAMPLE Ted McAllister, a hunter, captures an African lion and agrees to sell it to the Bronx Zoo. The Bronx Zoo assigns their right to possession of the lion to the San Diego Zoo on July 4. On July 11, the lion is delivered to the Bronx Zoo. On July 17, Ted receives notice of the assignment. Has the San Diego Zoo, as the assignee, any rights against Ted? No! Prompt notice of the assignment was not given. The San Diego Zoo must look to the Bronx Zoo to claim the lion.

Nolan v. Williamson Music, Inc.
300 F. Supp. 1311 (S.D. N.Y. 1969)

Nolan brought an action to prevent Sam Fox Publishing Company from assigning the rights to "Tumbling Tumbleweeds," a song that Nolan composed. Nolan alleges that Sam Fox breached the contract by making an assignment to the Williamson Music Company without his consent.

The contract between Nolan and Fox was signed on July 11, 1934. It provided that the composers, Nolan, Walker, and Hall, grant to the "Publisher (defined as Sam Fox Publishing Company), its successors and assigns forever, all the right, title and interest of every kind, nature and description including the copyright therein, throughout the world, of the Composers in 'Tumbling Tumbleweeds'." The contract also stated that it was the intention of the parties that no rights of any kind would be reserved by the Composers. In consideration of the transfer, the Publisher agreed to pay royalties to the Composers.

In 1946, Sam Fox assigned the contract to the defendant, Williamson Music Company, without giving notice to Nolan. Nolan argued that Fox's concealment of the assignment was fraudulent.

The issues presented are (1) whether the assignment is effective without consent, and (2) whether lack of notice constitutes fraud.

The court stated the assignment is effective without requiring notice to Nolan, or his consent. This is clear from the words of the contract, which granted all rights in the song to the "Publishers, its successors and assigns forever." Judgment for Williamson.

A more serious difficulty arises when the assignor assigns the same contract rights to two or more assignees. The obligor will only be liable for payment or performance once. This is why immediate notice should be given to the obligor. Most states require performance to be rendered to the first assignee to whom the assignor assigns the contract rights, even though this assignee may not have been the first to give notice to the obligor. This is based on the theory that once the assignment is made to the first assignee, the assignor has no more "rights" to assign, thereby causing the subsequent assignments to be void. However, there are exceptions to this theory if a subsequent assignee gives valuable consideration and acts without notice of the first assignment.

A subsequent assignee who receives from the obligor either payment or a document essential to the enforcement of the contract, such as a deed, mortgage, or bankbook, will prevail. This is similarly true of one who enters into a novation with the obligor and assignor, or who obtains a judgment against an obligor. Some states allow a subsequent assignee to recover if he or she is the first to notify the obligor and has given valuable consideration while acting without notice of the first assignment. The burden of proving this will be on that assignee. To avoid this predicament, a prudent assignee will inform the obligor of the prospective assignment and inquire if any previous assignments have been made by the assignor.

EXAMPLE | Jacob Cod arrives back in a New England port with 1,000 pounds of shad roe caviar. He agrees to sell the entire catch to a new restaurant called the Scorpion's Delight. The Scorpion's Delight assigns the same contract to both the Crab Palace and Pisces Emporium. The Crab Palace is the first to receive the assignment, but the Emporium is the first to give notice to Cod. Who gets the caviar? Most states would give it to the Crab Palace, even though they were not the first to give notice, because they were the first to receive the assignment.

The assignee also has a duty to perform any delegation of duties he or she has agreed to assume. If the assignee fails to perform the obligation, the obligor has a cause of action for breach of contract against both the assignor and the assignee for failure to perform in cases where consideration is given.

EXAMPLE | Universal Pictures wants to make a space movie about James Bond. Starlite agrees to deliver certain space props, but thereafter assigns the contract to Tops in Props, who is three days late in delivery. Who is accountable for the damages caused by the delay? Both Starlite and Tops in Props, although Tops in Props is primarily liable. If Starlite pays the damages, Tops in Props must indemnify them because Tops in Props has breached its delegated duty to deliver the props under the assigned contract.

DUTIES OF AN ASSIGNOR

An assignor has a duty to the obligor to guarantee that performance is completed by the assignee. This is why the assignor remains liable on the contract after the assignment has been made. In making an assignment, an assignor impliedly warrants to an assignee: that the assigned claim is valid; that any signed writing evidencing the assignment is authentic; and that no interference will be made to impair the value of the assignment. However, no warranty is made guaranteeing the obligor's solvency and performance. The assignee has a cause of action against the assignor if any of warranties made by the assignor are breached. An assignor who receives payment or performance from the obligor is accountable to the assignee and must hold it in trust. An assignor who assigns his or her rights under a contract to more than one assignee will be liable to those assignees who do not receive performance from the obligor.

REVIEW QUESTIONS

1. Define third-party beneficiary contracts, creditor, incidental and donee beneficiaries, assignment, assignor, assignee, obligor, and novation.

2. Which contract rights are not assignable?

3. Cunningham entered into a contract to play basketball for the Carolina Cougars for three years. The contract contained a provision that it could not be assigned without Cunningham's consent. Southern Sports Corporation, owner of the Cougars, sold the team to Munchak Corporation. Cunningham's contract was assigned to Munchak. Subsequently, Cunningham refused to play for the new owner. He claimed the assignment was a breach of contract because it was made without his consent. What result? Munchak v. Cunningham, 457 F.2d 721 (4th Cir. 1972).

4. Rose owned a cement business and a stone quarry with a rock-crushing business. He agreed to sell his rock-crushing business and lease the quarry for ten years to Dooley, if Dooley would supply him with a sufficient amount of stone to satisfy the needs of his cement business for the next ten years, at a set price. Subsequently, Dooley sold the business to Vulcan Company and assigned the rights under the quarry lease as well. Vulcan raised the price on the stone delivered to Rose. Rose asserts that Vulcan is bound by the original agreement made between Rose and Dooley. What result? Rose v. Vulcan Materials Co., 282 N.C. 643, 194 S.E.2d 521 (1973).

5. In 1930, the Wetherall Brothers Company had the exclusive right to sell steel in New England for United States Steel. This contract was indefinite, subject only to termination by either party on two years' notice. In 1950, Wetherall Brothers liquidated their corporation and assigned the exclusive right to represent United States Steel to a Pennsylvania corporation who assumed the name Wetherall Brothers. United States Steel was not given notice of the assignment, but subsequently learned of it and terminated the contract. The new Wetherall Brothers brought an action for breach of contract. Was the assignment effective? Wetherall Brothers Co. v. United States Steel Corp., 105 F. Supp. 81 (1952).

6. American Fire agreed to guarantee Air Metals's performance as subcontractors on a construction project. Air Metals assigned their right to payment as collateral for the guarantee. Almost a year later, Air Metals received a loan from Boulevard Bank. Air Metals assigned the same right to payment for their work on the project to the bank as collateral for the loan. In June of that year, Air Metals defaulted on the construction contract. Notification was given to the general contractor by American Fire in July and by Boulevard Bank in August. In October, the general contractor paid American Fire the reasonable value of the services rendered by Air Metals. As a result, Boulevard Bank brought suit against the general contractor. What result? Boulevard National Bank of Miami v. Air Metals Industries, 176 So. 2d 94 (1965).

7. Powder Power Tool Corporation promised to raise the wages of its employees as a result of an agreement with the labor union. Certain employees did not receive the agreed-upon raise. One of them, named Springer, brought an action to get the appropriate wage increment. Powder Tool claimed that Springer could not bring an action because he was not a party to the wage agreement. What result? Springer v. Powder Power Tool Corp., 220 Ore. 102, 348 P.2d 1112 (1960).

8. Murray entered into a contract with McDonald Construction Company for the purpose of building an addition to the building he owned. The contract provided that construction was to be completed in forty-five days. Murray leased the premises to a newspaper company, but the addition was not finished until six months later. Murray and the newspaper company sued the construction company. What result? McDonald Construction Co. v. Murray, 5 Wash. App. 68 485 P.2d 626 (1971).

9. Holly owed Fox $300. Lawrence asked Holly if he could borrow $300. Holly loaned Lawrence the money and told him to repay the money to Fox. Lawrence never paid Fox. Fox sued Lawrence for nonpayment. What result? Lawrence v. Fox, 20 N.Y. 268 (1859).

10. Landes bought goods on credit from a department store, which subsequently assigned the right to payment to Peoples Finance Company. Before receiving notice of the assignment, Landes returned the goods to the department store which accepted the goods and cancelled the debt owed. The Finance Company sued Landes to recover the purchase price of the goods. What result? Peoples Finance & Thrift Co. v. Landes, 28 Utah 2d 392, 503 P.2d 444. (1972).

13

REMEDIES FOR BREACH OF CONTRACT

INTRODUCTION

BREACH OF CONTRACT

Most contracts are completed without significant problems. Parties generally fulfill their promises under the contract. Breach of contract occurs when a party does not fulfill his or her promise to perform. The breach is a failure to perform a material contractual obligation. It may take the form of renunciation of the contract, restraining the other party's performance, as well as failure to perform. A breach may be either partial or total. It may be material, incidental, or anticipatory.

A material breach is substantial and goes to the heart of the contract. The other party may treat the contract as cancelled and terminate performance.

EXAMPLE | Eleanor Hanley is eighty-five years old and lives alone. On a Monday afternoon, while she is watching "General Hospital," the picture suddenly disappears. Eleanor quickly telephones Artie's Television Repair Shop. He comes down and after inspecting the set tells her he can make it work perfectly for $75. He makes the adjustment. She pays him. Fifteen minutes later, the picture abruptly disappears again. In a state of agitation, she telephones Artie and he returns to her apartment. This time he tells her he must take the set back to his shop. An hour later, he calls to say he has encountered major complications with her set and the cost to repair it will be $150. Eleanor tells him she does not want to spend that much money on it and will he please return the set and refund her $75. He returns the set, but refuses to refund the $75. Has Eleanor Hanley any recourse? Yes! He promised to repair the set for $75 and failed to make good on it. Because he has materially breached the contract, she is entitled to a return of her $75.

Incidental breaches involving minor defects occur where substantial performance has been rendered. The party for whom performance was rendered still has a duty to perform. However, he or she has a cause of action for damages to remedy the incidental defects.

Donna Eastwood brings her 1966 Plymouth Fury to Max's Service Station. The car has 108,000 miles on it. Donna asks Max to inspect the car and inform her of the necessary repairs. Max tells her the car needs a rebuilt transmission, shock absorbers, new windshield wipers, and replacement of radiator hoses. Donna authorizes the repairs, which total $875. When she drives the car home, it begins to rain and she notices the windshield wipers have not been replaced. She decides to stop payment on the check. Would she be well advised to do so? No! All the major repairs have been made. This is an incidental breach. Donna should either return to the service station and demand they replace the windshield wipers; or issue a new check for the cost of all repairs made except the wipers, and request the return of her original check.

An anticipatory breach occurs prior to the time when the contract is to commence. It is typified by a clear inability or unwillingness to perform. However, a request to renegotiate is not a manifestation of unwillingness. Aggrieved parties may treat the anticipatory breach as a full breach by establishing that they themselves were ready, willing, and able to perform.

Regina Talbot and Margaret O'Hara were playing pinochle at the Senior Citizen's Center on a Friday afternoon. Regina was informing Margaret of her gallbladder operation, which was scheduled for the following Thursday. She said Dr. Cotton was her physician and how fortunate she was to have him performing the operation. Margaret's eyes lit up. She replied that Mary Porter was also having her gallbladder removed by Dr. Cotton next Thursday, but she was not sure of the time. They signaled to Mary Porter, who came over after finishing her shuffleboard game. Mary confirmed what Margaret had said and the two patients were amazed to discover that Dr. Cotton had scheduled both operations at the same time, but at different hospitals. What can Regina and Mary do? They should notify the administrators of both hospitals that Dr. Cotton be sanctioned for his conduct, and they may treat the contract as breached before the operations take place.

A retraction may be made by the breaching party only if: 1) notification is received by the innocent party prior to the innocent party's commencement of a lawsuit; 2) there has been no change in the innocent party's position, such as entering a new contract; and 3) no communication has been sent to the breaching party that the breach is looked upon as final. A cause of action is a right to sue in court for a remedy. Breach of contract gives rise to a cause of action.

Remedies

Contractual remedies are the means by which a legal right is enforced where there has been a breach of contract. The purpose of a remedy is to restore the party harmed by the breach to as favorable a position as would have been the case had the contract been carried out as promised, or to the same position he or she had been in before the contract came about. This may be accomplished either through compensation or through prevention of the breach. There are two categories of remedies: legal and equitable.

Legal remedies are enacted by the federal and state legislatures and are found in statutes. Equitable remedies can also be granted by the courts for reasons of fairness and justice.

Equitable remedies are granted when the legal remedy that is usually provided would result harshly upon the innocent party. In requesting an equitable remedy, the party must have acted in good faith and commenced the lawsuit without unnecessary delay. Equitable remedies are preferable especially where the breaching party has little or no money to pay for the loss. These remedies also prevent a party who is breaching the contract from becoming unjustly enriched at the expense of the party who is suffering the loss. In many cases, parties may elect the remedies which they prefer. However, where remedies are conflicting, parties are limited to choosing only one. For example, in a breach of contract involving refusal to sell a house, the aggrieved party is not entitled to specific performance as well as money damages.

The equitable and legal remedies are:

Injunction

Quasi contract

Specific performance

Rescission

Restitution

Reformation

UCC remedies

Money damages

INJUNCTION

An injunction is an equitable remedy which prevents a party breaching a contract from rendering the same performance elsewhere. An injunction is personal in nature and negative in effect in that it precludes a person from performing certain acts. In cases involving personal service contracts, this remedy is used instead of the remedy of specific performance, because specific performance cannot be granted to compel parties to perform services against their will. However, since the breaching party cannot be *compelled* to perform a certain act, an injunction can prohibit them from performing the same act elsewhere. An injunction acts as a restraint against a party breaching a personal service contract.

EXAMPLE Wild Bill Cary is under a five-year contract with the Green Bay Packers to play quarterback for them for $100,000 per year. After leading his team to successive central division titles, he is offered a four-year contract from the Atlanta Falcons for $500,000 per year. There are still three years remaining on Wild Bill's contract with Green Bay, but he decides to accept Atlanta's offer. Can Green Bay prevent Wild Bill from quarterbacking for Atlanta? Yes! An injunction can be granted, but Green Bay can not legally force Wild Bill to quarterback for them through specific performance. Wild Bill is bound to Green Bay for the three years remaining on his contract unless they renegotiate his contract or trade him. The terms of Wild Bill's original contract were designed to protect him from being cut from the team while insuring him a substantial yearly salary. After the contract expires, Wild Bill will have free agent status.

Madison Square Garden Corporation
v. Carnera
52 F.2d 47 (2d Cir. 1931)

Madison Square Garden asked for an injunction to restrain Carnera from engaging in a boxing match with Sharkey. The Garden alleged that to permit such a match would be a breach of the restrictive covenant, which would cause them irreparable harm.

Primo Carnera was a professional heavyweight boxer. He entered into an exclusive contract with the Garden to fight the winner of the Schmeling-Stribling contest for the heavyweight title of the world. The contract provided that if the fight with either Schmeling or Stribling did not occur within nine months, Carnera would no longer be bound by the contract's terms. The restrictive covenant provides:

> 1. Carnera agrees that he will render services as a boxer in his next contest, which contest shall be with the winner of the proposed Schmeling-Stribling contest . . . at such time, not, however, later than midnight of September 30, 1931, as the Garden may direct . . .
>
> 9. Carnera shall not, pending the holding of the First Contest, render services as a boxer in any major boxing contest, without the written permission of the Garden in each case had and obtained. A major contest is understood to be one with Sharkey, Baer, Campole, Godfrey, or like grade heavyweights . . .

Subsequently Carnera entered into a contract to box Sharkey before the match with either Schmeling or Stribling. Carnera contends that nowhere in the contract is a match with Schmeling or Stribling agreed upon. Carnera is pledging his services to the Garden for nine months with the hope that such a match can be arranged. If the match does not materialize, Carnera receives no compensation.

The issue is whether Carnera is bound by the restrictive covenant and whether an injunction is the appropriate remedy to enforce it.

The court held that the restrictive covenant is enforceable because its terms were reasonable and voluntarily agreed upon by the parties. An injunction is the appropriate remedy because Carnera's services are unique, and because money damages cannot be easily measured. The court also required the Garden to give Carnera a bond for $35,000. This amount is to compensate Carnera for the loss he would sustain because of the injunction, if the heavyweight title contest never materialized.

QUASI CONTRACT

The word *quasi* means seemingly. A quasi contract seems to be a contract. Quasi contracts are not actually contracts, but rather obligations implied in law for reasons of fairness and justice, and to prevent unjust enrichment at the expense of another.

Although quasi contracts lack the elements of a contract, they have the binding effect of a contract. In a quasi contract, an obligation arises in the party receiving performance to pay for the reasonable value of the services rendered or the goods delivered. It would be unjust to deny compensation to a person who performs a benefit for another, in good faith, because there is no formal contract.

EXAMPLE On a Friday afternoon during rush hour, the New Springville Hospital Ambulance Service is rushing to the hospital with an unconscious patient who has a very low pulse. While trying to gain time, the ambulance driver turns off the congested interstate onto a bumpy back road. After the ambulance hits a deep pothole, the bolts holding a rear shock absorber snap. The driver is afraid to proceed because, without the shock absorber, the vibrations from the bumpy road may cause serious complications for their patient. Jack Bradley, a car mechanic, lives across the road from where the ambulance has stopped. He works frantically for two hours to bolt the shock absorbers to the upper and lower control arms, while the medics keep the patient alive. All the other ambulances were out on call, and were therefore unable to come to this patient's aid. Subsequently, the ambulance arrives safely at the hospital and the patient's life is saved. Everyone is happy, but Jack! They acknowledge the good deed he did, but when he requests payment for his services, the hospital refuses, claiming they had no contract with Jack. Is Jack entitled to compensation for the services he rendered? Yes! Jack may recover the reasonable value of the services he rendered under the theory of quasi contract. Although no actual contract exists between Jack and the hospital, the law will imply a contract for reasons of fairness and justice, in order to prevent the hospital from becoming unjustly enriched at Jack's expenses. The services rendered by Jack were essential to the ambulance's performance, and the hospital would have had to pay for them in any event.

SPECIFIC PERFORMANCE

Specific performance is granted where the only way to fulfill the party's reasonable expectations is to force the breaching party to perform the contract, and where the remedies of money damages and rescission are inadequate. Specific performance can be obtained only in contracts involving something unique. Subject matters which are unique include: real estate, art, antiques, other rare items, and stock of a closely held corporation. The latter is considered unique because there is a restricted number of shares; the stock cannot be obtained through a public exchange; and the power to exercise control over the corporation's affairs is inherent in the stock.

EXAMPLE Juan Cortez, an antique dealer, agrees to purchase genuine Aztec treasures from Ricardo Montezuma. Montezuma inherited the treasures from his ancestors. Before delivery, Montezuma gets a better offer from Velasquez, a fierce competitor of Cortez. Can Cortez still lay claim to the treasures? Yes! Since the Aztec treasures are unique, specific performance will be granted because money damages are inadequate.

The remedy of specific performance does not apply to personal service contracts, including employment and construction contracts. Although these contracts are unique, parties in breach cannot be forced personally to perform them. To do so, would relegate a breaching party to involuntary servitude, which is in violation of the United States Constitution. A meaningful performance could not be assured because the courts do not have the capabilities to monitor mandatory personal performance or to judge whether or not it is adequate. The equitable remedy of specific performance will also not be granted where the result would be unconscionable.

EXAMPLE In the previous example, suppose that Cortez, the expert in antique treasures, misrepresents the value of the Aztec treasures to Montezuma and persuades him to sell the treasures for a low price. After signing the contract, Montezuma learns of the fraud and refuses to perform. Will specific performance be granted for Cortez? No! The result would be unconscionable. The use of fraud precludes Cortez from taking advantage of an equitable remedy.

RESCISSION AND RESTITUTION

Rescission and restitution can be both legal and equitable remedies, depending upon whether they are provided by statute or invoked equitably by the court's discretion. Rescission is the cancellation of the contract; restitution is the returning of the parties to the position they were in before the contract came about. Restitution requires each party to give back the consideration they received and return to the status quo. The right to rescind will expire if the party continues to perform under the contract. This right will also expire if not exercised within a reasonable time. The party wishing to rescind must evidence his or her intent by giving prompt notice.

EXAMPLE Kubla Khan hires Marco Polo to build the Great Wall of China, which is intended to keep out unfriendly neighbors. The Khan pays Marco $100,000. Marco agrees to use a strong bonding cement. Upon inspection, the Khan discovers that Marco is using the cheapest cement available. This cement will crack and can easily be demolished by the neighboring Mongolians. What recourse does the Khan have against Marco? The Khan can rescind the contract because of the material breach caused by Marco's fraud. Marco must make restitution by returning the $100,000 and he may also be liable for money damages caused by the delay in construction which will result because of his breach.

REFORMATION

Reformation is the rewriting of a contract to reflect the true intention of the parties, where the terms are incorrectly stated. It is usually applied in cases where parties have made a mutual mistake as to a material fact. The remedy is available only for an error in writing, not in meaning. Even if the contract falls within the statute of frauds, reformation is available to correct the written mistake. If one party has made a material mistake which the other party is aware of, or should be aware of, the contract can be reformed to evidence the mistaken party's true intent. Contracts can also be reformed without resort to a lawsuit if the parties mutually agree to the reformation.

EXAMPLE | Lockheed agrees to build 40 MX missiles for the United States government for $5 billion. When the government secretary typed the contract, it read 400 MX missiles. What remedy is available to Lockheed? The contract may be reformed to evidence the intention of the parties: 40 MX missiles.

UCC REMEDIES

The UCC remedies will be discussed in Chapter 18 and Chapter 19.

MONEY DAMAGES

Money damages are awarded to compensate a party for the loss sustained. The innocent party has the burden of proving that he or she suffered damages as a result of the other party's breach. Money will usually be a satisfactory substitute for performance if a breach occurs, but when it is not, an equitable remedy may be granted for reasons of fairness and justice. For example, when an individual refuses to perform a personal service contract, an injunction may be granted; and when a party refuses to perform a contract involving something unique, specific performance will be granted. Money damages may be awarded by one or more of the following methods, as appropriate to redressing the loss:

Compensatory damages
Resulting damages
Incidental damages
Stipulated damages
Punitive damages
Nominal damages

Compensatory Damages

The parties to a contract have the right to have their reasonable expectations fulfilled in accordance with the contract. Compensatory damages have the effect of awarding the injured party the same benefits that he or she would have received had the contract been carried out as promised.

The benefit of the bargain is the difference between the value of the performance received as a result of the breach and the actual value of the performance promised in the contract. The actual value of the performance promised is the value the innocent party would have received had the breach not been committed. The performance received, plus the difference between that value and the actual value of what was promised in the contract, will give the aggrieved party the benefit of the bargain.

EXAMPLE | John Dorsey, an extremely tall and slender young man, was to be married at 4 P.M. on a Saturday afternoon. At 2 P.M., when he went to get dressed in the tuxedo he had rented from Penguin Rentals for $75, he found to his dismay that they had sent him a tuxedo for a very small, portly man. He telephoned Penguin Rentals, who apologetically said they must have sent his tuxedo to someone else. There was not a moment to waste. John rushed out and drove from one rental establishment to another before he located a tuxedo in his size. The cost of this rental was $125, which exceeded his contract with Penguin by $50. What is Dorsey's measure of damages? Dorsey is entitled to the benefit of his contract with Penguin. Since he must pay $125 in the market, he may recover the difference between the contract price and the market price, $50, plus a return of his $75 payment.

Out-of-pocket damages are the reimbursement for the difference between the contract price and the value of what was received. The value received would have to be lower; otherwise the party would not be asking for damages.

In the previous example, assume that John Dorsey was able to rent a tuxedo at the same price as his contract with Penguin. What would his measure of damages be? He would get $75—his out-of-pocket expenses.

Resulting Damages

Resulting or consequential damages are awarded where a direct financial loss can be attributed to the breach. This remedy is granted in addition to compensatory damages. Loss of profits is a consequence of many breached contracts. The party suffering the detriment must establish that the loss of profits stemmed directly from the breach. The party in breach must know, or should have known, that a breach would result in additional losses to the other party. In other words, the damages arising from the breach must be reasonably foreseeable. Under this theory, a party in breach will be liable to an innocent party for any damages the innocent party must pay to a third person who sues the innocent party because of an unintentional breach. The innocent party's unintentional breach must directly result from the breach of contract by the first party. Parties may also recover interest lost on their money as a result of the breach.

We will now examine the formula for recovery of damages where a breach is committed, at various stages, by both the person performing services and the recipient of those services. When a breach is committed by the recipient of the services, before performance, the person performing the services is entitled to loss of profits. Loss of profits is generally the difference between the contract price and the cost of performance. The cost of performance includes expenses for materials, labor, and other such costs incurred in carrying out the contract. For a breach during performance, damages include loss of profits plus the cost of performance incurred to the date of the breach. Recovery for a breach after performance is the entire contract price.

EXAMPLE | Columbus has a contract with three different shipbuilders. Each shipbuilder is to construct a ship for Columbus's voyage. Subsequently, Columbus receives a better deal elsewhere and cancels all three contracts. What will the shipbuilders' measure of damages be? The builders of the *Nina* have not yet commenced construction. Their measure of damages will be loss of profits on the contract. The company constructing the *Pinta* has commenced performance. Their measure of damages will be loss of profits plus the cost of performance to the date of the breach, less the market value of the partially completed ship. The third firm has completed the construction of the *Santa Maria*. They will be entitled to recover the full contract price.

The damages for a breach committed by a person performing the services, before performance commences, are limited to the difference between the contract price and the market price. The market price is the ordinary price charged for the same services in the general vicinity where performance was to take place. Where only partial performance is rendered and the breach is unintentional, the recipient of those services must pay the breaching party the reasonable value for the services performed. This is equivalent to the contract price less the cost of completion. However, many states hold that no consideration need be paid to a party who breaches the contract intentionally. If the contract is substantially performed with only an incidental breach, the innocent party must pay the contract price less the amount of damages necessary to cover the incidental defects. The nonbreaching party is entitled to have his or her reasonable expectations fulfilled. This includes complete performance in accordance with the terms of the contract. For a late performance, recovery will be limited to loss of use caused by the delay.

EXAMPLE In the previous example, if each of the three shipbuilders breached their contract with Columbus what would his measure of damages be? For the *Nina*, because performance has not yet begun, Columbus will recover the difference between the contract price and the price he must pay to another shipbuilder (market price). Columbus is entitled to have the ship built at the original contract price. For the *Pinta*, he will have to hire another contractor to complete the ship. He need only pay the original contractor the contract price less the cost of completion. For the *Santa Maria*, which has been substantially completed, Columbus will have to pay the contract price less the cost to repair any incidental defects.

Incidental Damages

The awarding of incidental damages is to reimburse an innocent party for expenses caused by a breach of contract in connection with inspection, storage, and transportation. The expenses incurred by the party in attempting to locate substituted performance may also be recovered from the party in breach.

EXAMPLE The Pacific Northwest Salmon Corporation in Alaska agrees to sell and deliver 500 pounds of salmon to The Catch of the Day, a seafood restaurant on Fisherman's Wharf in San Francisco. The Catch of the Day refuses to accept delivery after the goods have been shipped to San Francisco. Five days later, the Salmon Corporation finds a buyer in Sacramento who is willing to pay the same price. May they recover the transportation costs to Sacramento and the storage costs for the five days? Yes! Damages incidental to the breach may be recovered.

Stipulated Damages

Stipulated or liquidated damages are an estimate by the parties at the time the contract is made of what the damages might be should a breach take place. The reason for stipulating damages in the contract is for the sake of convenience. It avoids the expense of a lawsuit to determine damages, where damages might otherwise be difficult to prove. Parties can agree to limit damages as long as the amount stipulated is reasonable. Damages are reasonable when they approach what the actual loss might be, should a breach occur. Reasonableness takes into consideration the date of the contract, not the date of the breach. A determination must be made as to whether the stipulated damages were reasonable on the date the contract was made. A fair estimate of loss of profits may also be stipulated.

A figure that is so excessive as to constitute a penalty, need not be adhered to by the parties. Neither does a figure which is too low restrict a party from commencing a lawsuit for the recovery of reasonable damages. Where the stipulated damage clause is nullified because of unfairness, the aggrieved party may recover damages which are fair under the circumstances. Parties may modify or limit remedies through a liquidated damage clause. However, any attempt by a party to use this clause as an exculpatory clause to disclaim liability is void because of unconscionability. This is especially true in consumer contracts.

EXAMPLE | Johnny Appleseed had a contract with a man named MacIntosh, to plant apple seeds along the east coast of the United States, which is 2,000 miles in length. His fee was $10 per mile, but for every mile not covered before the end of the year, he had to repay $1. An early winter caused Johnny to abandon his journey in New York, 500 miles short of his destination. It was here that he dumped all of the remaining seed. That is how New York became known as the Big Apple. What are the damages recoverable by MacIntosh? Five hundred dollars. The damages stipulated in the contract may be recovered because the parties agreed to these damages, and they are reasonable.

Punitive Damages

Punitive damages are awarded to penalize the party who commits a wrong that injures the general public. These damages are assessed in addition to the compensatory damages awarded to the injured party, usually in cases involving fraud. Punitive damages are not actually a contract remedy, because the law does not exact punishment for breach of contract by itself. When the breach of contract also constitutes a tort, then the court may award punitive damages for the tort in addition to the compensatory damages for the breach of contract. The purpose of the punitive damages is to act as a deterrent to future offenses of a similar nature, and to compensate the victim for the mental anguish suffered.

EXAMPLE | Daniel Revson lives in Forest Hills, Queens, and has been working for General Motors in New York for twenty-five years. He receives a promotion and is transferred to Detroit to oversee assembly production. He calls a branch office of Find-A-Home real estate and asks them to find him a six-room apartment in Grosse Point. Five days later, the real estate saleswoman telephones Mr. Revson to notify him of such an apartment for

$1,200 a month, which is the going rate for a luxury apartment in the heart of Grosse Point. A lease and a letter of explanation arrive two days later. Revson signs the lease and mails it to the Find-A-Home, along with a check for $3,600: one month's rent, one month's security, and the brokerage fee. Two weeks later, Revson moves to Grosse Point, or so he thought. The address on his copy of the lease proves to be a floor in a modest house on the fringe of Grosse Point. Revson sues the brokerage for compensation and asks the court to award punitive damage. Will they be granted? Yes! Revson is entitled to the return of his $3,600 together with any incidental expenses, such as hotel bills, incurred in trying to find another apartment in Grosse Point. Punitive damages may also be awarded to punish Find-A-Home real estate for the fraud committed and to deter them from committing any future harm.

Boise Dodge, Inc. v. Clark
92 Idaho 902, 453 P.2d 551 (1969)

Boise Dodge sued Clark for nonpayment on a Dodge Monaco. Mr. Clark counterclaimed against Boise Dodge for breach of contract resulting from their fraudulent actions with respect to a car he purchased. The plaintiff, Clark, alleges that Boise Dodge purposely turned back the odometer 7,000 miles in order to induce a sale. He asked the court to award compensatory damages as well as punitive damages.

The service manager testified that he was instructed by the general manager of Boise Dodge to turn back the mileage on thirteen demonstration cars in order to make them more saleable. Clark purchased one of these cars, a Dodge Monaco, by trading in his Pontiac and paying the balance by check. He stopped payment on the check, but Boise Dodge still had possession of his Pontiac.

The issue concerning punitive damages is whether the fraud committed was perpetrated against the general public rather than a specific individual.

Boise Dodge's action in turning back the odometers is a public wrong. The court awarded Clark $12,000 in punitive damages to discourage future actions of this nature. Clark was required to pay the balance owed on the contract, $2,400 less a deduction of $350 to compensate for the car's lower value as a result of 7,000 extra miles on the odometer.

Nominal Damages

Where the innocent party has suffered no loss, nominal damages will be awarded—not for compensation, but as a sign of the breaching party's wrongdoing. This happens in situations where the breach has put the innocent party in a better position than he or she would have been in had the contract been completed.

EXAMPLE | Under a contract with a resort development company, Ponce de Leon departs in early April on an expedition to discover new areas to build community settlements. Ponce is to return by August 31, but he delays his return in order to pursue his quest for the Fountain of Youth, which he discovers one month later. As a result of his discovery, many elderly people settle in Florida. Since Ponce's breach actually enhanced the position of the resort development company, are they entitled to any damages? Yes!

But, their recovery will be limited to nominal damages, which are awarded only to evidence the wrongdoing committed by the party in breach.

DUTY TO MITIGATE DAMAGES

Upon learning of a breach, an innocent party has a duty to mitigate damages. This means that the innocent party must, in good faith, attempt to keep the damages as low as possible without incurring any undue risk or expense. A party who does not make a reasonable attempt to mitigate damages will be barred from recovery. A seller's duty may be fulfilled by stopping production, and by attempting to resell the goods at a fair and reasonable price. A seller who continues production regardless of the fact of having been notified of the breach, will be limited to recovery of damages suffered at the time of the breach. This is because of the failure to mitigate damages. In certain instances, mitigation of damages may require the seller to complete manufacture of the goods where the goods have no value unless completed. A seller who does not make an attempt to resell the goods for a reasonable price after notification of the breach will be barred from recovery.

In a case where the breach concerns nonconforming goods, buyers may not continue to use these goods once they discover the goods are nonconforming. Buyers may satisfy their duty to mitigate damages by attempting to obtain substitute performance at a reasonable price. Buyers who continue to use the goods may be limited in their recovery of damages, or may be barred completely. A situation may arise, as the next example illustrates, where mitigation of damages would require the buyer to use the nonconforming goods until a suitable replacement can be furnished.

Employees under contract who have been terminated without cause have a duty to mitigate damages by making a good faith effort to seek similar employment elsewhere. The employee need not, however, accept a lower position or look for employment beyond the general vicinity.

EXAMPLE

On February 17, Wilson Athletic Corporation contracts to purchase a machine which manufactures fifty baseballs per hour, from McNeil Machinery Corporation. Wilson needs the machine by April 1, in order to fill an order for the entire Major League Baseball season. On April 1, McNeil mistakenly sends a machine which produces only twenty-five baseballs per hour. Wilson immediately notifies McNeil of the nonconformity, but continues to use the machine. Will this bar Wilson from recovery? No! Wilson acted wisely to mitigate damages. Wilson's damages will be based on loss of profits or the consequences of a late delivery resulting from delivery of the slower machine.

REVIEW QUESTIONS

1. Define remedies, breach of contract, injunction, quasi contract, rescission, restitution, reformation, specific performance, and money damages.
2. List and explain the various types of money damages.
3. Evergreen Amusement wanted to convert a parcel of land it owned into a drive-in movie. They entered into a contract with Milstead to clear the land and grade

it according to the specifications given. The work was to be completed by June 1, in time for the busy summer season. Milstead did not finish the job until late August. Can Evergreen Amusement recover lost profits for the summer months? Evergreen Amusement Corp. v. Milstead, 206 Md. 610, 112 A.2d 901 (1955).

4. Chaplin was a beauty contestant in the Miss America pageant. Hicks was Chaplin's agent. One of his duties was to notify her of the time that each event would begin. Hicks forgot to tell Chaplin that the bathing suit competition was to begin at 8:00 P.M. on Sunday night. Chaplin missed the competition and lost all hope of winning any prizes. She sued Hicks for breach of contract. What result? What kind of damages should Chaplin recover, if any? Chaplin v. Hicks, 2 K.B. 786 (1911).

5. The Raft Brothers signed a personal service contract to perform exclusively for the Shubert Theatrical Company. The contract contained a clause granting Shubert an option to renew the contract for an additional year at a stipulated price. The Raft Brothers refused to perform, stating they had signed another agreement. What recourse does Shubert have against the Raft Brothers? Shubert Theatrical Co. v. Raft et al., 271 Fed. Rep. 827 (1921).

6. Denver Burglar Alarm installed a system in Niccoli's house. The contract provided that when the alarm sounded, an agent of Denver Alarm would be sent to the house. If the agent failed to appear, Denver's liability would be fixed at $50. Subsequently, Niccoli's alarm went off and the house was burglarized, but no agent was ever sent by Denver Alarm. Denver Alarm refuses to pay the $50, stating it was unreasonable. What result? Niccoli v. Denver Burglar Alarm, Inc., 490 P.2d 304 (Colo.App.) 1971.

7. Rixse, an architect, agreed to draw plans for the proposed construction of a new building by Wetzel. Wetzel breached the contract by refusing to perform. At the time of the breach, Rixse had completed only the preliminary drawings. He continued to prepare the remainder of the plans after he was notified of the breach. Rixse sues Wetzel for non-payment of the entire contract price. What result? Wetzel v. Rixse, 93 Okla. 216, 220 P. 607 (1923).

8. The public defender of Champaign County represented Hanks in a criminal prosecution because Hanks claimed he was indigent. The county later discovered that Hanks was worth over $50,000. The county sued Hanks for the reasonable value of the services rendered by the public defender. Hanks contended that he never entered into a contract with the public defender. What result? County of Champaign v. Hanks, 41 Ill. App. 3rd 679, 353 N.E.2d 405 (1976).

9. Williams entered into a contract to build a house for Hillerich. The house was built defectively. When Hillerich refused to pay Williams refused to convey title to the house to Hillerich. Hillerich sued Williams for specific performance of the contract for the sale of the house and for damages arising from the defective construction. Williams argued that both remedies could not be awarded because they are inconsistent. What result? Billy Williams Builders & Developers, Inc. v. Hillerich, 446 S.W.2d 860 (Ky.) 1969.

10. Hadley ran a flour mill in Gloucester, England. The crankshaft of the steam engine broke. Hadley hired Baxendale to transport the crankshaft to a foundry in Greenwich, England. Baxendale promised to deliver it the next day. Until the crankshaft was repaired, the mill could not operate. Delivery was not made until several days later, which resulted in the mill's being shut down for a comparable amount of time. Hadley sued Baxendale for lost profits during the shutdown. What result? Hadley v. Baxendale, 156 Eng. Rep. 145 (1854).

14

CONTRACTUAL DEFENSES

INTRODUCTION

People enter into contracts in order to receive valuable consideration in the form of performance, forbearance, or payment from other people. A party who has not received valuable consideration from the other, has a cause of action against that party for breach of contract. The nonperforming party will be liable for the breach unless he or she has a justifiable reason to excuse the failure to perform. Justifiable reasons for nonperformance are known as contractual defenses and may be either real or personal. Real defenses are absolute defenses provided by statute for the protection of a certain class of people. They include bankruptcy discharge, duress, illegality, statute of limitations, statute of frauds, infancy, and when sanity is lacking. Real defenses can not be waived. Personal defenses arise during the performance of a contract and may be asserted only by the aggrieved party. They include agreement in jest, misrepresentation and fraudulent inducement, stop in performance, insufficient consideration, performance of a condition fails, payment is not made, impossibility, release, unconscionability, and mistake. Real and personal defenses are raised in response to a cause of action that is brought by the other party. The burden of proving the validity of the defenses is on the party affirming it. If the contractual defense is successfully proven, the cause of action will be dismissed. Most contractual defenses may be used in the affirmative by a party rescinding the contract. There are many contractual defenses including:

> Bankruptcy discharge
> Agreement in jest
> Duress and undue influence

Misrepresentation and fraudulent inducement

Illegality

Statute of limitations

Statute of frauds

Infancy

Stop in performance

Sanity is lacking

Insufficient consideration

Performance of a condition fails

Payment is not made

Impossibility

Release

Unconscionability

Mistake

BANKRUPTCY DISCHARGE

Bankruptcy occurs when a person is unable to pay his or her debts. The bankruptcy law, which is invoked by the filing of either a voluntary or involuntory petition, provides for a fair distribution of the debtor's assets among the creditors. The bankrupt's debts are discharged in bankruptcy, which protects the debtor from all future claims made by creditors for past debts. This protection operates as a defense to a cause of action for breach of contract brought by a creditor.

EXAMPLE Mrs. Henrietta Mulholland, a seventy-nine-year-old philanthropist, filed for bankruptcy when she found she had no money left. Among those to whom she owed wages were her housekeeper, chauffeur, maid, gardener, and masseuse. All received notice of the bankruptcy proceedings, but the masseuse decided to sue. In a suit by the masseuse for nonpayment of wages, is bankruptcy a good defense? Yes! Mrs. Mulholland's debts, including the one owed to the masseuse, have all been discharged in bankruptcy.

AGREEMENT IN JEST

Parties contracting with each other must have the requisite legal capacity to make a contract. An agreement made in jest lacks the necessary legal capacity because there is no intent to perform. Intent to perform is manifested through the outward expressions of the parties. The requirement of intent is satisfied if the offeree is reasonable in believing the offeror to be serious. A contract which lacks a party's intention to agree is voidable. The party setting forth the defense of jest has the right to disaffirm the contract if the defense can be proved. But, in any event, people would be wise not to make offers in jest.

The Sheriff of Nottingham was having a few beers with Robin Hood. Robin asked the sheriff if he would sell Sherwood Forest for $100,000. The sheriff replied, "Sure!" Then he laughingly continued, "But where would a peasant like you get the money?" Robin replied, "You'd be surprised" whereupon he produced the $100,000. The sheriff, struck with awe, protested that the agreement had been made in jest. Is this a good defense? Yes! Looking at the objective actions of the parties, the sheriff's laughter while assenting to Robin's offer coupled with the fact that they had a few beers would tend to prove that the sheriff was not serious and that Robin was not reasonable in believing him to be serious. Furthermore, there was nothing in writing to evidence the sheriff's intention to be bound.

DURESS AND UNDUE INFLUENCE

Duress is the wrongful or illegal use of coercion by one party to force another party into entering a contract or making a payment greater than the contract provided for, out of fear of harm. The fear may arise from the threat of physical, social, or economic harm, but it must be genuine, not illusory. The threat of physical harm, which is often closely associated with extortion, may be directed at the person, a family member, or the person's property, where the damage threatened is severe. Social duress is accomplished through blackmail: the threat of exposing personal secrets that will result in public humiliation, disgrace, embarrassment, or possible loss of membership in societies, clubs, and associations. Economic duress arises where one party threatens to withhold performance unless a greater sum is paid and the aggrieved party cannot locate a satisfactory substitute within the time limits set forth in the contract. The aggrieved party may be in need of performance immediately. The other party, with knowledge of the immediate need for performance, seizes the opportunity to exploit the victim in his moment of weakness.

EXAMPLE Joan Enwright, a registered nurse, who once worked in a doctor's office, threatens Howard Smithwick that unless he signs a promissory note for $5,000, she will reveal to the Federal Bureau of Investigation, where he is now applying for a job, that he was treated several years ago for drug addiction. Howard Smithwick signs the note, but later refuses to pay, asserting duress. Is duress a good defense? Yes! Howard Smithwick felt an immediate and justifiable fear of economic and social harm.

Undue influence is the use of a confidential or fiduciary relationship, based on trust and confidence, by one person to obtain a benefit by inducing another person to enter into a contract. The key to undue influence, as well as to duress, is the victim's lack of freedom to make a decision.

People susceptible to undue influence are those who place their faith in another because of the other party's status or because of their close relationship with the other party. These relationships include: attorney-client, doctor-patient, executor-beneficiaries, and the like. But the most vulnerable groups are the infants and elderly persons who rely on family members or guardians to act on their behalf. They run the greatest risk of being exploited. There is a presumption of undue influence where fiduciaries enter into contracts with their beneficiaries. Individuals in a fiduciary capacity can rebut the presumption of undue influence by proving that full disclosure was made; that consideration was adequate; and that the aggrieved party had independent counselling before entering into the contract.

EXAMPLE

On hearing that his elderly aunt, Catherine Forbes, has been hospitalized with a severe stroke, William Danihy flies across the country to be with her. She is wealthy and he knows she is leaving him and his two cousins equal shares in her estate. At her bedside, seeing that her mind is wandering and not too strong, he tells her repeatedly and untruthfully that his two cousins have been very successful of late and are in no need of money, whereas he and his family are in dire straits. While dinning this into her mind, he discourages his cousins from coming to see her by making light of her illness. He brings a lawyer to his aunt's bedside and convinces her to change her will to favor only him. She does so and dies that evening. The two cousins sue to reclaim their share. If, with the aid of the trained nurses, they can prove that William Danihy unduly influenced his aunt to change her will, would this be a good defense? Yes!

MISREPRESENTATION AND FRAUDULENT INDUCEMENT

Misrepresentation is a false statement of a material fact which is justifiably relied on by a person to his or her detriment. If the misrepresentation is intentional, then it is fraudulent. The elements of fraud are as follows:

Intent to deceive
False representation of a material fact
Justifiable reliance
Detriment

Intent to Deceive

Intent to deceive is the characteristic that separates a fraudulent misrepresentation from an innocent one. Intent to deceive is established by proving the falsity of the representation at the time it was made. The knowledge will be imputed to the party making the statement where that party should have known that the statement was false, or that party made the statement in reckless disregard of whether it was false or not.

False Representation of a Material Fact

False representations may be made innocently (misrepresentation) or intentionally (fraud), through actions as well as speech. Concealment of material alterations or defects which would not be generally noticed is an example of fraud. Material facts are those facts which influence parties in their decision to enter into contracts. Although silence usually does not constitute fraud, a duty to speak will arise in situations when a person, having knowledge that an essential fact is false, knows that the other party believes that fact to be true. Individuals who have a duty to speak include a fiduciary; a person with knowledge of an alteration, or a hidden defect; and a person who discovers a previous misstatement. These individuals must apprise the potential victim of the truth; otherwise their silence will constitute fraud. Parties may not disclaim their fraudulent or innocent misrepresentations at the expense of others.

Justifiable Reliance

Statements regarding predictions of future happenings or opinions as to value are generally not categorized as fraudulent because a party is not justified in relying upon these types of statements. However, in the case where the false opinion is given by an expert in the field, such as a lawyer or physician; a fiduciary in a relationship of trust and confidence; or a person with superior knowledge of the product or service, then the false opinion will constitute fraud. People are justified in relying upon the opinions of these three types of individuals unless the facts of the case arouse suspicion. A person has a duty to investigate suspicious facts before entering into a contract. An individual who discovers fraud before entering into the contract may not enter into the contract and thereafter seek to abrogate it on the basis of fraud.

Detriment

The defrauded or misrepresented party must have suffered some financial loss, and be able to prove it, in order to have a cause of action.

The remedy for misrepresentation is rescission. Rescission has the effect of cancelling the contract and returning the parties to status quo. Inherent in this remedy is the return of consideration by both parties. Rescission is also available as a remedy for fraud, but the defrauded party may, on the other hand, sue for money damages. The remedy of money damages has two basic forms: benefit of the bargain and out-of-pocket damages.

Benefit of the bargain is the difference between the value of the performance received as a result of the fraud and the actual value represented. The actual value represented is the value the defrauded party would have received had the fraud not been committed. The performance received plus the difference between that value and the actual value represented will give the aggrieved party the benefit of the bargain. The defrauded party is entitled to receive that difference in value as damages.

Out-of-pocket damages are the reimbursement for the difference between what was paid under the fraudulent contract and the actual value of what was received. The actual value would be lower, otherwise the party would not be asking for damages. Courts, at their discretion, may also award punitive damages. Punitive damages are penalties to punish those who commit fraud, and to discourage them from doing it again.

EXAMPLE The Artful Dodger is a con artist, who devises a scheme and employs his innocent young friend, Oliver Twist, to carry it out for him. The Dodger knows that Mr. Bumble, a wealthy gentleman, is interested in purchasing a thoroughbred horse. He tells Oliver to inform Mr. Bumble that for $10,000 they will deliver a fine one. Mr. Bumble realizes that this is a good deal and gives Oliver the $10,000. Bumble trusts Oliver's judgment because he has known him since he was a small boy. Oliver believes that his representations are true. The next day, an old mare is delivered to Mr. Bumble and he refuses to pay for it. In a suit brought by Oliver and the Artful Dodger for nonpayment, what defenses could Mr. Bumble raise? Bumble could raise the defense of fraud against the Artful Dodger because the Dodger intentionally deceived Bumble through the false representations he had Oliver make concerning the horse. Bumble's reliance was justified because of his trust in Oliver. Bumble could raise the defense of misrepresentation against Oliver even though Oliver acted innocently. Bumble's remedy against both parties would be rescission and out-of-pocket damages—$10,000 less the value of the horse received. Bumble would probably not be entitled to punitive damages because the fraud was personal and not perpetrated against the general public. If the particular thoroughbred described in this contract existed, Mr. Bumble would be entitled to the benefit of the bargain—the difference in the value of the horse received and the value of the horse he would have received had the representation been true.

Vokes v. Arthur Murray, Inc.
212 So.2d 906, (D. Ct. App. Fla. 1968)

Vokes sued the Arthur Murray School of Dancing for rescission of a contract for dance lessons. The plaintiff contends that she entered into the contract because of fraudulent representations made about her dancing ability.

Audrey Vokes, a widow for over fifty years, had no family. She had a yearning to become "an accomplished dancer" and to develop a new interest in life. She was invited to a dance at Davenport's Dance School, a local franchise of Arthur Murray's School for Dancing. She took free dancing lessons with the instructors while constantly being barraged with flattery and compliments about her dancing potential. She was baited with a trial offer of eight half-hour lessons for $14.50. The come-on worked over a period of time, for the dance school was able to induce her to buy fourteen dance courses, totaling over 2,300 hours of lessons. The cost was over $31,000. The fourteen course enrollments are evidenced by Arthur Murray's School of Dancing Enrollment Agreement.

The inducement used by the dance school included compliments concerning her grace and poise, and about her rapidly improving and developing dancing skill. She was informed that the lessons would "make her a beautiful dancer, capable of dancing with the most accomplished dancers." The plaintiff was even given dance aptitude tests to determine how many additional hours she needed.

She was sold 545 additional hours at one stage, which qualified her for the "Bronze Medal." Thereafter, 926 hours were added for the "Silver Medal," 347 hours for the "Gold Medal," and finally 481 hours for the classification "as a Gold Bar Member, the ultimate achievement of the dancing studio." The defendant also cajoled the widow into buying a life membership which allowed her to take a trip to Miami at her own expense, where she was "given the opportunity to dance with members of the Miami Studio." She was also talked into buying still more hours in order to be eligible for trips to Trinidad and Mexico, again both at her own expense. In reality, Mrs. Vokes had no "dance aptitude" and actually had difficulty in "hearing the musical beat." She was told she was entering into the "spring of her life," but actually there was no spring in her life or her feet.

The defendants contend that their misrepresentations relate to opinions, not facts.

The issue is whether a contract can be rescinded where it was entered into through reliance on fraudulent opinions.

The court held that the parties were not of equal bargaining strength, and that the dance studio used their greater strength to their advantage. The studio's opinion of the plaintiff's dancing ability is considered to be one of superior knowledge, equivalent to a statement of fact, because of the studio's expertise. The hours of instruction were unjustified, because Mrs. Vokes lacked ability for improvement. If they had told her the truth, she would have realized this. The widow justifiably relied on their opinion to her detriment. Judgment for Vokes.

ILLEGALITY

The purpose of a contract must be lawful. This is one of the elements of a contract. Where either the acts to be performed, or the purpose to be achieved is illegal, the contract will be unenforceable. Illegal contracts are prohibited by federal, state, and local statutes; and by public policy. The defense of illegality may be invoked by either party without resort to a court of law because all illegal contracts are void. Courts generally do not decide matters of illegality except where an innocent party is asking for restitution. A more detailed discussion of the defense of illegality was presented in Chapter 10, Lawful Purpose.

STATUTE OF LIMITATIONS

A statute of limitations is the duration of time within which a person must exercise his or her cause of action; that is, the time within which the injured party must serve the summons on the other party. The time limitation begins to run from the time the harm is committed, or, in some cases, discovered. Its duration varies according to the type of action brought. Contracts for the sale of goods have a four-year statute of limitations. All other contract actions are governed by the particular statute of limitations of the state having jurisdiction. Some states have a special statute of limitations for fraud: six years from the time the fraud was committed, or two years from its discovery, whichever is longer. The statute of limitations may be raised as a defense to a contract action which has been brought after the appropriate time limitation has lapsed.

EXAMPLE | Robinson Crusoe sells a bunch of coconuts to his friend, Friday. Friday is to make payment after Crusoe returns from a trip to the Bahamas. However, Crusoe gets caught in a storm and ends up on Galapagos Island with a bunch of overgrown turtles. Twenty-seven years later, Crusoe returns and seeks to enforce Friday's promise to pay for the coconuts. Friday raises the defense of the statute of limitations. Is this a good defense? Yes! Because this was a contract for the sale of goods, the statute of limitations expires four years after the date that payment was due.

STATUTE OF FRAUDS

The defense of the statute of frauds may be raised against an action based on an oral contract which the statute requires to be in writing. It may also be used affirmatively in an action for rescission where one party is seeking to cancel the contract. The statute of frauds is discussed more fully in Chapter 11, Form and Interpretation.

INFANCY

The defense of infancy—which is explained more fully in Chapter 9, Legal Capacity—can be raised only by an infant. Infants may use the defense affirmatively in their own actions for rescission, or defensively in an action brought by an adult for enforcement of the contract or for damages. The basis for the defense is to protect infants because of their lack of experience in dealing with adults. The age of majority is set by statute. Infants are those individuals who have not yet attained majority. They are still in their minority.

STOP IN PERFORMANCE

A stop in performance by one party for no justifiable reason is sufficient cause for the other party to halt payment or performance. The defense can be raised by the aggrieved party in an action for payment brought by the party who stopped performance. The aggrieved party may rescind or cancel the contract by asserting a stop in performaance.

EXAMPLE Claudia Richardson hired Superior Home Repairs, Inc., to convert her cellar into a finished basement. Superior estimated the work would take twenty days and promised to begin February 1. Claudia was to pay them in four installments: on February 5, 10, 15, and 20. Claudia made the payments on February 5 and the 10. However, the workers failed to show for the next five days. Claudia refused to pay the February 15 installment and was sued for nonpayment according to the contract schedule. Has she any recourse? Yes! Superior Home Repairs was not justified in stopping their perform-ance. Claudia is entitled to withhold the scheduled payment until the work is completed.

A party who substantially performs will be entitled to the reasonable value for the work completed if the breach was unintentional. The same may be said for partially performed contracts which were breached unintentionally if the contract can be divided into more than one contract, or can be made into a separate contract.

EXAMPLE In the previous example, assume Superior Home Repairs had been hired to modernize the first-floor kitchen and bathroom in addition to finishing the basement, and that total payment was to be made upon completion of both jobs. Superior Home Repairs finished the basement, but never returned to modernize the first-floor kitchen and bath. Claudia refuses to make any payment. Superior Home Repairs sues her for the reasonable value of their services. Are they entitled to it? Yes! The performance required can be divided into two separate contracts; one of which was completed. Superior Home Repairs is entitled to the reasonable value of the services they rendered in completing the base-ment, as long as their breach in regard to the first-floor apartment was unintentional. They may still be liable for damages caused by their unintentional breach; that is, the difference between their contract price for modernizing the first-floor kitchen and bath and the market price Claudia will have to pay.

SANITY IS LACKING

Sanity is a requisite for legal capacity, which is one of the elements of a contract. The defense of insanity is available only to the insane for their protection. It may be raised by the insane individual, either personally in a lucid interval, or by his or her guardian. Chapter 9, Legal Capacity, provides a more definitive explanation.

INSUFFICIENT CONSIDERATION

A party whose performance does not fulfill his or her promise under the contract, is said to have given insufficient consideration. The other party may withhold consideration until payment is made or performance is completed. If an action is brought against the party withholding consideration, the defense of insufficient consideration may be raised. If it is reasonable to assume that performance will not be completed, the contract may be rescinded or an action for money damages may be brought.

EXAMPLE Dr. Watson kept his narcotic drugs in a locked safe in his medical office. Each Friday morning, on opening the safe, he found one bottle missing. Watson hired Sherlock Holmes, a private investigator, to solve the mystery. Holmes was to be paid only if the case was solved. Upon arriving on the scene, Holmes said "Dr. Watson, I presume." After being briefed about the drug thefts, Holmes went to work. He discovered that Watson's nurse had left the medical office door open a crack. By using a miniature telescope, she had observed the combination to the safe when Watson turned the dial. Late in the day, she would slip in and remove one bottle. Watson was astounded by Holmes' brilliance, but he was even more astounded when he received the bill for $10,000. Watson refused to pay and Holmes sued for breach of contract. Then an amazing event took place. Another bottle was removed from the safe a week later, and another the following week. Holmes had not solved the mystery after all. Watson raised this as a defense to the suit for nonpayment. Is this a good defense? Yes! Holmes was only entitled to the fee if he solved the case. Since, he did not, he gave insufficient consideration in return for Watson's promise to pay.

PERFORMANCE OF A CONDITION FAILS

A condition occurs where the parties' contractual duties are contingent upon the occurrence of a future event. Parties must expressly agree when making the contract if they are conditioning their obligations on the occurrence of a particular event. Depending on whether the condition is worded positively or negatively, the occurrence of the future event may or may not require the parties to perform their contractual obligations. The condition may be expressed that if the event occurs, contractual obligations exist. Here, failure of the condition would discharge the parties from their obligations. The party who must satisfy the condition has a duty to make a good-faith effort in that direction by taking positive steps. There are three types of conditions: conditions precedent, conditions concurrent, and conditions subsequent.

Conditions precedent require a future event to occur before parties are obligated to perform their contractual duties. The condition must be satisfied before the contract can be performed. If the condition is not satisfied, the contract is unenforceable.

EXAMPLE | The Three Musketeers agreed to serve as bodyguards for Cardinal Richelieu while he traveled through the kingdom, on the condition he could locate D'Artagnan, the fourth Musketeer. The cardinal was not able to find D'Artagnan. The Three Musketeers refused to honor their contract. The cardinal sued them for breach of contract and The Musketeers raised the defense of failure of a condition precedent. Is this a good defense? Yes! This is a good defense because the condition had to be complied with before the Three Musketeers would be bound by the contract.

Conditions concurrent require that performance by both parties occur at the same time in order for the contract to be enforceable. Performance is contingent on payment and payment is contingent on performance. If any condition material to the contract is not fulfilled, the defense of failure of condition may be raised by either one of the parties, either affirmatively in an action for rescission, or defensively in an action for breach of contract.

EXAMPLE | Mitch Miller and his merry band have a standing contract to perform at Friar Tuck's Inn on Saturday night if a crowd of fifty or more gather. Mitch and his merry band reside in Sherwood Forest, near Friar Tuck's Inn, so it is always easy to call upon Mitch for a sing-a-long at the last minute. This is an example of a condition which runs concurrently with performance. Each Saturday night the condition must be satisfied (fifty people must gather) or performance will not be required.

Conditions subsequent involve existing contracts where parties must continue to perform their contractual obligations until the condition is not satisfied. Once the condition is not satisfied, the contract can no longer be enforced and the parties are excused from performing their duties under the contract. The difference with a condition subsequent is that there is an existing contract and, as long as the condition is satisfied, the contract will be enforceable.

EXAMPLE | Michael Caruso hires Susan Wood, through a local employment agency to be his all-purpose secretary until Theresa Mackey, his original secretary, returns from an extended illness. When Theresa returns, the condition subsequent will be satisfied and the employment contract with Susan Wood will terminate.

Conditions may be implied where the circumstances reasonably indicate that the parties assumed the contract would be conditioned on some stipulated event. Conditions may also be implied where the type of contract entered into necessitates implying certain conditions. Courts may likewise imply conditions for reasons of fairness and justice. Where one party has substantially performed, the fact that every detail was not completed may not be raised as a failure of condition.

EXAMPLE | The *Bounty* was to set sail for Tahiti. Before departure, Captain Cook contracted with Fletcher Christian, the first mate, to procure fifty barrels of coconut oil. He also contracted with Captain Bligh to obtain a large supply of conch shells, which Captain Cook would use to hear the ocean roar. On board the ship were breadfruit trees which the natives had contracted to buy. Half way to Tahiti, a mutiny broke out. The mutineers sent Captain Bligh adrift in a rowboat, while they continued to Tahiti. The hot sun and the occasional stormy weather withered the breadfruit trees. Upon arriving in Tahiti, Christian and his crew decided to remain there, knowing their lives would be worthless back home. Meanwhile, Captain Bligh arrived back in England. Are any of the contracts viable? No! The contract for the conch shells was cancelled because Captain Bligh never reached Tahiti. This condition was implied because the parties assumed the contract would be carried out only if Bligh reached Tahiti. The contract for the coconut oil was cancelled because Christian never returned to England. Many seamen remained on the islands after voyages. Enforcement of this contract necessitated implying that Christian would return home. Since he did not, the condition failed and he is excused from performing. Finally, the contract for the breadfruit trees was cancelled because they withered and died from the long journey. Neither party was aware that the journey would kill the breadfruit trees, so the court will imply a condition, (that if the trees withered and died, the contract would be cancelled), for reasons of fairness and justice.

PAYMENT IS NOT MADE

When one party to a contract was to receive payment in advance, and did not receive it, this party may use the defense of nonpayment if the other party brings a lawsuit against him or her.

EXAMPLE Richard Eastman is a broker at E.F. Hutton. At 10 A.M., he receives a call from Bob Matson who is offering to purchase 1,000 shares of IBM at the current market price, which is $100 per share. Eastman asks Bob Matson whether he has an account with E.F. Hutton. Matson replies that he does not. Eastman notifies him that payment must be made in advance when a customer does not have an account. Matson replies that he understands and that he will drop by on his lunch hour with a check for $100,000. When Matson arrives at 1 P.M., the price of IBM has risen to 108. Matson, thinking that Eastman had bought the stock at 100, which would give him a profit of $8,000, greets Eastman as if they were old friends. Eastman quickly explains that the stock was not purchased because payment had not been made. In a suit by Bob Matson, will this be a good defense for Eastman? Yes! Since it was agreed that payment was to be received by Eastman before he was required to buy the IBM stock, then nonpayment will excuse Eastman from performing.

IMPOSSIBILITY

Impossibility of performance refers to situations in which it is impossible for the contract to be performed either by the party under contract or by anyone else. Impossibility may be of a permanent or a temporary nature. Permanent impossibility will discharge the parties from their contractual obligations. Temporary impossibility will generally suspend the duty to perform until the impossibility diminishes. At that point, the duty to perform is revived. Personal inability to perform, alone, will not release the parties from their contractual obligations.

The people of Camelot hired Sir Kay and Sir Hector, specialists in metallurgy, to remove the sword Excalibur from the stone. Sir Kay and Sir Hector used various heating procedures and other methods, but were unsuccessful in their attempts. The people sued them for breach of contract. Sir Kay and Sir Hector claimed the defense of impossibility. In the meantime, the people of Camelot hired Arthur, at a greater cost, to remove the sword. Arthur was successful in his first attempt and the people rejoiced. Is the defense used by Sir Kay and Sir Hector viable? No! Personal inability to perform is not equivalent to impossibility.

The event causing impossibility must be brought about by an independent intervening cause. Examples of independent intervening causes are: a change in a law that makes performance illegal; the destruction of subject matter which is unique, or is specially designated for a particular contract; or the illness, incapacity, or death of one party whose special skills were required in a personal service contract. Under these circumstances, impossibility does not exist at the time the contract is made, but arises sometime thereafter. However, in certain instances of commercial impracticability, the impossibility may exist, but is not reasonably evident to the parties. The parties must not have foreseen the event nor have assumed the risk of its occurrence. Foreseeability refers to the fact that the event was anticipated or should have been anticipated and that since nothing was done to prevent the risk of loss, it was assumed. A party may assume the risk impliedly, as stated above, or expressly, if provided for in the contract.

There is a trend to equate impossibility with impracticability. The requirements of impracticability are as follows: a contingency, which is unforeseen, must have occurred; the risk of the unforeseen occurrence must not have been allocated to either party by agreement or custom; and the occurrence of the contingency must have rendered performance commercially impracticable. Commercially impracticable means performance can only be completed at a really excessive and unreasonable cost.

Northern Corporation v. Chugach Electric Association
518 P.2d 76, *rehearing*, 523 P.2d 1243 (Alaska) 1974

Northern sued Chugach to recover the costs they incurred in attempting to complete the contract. They allege that the contract is impossible to perform and that their damages stem from the defendant's insistence that they perform.

Northern entered into a contract with Chugach to repair the Cooper Lake Dam, using rock from a designated quarry, in August 1966. After testing the rock, both parties agreed that it was not suitable and they chose a new sight at the opposite end of Cooper Lake. It was contemplated by the parties that the rock would be transported by truck when the lake froze to a sufficient depth. Northern complained of unsafe conditions, but Chugach insisted on performance. In March 1967, Northern loaded two trucks and sent them across the lake. The ice broke, causing the loss of the trucks and the death of the drivers. Northern suspended all operations.

The issue is whether the condition of the lake made performance under the contract impossible, and whether Northern had an obligation to find other means of transporting the rock to the dam site.

The court decided that the parties were discharged from performance because of impossibility. The concept of impossibility is now equated with commercial impracticability—that which can only be done at excessive and unreasonable costs. Chugach's argument that an alternate means of performance should have been used is without merit because the only method of transportation contemplated by the parties was by truck. Furthermore, alternate performance would be commercially impracticable.

In regard to damages, the court held that Northern may recover the additional costs incurred after Chugach insisted on performance unless Northern knew or should have known that transporting the rocks in trucks across the ice was impossible. Judgment for Northern Corporation.

RELEASE

Parties may release each other from their duties to perform by mutual agreement. One party may release the other party from his or her obligation to continue performance after it has been partially or substantially completed. A party's right to release another is part of the freedom to contract. The release must be supported by consideration, in writing, and signed by the releasing party. The UCC requires delivery of a signed writing, but it need not be supported by consideration. The form of a release may be as simple as writing "paid in full" on a check. This is illustrated by an accord and satisfaction, which is dealt with in Chapter 8, Consideration.

EXAMPLE | Robin Hood engaged in a marksmanship contest with the king's guard. Gilbert, the finest marksman of the guards, shot an arrow into the bullseye. Robin Hood also hit the bullseye, and split Gilbert's arrow in two. King Richard the Lionhearted was amazed at Robin Hood's proficiency and offered to release him from all the debts he owed the kingdom if he would serve in the palace guard for one year. Robin Hood accepted and King Richard signed a written release form. Later, Richard's brother, John, overtook the throne and called Robin to account for his debts. Robin argued that he was released from all his debts and produced the release form. Is this a good defense? Yes! A written release signed by King Richard in return for Robin's consideration—agreeing to work in the palace guard for one year—is valid.

UNCONSCIONABILITY

Unconscionability is involved in those contracts which are so unduly harsh or one-sided as to constitute a violation of conscience. Unconscionable contracts usually involve parties of unequal bargaining strength, where the stronger parties use this to their advantage. This is evident in many consumer contracts between individuals and large corporations where the corporations are providing goods or services to individuals. Unconscionable contracts are voidable contracts. They are against public policy and are specifically in violation of the UCC in respect to contracts involving the sale of goods. The victimized party has the special right to rescind the contract.

EXAMPLE Injun Jo employs Tom Sawyer, Huckleberry Finn, and Becky Thatcher to work as his assistants in a cemetery. The contract provides that Injun Jo shall have the authority to determine how long they work each day, what work they do, and the duration of the contract. Another clause in the contract provides that if Tom, Huck, and Becky abrogate the contract, they must return to Injun Jo all monies paid to that point. After two months of digging graves twelve hours a day, Tom, Huck, and Becky are at the point of exhaustion. They decide to cancel the contract and decide to raise the defense of unconscionability if Injun Jo sues them for a return of the money already paid. Will this be a successful defense? Yes! This contract is definitely unconscionable. It is truly harsh and one-sided.

MISTAKE

Mistake is a belief which is not in accordance with the actual facts. Mistakes must be material, not incidental. This means if not for the mistake, the contract would not have been entered into. Parties may have a mistaken belief as to the facts, or may make a mistake in judgment as to the value of the contract. There is generally no relief afforded to a party who makes a mistake in judgment as to value. Otherwise, contracts would not be binding if everytime a person made a bad deal he or she could rescind the contract claiming mistake. However, where a factual mistake is made, parties may be allowed to rescind the contract. This depends on whether there is a mutual mistake or a mistake made by only one party.

Mutual mistakes occur when both parties erroneously believe the contract can be performed as agreed, or where the actual identity of the subject matter is mistaken by both parties. The contract will be cancelled if a mutual mistake occurs. Since both parties did not actually agree on what they were contracting for, the court will not bind them to the contract. They will be returned to the position they were in before the contract came about. Reformation is available as an alternative to rescission in cases of typographical mistakes in a written contract where the error is reasonably clear to both parties.

When one party enters into a contract with a mistaken belief about certain material facts, that party will not be allowed to rescind or reform the contract unless the other party has committed fraud, or unless the other party knew, or should have known, of the mistake. A party should have known of the mistake in cases where there is a noticeable discrepancy between what the mistaken party promises, and what is promised by others who have knowledge of the actual facts. The question is who should suffer for the mistake. If the mistaken party is forced to perform, he or she will suffer. If the mistaken party is excused, the other party will suffer. Since one party is going to suffer, the burden of loss falls upon the party who made the mistake. This reinforces the precept of exercising due care when entering into a contract. A person can exercise due care by examining all the facts and by making sure they are what they seem to be. This will help avoid mistakes of negligence.

EXAMPLE | Harrison Whitney is a security analyst at Merrill Lynch. He is very dedicated to his work. On the morning of May 24, while he is diligently analyzing a new issue on the Big Board, his wife telephones to remind him to leave the office on time because she has a special dinner planned for him. He hangs up and begins to wonder why she would have a special dinner on the twenty-fourth of May. Then he suddenly remembers it's her birthday. On his lunch hour, he goes to the jeweler just off Wall Street to buy his wife a birthstone ring. There is a discrete sign which says, "All Sales Final." He tells the clerk, who was newly hired, "My wife's birthday is today; I wish to purchase a sapphire birthstone ring." The clerk, believing sapphire was the correct birthstone, sold Whitney the ring. When Whitney presents the gift to his wife, to his astonishment, she throws it at him crying, "My birthstone is an emerald! How could you be so thoughtless? I've said I don't like sapphires at all." Whitney attempts to return the ring to the jewelers. They claim it was a final sale. Has he any recourse? Yes! Both Whitney and the clerk made a mutual mistake of fact concerning the proper birthstone for May. The contract may be rescinded. If Whitney had requested the sapphire ring without asking the clerk whether it was the birthstone for May, then it would have been a unilateral mistake and Whitney would be without recourse.

REVIEW QUESTIONS

1. Define duress, undue influence, misrepresentation, fraud, condition precedent, condition subsequent, condition concurrent, impossibility, and mistake.

2. List and explain each of the contractual defenses.

3. In 1960, Hoeflich purchased a drug prescribed by his doctor. The drug had side effects which resulted in skin irritation, hair loss, and cataracts. Hoeflich suffered from these side effects for four years. Two years after this, in 1966, Hoeflich discovered that the cause of the problem was related to the prescription drug he had taken in 1960. He brought an action for breach of contract against the manufacturer of the drug, Merrell Company. Is he entitled to damages? Hoeflich v. William S. Merrell Co., 288 F. Supp. 659 (E.D. Pa. 1968).

4. Christy entered into a contract with Pilkinton to purchase her house for $30,000. The Christys were planning to pay for the house with profits obtained from their used-car business. However, due to a subsequent decline in their business, they were unable to come up with the cash. The Christys contend that they should be excused from performance because it is impossible for them to pay. What result? Christy v. Pilkinton, 224 Ark. 407, 273 S.W.2d 533 (1954).

5. The Transatlantic Financing Corporation entered into a contract with the U.S. government to haul cargo from the U.S. to a port in Iran. The usual route was through the Suez Canal. As a result of an international crisis, the canal was closed and it was necessary for Transatlantic to go around Africa to get to the destination. It then sued for additional compensation, because of the longer route. The suit was based on the premise that Transatlantic had been discharged from its obligation because of impossibility. What result? Transatlantic Financing Corp. v. U.S., 363 F2d 312 (D.C. Cir. 1966).

6. Whipp entered into a contract with Iverson, the owner of an auto repair company which also sold Oldsmobiles and Ramblers. Iverson falsely represented to Whipp that the sale of the business included the Oldsmobile franchise. This induced Whipp to sign the contract. Subsequently, Oldsmobile refused to transfer the franchise to Whipp. Whipp returned possession of the auto repair business and brought an action for rescission. What result? Whipp v. Iverson, 43 Wis.2d 166, 168 N.W.2d 201 (1969).

7. Wirth, a real estate owner, signed a contract giving Clarkson, a real estate broker, an exclusive listing on his property. Through Clarkson, the Grimes brothers contracted with Wirth to buy the property subject to the following conditions: (1) Buyer must sell certain properties prior to the closing of this contract, and (2) closing of this contract of sale must take place prior to October 1. Neither condition was satisfied. Six months later, the Grimes brothers purchased Wirth's property without going through Clarkson. Clarkson sued Wirth for the commission. Is he entitled to it? Clarkson v. Wirth, 4 Wash. App. 401, 481 P.2d 920 (1971).

8. Giller and Shurtleff were both employees of the Thorn Tool Company. Shurtleff was Giller's foreman. They entered into a joint venture on their own to construct an apartment house. A bank loaned them the money in return for their signed promissory note for $170,000. After all but $60,000 had been paid, Giller and Shurtleff agreed to dissolve the joint venture with Giller receiving the assets and assuming the debt. The bank requested payment of the $60,000 from Shurtleff. He paid the bank and then asked Giller to sign a note for more than $60,000 with 9 percent interest—an unusually high rate at the time. He threatened to have Giller fired from his job, at a time when he knew Giller's daughter was hospitalized. Giller's employment contract contained a covenant not to compete for two years, so Giller would have been unable to open his own business if he was fired. Giller signed the note but refused to pay. What result? Shurtleff v. Giller, 527 S.W.2d 214 (Tex. Civ. App. 1975).

9. Raffles sold Wichelhaus cotton which he agreed to ship on the *Peerless*. No date was mentioned. Wichelhaus waited at the pier in October, when the *Peerless* arrived, but there was no cotton. In December, the cotton arrived on another ship also called the *Peerless*. Wichelhaus refused to accept the goods, claiming he needed them in October. What result? Raffles v. Wichelhaus and Another, 2 H. & C. 908 (1864).

10. Villella maintained a brokerage account with First Regional Securities. Villella's son, having authority to trade for his father, sold 2,000 shares of General Energy Corporation of Delaware when he saw it selling at $7 per share. Later, it was discovered that his father owned General Energy Corporation of *Arizona*, a stock not publicly traded. Since the shares were not in Villella's account, the brokerage had to buy 2,000 shares to cover the sale. Villella refused to pay for the 2,000 shares. What result? First Regional Securities, Inc. v. Villella, 84 Misc.2d 790, 377 N.Y.S.2d 424 (Civ. Ct. N.Y. 1975).

15

SALES: TITLE
AND WARRANTIES

INTRODUCTION

Article 2 of the Uniform Commercial Code applies to sales. Sales is the codification of contract law with respect to the sale of goods. It is one of the four types of contracts:

> Real property contracts
> Sales contracts
> Personal service contracts
> Special contracts

Since the sale of goods is a contract, the elements of a contract must be present for the sale to be valid.

> Purpose (lawful)
> Agreement
> Legal capacity
> Act (promise to perform)
> Consideration
> Executed in proper form

The law of contracts is applicable to sales except for those areas which have been changed by the UCC. The previous section of this book deals with contract law. In the individual chapters of that section, references are made to the changes brought about by the UCC with respect to contracts for the sale of goods. Those chapters in conjunction with these, form an overall picture of the law of sales.

A sale consists of the passing of title to goods from a seller to a buyer, for consideration. Goods are all existing movable things which have been identified to the contract of sale. An obligation to act in good faith is imposed on every party to a commercial transaction. *Commercial transaction* is a broad term encompassing contracts for the sale of goods as well as the special contracts covered by the other articles of the UCC.

Good faith means honesty in fact; it requires a person to act in an honest manner when entering, performing, or enforcing a commercial transaction. With regard to merchants, the obligation of good faith requires honesty in fact plus the adherence to the reasonable commercial standards of fair dealing prevalent in the marketplace. A merchant is a person who regularly deals in a certain kind of goods or one who proclaims that he or she possesses a skill or knowledge peculiar to a certain kind of goods. This does not refer to a person making an isolated sale of goods. Goods are merchantable when they can pass without objection in the trade under the description of the contract.

DOCTRINE OF CAVEAT EMPTOR

The doctrine of caveat emptor, "Let the buyer beware," has been minimized over the past twenty years with the development of consumer rights. This chapter on warranties illustrates the rights consumers have when they purchase a product. These rights have even been extended to give consumers the right to sue for property damages or personal injuries caused by defective products. Chapter 17—Sales: Products Liability—is devoted to this topic. It is important for consumers to be aware of the warranties imposed by law and the way the law has changed from strict adherence to the doctrine of caveat emptor. Now it is the obligation of the sellers to market a product to which they have good title and which will be fit for the use for which it was intended.

TITLE

Title is the right to ownership of property. In sales, it is evidence of the right a buyer or a seller has to the possession of goods. Title passes from the seller to the buyer at the time and place the seller physically delivers the goods to the buyer in accordance with the contract. Physical delivery may occur when the buyer picks up the goods at the seller's place of business or when the seller delivers the goods to a particular destination. If the seller is required to ship the goods, title passes to the buyer at the time and place shipment is made. The goods must be identified to the contract before title may pass.

Identification is the setting aside of goods for the purchaser. Identification occurs in a contract for existing goods when the contract is made; in a contract for future goods when the goods are shipped; and in a contract for crops when the crops are planted. When goods are identified to the contract, the buyer obtains an insurable interest in the goods. An insurable interest is the right of a person to insure the goods because of his or her real and substantial interest in those goods. Even though the buyer has an insurable interest in the goods after signing the contract, buyers will usually request that the insurance become effective when the goods are in their possession.

An insurable interest remains with the seller as long as the seller has title to the goods, or a security interest in the goods. Therefore, it is possible for both the buyer and the seller to have an insurable interest in the same goods between the time the goods are identified to the contract, and the time title to the goods passes, or the security interest in the goods is satisfied. A security interest is the interest the seller (creditor) has in goods which are transferred to the buyer (debtor) in a credit sale. This security interest secures the obligation of the buyer to pay for the goods; that is, the goods act as collateral for the credit extended.

EXAMPLE On May 28, Paul Michaels walked into an art gallery and informed the proprietor, Vincent Vandermere, that he would like to buy a Renoir. Vandermere showed him his collection of Renoir paintings. Michaels selected a portrait of a girl, priced at $400,000. He made a down payment of $200,000 and promised to pay the remainder in monthly installments. He told Vandermere that he was flying to Paris for the month of June and when he returned he would pick up the painting. Before he departed for Paris, Michaels insured the painting with the policy to commence on July 1, the day of his return. Do both parties have an insurable interest in the goods on May 28? Yes! This is true even though Michaels chose not to insure the painting until he took possession of it. When will Vandermere's insurable interest expire? Since this is a credit sale involving installment payments, Vandermere has a security interest in the painting up until the last payment is made. Vandermere's insurable interest will expire when the security interest is satisfied.

DOCTRINE OF ENTRUSTING

The Doctrine of Entrusting is one in which a merchant who deals in goods of that particular kind is endowed with the power to transfer title to goods received from the original owner for storage, repairs, or safekeeping. The transfer must be made to a good-faith purchaser for value. The doctrine of entrusting applies even where the merchant obtained the goods by larceny or sold them with that intent.

The reason for the doctrine is to insure that good-faith purchasers will not be inhibited from buying from merchants out of fear that the goods may have been stolen. This preserves the smooth flow of business. A good-faith purchaser is a person who buys for value in the ordinary course of business without knowledge that the goods are stolen or that any contractual defenses exist.

EXAMPLE Paul Monroe brought one of his paintings to Thomas Brolin, an art dealer, to have a new frame constructed for it. He was told to come back in three weeks. In the meantime, Brolin sold the painting to Barbara Fisher for $50,000, a reasonable price. Monroe returned to find the painting gone. Can Monroe recover his painting? No! Since, Thomas Brolin is a merchant who regularly deals in the sale of art, he may pass title to goods entrusted to him to Barbara Fisher, as long as Barbara is a good-faith purchaser who buys for value in the ordinary course of business. Monroe's only recourse would be to sue Thomas Brolin for the value of the painting.

WARRANTIES: DEFINED

A warranty is a guarantee; an assurance that the facts, as stated, are true. The purpose of a warranty is to establish the seller's liability for the marketability, quality, and suitability of the goods sold. This liability may be assumed by the seller through the making of an express warranty, or may be imposed on the seller by law through one of the implied warranties set forth in the UCC. The following warranties exist in all contracts for the sale of goods unless properly disclaimed:

Warranty of merchantability
Warranty of fitness for a particular purpose
Express warranties
Warranty against encumbrances
Warranty of title

WARRANTY OF MERCHANTABILITY

The warranty of merchantability is an implied warranty given only by merchants in contracts for the sale of goods. The warranty extends to food and drink served by merchants to be consumed on their premises or elsewhere. A merchant impliedly warrants that the goods are merchantable. Goods are merchantable when they are fit for the ordinary use for which they are intended. They must be able to pass without objection in the trade. This means they must be of average quality in comparison to that which is generally accepted in the trade under the description of the contract. If the goods are sold in units, each unit must be of the same kind, quality, and quantity as the rest. If the goods require packaging and labeling, then the packaging must be done in an adequate manner to avoid tampering, as in the famous Tylenol case, spoilage, or infestation; and the labeling must conform to the factual statements and promises made by the seller.

Webster v. Blue Ship Tea Room
347 Mass. 421, 198 N.E.2d 309 (1964)

Webster brought an action based on breach of implied warranty of merchantability, for injuries she sustained while eating a bowl of fish chowder.

On Saturday, April 25, 1959, Webster entered a quaint restaurant called the Blue Ship Tea Room, with her sister and her aunt. They were seated at a table and supplied with menus. Webster ordered a cup of fish chowder to accompany her crabmeat salad. After eating a few spoonfuls of chowder, she felt something lodge in her throat that prevented her from swallowing.

She was rushed to Massachusetts General Hospital, where a fish bone was discovered in her throat and removed.

The court stated that the issue is whether "a fish bone lurking in a fish chowder . . . constitutes a breach of implied warranty" of merchantability.

The judge charged the jury, "But the bone of contention here—I don't mean that for a pun—but was this fish bone a foreign substance that made the fish chowder unwholesome or not fit to be eaten?"

The court held

> . . . It is not too much to say that a person sitting down in New England to consume a good New England fish chowder embarks on a gustatory adventure which may entail the removal of some fish bones from his bowl as he proceeds. We are not inclined to tamper with age old recipes . . . Certain Massachusetts cooks might cavil at the ingredients contained in the chowder in this case in that it lacked the heartening lift of salt pork. In any event, we consider that the joys of life in New England include the ready availability of fresh fish chowder. We should be prepared to cope with the hazards of fish bones, the occasional presence of which in chowders is, it seems to us, to be anticipated, and which, in the light of a hallowed tradition, do not impair their fitness or merchantability.

Webster was not entitled to recover any damages for the injuries sustained to her throat. Judgment for the Blue Ship Tea Room.

A person who makes an isolated sale of goods does not impliedly warrant that the goods are merchantable because such a person is not considered a merchant. However, the person selling the goods may make an express warranty of merchantability, if he or she states that the goods are guaranteed.

EXAMPLE After the death of Charles Rubens, his widow, Margaret, sold his snowplow, power tools, and gardening equipment to a neighbor, Anthony Lerman. She assured him the items were of the very finest quality. Lerman used the tools and gardening equipment and then complained that many of them did not function properly. He sued her for breach of warranty in that she sold him goods that were not merchantable. Margaret Rubens protested that she was not a merchant. What result? In an isolated sale, a nonmerchant makes no implied warranty of merchantability unless expressly stated. Margaret Rubens's statement that the goods were of the finest quality constitutes an express warranty of merchantability, which she violated.

The implied warranty of merchantability may be excluded only by using the word "merchantability" in the disclaimer or by stating the sale of the goods to be "as is."

Henningsen v. Bloomfield Motors, Inc.
32 N.J. 358, 161 A.2d 69 (1960)

Henningsen sued Bloomfield Motors and Chrysler Corporation based on breach of warranty for injuries to his wife caused by a defect in the new Plymouth he purchased from them. The defendants contend that they are not liable because of a disclaimer provision in the contract.

On May 7, Henningsen purchased the car for his wife as a Mother's Day present. Two days later, it was delivered. The Henningsens used the car for ten days without any signs of difficulty. On May 19, Mrs. Henningsen drove to Asbury

Park when, she stated, it "felt as if something cracked." The car swerved sharply to the right, hit a brick wall, and was totally wrecked.

The standardized contract contained a provision which stated that there were no express or implied warranties made by either the dealer or the manufacturer concerning the vehicle, its chassis, or parts except that they are free of defects in material and workmanship. The warranty limited the obligation of Bloomfield Motors and Chrysler to replacement of parts within the first ninety days or 4,000 miles, whichever comes first.

The issue is whether their disclaimer of the implied warranty of merchantability is effective.

The court held, ". . . when a manufacturer puts a new automobile in the stream of trade and promotes its purchase by the public, an implied warranty that it is reasonably suitable for use as such accompanies it into the hands of the ultimate purchaser." The court concluded that the disclaimer of the warranty of merchantability and the elimination of all other responsibility, save for the replacement of defective parts by Bloomfield Motors and Chrysler, is void because it violates public policy. Mrs. Henningsen may recover for the injuries she sustained as a result of the defective automobile. Judgment for Henningsen.

WARRANTY OF FITNESS FOR A PARTICULAR PURPOSE

The warranty of fitness for a particular use arises when the seller has reason to know that the buyer is relying upon his or her expertise or judgment in selecting or furnishing goods suitable to the buyer's particular purpose. This warranty is implied from the facts and applies to both merchants and nonmerchants. The buyer must prove the seller's expertise and the buyer's own reliance on it. If the buyer insists on a particular brand name, no reliance is placed on the seller's expertise or judgment. However, the warranty does apply to a brand name purchased by the buyer on the seller's recommendation.

EXAMPLE | Christopher Larchmont was planning to go on a two-week ski vacation to the Swiss Alps. Before the trip, he went to Joe Cool's Ski and Camera Shop to purchase equipment. He advised Joe Cool, the store owner, that he wanted a camera that could take pictures in the subfreezing weather. Joe Cool recommended an expensive Japanese model. Larchmont also asked Joe Cool to select a pair of skis of the proper length for him and explained that he was a novice. Joe Cool was out of the shorter length of skis that are recommended for beginners, so he sold him a long pair. Christopher Larchmont thanked Joe Cool for his help and bid him farewell. During his first two days on the Alps, he shot two rolls of film which, because of the extreme cold, could never be developed. On the third day, he was still trying to negotiate the long skis when the tips crossed, sending him head over heels. He suffered severe head and back injuries as a result. Has Larchmont any recourse? Yes! Larchmont may sue Joe Cool, the store owner, but not the manufacturer of the skis or the camera. The manufacturers are not liable because the goods were merchantable. They were fit for the ordinary use for which they were intended. However, they were not fit for the particular purpose that Larchmont intended. He had informed Joe Cool of his special needs and relied on Joe's selection.

Larchmont was justified in doing so because Joe was a merchant who regularly dealt in cameras and skis. Joe will be liable for the purchase price of the camera and skis, as well as for the injuries caused by his recommending improper skis.

The warranty of fitness for a particular purpose may be modified or excluded only by conspicuous language in writing; for example, "There are no warranties which extend beyond the description of the face hereof," or "All goods are sold 'as is'." The disclaimer may be printed on a sales slip or in a formal contract.

EXPRESS WARRANTIES

Express warranties are created through (1) any factual statements or promises made by the seller about the goods; (2) any description of the goods made by the seller; or (3) any samples or models exhibited by the seller during the contract negotiations which become part of the basis of the contract. There is no need to prove reliance on the factual statements and promises made by the seller during the contract negotiations, because these are looked upon as a description of the goods. A description of the goods encompasses more than just words. It includes blueprints and other technical diagrams, specifications, and plans. A sample is a selection of goods indiscriminately drawn from the bulk of goods identified to the contract, while a model is an imitation or copy offered for inspection when the actual goods are not available.

The seller may not have intended to make any warranties, but express warranties will be created by any of the previously mentioned statements, promises, descriptions, samples, or models introduced by the seller during the contract negotiations, unless a good reason is shown to the contrary. No formal language involving the words "warranty" or "guarantee" is required, but statements made by the seller concerning his or her opinion of the quality of the goods or their value are looked upon as mere puffing and do not create an express warranty. Once an express warranty is created, it may not be limited or negated.

EXAMPLE On seeing the portrait of Whistler's mother, Muriel Astor approached the artist and asked if he would do a portrait of her. After considerable dickering over the price, Whistler agreed to do the painting for $250,000 and guaranteed Muriel Astor's approval. Five sittings were completed and Muriel Astor cried "What is this? You have made me look older than your mother." She refused to continue the sittings. Whistler, steaming mad, sued Muriel Astor for the full price of the portrait. What result? Whistler has not a leg to stand on because he expressly guaranteed her approval and could not earn it.

WARRANTY AGAINST ENCUMBRANCES

The warranty against encumbrances implies that the goods shall be delivered to the buyer free of any security interest or other lien of which the buyer has no knowledge at the time the contract is made. This warranty may be modified or excluded only by specific language or if the circumstances give the buyer reason to know that a security interest or other encumbrance or lien exists against the property.

EXAMPLE | Henri Matisse purchased a copy of the enormous sculpture, *The Thinker*, for $750,000 from Auguste Rodin. Matisse made a $250,000 down payment with Rodin, who retained a security interest in the sculpture for the balance. Matisse sells the statue to Picasso for $800,000, guaranteeing it to be free of encumbrances. To his astonishment, Picasso learns that Rodin has a security interest in *The Thinker* and sues Matisse for breach of warranty. What result? Matisse has breached the implied warranty against encumbrances by not acknowledging the existence of Rodin's security interest in the sculpture.

WARRANTY OF TITLE

This warranty guarantees that the seller has clear title to the goods he or she has contracted to transfer to the buyer. The warranty of good title is implied in all contracts for the sale of goods and cannot be excluded by the phrase "as is." This is to insure that the buyer's expectations are fulfilled, and to protect buyers against lawsuits questioning the validity of the title. A buyer acquires no better title than that which he or she receives from the seller. Title does not pass through a thief with the exception of the doctrine of entrusting. This warranty may be modified or excluded only by specific language or circumstances which apprise the buyer of the fact that the seller does not have good title to the goods.

EXAMPLE | Roy Barr sold da Vinci's portrait *Mona Lisa* to the Louvre in Paris for $1.5 million. He guaranteed he had clear title to the painting. Subsequently, it was proven that Roy Barr had stolen the painting from George Raphaelson, the true owner of the painting. The Louvre sued Barr for breach of warranty of title. What result? The Louvre returned the painting to Raphaelson and recovered the $1.5 million from Barr for breach of warranty of title.

BREACH OF WARRANTY

An action for breach of warranty may be brought by the buyer of the goods on the basis of either an express warranty made by the seller, or one of the implied warranties the UCC imposes on the seller. A breach may occur because the seller did not have proper title to the goods that were sold; because there was a lien or other encumbrance against the goods; because the goods were not merchantable; or because the goods were not fit for the particular purpose requested. A breach will give the buyer the right to sue for a remedy. Buyer's remedies will be discussed in Chapter 18. A buyer who has not sustained any damages will be permitted to cancel the contract by returning the goods and regaining his or her purchase price. If property damage resulted from the use of the goods, then the buyer may sue for consequential damages. A buyer who was forced to cover by purchasing the goods elsewhere will be entitled to the difference between the contract price and the cover price. If personal injury results from the use of the product, the person injured—who may even be someone other than the buyer—has a right to sue based on breach of warranty, negligence, or strict products liability. Although we have discussed personal injury caused by breach of warranty in this chapter (the cases of *Webster v. Blue Ship Tea Room* and *Henningsen v. Bloomfield Motors*), Chapter 17, Products

Liability, will zero in on all the remedies available to a person who is injured by a product, including breach of warranty.

REVIEW QUESTIONS

1. Define sales, goods, commercial transaction, good faith, merchant, merchantable, title, identification, insurable interest, and warranty.

2. List and explain the various types of warranties.

3. Medico Leasing Company transferred possession of an automobile they owned to a used-car dealer named Smith in return for a percentage of the sale. Smith sold the car to Wessell Buick Company, representing that he was the true owner. Smith never paid Medico Leasing the money he owed them. Subsequently, Wessell Buick resold the car to Country Cousins Motors. W. C. and Doreen Carter purchased the car from Country Cousins Motors. Did Smith have good title to convey the car to Wessell Buick and is Medico Leasing precluded from regaining possession of the car? Medico Leasing Company v. Smith, 457 P.2d 548 (Okla.) 1969.

4. Honeycutt was in the business of selling boats. He sold a new boat, motor, and trailer to a person who identified himself as Willis, for a price of over $6,000. Willis took possession of the boat and paid for it with a check, which was later dishonored. Six months later, Lane bought the same boat from a man who identified himself as Garrett, for a mere $2,500. Garrett represented to Lane that he was selling the boat for someone else. When Lane delivered the money, Garrett signed the alleged owner's name on a document which he suggested was the title. The document was the certificate of number, not the certificate of title. Honeycutt brought an action against Lane to reclaim the boat. Does Lane qualify as a good-faith purchaser? Lane v. Honeycutt, 14 N.C. App. 436, 188 S.E.2d 604 (1972).

5. Catania was looking to buy paint for the exterior of his stucco home. He went into a paint store and informed Brown, the proprietor, of his needs. Brown recommended "Pierce's Shingle and Shake" paint and advised Catania how to prepare the exterior and how to mix the paint to the right consistency using thinner. Catania followed Brown's instructions, but the paint blistered and peeled. Catania sued Brown for breach of warranty. What result? Catania v. Brown, 4 Conn. Cir. 344, 231 A.2d 668 (1967).

6. Connelly made repairs on a trailer, at the request of the purported owner. After the repairs were completed, the trailer was never claimed. Connelly brought a foreclosure action in order to receive payment for the repairs he made. The trailer was auctioned at a judicial sale with the proceeds going to pay for the repair bill. Connelly bought the trailer at that sale and subsequently sold it to Marvin. Thereafter, it was discovered that the vehicle was stolen. Neither one of the parties had known this. Marvin sued Connelly for breach of warranty of title. Did Connelly have good title to the trailer? Marvin v. Connelly, 272 S.C. 425, 252 S.E.2d 562 (1979).

7. V-M Corporation, a manufacturer of phonographs, contracted with Massachusetts Gas & Electric Light Supply Corporation, a distributor, to deliver a reasonable inventory of phonographs. In the past, the distributor normally required 100 phonographs each month. The contract contained a thirty-day cancellation clause. The manufacturer exercised its option and cancelled the contract. Before cancellation, the distributor placed a large order sufficient to meet its needs for the next six months. V-M refused to fill the order because it was unreasonably high. Did the distributor act in good faith when placing the order? Massachusetts Gas & Electric Light Supply Corp. v. V-M Corp., 387 F.2d 605 (1st Cir. 1967).

16

SALES: PERFORMANCE AND RISK OF LOSS

INTRODUCTION

Both parties have a general obligation to act in accordance with the contract. The seller has a duty to transfer title to the goods and to deliver them to the buyer; the buyer has a duty to accept the goods delivered and to pay for them.

Document of title is a document that evidences ownership of goods. It is used in the regular course of business to prove that the person presenting the document of title is entitled to possession and ownership of the goods it covers. Documents of title include bills of lading, warehouse receipts, and orders for delivery of goods. These documents may also be transferred by sale, exchange, or gift.

Bill of lading is a document of title evidencing the receipt of goods for shipment. It is issued by a common carrier. A common carrier is a company engaged in the business of transporting goods. A negotiable bill of lading specifies that delivery must be made to either the person named in the bill of lading or to the person in possession of the bill of lading, who is commonly known as the bearer. A negotiable bill of lading can be transferred by sale, gift, or exchange. A bill of lading in any other form is nonnegotiable. A nonnegotiable, or straight, bill of lading may not be transferred.

Warehouse receipt is a document of title issued by a warehouseman upon receipt of goods. A warehouseman is a person who is engaged in the business of storing goods.

Bailment is a contract to deliver goods or to hold them for safekeeping in return for a fee. A bailee is the person to whom they have been entrusted. The bailee will deliver the goods to the buyer upon the buyer's presentation of a document of title.

Documents of title are required only where: (1) the seller and purchaser expressly provide for them in the contract of sale or (2) the circumstances of the case or usage of trade dictate that the documents of title are necessary. A further discussion of bailees, common carriers, and warehousemen may be found in Chapter 25, Bailments.

TENDER OF DELIVERY

Tender is the seller's notice to the buyer of willingness and ability to perform. This must be followed by the actual performance which consists of delivery of the goods. The buyer need not pay if tender of delivery is not made. When tender is made, the buyer must accept the goods, if they conform to the contract, and pay for them; otherwise the buyer will have breached the contract.

Tender of delivery may be made when the seller holds conforming goods for the buyer and gives the buyer notice that he or she may take delivery. The tender of delivery must be made at a reasonable hour and the buyer must be given adequate time to take possession of the goods. It is the buyer's obligation to furnish sufficient facilities to store the goods upon receipt; this does not affect the seller's tender.

EXAMPLE | Bob Smallwood, a Texas gentleman, is a rancher living in Dallas. He owns several cattle farms throughout the state. All deliveries are made through the Dallas ranch. On March 30, he enters into a contract to sell 1,500 head of cattle to John Long. On April 3, Bob Smallwood notifies John Long that the cattle are at his Dallas ranch waiting to be picked up. John arrives and picks up the cattle the very next day. Has proper tender of delivery been made? Yes!

In destination contracts, the seller must tender the appropriate document of title in correct form to the buyer. A negotiable document of title is one in bearer form. The bailee must transfer the goods covered by the document of title to any person who presents it. A negotiable document of title may also be assigned. A nonnegotiable document of title is payable to only the person named on the document. It may not be assigned. A nonnegotiable document of title or a written direction to the bailee to make delivery will suffice as tender unless the buyer objects. If the bailee refuses to honor either the document or the direction, tender has not been made.

EXAMPLE | Rose Leigh is working as a stripper in the Silver Spoon Saloon on the Barbary Coast in San Francisco. She contracts with La Boudoir, Madame Celeste's lingerie shop in Crystal City, Colorado, to furnish her with twelve stunning costumes with "lots of lace and space." Madame Celeste ships the goods via the Union Pacific Railroad, with written instructions directing the carrier to deliver the goods to Rose Leigh on the Barbary Coast. When the goods arrive, the carrier refuses to deliver them to Rose Leigh. Has tender of delivery been made? No! The carrier refused to honor the written instructions given by Madame Celeste.

The buyer has a right to reject a tender of delivery which fails to conform to the contract. The seller may cure an improper tender or delivery which is rejected because the goods are nonconforming. The seller must notify the buyer of his or her intention to deliver conforming goods and make delivery before the expiration of the time for performance.

In the previous example, suppose the contract called for delivery on or before July 17. Rose Leigh receives the shipment on July 11 but rejects the costumes because there is too much space and not enough lace. Madame Celeste informs Rose that she will send her another shipment of costumes with more lace and less space. The shipment arrives on July 15, and this shipment conforms to the contract. Is Rose bound to accept this shipment? Yes! Since the expiration date has not expired, Madame Celeste must be afforded the chance to cure the nonconformity. She accomplished this by notifying Rose of her intention to cure and by delivering conforming goods before July 17.

The risk of loss remains on the seller until a cure of either the goods or the document of title is made. The seller may not shift the risk of loss until his or her performance conforms to the contract. If the seller had reasonable grounds to believe the original tender would be accepted, the seller may be afforded a reasonable time beyond the expiration date for performance to cure the nonconformity. A determination as to whether the seller had reasonable grounds to believe that the tender would be accepted can be made from prior course of dealing or from the circumstances surrounding the contract.

In the ongoing tale of Rose Leigh and Madame Celeste, suppose Madame Celeste had made annual deliveries of costumes to Rose for the last five years. Rose accepted the delivery each time, relying on Madame Celeste's taste in selection. This time, Madame Celeste cannot cure the nonconformity by July 17. What result? Since Madame Celeste had reasonable grounds to believe that her tendered delivery would be accepted, she will be allowed a reasonable time beyond the expiration date to cure the nonconformity.

TENDER OF PAYMENT

Tender of payment must be made before the seller is required to deliver the goods, unless the contract provides that delivery is to be made first, as in the majority of cases with credit sales. Tender of payment may be made in any ordinary business manner. If the payment is made by check and, upon presentment of the check to a bank, it is dishonored, then tender of payment has not been made.

A buyer who wishes to purchase goods on credit is often required to secure a letter of credit from a bank which is willing to act as a surety and assume the risk of nonpayment by the buyer. The buyer must then deliver the letter of credit to the seller.

Diamond Jim Brady, a big spender, wants to purchase a diamond necklace from Tiffany's for his new girlfriend, Darlin' Lil. The necklace costs $30,000 and Diamond Jim promises to pay for it in thirty equal installments. Tiffany's asks Diamond Jim to obtain a letter of credit from his bank, guaranteeing the extension of credit. Diamond Jim secures the letter of credit from the Franklin Savings Bank. Will Darlin' Lil now become Diamond

Lil? Yes! By all means! The bank's issuance of a letter of credit means it will honor all checks drafted by Diamond Jim in regard to the installment payments.

INSPECTION OF GOODS

The buyer has a right, before payment or acceptance, to inspect the goods at a reasonable place and time, and in a reasonable manner to discover any defects which do not appear on the surface. When the seller is sending the goods to the buyer, the buyer may inspect them after arrival. If the contract requires payment before inspection, the buyer must pay, but later may revoke acceptance if the goods are nonconforming. The buyer has the responsibility of paying for the inspection. If the goods are found to be nonconforming, the buyer may be reimbursed for his or her inspection expenses.

EXAMPLE | Little Joe from Kokomo agrees to purchase 100 pounds of Boston Baked Beans for $200 from Boston Blackie, who is the proprietor of the Boston Beanery. Little Joe sends the money to Blackie, who in turn ships the beans to Kokomo. After the beans arrive, Little Joe tastes them and discovers they are actually jumping beans and not the baked beans he ordered. Now he is known as Jumpin' Joe from Kokomo. Has Jumpin' Joe any recourse? Yes! Even though Jumpin' Joe paid for and accepted the beans, his acceptance was conditioned on his right to inspect them after arrival. He may revoke his acceptance and recover his payment together with any incidental expenses incurred for the inspection.

When there is a dispute as to the quality of the goods after the buyer has paid for, inspected, and rejected them, each party has the right to inspect, test, and sample the goods to establish evidence for his or her case. The parties may agree to have an arbitrator inspect the goods to determine their condition and conformity, and the parties may also agree to be bound by the arbitrator's decision.

RISK OF LOSS

Risk of loss is the placement of the financial responsibility for lost, damaged, or destroyed goods. Actually, anyone who has an interest in the goods suffers by their destruction. A person having a security interest loses the right to exercise it as well as the right to resell or reclaim the goods on the buyer's default if the goods are destroyed. When the risk of loss falls on the buyer, he or she must pay for the goods without receiving them. When the risk of loss falls on the seller, he or she loses the right to the goods even though no payment is received.

SHIPMENT CONTRACTS

In a shipment contract, the risk of loss is transferred to the buyer when the goods are delivered by the seller to the carrier at the place of shipment. The expense of transferring the goods to the carrier is also borne by the seller. Shipment contracts are denoted by the following terms.

F.O.B.

The term *F.O.B.* means free on board. It requires the seller to deliver the goods to the F.O.B. point, the place of shipment or destination. It is usually written as F.O.B. Charlotte (place of shipment) or F.O.B. Milwaukee (place of destination). The seller must bear the expense and risk of transferring the goods into the possession of a carrier. The seller also has the responsibility for contracting with the carrier who will deliver the goods to the place of destination. In a shipment contract, the risk of loss is placed on the seller until the time the goods are transferred to the carrier at the place of shipment. After the goods are in the carrier's possession, the risk of loss transfers to the buyer.

In a destination contract, the seller must be responsible for the expense and risk of loss until the goods are delivered to the place of destination. The seller must notify the buyer when the goods arrive at the place of destination so that the buyer may take delivery of the goods. When the buyer takes delivery at the place of destination, it is only at this point that the risk of loss passes from the seller to the buyer.

Ninth Street East, Ltd. v. Harrison
5 Conn. Cir. 597, 259 A2d 772 (1968)

Ninth Street East brought an action to recover the purchase price for goods which were delivered to Harrison, were not accepted, and were later lost.

Ninth Street East, a Los Angeles manufacturer of men's clothing, agreed to supply The Rage, a Connecticut men's clothing store owned by Harrison, with the clothing that Harrison ordered, for $2,216. The goods were delivered to the Denver-Chicago Trucking Company who issued a bill of lading for the goods. Ninth Street East mailed the bill of lading together with four invoices covering the total sale, to Harrison. In Massachusetts, Denver-Chicago Trucking transferred the shipment to Old Colony Transportation Company, who delivered the clothing to Harrison's store. Harrison's wife refused delivery because Old Colony would not make delivery inside the store. Old Colony drove off with the clothing and after that, the clothing was never seen again.

The issue is whether the buyer made a rightful rejection of the goods and on whom the risk of loss will fall.

The court held that the buyer, Harrison, wrongfully rejected the goods and that the risk of loss remains on him. Ninth Street East may recover the entire purchase price for the clothing. Judgment for Ninth Street East.

F.A.S.

The term *F.A.S.* means free alongside ship. F.A.S. is a delivery term in a shipment contract which obligates the seller to transport goods to the place of shipment at the seller's expense and risk. The seller must make delivery on the dock alongside the ship. The name of the ship and the port must be specified.

Dapper Dan runs the Masquerade House in St. Louis. He contracts with the city of New Orleans to supply all the costumes for the annual Mardi Gras on Bourbon Street. The terms of the contract state: F.A.S. Kansas City on the *Riverboat Queen*. Dapper Dan delivers the costumes to the dock in Kansas City, alongside the steamboat. The costumes are loaded on board and the *Riverboat Queen* sets sail for New Orleans. During the course of the journey, a masked villain makes off with the costumes. Who must bear the risk of loss? Although the carrier will ultimately be responsible for the stolen costumes because it failed to exercise reasonable care for their protection, the risk of loss initially falls on the city of New Orleans as the buyer. An F.A.S. contract is a shipment contract. Dapper Dan, as seller, must bear the risk of loss only until the time he delivered the goods to the dock alongside the *Riverboat Queen*. After that, the city of New Orleans assumed the risk of loss.

C.I.F. and C.&F.

The terms *C.I.F.* and *C.&F.* mean cost, insurance, and freight, and cost and freight, respectively. Both terms indicate shipment contracts where the seller is obligated to pay all costs for transportation, insurance, and freight to the place of destination. These costs will be reflected in the price charged.

EXAMPLE Tucker's Inn located in Skagway, Alaska, ordered 300 pounds of sourdough from Yukon Distributors in Dawson City. Sourdough was used as a substitute for yeast in baking. The terms of the contract were: C.I.F. Skagway. While crossing the Chilkoot Pass, en route to Skagway, an avalanche of snow destroyed the shipment. Is Tucker covered for the loss? Yes! A C.I.F. contract is a shipment contract with the risk of loss falling on Tucker; however, as a part of the C.I.F. contract, Yukon Distributors had procured insurance for the goods being shipped. This is for Tucker's protection.

In a shipment contract, the seller must (1) assume the risk and expense of transporting goods to a common carrier; (2) transfer the goods to the carrier; (3) make a reasonable contract for their transportation; (4) forward to the buyer any document of title which will be necessary for him or her to get possession; and (5) promptly notify the buyer of shipment. Notification may be satisfied by sending the documents of title. In cases where there are no required documents, an invoice may be sent.

DESTINATION CONTRACTS

In destination contracts, the risk of loss remains with the seller until the goods are delivered to the buyer at the place of destination; only at that time does the risk of loss pass to the buyer.

In either a shipment or destination contract, if the goods are destroyed while in transit, the buyer and/or the seller having an insurable interest in the goods has a cause of action against the common carrier transporting the goods. The party upon whom the risk of loss falls may collect from his or her insurance company for the damaged or destroyed goods. The insurance company will then have a right of subrogation against the common carrier. A right of subrogation accrues when the insurance company pays the proceeds of the policy to the insured. The insured then assigns his or her cause of action to the insurance company pursuant to the subrogation agreement contained in the insurance policy.

EXAMPLE John Sutter enters into a contract to purchase fifty gold nuggets from Jim Walton. The terms of the contract are: F.O.B. Sutter's Mill, California. Jim Walton arranges to transport the nuggets by a team of huskies to Whitehorse, and then by stagecoach to California. En route to California, Dangerous Dan McGrew attacks the stagecoach up at Donner's Pass and steals the gold. Who must bear the risk of loss? This is a destination contract, so Jim Walton, as seller, must bear the risk of loss. If Walton is insured, he will be compensated on proof of loss. The insurance company will then have a right of subrogation and may exercise that right by suing the operators of the stagecoach, which is a common carrier, for failing to exercise reasonable care in the delivery of the gold against the likes of Dangerous Dan McGrew.

Contracts which specify neither a shipment term nor a destination term are presumed to be shipment contracts.

Eberhard Manufacturing Company v. Brown
61 Mich. App. 268, 232 N.W.2d 378 (1975)

Eberhard Manufacturing Company sued Brown to recover the price of goods sold which were lost in transit.

The parties did not expressly agree as to who would bear the risk of loss, since the contract contained no written evidence of an F.O.B. term. Eberhard Manufacturing claimed that delivery was F.O.B. their factory. This may be considered as usage of trade.

The issue is who must bear the risk of loss when the contract contains no F.O.B. term.

The court held,

> Under Article 2 of the Uniform Commercial Code, the "shipment" contract is regarded as the normal one and the "destination" contract as the variant type. The seller is not obligated to deliver at a named destination and bear the concurrent risk of loss until arrival, unless he has specifically agreed so to deliver, or the commercial understanding of the terms used by the parties contemplates such delivery. Thus, a contract which contains neither an F.O.B. term nor any other term explicitly allocating loss is a shipment contract.

Furthermore, the court stated that Brown's argument that the words "ship to" are equivalent to F.O.B. place of destination, is without merit because ". . . a 'ship to' term has no significance in determining whether a contract is a shipment or destination contract for risk of loss purposes. . . . Since the presumption of a shipment contract controls in this case", the seller, Eberhard, may recover the price from Brown for the goods lost in transit. Judgment for Eberhard Manufacturing Company.

STATIONARY CONTRACTS

When stationary goods are to be picked up by the buyer at the seller's place of business or at the place where the goods are located, the risk of loss remains on the merchant seller until actual receipt of the goods by the buyer. This is true even though the buyer has made full payment for the goods and has been notified that he or she may take possession of them. The reason for this is that the merchant is still in physical control of the goods and he or she is in the best position to have the goods insured. It is unusual for a buyer to insure goods before taking possession of them.

EXAMPLE | The Crystal Palace Saloon, located on the Barbary Coast in San Francisco, was a distributor and retailer of distilled spirits. On April 14, a group of descendants of the original Forty-Niners contracted to purchase 100 cases of distilled spirits from the Crystal Palace for $5,000. They paid the contract price and informed the Crystal Palace they would take possession of the liquor on April 21, the night of their annual reunion. On April 18 and April 19, an earthquake erupted in San Francisco that devastated the Barbary Coast region including the Crystal Palace Saloon. Who must bear the risk of loss? The risk of loss remains on the Crystal Palace because they were in the best position to have the liquor insured until the Forty-Niners took possession of it.

When the goods are held by a bailee without physically being moved, pending receipt of the buyer, performance is complete and risk of loss passes to the buyer when he or she receives the document of title, or the bailee acknowledges that the buyer has the right to possession of the goods.

EXAMPLE | Christopher Walters owned a tobacco plantation in Virginia. He entered into a contract to sell Beauregard Clayton five tons of tobacco leaves. Walters told Clayton to pick up the tobacco at a warehouse on the outskirts of Roanoke, where it was stored. He gave Clayton the warehouse receipt. That evening a forest fire swept across the Blue Ridge Mountains and consumed the warehouse. Who must bear the risk of loss? The risk of loss passed to Beauregard Clayton when he received the warehouse receipt for the tobacco.

The risk of loss is placed on the person who is in the best position to guard against the loss, and who is most likely to have the goods insured. The risk of loss may be altered by the agreement of the parties. In the contract, the risk of loss may be directly allocated or the parties may use any of the delivery terms which fix the risk of loss, such as F.O.B.

CONDITIONAL SALES CONTRACTS

Sale on Approval

In a contract providing for sale on approval, goods are transferred to the buyer for a certain period of time during which the buyer may use the goods to determine whether he or she wishes to purchase them. The buyer must be the ultimate consumer—the person who is going to use the product—rather than a merchant who is purchasing the product for resale.

The reason behind sale on approval contracts is that sellers want to entice buyers to try their product by providing a money-back guarantee if the purchaser is not satisfied. This is a personal test to be applied by the consumer. The product may be returned even if it conforms to the contract. During the approval period, title and risk of loss remain with the seller because the sale is not complete. Title and risk of loss pass to the buyer when he or she accepts the goods by making payment.

EXAMPLE | Muriel Shubert was watching Benny Hill one night on television. During a commercial break, she listened to an advertisement for a wok and its related implements. (A wok, which originated in China, is a round-bottomed pan used for frying.) The total package cost was $19.95 with a money-back guarantee. Muriel called right away. When Muriel received the products, she discovered this wok was nothing more than an ordinary, large frying pan. She returned the "wok" and requested her money back. Is she entitled to it? Yes! This is a sale on approval contract. The goods may be returned by the consumer even though they conform to the contract, because the consumer was not satisfied. Is this true even when the returned goods are lost in the mail? Yes! The risk of loss remains on the seller until the goods have been accepted and paid for by the consumer.

Sale or Return

In a sale or return contract, goods are transferred to the buyer on consignment. If the buyer is unable to resell them, he or she may return them to the seller. A sale or return contract usually occurs between merchants where the buyer is purchasing the goods for the purpose of resale. During the period of consignment, the title and risk remain with the buyer because the sale is considered complete even though the buyer may return the goods. If the goods are returned, it must be at the buyer's risk and expense.

EXAMPLE | Old Zeke from Cabin Creek was the manufacturer of Louisiana Lightning, a distilled spirit made from potatoes. Zeke agreed to sell 100 cases of the potato whiskey on consignment to Johnny Walker Red, a city slicker from Memphis. The Louisiana Lightning proved so potent that when a customer at the Red Garter, owned by Johnny Walker Red, lit a cigarette near an open bottle, that bottle exploded and ignited 50 of the 100 cases delivered. The 50 cases burst into flames. Who must bear the risk of loss? Johnny Walker Red, as buyer, must bear the loss on a consignment contract because the goods were accepted and the risk of loss remains with the buyer until the goods are returned, if ever. If Johnny Walker Red returns the other 50 cases because he could not sell them is he entitled to reimbursement? Yes! This is a sale or return contract. Even though risk of loss falls on the buyer while the goods are in his or her possession, the remaining goods may be returned even though they are conforming.

THE RISK OF LOSS AFTER BREACH

The previous discussion assumed that there was no breach of contract. If the buyer breaches the contract by repudiating it after the goods have been identified to the contract, but before the risk of loss normally passes to him or her, then the risk of loss will rest with the buyer for a reasonable time. The buyer will assume this risk of loss only to the extent of any deficiency in the seller's insurance coverage. If the seller breaches the contract and the buyer revokes his or her acceptance, then the risk of loss will rest on the seller for a reasonable time; but only to the extent the buyer's insurance is not sufficient to cover the loss.

EXAMPLE The Hatfields and the McCoys are at peace. The McCoys are in the coal mining business in the hills of Kentucky, and are planning to build a new mine shaft. The Hatfields, who are in the construction business, agree to supply them with two tons of dynamite for $4,000. The terms of the contract are F.O.B. Hills of Kentucky. After shipping the goods, the Hatfields receive a call from the McCoys repudiating the contract. An hour later, the dynamite blows up en route to the hills of Kentucky. The Hatfields have insurance coverage of $1,000. Who must bear the loss? The feud between the Hatfields and the McCoys is on again. The contract is a destination contract. The risk of loss is usually on the seller, but because of the McCoys's breach, they are liable for $3,000— the extent to which the Hatfield's insurance does not cover the loss.

REVIEW QUESTIONS

1. Define document of title, bill of lading, common carrier, tender of delivery, risk of loss, shipment contract, destination contract, F.O.B., F.A.S., C.I.F., C.&F., sale on approval, and sale or return.

2. Klein, a wholesale jeweler, sued Lopardo, a retail jeweler, for the wholesale price of two diamonds. Lopardo bought the diamonds with the understanding that if he were unable to sell them, they would be returned. Ten days after Lopardo received the diamonds, they were stolen from his store. Who must bear the risk of loss? Harold Klein & Co., Inc. v. Lopardo, 113 N.H. 400, 308 A.2d 538 (1973).

3. Multiplastics contracted to manufacture and deliver 40,000 pounds of brown-styrene pellets to Arch Industries for $.19 per pound. Arch Industries agreed to accept delivery of 1,000 pounds per day after production had been completed. Arch Industries refused to accept delivery in accordance with the terms of the contract. Multiplastics advised Arch Industries to pick up the brown styrene pellets since they had stored them for more than forty days. One month later, the Multiplastics plant was destroyed by fire. Their insurance did not cover the pellets. Multiplastics sued for the contract price plus interest. Did Multiplastics make a valid tender of delivery and on whom should the risk of loss fall? Multiplastics v. Arch Industries, Inc., 166 Conn. 152, 348 A.2d 618 (1974).

4. On June 11, 1974, Martin, a farmer, agreed to purchase a truck and haystack mover for over $35,000 from Melland's dealership. Martin was to receive over $17,000 as a trade-in allowance on his old unit. Since the new unit would not be ready for two to three months, Martin was allowed to retain the old unit. In August, a fire destroyed the truck and haystack mover unit. The parties had no risk of loss provision in their contract. Did Martin tender delivery of his old unit, and on whom does the risk of loss fall? Martin v. Melland's Inc., 283 N.W.2d 76 (N.D.) 1979.

5. Scampoli purchased a television set from Wilson. The set was warranted for ninety days of free service. After the set was delivered, there was a reddish tint to the picture. A service representative arrived to adjust the color, but after encountering some difficulty, he maintained that he would have to remove the television chassis and bring it to the shop. Scampoli's adult daughter, who was home at the time, refused to allow Wilson's representatives to remove the chassis, insisting she wanted a brand new set, not a repaired one. Scampoli later demanded a return of her purchase price, but Wilson refused, and again offered to cure the defect. What result? Wilson v. Scampoli, 228 A.2d 848 (D.C.) 1967.

6. Sterling agreed to ship goods to Electric Regulator F.O.B. Norwalk, Connecticut, which was the seller's place of business. The goods were damaged during shipment. Electric Regulator asserted that the contract is a destination contract rather than a shipment contract because the "ship to" addresses take precedence over the F.O.B. term. Sterling argued that the contract must state the destination and the carrier must be supplied with the destination in order for the goods to be delivered. This is the only purpose fulfilled by the "ship to" addresses. Who must bear the risk of loss for the damages to the shipment? Electric Regulator Corp. v. Sterling Extruder Corp., 280 F. Supp. 550, (D. Conn.) 1968.

7. Ramos contracted to buy a motorcycle from Wheel Sports Center and tendered payment of $893. Delivery was to be made June 30. Ramos was given the papers necessary to register the motorcycle and to obtain insurance for it. On July 11, a power blackout occurred and the motorcycle was stolen by looters. Who must bear the risk of loss? Ramos v. Wheel Sports Center, 96 Misc. 2d 646, 409 N.Y.S.2d 505 (1978).

17

SALES:
PRODUCTS LIABILITY

INTRODUCTION

Products liability is a separate area of the law. It incorporates principles of contracts; sales, specifically warranties; and the torts of negligence and strict liability. Products liability was developed to insure that a consumer who sustains personal injury caused by a defective product will be compensated for the injury.

Businesses are extremely concerned over products liability. This is evidenced by the huge amounts of insurance written to protect businesses against losses resulting from liability suits.

A person injured by a defective product may bring a lawsuit under any or all three of the following causes of action: breach of warranty, negligence, and strict products liability. Breach of warranty is a contract action which encompasses the express and implied warranties discussed in Chapter 15. Negligence and strict products liability are tort actions. Injured parties who may proceed under these causes of action include the purchaser, a user other than the purchaser, and innocent bystanders. The parties against whom they may seek redress are the manufacturer, including manufacturers of component parts; distributors and other middlemen; and the retailers—merchants who sell the goods.

In Chapter 15, we considered warranties covering defective products where the product was merely defective and, to an extent, those cases where the product caused personal injury. In this chapter, we are going to zero in more thoroughly on warranties covering defective products that bring about personal injuries.

BREACH OF WARRANTY

Breach of warranty is a contract action brought by the purchaser of the goods for personal injury and/or property damage based on either the express warranties made by the seller or the implied warranties imposed on the seller by the UCC. See the *Webster v. Blue Ship Tea Room* case in Chapter 15.

A breach of warranty action may also be brought by any member of the buyer's family or any guest in the buyer's home if it would be reasonable to expect them to use the goods or to be affected by them. Some states have extended the warranty to include personal injury and property damage suffered by any person who would reasonably be expected to use the goods or be affected by them. In those states restricting recovery to family members and guests, outsiders would be relegated to suing based on negligence or strict products liability.

EXAMPLE | Jim Brandt engaged an architect to design and build a little summer house for his garden. After its construction, a family gathering was held. Jim's grandmother was sitting having tea when the railing in back of her gave way. She landed in the flower bed and broke her hip. Has Grandma any recourse? Yes! Since she was a member of the family, she may sue the architect for breach of warranty.

A breach of warranty action may be brought against the seller and/or the manufacturer even though the person bringing the suit has not dealt with either of them, as was the case with Mrs. Henningsen in the *Henningsen v. Bloomfield Motors* case discussed in Chapter 15. To establish breach of warranty, the injured person must prove that the warranty existed; that it was breached by the seller; and that the seller's breach was the proximate cause of the injury. The seller or manufacturer will attempt to rebut the buyer's allegations by establishing that he or she exercised due care in the manufacturing, processing, or selection of the goods.

NEGLIGENCE

A manufacturer will be liable to any person for reasonably foreseeable injuries and property damage (see the Palsgraph test in Chapter 5) that were proximately caused by products reasonably certain to place life and limb in danger when negligently made. This may include almost any product. The term *manufacturer* applies to both the manufacturer of the finished product and the manufacturers of component parts. The injured person must prove that the defect in the product was caused by the manufacturer's negligence in failing to exercise reasonable care in designing the product, and in failing to make a reasonable inspection that would have revealed the defect.

MacPherson v. Buick Motor Company
217 N.Y. 382, 111 N.E. 1050 (1916)

MacPherson sued Buick for injuries sustained during an automobile accident. MacPherson alleges that Buick was negligent in failing to make a reasonable inspection of the automobile prior to sale.

MacPherson purchased an automobile from a Buick dealership. The spokes of the wheels were made of wood. While he was driving, the spokes of one of the wheels fragmented and caused MacPherson to be thrown from the auto. Even though MacPherson bought the auto through a Buick dealership, he decided to sue Buick directly. Buick contended that they had no knowledge of the defective wheel and that they are not responsible, since MacPherson did not purchase the auto directly from them. MacPherson retorted that Buick was negligent in failing to make a reasonable inspection that would have made them aware the wheel was defective. He further alleged that Buick's negligence resulted in placing a human life in imminent danger.

The issue is whether Buick owed a duty of care to someone who is not the immediate purchaser.

The court held that a thing of danger is something which, if negligently constructed, will place life and limb in danger. Manufacturers of things of danger are under a duty to make them carefully. This rule extends to those other than the immediate purchaser when the manufacturer has knowledge that the product will be used by someone other than the immediate purchaser. Buick was responsible for the finished product, and therefore had a duty to make a reasonable inspection of the wooden spokes. Since Buick failed to inspect, they were held liable to MacPherson for the injuries he sustained. Judgment for MacPherson.

The manufacturer also has a duty to adequately warn the prospective user of the potential danger of the product, and to recall the product upon discovery that it is defective. The manufacturer's failure to warn or to recall amounts to negligence. There must be knowledge that danger is probable. A manufacturer is not compelled to put a reliable product on the market; just one that is free of negligence. If the injury is caused to someone other than the purchaser, that person must also establish that the item was used for the purpose for which it was intended and that the manufacturer had knowledge that the item would be used by a person other than the purchaser without that person's examining it to see if it was defective. Often, injured persons will be unable to recover from the manufacturer in negligence cases because of intervening inspectors. The inspectors will be liable instead.

STRICT PRODUCTS LIABILITY

Strict products liability developed out of the theory of strict liability in tort. Even without proof of negligence, a manufacturer, distributor, and seller are strictly liable for injuries which occur when they place an article on the market knowing it is to be used without the kind of inspection likely to uncover the defect. The term *manufacturer* includes manufacturers of component parts. These merchants are strictly liable even though they have exercised due care in the preparation, inspection, and sale of the product regardless of whether the person who used it is the purchaser. This is the case provided that the seller is engaged in the business of selling the product which caused the injury; the product was used in the way it was intended to be used; the injury arose from a defect in either the design or manufacture of the product; and the person who was injured was not aware of the defect. A defect in design occurs when the product as produced is inadequate to serve the purpose for which it was intended. A defect in manufacture occurs when the product is not properly made.

The injured party has the burden of proving that the defect in design or manufacture existed at the time the product left the hands of the seller. The injured party may rely on circumstantial evidence to prove this. Evidence must also be submitted that tends to prove the relationship between the defect and the injury. The court will decide whether or not the accident caused the injury, on the basis of expert testimony coupled with other evidence that indicates the circumstances surrounding the accident. Some courts also require that the injured party prove that the defective condition made the product unreasonably dangerous. This concept limits the doctrine of products liability in situations involving the extent of the duty of a manufacturer with regard to safe design. Similarly, it limits the doctrine of products liability where the type of injury sustained is not commonly caused by the defect and the possibility that the injured party misused the product is in issue.

There are several tests applied to determine whether the defect is unreasonably dangerous. One of the foremost tests considers whether a reasonable manufacturer would continue to produce and sell the product in the same condition, and do so with the knowledge he or she now possesses of the potentially dangerous consequences. Other tests consider such factors as the usefulness of the product, the availability of safer products, the potential risk of injury and the knowledge and acceptance of this risk by the public.

EXAMPLE A merchant of Venice borrows a large sum of money from Paul Marco and signs a contract agreeing to hand over his gondola rental and manufacturing business if the money is not returned within three months. The merchant of Venice, who is having financial difficulties because of a decline in the tourist trade, cannot meet his payments. He offers to substitute one of the gondolas he manufactured as payment for the loan. Marco is paddling around the canals in the gondola when he suddenly realizes it is sinking because of a defect in the design. Unfortunately he cannot swim so, like a captain, he goes down with the ship. Does his estate have any recourse against the merchant of Venice? Yes! They may sue the merchant for Marco's wrongful death based on the theory of strict products liability. The gondola manufactured by the merchant had a defect in its design. The defect in construction was unreasonably dangerous because it caused the boat to sink, resulting in Marco's death.

Some states have extended this rule to innocent bystanders for damages sustained as a consequence of a defect that is reasonably foreseeable, provided that the item was properly used; the defect could not have been discovered with reasonable care; and the injury to the bystander could not have been averted with reasonable care. A bystander deserves better protection than a user because the bystander does not have the opportunity to inspect.

A lessor is also liable for injuries which result from property that is leased to a consumer in a defective condition. However, if the person had knowledge of the defect before use, or used it in an abnormal way, the consumer would be barred from recovery.

A person or company that is engaged in the business of selling food or other products for intimate bodily use, which sells such a product in a defective condition that is unreasonably dangerous to the consumer, is liable for the bodily harm which results. A merchant selling food has an affirmative duty to check the food, thus assuring the consumer that it is safe to eat.

EXAMPLE   Tom Jones runs a restaurant in California. Before discoing the night away, Monica Vermil stops in for dinner, orders a bowl of chili and two giant meatballs. The dinner is delicious until she bites into the second giant meatball and finds a decomposed mouse. As a result, she is continuously nauseous and cannot eat for weeks. She has constant nightmares about a mouse attacking her. Has she any recourse? Yes! Based on the theory of strict products liability, Monica may sue Tom Jones for her physical injuries as well as the mental distress she suffered because of the mouse.

Embs v. Pepsi-Cola Bottling Co. of Lexington, Kentucky, Inc. 528 S.W.2d 703 (Ky.) 1975

Mrs. Embs sued Pepsi-Cola for the injuries she sustained when a bottle of soda exploded near her. Mrs Embs's cause of action is predicated on the theory of strict products liability.

Mrs. Embs entered Stamper's Cash Market to purchase soda pop for her children. After she removed the soda from the cooler, a carton of 7-UP near her exploded, causing pieces of glass to become imbedded in her leg. Mrs. Stamper, the store manager, drove Mrs. Embs to the hospital, leaving instructions for one of her children to clean up the mess. She told Mrs. Embs that during the past week, other bottles of 7-UP had exploded. Mrs. Embs decided to sue Pepsi-Cola, the manufacturer, who also bottled the soda; Arnold Lee Vice, the distributor of 7-UP in the county; and Stamper's Cash Market, the merchant-retailer, who owned the store in which the 7-UP exploded.

The issue is whether the theory of strict products liability extends to bystanders and upon whom responsibility for injury should fall.

The court held that a bystander may recover for injuries caused by a defective product if the injuries were reasonably foreseeable. Mrs. Embs is entitled to recover for the injuries she sustained because it is reasonably foreseeable that a bottle exploding in a market could injure a person (bystander) shopping there. Mrs. Embs was entitled to recover for the harm she suffered, even though the evidence had been cleaned up, because this is one of those accidents which usually does not occur unless caused by a defect. Concerning the responsibility for Mrs. Embs's injury, the court stated,

> As a matter of public policy the retailer or middleman as well as the manufacturer should be liable since the loss for injuries resulting from defective products should be placed on those members of the marketing chain best able to pay the loss, who can then distribute such risk among themselves by means of insurance and indemnity agreements.

Judgment for Embs.

STATUTE OF LIMITATIONS

A statute of limitations is the length of time an aggrieved party has in which to begin a lawsuit. Statute of limitations vary depending upon the cause of action. Breach of express and implied warranties pertain to contracts for the sale of goods; therefore a four-year statute of limitations applies. The four-year period begins to run from the date the goods were sold. In a suit based on the torts of strict products liability or negligence, a three-year statute of limitations applies, but it does not begin to run until the date of injury. If the injury occurs five years after the date the defective product was purchased, a suit based on breach of warranty would fail because the four-year statute of limitations would have run, but a suit based on negligence or strict products liability would prevail because the three-year statute of limitations would not have begun to run until the date of injury. This may allow an aggrieved person to recover where he or she would otherwise be barred.

REVIEW QUESTIONS ——————————————————————————————

1. Define products liability, breach of warranty, negligence, and manufacturer.

2. Mrs. Manzoni purchased a case of Coca-Cola from a grocery store. She opened a bottle and gave some of it to her daughter, and finished the rest of it herself. It did not taste right. She examined the bottle and found something that was brown and slimy. She felt nauseous and began to vomit. She required medical attention. The Detroit Board of Health examined the bottle and analyzed the slimy substances as mold spores. Mrs. Manzoni sued Coca-Cola, alleging the drink was not fit for human consumption. What result? Manzoni v. Detroit Coca-Cola Bottling Co., 363 Mich. 235, 109 N.W.2d 918 (1961).

3. Mrs. Hauter bought the "Golfing Gizmo" for her thirteen-year-old son, Fred. The Golfing Gizmo was designed to help improve the games of unskilled golfers. It consisted of two pegs driven into the ground about two feet apart; an elastic cord extending between them; and another cord with a golf ball on its end, tied to the middle of the elastic cord. The Golfing Gizmo resembled a large letter T with the golf ball at its base. The Golfing Gizmo is set up so that the ball will spring back after it is hit. The instruction booklet states that players should "drive the ball with full power" and furthermore asserts that the Golfing Gizmo is "COMPLETELY SAFE. BALL WILL NOT HIT PLAYER." Fred used the Golfing Gizmo several times after reading the instruction booklet. On one swing, Fred hit underneath the ball and caught the cord with his golf club. This looped the ball over the top of the club striking Fred on the left temple. He suffered brain damage. Fred's parents sued the manufacturer for breach of warranty. What result? Hauter v. Zogarts, 14 Cal. 3d 104, 120 Cal. Rptr. 681, 534 P.2d 377 (1975).

4. Rooney was correcting a water leak in a New York City sewer. He was fatally stricken by lethal gas present in the sewer when his oxygen mask failed to function properly. A companion worker shouted for help and two other workers responded. In their attempt to rescue Rooney, they entered the sewer without masks and were fatally stricken. The families of the two decedents who attempted to rescue

Rooney sued the manufacturer of the oxygen masks. The manufacturer contended that it had no liability to the two men because they were not wearing oxygen masks. What result? Guarino v. Mine Safety Appliance Co., 25 N.Y.2d 460, 306 N.Y.S.2d 942, 255 N.E.2d 173 (1969).

5. Price was employed as an aircraft mechanic for Flying Tiger. Flying Tiger leased a gasoline tank truck from Shell. The truck had a movable ladder mounted on it which was used for refueling airplanes. The lease provided that Flying Tiger was obligated to maintain the equipment in a safe condition. Four years later, a replacement ladder was installed by Shell and inspected by Flying Tiger. Two years later, Price climbed the ladder in an attempt to reach the wing of an airplane. The legs of the ladder split, causing Price to fall against the gasoline tank. He sustained severe physical injuries. Price sued Shell based on causes of action in negligence and breach of implied warranty of merchantability. What result? May Price recover under the theory of strict products liability? Shell argues that Flying Tiger should be responsible under the terms of the lease. Are they correct? Price v. Shell Oil Company, 2 Cal. 3d 245, 85 Cal Rptr. 178, 466 P.2d 722 (1970).

6. Mildred Lettieri purchased a jacket from Krogers for her nephew, John La Gorga. There was no label on the jacket identifying the fabrics used in its manufacture, nor was there a warning that the jacket was not flame retardant. John was wearing the jacket one day while playing in a schoolyard when a spark from a waste barrel ignited the jacket. John's friends attempted to remove the jacket, but their efforts were impeded by the defective zipper. As a result, John sustained severe burns to 80 percent of his body. John's parents sued Kroger on his behalf. What result? La Gorga v. Kroger Company, 275 F. Supp. 373 (W.D. Pa. 1967).

7. Three Rivers Builders & Masonry Supply agreed to deliver to a contractor an amount of cinder blocks necessary to construct a house. The contractor was building the house for Spence. Spence had no contract with Three Rivers. Thereafter, Spence's home collapsed because of a defect in the manufacture of the cinder blocks. In a lawsuit brought by Spence against Three Rivers, will Three Rivers be responsible even though they did not manufacture the cinder blocks? Spence v. Three Rivers Builders & Masonry Supply, Inc., 353 Mich. 120, 90 N.W.2d 873 (1958).

18

SALES: BUYER'S REMEDIES

INTRODUCTION

The buyer is entitled to a remedy when the seller breaches the contract. A breach of contract by the seller occurs when the seller

1. Repudiates the contract
2. Fails to make delivery
3. Delivers nonconforming goods

The seller's repudiation or failure to make a delivery is an automatic breach of contract, and the buyer may immediately exercise his or her right to a remedy. With respect to nonconforming goods, the buyer has the right to

1. Reject the goods upon inspection
2. Accept the goods and later revoke
3. Accept the goods and recover damages

Any action taken by the buyer is not effective until the seller receives notification.

BUYER'S REJECTION

The buyer's rejection of nonconforming goods must be in relation to commercial units. A buyer may reject an unlimited number of units, but may not reject part of any one unit. The whole unit must be rejected, otherwise it is considered accepted.

To make an effective rejection, the buyer must

1. Reject the goods within a reasonable time after they have been tendered or delivered

2. Notify the seller of the particular defects in order to give the seller the opportunity to cure them

3. Refrain from exercising any ownership over the goods which would be inconsistant with his or her rejection

4. Exercise reasonable care with regard to the rejected goods and hold them for a reasonable time to allow the seller to reclaim them

If the buyer is a merchant, that person has a further duty to follow the seller's reasonable instructions with respect to the rejected goods. The merchant must make a good-faith effort to salvage the value of perishable goods and other goods rapidly declining in value, by selling them and applying the proceeds to the seller's account. The buyer may deduct the expenses incurred in selling the goods.

EXAMPLE Rick Boon, a butcher, orders 1,000 pounds of beef from Thompson Meatpackers Company. Both parties are merchants dealing in the sale of meat. After delivery is made by the Thompson Meatpackers, Rick inspects the meat and discovers that the so-called beef is horse meat. He promptly notifies Thompson Meatpackers of the defect. Thompson instructs Rick to sell the horse meat at a nearby market. Does Rick have to follow the instructions? Yes! Rick Boon, as a merchant, has a duty to follow the instructions if they are reasonable. If Rick sells the goods as instructed and applies the proceeds to Thompson Meatpackers' account, has he made a valid rejection? Yes! He promptly notified Thompson Meatpackers of the defect, followed their instructions with respect to the goods, and did not exercise any ownership over the goods inconsistant with Thompson Meatpackers' wishes.

A buyer who receives no instructions may reship the rejected goods to the seller; resell them and apply the proceeds to the seller's account; or store the rejected goods for the seller.

BUYER'S REMEDIES PRIOR TO ACCEPTANCE

In cases where the seller has breached the contract by repudiating it, by failing to make delivery, or by delivering nonconforming goods which are properly rejected, the buyer's remedies prior to acceptance are:

Cancel

Cover

Recover goods from an insolvent seller

Interest, security

Damages for non-delivery

Expenses incidental to the breach

Resulting damages

Specific performance and replevin

Cancel

The buyer may cancel the breached contract and recover any consideration given. This is equivalent to rescission and reimbursement for out-of-pocket expenses. In addition to this remedy, the buyer may also cover or recover damages for non-delivery.

Garfinkel v. Lehman Floor Covering Company
60 Misc.2d 72, 302 N.Y.S.2d 167 (1969)

Garfinkel sued Lehman Floor Covering Company for reimbursement of the purchase price paid for the installation of carpeting. Garfinkel alleged that the carpeting was installed in a defective condition and sought to cancel the contract.

On March 8, 1967, Lehman installed the carpet in Garfinkel's home. After installation, Garfinkel immediately informed Lehman that he noticed an unsightly condition about the carpet. Lehman's representative's attempted to cure the defect on two occasions without success. Garfinkel alleged that he is entitled to a return of his purchase price because his rejection and immediate notification were timely made. Lehman contended their ownership rights were interfered with by Garfinkel's retention and use of the carpet.

The issue is whether the buyer, after notifying the seller of his or her rejection, has any further duty with respect to the rejected goods other than to hold them with reasonable care until the seller removes them.

The court held the buyer has no further obligation concerning the goods. After notifying Lehman that the goods were defective and nonconforming, Garfinkel was allowed to retain the carpet and to use it until Lehman removed it. Lehman delivered the carpet and it is fair that he should bear the burden of removing it. Judgment for Garfinkel.

Cover

The buyer may cover by purchasing substitute goods elsewhere in good faith, and in a reasonable manner, without delay. The buyer is entitled to the difference between the contract price and the cost of cover together with incidental damages, less any expenses saved because of the seller's breach. Consequential damages may be awarded only if the buyer is unable to cover, or for damages occurring between the time of the breach and the time adequate cover is made.

EXAMPLE In the previous example, let us assume Thompson Meatpackers does not cure the defect by the delivery date specified in the contract. Rick Boon thereupon purchases the 1,000 pounds of beef elsewhere for $2,500. The original contract price was $2,000. What will Rick's measure of damage be? $500! The difference between the contract price, $2,000 and the cost of cover, $2,500, which must be reasonable under the circumstances.

Recover Goods from an Insolvent Seller

The buyer has the right to recover goods identified to the contract if the seller becomes insolvent within ten days after receiving the first installment of payment from the buyer. The buyer must tender the balance of the payment owed to the seller. This remedy is designed to prevent the seller from fraudulently inducing the buyer to enter into a contract shortly after the seller becomes insolvent.

EXAMPLE Custer is an ice cream manufacturer located in Montana. He has a franchise of ice cream stands bearing his name throughout the state. His chief competition comes from Tom Carmel. Carmel, through price wars, is slowly putting Custer out of business. He is down to his last stand. The operator of the last stand, located in Little Big Horn, orders 500 gallons of ice cream from Custer at $1 per gallon and sends $300 as a down payment. One week later, after the goods have been identified to the contract, Custer files for bankruptcy. Will Custer's last stand be able to recover the 500 gallons of ice cream from him? Yes! By tendering the balance owed, it may recover the ice cream because Custer became solvent within ten days after the down payment was made.

Security Interest

The buyer has a security interest in the rejected goods for any payments made on them, and for any incidental expenses incurred. Pursuant to that security interest, the buyer may resell the goods and recover the payments together with the incidental expenses. The amount that remains must be applied to the seller's account. The buyer is not permitted to determine what his or her measure of damages should be in addition to the payments made and retain the proceeds of the sale for that purpose.

EXAMPLE Joseph Winston, proprietor of Smokin' Joe's, orders ten dozen boxes of Havana cigars from a man named Castro, for $1,200. Winston sends a check for $500 with the order. When the cigars are delivered, they are found to be an inferior brand, worth much less than the contract price. Winston wants his money back. What recourse does he have against Castro? If Winston made a valid rejection of the cigars, he has a security interest in those goods for $500. The cigars will act as collateral until the $500 is returned by Castro. If Castro refuses to return the down payment, Winston may resell the cigars to recover it, and then apply the amount left over to Castro's account.

Damages for Nondelivery

As an alternative to the remedy of cover, the buyer may cancel the contract and sue for damages for nondelivery. The buyer is entitled to the benefit of the bargain when he or she makes a contract. This is achieved through awarding the buyer the difference between the contract price and the market price, along with any incidental or consequential damages which result from the breach. The market price is the prevailing price of goods when the breach occurs at the place where performance was to be made.

EXAMPLE | On May 28, Gerard Hughes contracts to purchase fifteen tons of tobacco from Anthony Mills, at $2,000 per ton—the current market price. Delivery is to be made on June 13. Mills breaches the contract by refusing to deliver on the date specified. Hughes opts for recovering damages caused by Mills's nondelivery. On June 13, the date of the breach, the market price of tobacco was $2,200 per ton. What will Hughes's measure of damages be? $200 per ton. Gerard Hughes will be entitled to the difference between the contract price ($2,000 per ton) and the market price ($2,200 per ton).

Expenses Incidental to the Breach

Incidental damages are awarded to compensate the buyer for expenses incurred because of the seller's breach of contract. Incidental damages include disbursements made for inspection, receipt, storage, transportation, care, custody, and resale of the rejected goods. The incidental expenditures made by a buyer in attempting to cover may also be recovered.

EXAMPLE | Thomas Tallchief operates a souvenir shop on a Navajo reservation. He orders and pays for 100 bow and arrow sets from the Pueblos. The Pueblos mistakenly send 100 tomahawks. Tallchief exercises his remedy of cover by purchasing the bow and arrow sets from the Iroquois. Tallchief makes a valid rejection of the tomahawks, but the Pueblos refuse to refund his money. Tallchief ships the tomahawks to the Cherokees in the Smokey Mountains. They operate the only other souvenir shop that could handle such a quantity. The Cherokees are able to sell all the tomahawks. The proceeds of the sale are $1,000. What damages are recoverable by Tallchief out of the proceeds of the sale, in addition to the cost of cover? Tallchief may recover any incidental expenses incurred in the inspection of the nonconforming goods; storage of the goods; transportation of the goods to the Smokey Mountains; resale of the goods by the Cherokees, and procurement of substitute goods through the remedy of cover.

Resulting Damages

Resulting damages, also known as consequential damages, are awarded to compensate the buyer for any direct financial loss he or she suffers as a result of the seller's breach. Consequential damages include any loss, stemming from the buyer's needs or requirements, which was reasonably foreseeable by the seller, and any injury proximately caused to a person or property by the seller's breach. If the buyer could have prevented the loss by utilizing the remedy of cover and obtaining substitute goods, he or she will not be allowed consequential damages.

EXAMPLE | In the previous example, suppose (1) Tallchief ordered all of his supplies from the Pueblos, (2) the Pueblos refused to deliver, and (3) Tallchief could not cover until the following week. Would Tallchief be entitled to the loss of profits for the week he was forced to shut down his souvenir shop? Yes! His loss of profits would result from the Pueblos' breach. The burden of proving the actual loss of profits would be on Tallchief.

Specific Performance and Replevin

The buyer may be awarded the equitable remedy of specific performance where the goods involved are unique and money damages are not a satisfactory substitute. *Replevin* is also an equitable remedy which is granted when the goods have been identified to the contract and the buyer is unable to cover because substitute goods cannot be found. Identification of goods to the contract occurs when the goods have been set aside specifically for the buyer. Both specific performance and replevin allow the purchaser to enforce the contract and recover the goods under the circumstances set forth above.

EXAMPLE | The Mohicans are the only tribe which continues to manufacture wigwams. Western World contracts to purchase five wigwams from the last of the Mohicans for use in the recreation of an Indian village, which they hope will prove to be an attraction for their entertainment park. After completing manufacture of the wigwams, the Mohicans get a better offer from The Land of Make Believe. Does Western World have any recourse against the Mohicans? Yes! Western World can regain possession of the wigwams through the remedy of replevin, since the goods have been identified to the contract and substitute goods cannot be found elsewhere.

BUYER'S ACCEPTANCE

Acceptance of goods by a buyer occurs in the following ways: (1) buyer signifies the goods are conforming after inspection, or decides to take the goods even though they are nonconforming; (2) buyer fails to reject the goods after having a reasonable opportunity to inspect them; and (3) buyer acts in a manner inconsistent with the seller's ownership of the goods.

If the buyer accepts the goods, he or she must pay the contract price. Although the buyer must keep the goods, acceptance does not deprive the buyer of the right to a remedy for the nonconforming goods he or she accepted.

BUYER'S REMEDIES AFTER ACCEPTANCE

The remedies available to a buyer after acceptance of nonconforming goods include:

Miscellaneous expenses incidental to the breach

Deduction from the price

Consequential damages

Recoupment

Acceptance revoked

Breach of warranty

Miscellaneous Damages Incidental to the Breach

Miscellaneous damages incidental to the breach is a fancy way of describing the incidental damages which were just discussed.

Deduction from the Price

The buyer may deduct all or part of the damages caused by the seller's breach if payment has not already been made. The buyer must notify the seller of his or her intention before any deduction may be made.

Shangri La, a catering establishment in Wappinger Falls, New York, orders 100 cases of white wine. By mistake, the Catawbas, distributors of fine wine, send 50 cases of white wine and 50 cases of rosé wine. The rosé wine is $2 per case less expensive than the white wine. But, in the billing, the Catawbas charge the same price for both red and white wine. Shangri La accepts the delivery, but notifies the Catawbas that they are deducting $100 from the price because of the inclusion of the less-expensive rosé wine. Is this valid? Yes! The buyer may deduct the damages caused by the seller's breach from the price after notification is given to the seller.

Consequential Damages

Consequential damages, which have been previously discussed under the heading of resulting damages, entitle the buyer to recover for any injury or damage caused by nonconforming goods which have been accepted.

Recoupment

The buyer who has accepted and paid for nonconforming goods, and who no longer has the option of revoking acceptance, may still recoup damages for the nonconformity. The measure of damages is the difference in value between conforming goods and the nonconforming goods which have been accepted. If payment has not already been made, the damges may be deducted from the price, as previously discussed.

EXAMPLE In the previous example, suppose Shangri La had already paid for the wine. Would they still be able to recover the $100 per case? Yes! Their remedy would be recoupment. They would be entitled to $2 per case, the difference in price between the fifty cases of the nonconforming rosé wine and the fifty cases of the conforming white wine for which they were charged.

Acceptance Revoked

Acceptance of the goods prevents the buyer from later rejecting them, unless he or she can revoke the acceptance. Revocation of acceptance may be made when the nonconformity could be cured by the seller and no attempt to cure it has been made. Acceptance may also be revoked when discovery of the defect was not made until after acceptance, whether because of the buyer's reliance on the reasonable assurances by the seller, or because of the buyer's difficulty in discovering the defect.

In order for the revocation of acceptance to be valid, the buyer must notify the seller within a reasonable time afer the buyer discovered the defect, or should have discovered the defect. A buyer, who effectively revokes, has the same remedies available as a person who rejected the goods before acceptance.

EXAMPLE James Dakota ordered 500 cases of mangos from a Hawaiian distributor. After the distributor makes delivery, Dakota inspects the shipment. Each case is marked "Mangos." The distributor had assured him that the mangos were the finest available. Dakota made payment on the mangos and began to sell them to fruit markets in the Black Hills of South Dakota. He soon discovered that almost half of the cases were filled with oranges, a less-expensive fruit. Does Dakota have any recourse against the Hawaiian distributor?

Yes! The defect was not discovered within a reasonable time because of the distributor's fraudulent assurances and labeling. Dakota may revoke his acceptance and proceed as though he had rejected the goods to begin with, thereby taking advantage of those remedies available to a buyer who makes a valid rejection.

Lanners v. Whitney
247 Ore. 223, 428 P.2d 398 (1967)

This is an action brought by the purchaser of an airplane for revocation of his acceptance due to the nonconformity of the goods (airplane) delivered.

Whitney sold his airplane to Lanners. An inspection undertaken by a mechanic from the Federal Aviation Agency (FAA) found that the airplane was suitable for flying. After Lanners received delivery, he found that the airplane burned an excessive amount of oil, overheated regularly, and had unusually high cylinder pressure. He sought to revoke his acceptance because the airplane did not conform to the assurances given by the seller. Whitney claimed that Lanners did not reject the nonconforming goods within a reasonable time.

The issue is whether Lanners could revoke his acceptance even though an unreasonable amount of time had passed.

The court held that Lanners could revoke his acceptance because his failure to inspect the airplane before he accepted it was due to his reliance on the assurances of Whitney and the FAA mechanic. This reliance was reasonable. Lanners may cancel the contract and recover the payments he made. Judgment for Lanners.

Breach of Warranty

The damages awarded for breach of warranty are explained in detail in Chapter 15, Title and Warranties.

REVIEW QUESTIONS

1. Explain each of the buyer's remedies prior to acceptance.
2. List the remedies available to the buyer after acceptance, and explain the significance of each remedy.
3. Thorstenson purchased a tractor and a loader which was to be mounted on the tractor, from Mobridge Iron Works. Mobridge contended that the loader could not be mounted on the tractor. Thorstenson claimed it could and offered to mount it himself. Mobridge refused to deliver the tractor and loader. Thorstenson bought the goods elsewhere at a $1,000 price increase and mounted them himself. What remedy is available to Thorstenson for Mobridge's breach of contract? Thorstenson v. Mobridge Iron Works Co., 87 S.D. 358, 208 N.W.2d 715 (1973).
4. Campbell purchased the machinery and equipment of an automatic car-wash business owned by Pollack, for $8,000. Pollack represented that the sale included everything within the four walls of the building; Pollack did not own the building

itself. After paying the purchase price, Campbell discovered that the heating and lighting equipment could not be removed because they were considered part of the building. What recourse does Campbell have? Campbell v. Pollack, 101 R.I. 223, 221 A.2d 615 (1966).

5. Oloffson, a grain dealer, contracted to purchase 40,000 bushels of corn from a farmer named Coomer, for $1.1225 per bushel. The contract was signed in April with delivery to be made in October. On June 3, Coomer notified Oloffson that he decided not to plant corn because of the wet season. The market price of a bushel of corn on June 3 was $1.16 per bushel. Oloffson waited until October before he covered by purchasing substitute corn at $1.35 and $1.49 per bushel. Oloffson then sued Coomer for the difference between the contract price and the respective cover prices. What result? Oloffson v. Coomer, 11 Ill. App. 3rd 918, 296 N.E.2d 871 (1973).

6. Steele purchased three new combine machines from J.I. Case Company in June 1960. The machines were warranted as to their quality. Any defect was to be repaired or replaced, or else the purchase price would be refunded. The warranty specifically limited damages to a return of the purchase price. The combines failed to function properly and several attempts made over a period of thirty days by Case's representatives to cure the defects failed. Steele's crops were harvested two weeks late and substantial damages resulted. Can Steele recover consequential damages for the loss of his crops despite the disclaimer in the warranty limiting damages to a recovery of the purchase price? Steele v. J.I. Case Co., 197 Kan. 554, 419 P.2d 902 (1966).

7. Traynor contracted to buy Christmas trees from Walters, who grew them. The contract specified that the trees were to be top quality. Traynor inspected the Christmas trees after receipt and discovered they were not top quality. Traynor immediately notified Walters of his rejection and resold the trees because he considered them to be perishable since Christmas was but a short time away. Walters had not given Traynor any instructions as to the disposition of the trees. Did Traynor act correctly by reselling them, and what must he do with the proceeds of the resale? Traynor v. Walters, 342 F. Supp. 455 (M.D. Pa. 1972).

19

SALES:
SELLER'S REMEDIES

INTRODUCTION

The seller in a contract for the sale of goods has a right to expect the buyer to accept and pay for the delivery of goods if they conform to the contract. The buyer may breach the contract by

1. Repudiating the contract
2. Failing to make timely payment
3. Wrongfully rejecting the goods
4. Inappropriately revoking acceptance

SELLER'S REMEDIES
UPON BUYER'S REJECTION

The seller must act in good faith in choosing and carrying out the available remedies:

Delivery withheld
Recall delivery in transit
Identify conforming goods to the contract
Promptly cancel
Damages for non-acceptance
Resell and recover damages
Occurrence of damages incidental to the breach
Price may be recovered

Delivery Withheld

Delivery may be withheld by the seller when the buyer repudiates the contract or fails to make a timely payment on or before delivery. The seller may then cancel the contract, resell the goods, and recover damages; or just recover damages for nonacceptance. The seller may also withhold delivery, when he or she discovers the buyer to be insolvent, except if the buyer pays in cash.

Recall Delivery in Transit

Goods in transit may be stopped and reclaimed by the seller when the buyer breaches the contract, or when the buyer becomes insolvent. The seller must notify the carrier or bailee of his or her intention to halt the delivery of the goods and the carrier or bailee must follow the seller's instructions. The seller's right to stop the goods in transit lapses when the buyer is in receipt of the goods; when the buyer is in receipt of a negotiable document of title; or when the carrier or bailee acknowledges that the goods are being held for the buyer.

EXAMPLE | The Kansas City Chiefs contract to purchase forty-five pairs of Jim Thorpe track sneakers from the Carlisle Shoe Palace for their contest with the Washington Redskins. After the goods are delivered to the railroad carrier for shipment, the Chiefs notify the Carlisle Shoe Palace of their intention to cancel the contract. What recourse does Carlisle have? They may recall delivery of the sneakers while in transit by notifying the railroad carrier. They must act promptly before their right to stop delivery in transit lapses.

Identify Conforming Goods to the Contract

The seller may identify conforming goods to the contract to make them available for resale. This means the seller has set aside certain goods for the purchaser. With respect to unfinished goods, the seller must use reasonable judgment to mitigate his or her losses by either completing them or stopping their manufacture. It will depend on how far the seller has progressed in manufacturing the goods. When unfinished goods are completed, they may be identified to the contract for the purpose of making them available for resale.

EXAMPLE | Martha's Craft Shop agrees to purchase eighty-five woolen blankets for $5,000 from the Florida Seminoles, a group of senior citizens who weave them for profit. After the Seminoles procured the necessary materials and the pattern is measured and cut, they begin work on the blankets. Martha then informs them of her intent to cancel the contract. What recourse is available to the Seminoles? They may finish manufacturing the blankets, identify them to the contract, and resell them. They may recover the difference between the contract price and the resale price.

Promptly Cancel

A material breach made by the buyer permits the seller to cancel the contract. The seller must promptly notify the buyer of the cancellation and, from that point on, the obligations of the parties are discharged. The seller may identify conforming goods to the contract, withhold delivery of the goods to be transferred, or stop delivery in transit. The seller may then proceed to recover damages for nonacceptance, resell the goods and recover damages, or sue for the price if the goods cannot be resold.

Damages for Non-Acceptance

The seller may choose not to resell the goods when the buyer repudiates the contract or refuses to accept the tendered goods. Instead, the seller may opt to retain the goods and sue the buyer for damages for his or her nonacceptance. These damages will be determined by measuring the difference between the market price at the time and place of tender, and the unpaid contract price together with incidental damages, but less any expenses saved by the seller because of the breach. The seller is entitled to be placed in a position as favorable as the one he or she would have held had the contract been carried out. If this measure of damages is not adequate, the seller will be reimbursed for the loss of profit resulting from the buyer's non-performance.

EXAMPLE A group of Eskimos contract to supply an Alaskan refinery with 150 tons of whale blubber at $800 per ton. Before delivery was made, the refinery refused the whale blubber because its need suddenly diminished. The market price for whale blubber had dropped to $750 per ton. The Eskimos chose to retain the whale blubber for their own use. Do they have any recourse against the refinery? Yes! The Eskimos may recover $50 per ton as damages for the refinery's nonacceptance. This amount is determined from the difference between the contrct price of $800, and the market price at the time of tender, $750.

Neri v. Retail Marine Corporation
30 N.Y.2d 393, 334 N.Y.S.2d 165,
285 N.E.2d 311 (1972)

Retail Marine Corporation sued Neri for lost profits resulting from Neri's nonacceptance of conforming goods.

Neri contracted to buy a boat from Retail Marine Corporation for $12,500. Less than a week later, Neri repudiated the contract and sued Retail Marine for the return of his $4,250 down payment. Retail Marine sold the boat for the same price to someone else. Retail Marine argues that they have lost the profit on the repudiated sale to Neri because they would have made the other sale anyway. Retail Marine also requests reimbursement for incidental damages of $675 incurred for storage, finance charges, and insurance until the resale.

The issue is whether a seller who has an unlimited supply of merchandise may recover loss of profit when the item is sold to another person for the same price.

The court held that where the difference between the market price and the unpaid contract price does not put the seller in as good a position as he would have been in if the sale was completed, the seller may recover the profits lost on account of the breach plus any incidental damages. Neri was entitled to a return of his down payment less Retail Marine's loss of profit and incidental damages. Judgment for Retail Marine Corporation.

Resell and Recover Damages

Goods which are finished and conform to specifications may be identified to the contract. The seller may resell these goods along with goods already identified to the contract which have been withheld or recalled from transit. The resale may be made at a public or private auction upon notification to the buyer. The seller may then recover the difference between the resale price and the contract price together with incidental damages, but less the expenses saved because of the buyer's breach. If the seller makes a profit on the sale, he or she does not have to apply it to the buyer's account.

A buyer cannot reclaim goods resold to a good-faith purchaser for value, even though the seller failed to notify the buyer of the resale or otherwise failed to comply with the resale requirements.

EXAMPLE | Newton Flour Company agrees to supply a bakery named Luscious Crepes and Cakes with 75 one hundred-pound bags of flour, for $2,200, on November 17. Payment is due on or before that date. On November 17, Newton Flour has not received payment. They sell the flour earmarked for Luscious Crepes and Cakes to the Donut Hole, a good-faith purchaser, for $1,600. Newton Flour then sues Luscious Crepes and Cakes for $600. Are they entitled to these damages? Yes! Newton Flour may resell the flour, and may recover the difference between the contract price of $2,200 and the resale price of $1,600. The resale was made without notice to Luscious Crepes and Cakes. Would this affect the outcome? No! Since the sale was made to a good-faith purchaser for value, Luscious Crepes and Cakes may not reclaim the goods and must pay the entire amount of damages.

Foster v. Colorado Radio Corp.
381 F.2d 222 (10th Cir. 1967)

This lawsuit was brought by a breaching party who seeks to be excused from paying damages because notice of a private resale was not given to her.

Rosemary Foster agreed to purchase certain assets of a New Mexico radio station from Colorado Radio. Foster agreed to make satisfactory arrangements concerning filing for the FCC's approval of the transfer. She did not use reasonable efforts to make these arrangements. A notice was sent to her by Colorado Radio demanding that she perform the contract. The notice stated,

> Our Washington, D.C., attorneys advise your FCC application required by our agreement dated 28 August, 1964, is still not ready for filing. Our material was ready in early September . . . We demand you use all diligence possible in preparation of application. Attorneys say five more days is reasonable . . .

Thereafter, Colorado Radio made a private resale of the New Mexico station to Walters. Colorado Radio then sued Rosemary Foster for the difference between the resale price and the contract price, which amounted to over $15,000.

Rosemary Foster contested the award on the grounds that, since Colorado did not give notice of the intended resale as required by the UCC, they are barred from recovering the difference between the resale price and the contract price.

The issue is whether the case comes under the UCC.

The court held that the UCC applies to those assets of the radio station which are movable and thereby constitute goods. This amounted to 10 percent of the total contract price. The court found in favor of Rosemary Foster because reasonable notice, which was not given, is required under the UCC in private resales as a condition precedent to the recovery of damages. The award granted to Colorado Radio was reduced by 10 percent, the value of the assets which constituted goods. Judgment in part for Foster.

Occurrence of Damages Incidental to the Breach

The seller may recover damages incidental to the breach including charges assessed by the carrier for stopping delivery; expenses for transportation, custody, and care of the goods halted in transit; and any disbursements resulting from the resale of the goods.

Price May Be Recovered

If the goods cannot be resold by the seller after making a reasonable attempt, the seller may sue the buyer for the contract price. The seller must hold the goods which are in his or her possession and which have been identified to the contract for the buyer. The seller must transfer the goods to the buyer upon recovery of the contract price from the buyer.

EXAMPLE

Larry Shields, a forty-two portly, orders a custom-made suit for $800 from his tailor, Jacques Monair. Jacques procures the necessary material and starts to work. After the material is cut in accordance with Larry Shields's measurements and is partially sewn, Shields notifies Jacques of his intention to repudiate the contract. What recourse is available to Jacques Monair? Jacques may sue Larry Shields for $800, the full cost of the suit, because custom-made clothing cannot be resold. When Jacques Monair recovers the purchase price, he must finish the suit, if Larry Shields requests it, and transfer it to him.

SELLER'S REMEDIES AFTER BUYER'S ACCEPTANCE

A buyer who accepts conforming goods for which he or she does not pay, is in breach of contract. The seller's rights against a buyer who has breached the contract after acceptance can be found in the following remedies:

Reclaim the goods

Demand cash or reclaim goods from insolvent buyers

Sue for contract price

Reclaim the Goods

The seller has the right to reclaim goods delivered to and accepted by the buyer, when the buyer does not pay for them. This rule applies to situations where payment is made by a check which is later dishonored. Payment by check is conditioned on the bank's honoring the check when it is presented.

Demand Cash or Reclaim Goods from Insolvent Buyers

Upon learning of the buyer's insolvency, the seller may refuse to deliver the goods except for cash. If delivery has been made and accepted, the seller may reclaim the goods by giving prompt notice of demand, within ten days after the buyer's receipt of the goods. The seller must discover the buyer's insolvency within the ten-day limitation or be precluded from reclaiming the goods.

Either party has the right to demand adequate assurances in writing that performance will be forthcoming where reasonable grounds for insecurity arise. If a response is not made within thirty days of receipt of the demand, the party making the request may consider the contract breached. This is to insure that the reasonable expectations of the parties will be fulfilled. If the buyer gives the seller adequate assurances, in writing, of his or her solvency within three months before delivery is tendered, the ten-day limitation does not apply.

A seller who elects to reclaim goods from an insolvent buyer will be barred from all other remedies because of the preferential treatment afforded the seller over the buyer's other creditors. The seller cannot reclaim goods delivered to an insolvent buyer if they are sold to a good-faith purchaser who buys them for value in the ordinary course of business.

EXAMPLE | Otto Baldwin, owner of the World of Shoes, enters into a contract to purchase twenty pairs of moccasins, on credit, from the Leather Factory. A week after making delivery, the Leather Factory learns of Otto's insolvency. Can it reclaim the moccasins? Yes! The Leather Factory can recover the moccasins by giving prompt notice of demand before the ten-day limit expires. If Otto Baldwin had given the Leather Factory an adequate assurance of his ability to pay, would the ten-day limit apply? No! Not as long as delivery was made within three months from the written assurance.

Price May Be Recovered

The seller has the right to sue for the price where the buyer has accepted conforming goods, but has not paid for them. This is the seller's main remedy after the buyer has accepted the goods.

REVIEW QUESTIONS

1. Explain each of the remedies available to the seller upon the buyer's improper rejection of the goods.
2. List the remedies available to the seller after the buyer accepts the goods and explain the significance of each.

3. Svihovec agreed to deliver 4,000 bushels of grain to Mott Equity Elevator in March for $1.86 per bushel. Mott refused delivery in March, April, and May claiming they were short on railroad boxcars used for storage. In June, Svihovec sold the grain to someone else for $2.20 per bushel. In September, when the market price of grain was $4.00 per bushel, Mott sued for nondelivery. What result? If Svihovec wins, will he have to account to Mott for the profit he made on the resale? Mott Equity Elevator v. Svihovec, 236 N.W.2d 900 (N.D.) 1975.

4. Cohn placed an ad in the newspaper to sell his boat. Fisher saw the ad and purchased the boat from Cohn for $4,650. Fisher gave Cohn a check for $2,535 as a down payment. On the check, Fisher noted that the purchase price was $4,650. Fisher decided not to go through with the contract and stopped payment on the check. Cohn placed another ad in the paper and resold the boat for $3,000, which was the best offer he received. Then Cohn sued Fisher for breach of contract. What will Cohn's measure of damages be? Cohn v. Fisher, 118 N.J. Super. 286, 287 A.2d 222 (1972).

5. Jagger Brothers contracted to purchase 20,000 pounds of yarn at $2.15 per pound from Technical Textile Company. After accepting delivery of 3,723 pounds of yarn, the buyer, Jagger Brothers, repudiated the contract. The seller, Technical Textile, stopped manufacturing the yarn and sued Jagger Brothers for breach of contract. The market price for the yarn at the time of the breach was $1.90 per pound. What result? Jagger Brothers, Inc. v. Technical Textile Co., 202 Pa. Super. 639, 198 A.2d 888 (1964).

6. French attended an auction in London given by Sotheby & Company, Auctioneers of Works of Art. French purchased eight antique guns through a bidding system, but then failed to pay for them. Sotheby's sued him for the price. French contends that his liability should be limited to the difference between the market price and the unpaid contract price. What result? French v. Sotheby & Co., 470 P.2d 318 (Okla.) 1970.

7. Stumbo delivered logs to Keystone Lumber Company under a contract of sale. Thereafter, a fire destroyed Keystone's lumber mill. Keystone could not continue to operate and the insurance proceeds were not sufficient to pay Stumbo the value of the logs. Stumbo removed his remaining logs from Keystone and sold them to Hult who made them into lumber. M.D.M. Corporation held a security interest in the logs and contested Stumbo's right to them. No demand was made by the seller to reclaim the goods within ten days after the buyer received the goods. Is Stumbo's claim, as seller, superior to M.D.M.'s claim, as a holder of a security interest? Stumbo v. Paul B. Hult Lumber Co., 251 Ore. 20, 444 P.2d 564 (1968).

20

COMMERCIAL PAPER: FORM AND NEGOTIATION

INTRODUCTION

Commercial paper is a negotiable instrument which is readily transferable between parties as a substitute for money. It is a contract creating an obligation on one party's part to pay another party a certain amount of money. There are four types of commercial paper: drafts, checks, notes, and certificates of deposit.

FORMS OF COMMERCIAL PAPER

Draft

A draft is an order to pay a certain amount of money. It involves three parties: the drawer, the drawee-payor, and the payee. The drawer is the person who is making the order; the drawee-payor is the person to whom it is made who must pay the amount of money stated in the draft; and the payee is the person to whom the money is paid.

Check

A check is a special form of a draft drawn on a bank and payable on demand. The drawer is the person making the check. The drawee-payor is the bank at which the drawer has a checking account, and who must pay the amount of money stated on the check upon presentment. The payee is the person to whom the bank must pay the money, usually the person who receives the check. If that person maintains an account at a different bank, the payee may be the bank in which the check was deposited or cashed.

Warren Robertson was Christmas shopping at Lord & Taylor for his wife, Kathleen. He bought her a woolen hat and scarf set for $45. Robertson paid for the gift with a check drawn on Citibank, the same bank at which Lord & Taylor maintains its account. Who are the respective parties to this check? Warren Robertson is the drawer, the person who is making out the check. Citibank is the drawee-payor, the bank against whom the check was drawn and who must pay the amount stated on the check upon presentment. The payee is Lord & Taylor. If Lord & Taylor had its account at Chase Manhattan Bank, who would be the payee? Chase Manahattan. After Lord & Taylor deposits or cashes the check, it is Chase Manhattan who is the one presenting the check to Citibank for payment.

Drafts and checks are three-party instruments, whereas notes and certificates of deposit involve two parties. A person could, however, draw a check on a bank payable to himself or herself. This would make two of the three parties, the drawer and the payee, the same.

Note

A note is a promise to pay a certain amount of money. A promissory note involves two parties. The maker of the note is the person making the promise to pay the amount stated, and the payee is the person to whom the promise to pay is made. Promissory notes range from IOUs to notes securing loans for automobiles, businesses, and houses, with the latter being referred to as a mortgage note.

EXAMPLE

Dawn McKenzie graduated from the University of Chicago and was working for an accounting firm. After six months, she had saved $2,000 and decided to put it toward a Chevrolet Corvette. The purchase price was $22,000 and she obtained financing from General Motors Acceptance Corporation. She signed a statement saying, "I agree to pay GMAC $20,000 plus 11% interest in equal installments over a period of thirty-six months." What is the effect of this statement? This is a promissory note in which Dawn as the maker of the note agrees to pay the amount stated to GMAC, the payee, in return for its $20,000 loan.

Certificate of Deposit

A certificate of deposit is a special form of a promissory note evidencing receipt of money by a bank with their promise to repay it at a future date with a guaranteed rate of interest, for example, six-month or two-and-a-half-year CDs. The bank is the maker of the certificate of deposit and the payee is the person who deposits the money with the bank.

REQUIREMENTS FOR NEGOTIABILITY

Commercial paper must meet certain requirements to be negotiable. Negotiable means the commercial paper may be transferred to another by indorsement or by delivery. The requirements are that the commercial paper must be signed by the drawer or maker; must contain an unconditional order or promise to pay a certain sum in money; and must be payable on demand or at a definite time to order or to bearer.

Signature

The drawer or the maker must sign the commercial paper. The signature may be in the usual written form or may be printed, typewritten, stamped, initialed, or fingerprinted. In cases of doubt, it is the court's function to determine whether the drawer or maker actually used or intended to use the symbol as his or her authentication of the commercial paper.

Unconditional Order or Promise

The order or promise to pay must be made without reservation, not subject to any other agreement. The holder of the commercial paper must be able to ascertain his or her right to payment from the instrument itself. Payment must also not be restricted to a particular fund. The holder must be confident in knowing the drawer or maker will be personally liable if the commercial paper is dishonored, without worrying whether a particular fund exists or is sufficient to make payment.

Certain Sum in Money

The holder of the commercial paper must be able to determine the amount payable from the face of the instrument. This includes any computation necessary to arrive at the correct figure. The amount must be payable in money. Money is currency, the agreed upon medium of exchange. Money refers to the dollar or any foreign currency which can be converted into dollars. It does not encompass precious metals, jewels, or other forms of personal property.

EXAMPLE Murray Steinman's Furniture Store was in need of cash. Steinman decided to reduce the rate of interest for those customers who repaid their notes within six months or less. Gloria and Barney Fisher, newleyweds, bought a dining room set for $3,500. They signed a promissory note which stated, "We agree to pay Murray Steinman $3,500 in twelve monthly installments with 14% interest; if however, the principal is repaid in six months or less, the interest rate shall be discounted to 12%." Is this promissory note negotiable? Yes! Although the interest on the amount owed may differ depending on when full repayment is made, it can be computed from the terms stated on the promissory note.

Roberts v. Smith and another
58 Vt. 492, 4 A. 709 (1886)

Roberts, the transferee, sued Smith, the maker of the note, for nonpayment.

E. P. Smith executed a promissory note to J. S. King which read "Two years from date, for value received, I promise to pay J. S. King, or bearer, one ounce of gold. E. P. Smith" Thereafter, J. S. King negotiated the note to Roberts for valuable consideration. Smith was advised of the transfer, but disregarded his promise and refused to pay the note when it came due. Smith argued that Roberts was not a holder because the note was nonnegotiable. This would prevent Roberts from enforcing the note against Smith. Smith's reasoning was based on the contention that the note did not set forth a certain sum payable in money.

The issue is whether one ounce of gold is a certain sum payable in money. The court held,

> It is but a promise to pay, that is, deliver, a certain article of merchandise definite in amount. Because gold enters into the composition of money we can not assume that "an ounce of gold" is money, or that it has a fixed and unvarying value. The contract in question lacks, not only the quality of negotiability, but certainty and precision as to the amount to be paid.

The note should be treated as a contract for the sale of goods, since gold is a commodity, not money. This would give Roberts a cause of action for breach of contract based on the assignment of contract rights from King to Roberts. Judgment for Smith.

Time for Payment

The commercial paper may state that time for payment is either on demand or at a definite time. Payable on demand means the payee must be paid at the time he or she presents the commercial paper for payment. Payable at a definite date means the time for payment is fixed and payment may not be demanded before that date. Notes and certificates of deposit are payable at a definite time in the future, while checks are usually payable on demand unless the check is postdated.

Payee: Order or Bearer

A drawer or maker may make the commercial paper payable to the order of himself or herself, to the drawee, or to a specific person or persons other than the above. In order to receive payment, the person to whom the commercial paper is payable must indorse the instrument by signing his or her name. Commercial paper may be made payable to two or more persons. If the payees are designated in the alternative, then anyone of them may indorse the instrument; if not, all of the payees must sign it. Commercial paper may also be made payable to bearer, to the order of bearer, to a specific person or bearer, or to cash. In these cases, to receive payment, the holder, who may be anyone in possession of the instrument, need only indorse his or her name and present it for payment. There is more of a risk that an instrument payable to bearer will be indorsed and presented for payment by someone other than the person to whom the drawer or maker intended because that person's name was not designated.

PURPOSE

The purpose of commercial paper is to act as a substitute for money and, in certain cases, as a credit device. Checks are the most popular and convenient substitute for money. Promissory notes serve as credit devices wherein money is loaned to a borrower in return for his or her promise to repay the loan in a lump sum or in certain installments at an agreed-upon rate of interest.

EXAMPLE | Mary Whitmore filled out an application for a VISA credit card. On the application it stated that the applicant agrees to pay all debts incurred through the use of this card within thirty days free of interest, or otherwise at the rate of $1\frac{1}{2}$ percent per month thereafter. Mary signed the application and was later accepted. What is the significance of the application she signed? It is a promissory note which remains open for as long as the credit card is authorized in her name. This promissory note is a credit device permitting Mary to purchase items on credit through the use of the VISA card.

NEGOTIATION

Negotiation occurs when commercial paper is properly transferred to a person (transferee), who then becomes a holder of the instrument. If the commercial paper is payable to the order of a specific person, an indorsement of that person's signature together with delivery of the instrument to the transferee are required for the transferee to become a holder. If the commercial paper is payable in bearer form to the person in possession of it, delivery of the instrument to the transferee is all that is required for him or her to become a holder. A holder is a transferee who has possession of commercial paper payable to his or her order or to bearer. A holder acquires all of the rights of the person who transferred the commercial paper to him or her. A holder may negotiate the commercial paper by transferring it in the required manner, or may enforce it for payment.

INDORSEMENTS

An indorsement is the signature of the person to whom the commercial paper is payable, which is required for the negotiation (transfer) of the instrument. The person to whom the commercial paper is payable may be any one of the following: the payee, the drawee, or the holder or accommodation indorser. An accommodation indorser is a person who extends his or her credit to the commercial paper to enable the holder to negotiate it to a person who is not satisfied with the holder's credibility.

EXAMPLE | Margaret Munson was food shopping at a Piggley Wiggley store in Buena Vista, Virginia. Her bill came to $65. She had only $55 in cash, so she attempted to indorse a $15 check made payable to her by her brother-in-law. The store manager refused to accept the indorsed check. Jim Stanton, the town postman, who was waiting in line, offered to vouch for Margaret Munson's credibility. The store manager requested Jim Stanton to indorse the check, as well. Jim acceded. What is his status? Jim is an accommodation indorser. He indorsed the check for Margaret's benefit to enable her to transfer it to Piggley Wiggley.

Special Indorsement

A special indorsement consists of the indorser's signature and specifies the person to whose order the instrument is payable. The person specified is the only one who can negotiate the instrument again. This may be done by his or her indorsement coupled with delivery to another.

Blank Indorsement

A blank indorsement is signed by the indorser but does not mention to whom the instrument is payable. Therefore it is payable to bearer—the person in possession of the instrument indorsed in blank.

EXAMPLE

Salvatore and Tina Palermo were separated. They were in the process of selling their home in St. Petersburg, Florida, when Salvatore moved to West Palm Beach. The net amount they were to receive from the sale of the house was $80,000. Salvatore and Tina agreed to divide the proceeds equally pursuant to a separation agreement. They informed the purchaser of this. At the closing of title, the deed was signed and delivered to the purchaser. Tina was present at the closing but Salvatore was not, because the house was in Tina's name. The purchaser brought two checks of equal amount made out to himself. On the first, he indorsed his name and handed it to Tina. On the second, he indorsed his name and then wrote "Pay to the order of Salvatore Palermo." He gave this check to the seller's attorney. What types of indorsements were made? The first was a blank indorsement which could be negotiated or presented for payment by the bearer, the person possessing it. The second was a special indorsement which could only be negotiated or presented for payment by Salvatore Palermo, even though his lawyer is in possession of it.

Restrictive Indorsement

There are four types of restrictive indorsements:

1. Conditional indorsements contain a condition precedent restricting the validity of the indorsement until the condition is fulfilled.
2. Indorsements which prohibit further transfers are not given any effect except to the extent they are treated as special indorsements.
3. Trust indorsements are indorsements which require payment to be made to an agent or trustee for the benefit of another.
4. Indorsements for deposit or collection restrict the commercial paper from being negotiated by anyone other than the bank to which it is presented. If the bank negotiates the instrument without crediting the depositor's account, it is guilty of conversion.

EXAMPLE

George Sommers was on his way home from work when he stopped at Picture Perfect Television Repair Shop, to pick up his set. This was the third time he left it there for repair. The bill was $75. Sommers made the check out to himself and then indorsed the back, "Pay to the order of Picture Perfect, if the television's picture is perfect for thirty days from the date of this check, signed George Sommers." George made a fast stop at the bank to deposit his salary check. He indorsed the check as follows, "George Sommers, For Deposit Only." His last stop was at his ex-wife's house to drop off the monthly checks for alimony and child support. He made the two checks payable to himself, then indorsed the back, "Pay to the order of Mary Sommers only" and "Pay to the order of Mary Sommers in trust for Timothy Sommers."

What is the effect of these restrictions? The television repair check contains a conditional indorsement. Picture Perfect must wait until the thirty days has lapsed before either negotiating the check or enforcing it for payment. If the set does not function properly within the thirty-day restriction, then Picture Perfect has no right to payment. The salary check contains an indorsement restricting anyone other than George's bank from negotiating the instrument or enforcing it for payment. The alimony check contains an indorsement which attempts to prohibit further negotiation. It will be treated as a special indorsement and Mary Sommers may negotiate it by signing and delivering it. The child support check is a trust indorsement. The proceeds of the check are payable to Mary Sommers for the benefit of her child, Timothy. If she negotiates the check to another and does not use the proceeds for Timothy, she may be compelled to account for Timothy's funds.

Fultz v. First National Bank in Graham
388 S.W.2d 405 (Tex.) 1965

Fultz sued the First National Bank for unauthorized payments made to his secretary from monies he had deposited in the bank with the restrictive indorsement, "For Deposit Only."

W. B. Fultz endorsed several checks, "Pay to the order of the First National Bank, Graham, Texas—For deposit only—W. B. Fultz." Fultz gave these checks to his secretary, Mrs. Fern McCoy, and asked her to make the deposit for him. The total amount of the checks credited to Fultz's account was $13,060, less certain unauthorized cash payments the bank made to Mrs. McCoy. Fultz contends these payments violated the specific instructions he gave the bank through his restrictive indorsement for deposit and collection. The bank argued Fultz did not report the violation within a reasonable time due to his negligence in failing to examine his banking statements.

The issue is whether the bank was responsible for making cash payments in violation of the restrictive indorsement "For Deposit Only."

The court held,

> The key to the first problem is the undisputed fact that the bank violated the written instructions of Fultz, and hence breached its deposit contract with him in each deposit transaction. In the exercise of care by Fultz, all of the checks which were deposited were endorsed "For Deposit Only." This was an unqualified direction to the bank to place the full amount of the checks in the account of Fultz. This instruction was violated when part of the amount of the checks was paid to Mrs. McCoy in cash. The bank had knowledge of its acts in violation of the instruction. Fultz as a depositor had the right to rely on the bank to honor the "For Deposit Only" instructions . . . he was under no duty to exercise further care to ascertain if the bank had followed his instructions. . . .

Judgment for Fultz.

Qualified Indorsement

A qualified indorsement is made by a person who transfers a negotiable instrument to another without guaranteeing that payment will be made. The qualified indorser may disclaim any contractual liability by signing the negotiable instrument, "without recourse."

Harry Morgan has his tax return prepared by Bob Robbins, an accountant for a large firm. Harry Morgan makes a check payable to Robbins. Robbins signs the check "Bob Robbins, without recourse" and hands it to the managing partner. What is the effect of Bob Robbins's indorsement? It is a qualified indorsement exempting Robbins from all contractual liability on the check. The check is still negotiable because Harry Morgan, the maker of the check, remains liable. This protects Robbins from being sued if the check bounces and Harry Morgan can not be located.

REVIEW QUESTIONS

1. Define commercial paper.
2. What are the four types of commercial paper?
3. Which ones are two-party instruments and which are three-party instruments?
4. Explain the requirements for negotiability.
5. List and explain the various types of indorsements.
6. What is the purpose of commercial paper?
7. Define negotiation, indorsements, holder, transferor, and transferee.
8. Lena Soma, an illiterate woman, received a check in return for the sale of land which she indorsed "for deposit Lena Soma." Her real estate agent advised her to leave the check with him for safekeeping. He then persuaded Alkoff to indorse it and deposit it with the Globe Bank. The Globe Bank accepted the check and credited Alkoff's account. Alkoff later wrote checks for the benefit of the real estate agent and herself. What recourse does Lena Soma have against the real estate agent, Alkoff, and the Globe Bank? Soma v. Handrulis et al., 277 N.Y. 223, 14 N.E.2d 46 (1938).
9. Roberts signed and delivered a promissory note payable to the Eastern States Warehouse and Cold Storage Company in return for services rendered. The Warehouse indorsed the note to the Chicopee National Bank, which held the note, along with other collateral, for the City National Bank. Roberts made a $1,500 payment on the note to the Warehouse which promptly presented the check to the Chicopee National Bank for payment. Chicopee did not know the check was given in payment of the note. The following year, City National Bank notified Roberts that it held the note and demanded payment. This was the first time Roberts had been notified that City National Bank was the owner of the note. What are the rights of City National Bank and Roberts in regard to each other? City National Bank v. Roberts et al., 266 Mass. 239, 165 N.E. 470 (1929).
10. Gordon signed the following check "Pay to the order of _____, Nine Hundred and Seventy Dollars—$970.00. Jno R. Gordon." This check was indorsed by Charles P. Downey and presented for payment at the Lansing State Savings Bank. The Bank refused to accept the check and make payment. The Bank asserted the check was not negotiable because no payee was designated either to the order of a specific person or to bearer. Is this a good defense to a suit for nonpayment? Gordon v. Lansing State Savings Bank, 133 Mich. 143, 94 N.W. 741 (1903).

21

COMMERCIAL PAPER: HOLDER IN DUE COURSE

INTRODUCTION

A holder is a person who is in possession of commercial paper and who has the power to negotiate it either by delivery or by indorsement and delivery.

A holder in due course (HDC) is a holder who acquires commercial paper for value; in good faith; and without notice that it is overdue, has been dishonored, or has any other defenses against it. The payee, as well as any subsequent person who receives the commercial paper, may qualify as a holder in due course by satisfying the following requirements.

REQUIREMENTS

Value

A holder must give valuable consideration in return for receiving the commercial paper, in order to qualify as a holder in due course. If the holder receives the instrument as a gift, he or she does not qualify as a holder in due course.

EXAMPLE Philip Brocton was to receive an inheritance of $1,200 in May. He informed his daughter Michelle that when the check arrived, he would negotiate it to her by indorsing it. On May 4, Philip Brocton received the check. He indorsed the check in blank and gave it to his daughter. Does Michelle qualify as a holder in due course? No! She is the recipient of a gift. This qualifies her as a mere holder because she gave no valuable consideration. If Philip Brocton negotiated the check to his daughter in return for her promise to repay the amount by doing clerical work in his office at the rate of $5 per hour for 240 hours would she be a holder in due course? No! The valuable consideration must be given at the time the commercial paper is negotiated. Michelle would still be a mere holder.

Good Faith

Good faith means honesty in fact. The purchaser must acquire the instrument in an honest manner. This does not preclude the transferor, the person from whom the holder received the commercial paper, from being an unscrupulous person or a thief. The good-faith requirement applies only to the transferee (purchaser).

EXAMPLE | Roger Thompson found a wallet on a street corner. Inside the wallet were several checks made payable to Harrison Whitney, which were already indorsed, and a deposit slip from Morgan Guaranty. As Thompson searched through the wallet, he came across Whitney's driver's license and registration. Thompson proceeded to Morgan Guaranty and cashed the checks against Whitney's account by providing the bank with proper identification. Does the bank qualify as a holder in due course? Yes! They acted in good faith when they paid valuable consideration to Thompson, whom they believed to be Whitney. If Thompson found no identification belonging to Whitney and offered to negotiate the checks, valued at $75, to a neighborhood liquor store for $30 worth of liquor, would the proprietor qualify as a holder in due course? No! The proprietor has not paid valuable consideration for the checks and has not acquired them in good faith. Good faith is lacking on the part of the proprietor because the suspicious circumstances through which he acquired the commercial paper, coupled with inadequate consideration requested, should have alerted him to refuse the instrument.

Manufacturers & Traders Trust Co. v. Sapowitch
296 N.Y. 226, 72 N.E.2d 166 (1947)

Manufacturers & Traders Trust Company sued Sapowitch for negotiable bonds which were pledged as collateral by a thief named Shuman who took a loan from the Trust Company.

Shuman applied for a loan from Manufacturers & Traders Trust Company. He offered as collateral certain negotiable bonds which he had stolen from Sapowitch. The theft was unknown to the bank. Shuman never repaid the outstanding loans, so the Trust Company attempted to foreclose their lien against the bonds. Sapowitch argued that the Trust Company had no right to the negotiable bonds beause it did not qualify as a holder in due course by virtue of the fact that it acquired the collateral in bad faith. The bank contended it was a holder in due course because it had no knowledge of the theft.

The issue is whether the bank acted in good faith, thus qualifying as a holder in due course.

The court held, "The requirement of the statute is good faith, and bad faith is not mere carelessness. It is nothing less than guilty knowledge or willful ignorance. . . . There is no claim of guilty knowledge in this case . . ."

The court reasoned,

One who purchases commercial paper for full value before maturity, without notice of any equities between the original parties, or of any defect of title; is to be deemed a bona fide holder. He is not bound at his peril to be upon the alert for circumstances which might possibly excite the suspicions of wary vigilance. He does not owe to the party who puts negotiable paper afloat the duty of active inquiry, to avert the imputation of bad faith. The rights of the holder are to be determined by the simple test of honesty and good faith, and not by speculations in regard to the purchaser's diligence or negligence. (Citations.)

The Trust Company qualified as a holder in due course, which entitled it to the bonds because the defense that the bonds were acquired from a thief is not good as against a holder in due course. Judgment for Manufacturers & Traders Trust Company.

No Notice of Defenses

The purchaser must acquire commercial paper without notice that it is overdue or has been dishonored, and without notice that a valid defense or claim exists against it. A purchaser has notice of a defense if the instrument is irregular. An instrument is irregular if it is visibly incomplete, forged, or altered.

EXAMPLE Alan McGuire was working as a temporary security guard at the Continental Illinois National Bank & Trust Company in Chicago. After business hours, he found a copy of a deposit slip made out by Martin Cromwell for $15,000. McGuire obtained a blank personal check from a bank officer's desk, wrote in the amount for $15,000, filled in Martin Cromwell's account number, and signed Martin Cromwell's name as it appeared on the deposit slip. A week later, McGuire indorsed the back of the check and presented it to the bank for payment. Does the bank qualify as a holder in due course? Yes! The bank was not on notice that the check had been forged because the forged signature was not visibly irregular. If McGuire had found or stolen one of Cromwell's signed checks and erased or whited out the amount, and then presented it to the bank for payment, would the bank be a holder in due course if it accepted the check? No! The bank would have noticed that the check had been altered from the visible erasure or white out. However, in either situation the bank will still be liable because the defense of forgery is valid against the claim of either a holder or a holder in due course.

RIGHTS OF A HOLDER IN DUE COURSE

Personal Defenses

The rights of a holder in due course are greater than those of a mere holder because a holder in due course *is not* subject to personal defenses, whereas a mere holder *is* subject to personal defenses. These personal defenses are:

Mistake

Unconscionability

Failure of a condition precedent

Fraudulent inducement

Lack of consideration

Expected delivery was not made

Release or discharge of debt

Stolen by a thief

If the drawer or maker or a prior transferor who indorsed the commercial paper raises any of the above defenses in a suit brought by a holder in due course, it will have no effect because of the special status of the holder in due course. If any of these defenses are raised against a holder, it will have the effect of nullifying his or her suit. Most of these defenses are discussed more fully in Chapter 14, Contractual Defenses.

Fraudulent Inducement   A drawer or maker who is induced to sign commercial paper based on the false representations of another has no defense if the instrument is negotiated to a holder in due course who requests payment. If the person requesting payment does not qualify as a holder in due course, the personal defense of fraudulent inducement will nullify his or her request.

EXAMPLE   Frank Carpenter is in a car accident in which severe body damage is done to the left fender on his Monte Carlo. Carpenter brings his car to Flashbright Auto Body. For $1,400, Flashbright agrees to replace the fender with a new one. Instead, they knock out the dents in the original fender, add a compound, sand and smooth out the indentations, and repaint the entire fender. The cost normally charged would be $400. Carpenter inspects the finished work, says, "Nice work," and gives a check for $1,400 to Flashbright. Flashbright quickly indorses and negotiates the check to one of its creditors, who qualifies as a holder in due course. Two days later, Carpenter notices some rough spots and realizes it is the same fender. He immediately stops payment on the check. In a suit brought by Flashbright's creditor, who is a holder in due course, would Carpenter's defense of fraudulent inducement be viable? No! A holder in due course is exempt from this defense. The reason for this is that, between the drawer or maker victimized by the fraudulent inducement and the holder in due course, the drawer or maker is in a better position to detect the fraud perpetrated by the payee. Carpenter's only recourse is to sue Flashbright for breach of contract and return of the $1,400.

Stolen by a Thief   A thief may negotiate commercial paper to another person; that person may even become a holder in due course. If that person becomes a holder in due course, then in a suit for payment against the drawer or maker, the fact that he or she acquired it from a thief will have no effect. Refer to the prior example in this chapter concerning Roger Thompson and Morgan Guaranty Bank. In that example, Thompson was a thief who presented checks signed by Harrison Whitney for payment. Morgan Guaranty made payment to Thompson because he possessed Whitney's identification. In that case, Morgan Guaranty would be a holder in due course.

Real Defenses

Both a holder and a holder in due course acquire commercial paper subject to real defenses. Real defenses include:

Forgery

Alterations

Duress

Statute of limitations has run

No capacity to contract either because of infancy or insanity

Fraud in the execution of the instrument

Illegality

Bankruptcy discharge

Forgery and Alteration   Forgery is the unauthorized signing of another person's signature. An alteration is something which materially changes the terms of the commercial paper, usually the amount. A holder has no right to payment when this defense is raised. A holder in due course has only the right to payment up to the orginal amount authorized before it was altered.

Fraud in the Execution   Fraud in the execution occurs when the drawer or maker does not know he or she is signing commercial paper. This is the difference between fraud in the execution and fraudulent inducement. In the latter, the drawer or maker knowingly and voluntarily signs a negotiable instrument. The fraud occurs when the consideration promised is not received or is not valuable.

EXAMPLE   John Braxton is a paralegal in a Park Avenue law firm. At Christmas time, Braxton finds himself low on cash. He takes one of the law firm's checks and tapes it underneath carbon paper. He then requests Errol Thorton, a partner in the firm to sign a legal document. Thorton's signature appears on the check as a result of the carbon paper trick. Braxton fills in the amount and then cashes the check at a local department store. When the firm is unable to balance its account, it discovers a missing check and issues a stop payment order. The department store presents the check, but it is dishonored because of the stop payment order. Assuming the department store is a holder in due course, what are its rights against the law firm? None! The law firm's defense of fraud in the execution of the commercial paper is a complete defense effective against holders and holders in due course alike.

Gross v. Ohio Savings & Trust Co.
116 Ohio 230, 156 N.E. 205 (1927)

Ohio Savings & Trust Company sued Gross for nonpayment on a note which Gross claims to have executed because of fraud.

Hill and Pittinger offered to sell Gross preferred stock in a drug store corporation they represented. After a quick glance at the paper, Gross agreed and signed what he thought was a contract for delivery of the shares of stock. The paper Gross signed was actually a promissory note which was conveyed to the Bank of Athens and then to the Ohio Savings & Trust Company. The latter qualifies as a holder in due course. Gross argued that he did not know he was signing a promissory note.

The issue is whether Gross's defense amounts to fraudulent inducement or fraud in the execution.

The court ruled,

> The distinction must be kept in mind between cases in which a party, through fraudulent representations, signs an instrument which he intends to be a negotiable promissory note, usually referred to as fraud in the inducement,

and those where through fraud and misrepresentation or deceit and trickery his signature is procured to a negotiable promissory note, when he had no intention or purpose to sign any such instrument, termed fraud in the inception of the instrument. It is quite well settled that fraud in the transaction out of which the instrument arose, or in respect to the consideration for which it was given, is no defense against a holder in due course. A different rule prevails where the signature of the maker of a negotiable instrument was obtained by fraudulent trick or device and the maker did not know that the paper he was signing was a negotiable instrument and had no intention of making or delivering such instrument. (Citation.)

In this case the court held that Gross was fraudulently induced to sign the note. This defense is valid against a holder, but not a holder in due course. The bank qualified as a holder in due course. If the signing of the note had been ruled to be fraud in the execution, rather than fraudulent inducement, this defense would have been valid against both holders and holders in due course including the bank.
The court decided,

[Citations] It is better that defendant [Gross], and others who so carelessly affix their names to paper, the contents of which are unknown to them, should suffer from the fraud which their recklessness invites, than that the character of commercial paper should be impaired, and the business of the country thus interfered with and unsettled.

Judgment for Ohio Savings & Trust Company.

SHELTER DOCTRINE

A transferee who acquires commercial paper from a holder in due course, but who does not qualify as one, is still entitled to the rights of a holder in due course under the shelter doctrine. The reason for this is because a transferee acquires all of the rights of his or her transferor.

EXAMPLE Christopher Shatner received a check made out to cash for $35 in a birthday card which read, "Have a drink on me, Tom." Shatner realized the check was mistakenly sent to him, but he decided to cash it anyway. He went down to the Drink and Be Merry liquor store where he purchased two bottles of his favorite scotch. Shatner indorsed his name on the back of the check and gave it to Robert Williams, the proprietor. That night, Williams's son asked to borrow his father's car for the big date he had the following evening. Williams assented, told his son to have a good time, and indorsed the $35 check that Shatner gave him over to his son. The following afternoon, the son took the check to the bank and found that payment had been stopped by the person who sent the birthday card. Is the son entitled to payment? Williams's son is a mere holder because he acquired the commercial paper by gift, not for value. Even so, he is still entitled to the rights of a holder in due course, under the shelter doctrine. This is because Williams, the son's transferor, is a holder in due course. The son, with the rights of a holder in due course, is not subject to any personal defenses, including mistake, and is entitled to payment. The drawer's recourse lies against Christopher Shatner, who negotiated the check with knowledge of the mistake.

REVIEW QUESTIONS

1. Define holder in due course, holder, value, good faith, and without notice of defenses.

2. What personal defenses are not valid against a holder in due course who is seeking to enforce the commercial paper for payment?

3. What real defenses are valid against a holder in due course?

4. Explain the difference between fraudulent inducement and fraud in the execution.

5. Can a person who acquires commercial paper from a thief qualify as a holder in due course?

6. What is the shelter doctrine?

7. Define forgery and alteration.

8. Smith asked Hardy to write his signature on a blank piece of paper. Hardy did so, but the paper turned out to be the back of a promissory note. Smith negotiated the note to Ouachita National Bank, which qualified as a holder in due course. The bank brought a lawsuit to enforce payment of the note against Hardy. Does Hardy have any valid defense? Hardy v. Ouachita National Bank, 165 Ark. 532, 265 S.W. 74.(1924).

9. Linick signed a blank check which was later stolen by Ryckoff and Silberman. They filled in the name of the payee and the sum, indorsed the payee's name on the back, and negotiated it to A. J. Nutting & Company. Nutting & Company cashed the check at the State Bank where Linick kept his account. Linick sued Nutting & Company for the value of the check, claiming the check had been stolen by a thief and altered. If Nutting & Company qualified as a holder in due course, would either of the defenses be good against it? Linick v. A. J. Nutting & Co., 140 App. Div. 265, 125 N.Y.S. 93 (1910).

10. Frank L. Fancher signed a note for $75 which was also indorsed by Lester, as an accommodation indorser. The check was subsequently altered to $375 and negotiated to the National Exchange Bank of Albany. The bank argued that Lester was liable if he had carelessly placed his name on the commercial paper without observing the spaces that Fancher left open, which would permit an alteration to the check. Lester contended that a drawer is not under a legal duty to prepare a check so carefully as to avoid any chance of alteration. Is the defense of alteration raised by Lester valid against the bank, who is a holder in due course? National Exchange Bank of Albany v. Lester, 194 N.Y. 461, 87 N.E. 779 (1909).

22

COMMERCIAL PAPER LIABILITY OF THE PARTIES, BANK DEPOSITS, AND COLLECTIONS

CONTRACTUAL LIABILITY OF PARTIES

Drawer and Maker

In a two-party instrument, it is the maker who is primarily liable for payment when the promissory note or certificate of deposit matures. In a three-party instrument, the drawer is only secondarily liable. He or she becomes liable to the holder of the check or draft if the drawee dishonors it.

Drawee

The bank or the drawee is primarily liable when it accepts a check or draft for payment. The reason the bank must accept the check before becoming primarily liable is to give the bank the opportunity to examine the drawer's account to verify that it contains sufficient funds to cover the check. If the drawer's account is maintained at a different bank, the depositor may cash the check against his or her own bank account. In that case, the depositor must have sufficient funds to cover the check if it bounces. A check bounces when the drawer does not have sufficient funds in the account to cover outstanding checks.

A bank has a contract with the drawer to pay all checks signed by the drawer where he or she maintains sufficient funds in an account to cover the checks issued. If a bank wrongfully dishonors a check by refusing to accept it where adequate funds were maintained, the drawer will be liable to the holder for payment, but the bank will be liable to the drawer for breach of contract. If the bank accepts a forged or altered instrument, it cannot charge the drawer's account, because the drawer is not liable for forgery or a subsequent alteration unless his or her negligence substantially contributed to the forgery or alteration.

Indorser

An indorser who signs an instrument agrees to pay its face value when it becomes due or upon presentment. This is a surety contract. A surety is a person who agrees to be liable for the debt of another. An indorser agrees to be liable for the debt of the maker or drawer of a negotiable instrument. For more information on suretyship, refer to Chapter 27.

An indorser is liable to the holder of the commercial paper or to any subsequent indorser who receives it from the holder, if the instrument is dishonored when presented for payment. Notice of dishonor must be given to the indorser by the holder. If there is more than one indorser, the indorsers are liable to each other in the order in which their signatures appear on the commercial paper. An indorser's liability is limited to the amount stated on the instrument when the indorsement was made. An indorser can disclaim his or her contractual liability by signing the check "without recourse." This protects the indorser from liability for any subsequent indorsement.

Accommodation Indorser

An accommodation indorser is a person who lends his or her signature to an instrument to help the holder negotiate it. As an indorser of the holder's instrument, the person making the accommodation is liable as a surety. Presentment and notice of dishonor are required. An accommodation indorser is considered to be a surety because he or she is guaranteeing the payment of another. An accommodation indorser is not liable to the person being accommodated; instead, the accommodation indorser has the right to reimbursement for any payments made on behalf of the person accommodated.

WARRANTY LIABILITY OF THE PARTIES

The UCC provides for certain warranties in regard to the transfer and presentment of commercial paper.

Transferor's Warranties

A transferor is a person who transfers commercial paper to another. In doing so, he or she warrants the following:

1. He or she has good title to the commercial paper.
2. All signatures on the commercial paper are genuine.
3. There has been no material alteration of the instrument.
4. No defenses exist against him or her. If the transferor indorses the instrument "without recourse," the warranty is limited to the transferor's knowledge.
5. He or she has no knowledge of any bankruptcy proceedings involving the drawer or maker.

These warranties are made either to a transferor's immediate transferee, if the transfer was made without indorsement; or to the transferee and any subsequent good-faith holder if the transfer was made by indorsement.

Warranties on Presentment

Any person who presents commercial paper and receives payment, warrants to the person or bank who made payment in good faith that:

1. He or she has good title to the commercial paper.
2. He or she has no knowledge that the signature has been forged.
3. The instrument has not been materially altered.

The warranties (2) and (3) against forgery and alteration, respectively, are not made by a holder in due course who is acting in good faith.

PRESENTMENT

Presentment is a demand by a holder either for payment from the maker or acceptance by the drawee. Commercial paper must be presented before a drawer or an indorser can be liable. The time of presentment must be reasonable. If an instrument matures on a definite date, presentment must be made on or before that date. With regard to checks, presentment must be made within thirty days from the date of issue or else the check will be considered stale. This puts the holder on notice that the check is overdue. The drawer's liability coincides with this rule, thirty days from the date of issue. An indorser's liability is limited to seven days after the date of his or her indorsement. Unexcused or unreasonable delay in presentment or notice of dishonor will result in discharge of the drawer or the indorser.

PROOF OF SIGNATURE

The signature on the instrument by the drawer or maker, or by an indorser, is deemed admitted by those parties unless it is specifically denied. The burden of proof is on the holder, but the holder is aided by the presumption of genuineness of a signature which applies in all cases except where the signer has died or has become imcompetent. The signer must then establish a real or personal defense to the holder's claim. If the holder can prove he or she fulfilled all the requirements of a holder in due course, or is entitled to the rights of a holder in due course under the shelter doctrine, then the holder will not be subject to any personal defense raised by the signer.

No person is liable unless his or her signature appears on the instrument. If the signature is forged or otherwise unauthorized, it is ineffective against the person whose name was unlawfully signed. This includes an agent exceeding his or her authority.

SIGNATURE OF AN AUTHORIZED AGENT

A signature by an authorized agent must be in his or her authorized capacity and the agent must also sign the name of the person he or she represents or else risk personal liability. Authorized capacity may be either express or implied.

LIABILITY UNDER SPECIAL CIRCUMSTANCES

Impostors

An indorsement by an impostor is effective if the impostor, through the use of the mails or in person, induces a drawer or maker to sign an instrument payable to the person whom the impostor is impersonating and to mail the instrument to the impostor. The person receiving the instrument (usually a check) from the impostor is entitled to payment from the maker or drawer if the receiver acted in good faith and exercised ordinary care in accepting the instrument. In other words, the person receiving it must be a holder in due course.

EXAMPLE | Scott Hanson sent Barbara Reynolds the following letter:

Dear Preferred Customer,
   We are writing to advise you of our liquidation of inventory of pots and pans, at greatly reduced prices. Our six-piece set, regularly $109, now only $69. Our twelve-piece set, regularly $179, now only $109. This offer good for thirty days only. Make checks payable to the signer as agent for Farberware.
Signed Thomas Josephson
   Barbara Reynolds ordered a set of each and mailed the check to the impostor, Scott Hanson, under the impression she was mailing it to an agent for Farberware. Hanson signed the name of the payee, Thomas Josephson, then indorsed the check to the Greensboro National Bank which paid him cash for it. Barbara sued the bank for wrongful payment. Is she entitled to recover the amount of the check from the bank? No! The impostor's indorsement is effective as long as the bank acted in good faith and exercised ordinary care in accepting the check. As between the bank and the drawer, Barbara Reynolds, the bank is the more innocent party and should be entitled to payment because the drawer had the opportunity to prevent the fraud by not dealing with the impostor.

Padded Payroll

A padded payroll is one to which a dishonest employee has added names that are unauthorized and frequently fictitious. Checks are issued to these fictitious payees and indorsed by the dishonest employee. An indorsement by an agent or employee who supplies the drawer or maker with the name of a payee, usually fictitious, and who induces the drawer or maker to issue a negotiable instrument to that person, is effective even though the impostor intends the named payee to have no interest in the commercial paper. The person or bank receiving the indorsed instrument is not liable if they acted in good faith and exercised ordinary care.

Jonathan Rhodes worked as treasurer for the Whitney and Myers Department Store. There were ninety-two employees of the store. Rhodes issued ninety-five checks each week. The three additional checks were issued to Moe, Larry, and Curly—fictitious employees of the department store who supposedly worked with mannequins. Rhodes indorsed the name of the payees and negotiated the checks to the Williamsburg Savings Bank in return for cash. When the department store discovered Rhodes's scheme, he had left for a permanent vacation in the Bahamas. Has the department store any recourse against the bank? No! The indorsements of Rhodes, the impostor, are effective against the company as long as the bank acted in good faith.

Conversion

Conversion is the theft of another's property. Conversion of commercial paper occurs when it is delivered to a person or bank which misappropriates it. A person or a bank is also guilty of conversion when they accept a forged instrument and credit the account of the person whose name was forged. The reason this amounts to conversion is because they are transferring funds from the account of the rightful owner to the forger even though they may have acted in good faith. Conversion does not require intent to steal; otherwise, it would be a crime. See Chapter 5, Torts, for a more detailed discussion of conversion.

Negligence

Any negligence of the drawer which substantially contributes to a forgery or alteration will prevent the drawer from asserting either of these defenses against a holder in due course, including a bank which makes payment in good faith. If the bank was also negligent in accepting the commercial paper for payment, this rule would not apply and the defenses of forgery and alteration could still be raised.

Certification

A bank is not under any obligation to certify a check, but when it does so, the certification operates as an acceptance of the check. This means the drawer and all prior indorsers are discharged from liability. The bank has agreed to honor the check as presented for payment.

Lost, Stolen, or Destroyed Instruments

A person who claims to be the owner of a lost, stolen, or destroyed instrument may recover from any person liable on the instrument (maker, drawer, indorser, or the bank that accepted the instrument for cash), if the person making the claim can prove the following:

Ownership of the instrument

Facts lending to the instrument's loss

Terms of the instrument

The court may require the purported owner to provide security indemnifying the person or bank from any future superior claims. When a check is stolen through the mails, the person who was to have received it must file a sworn affidavit testifying to the fact that the check was never received.

EXAMPLE | William Mayer lost his wallet while trying on a pair of pants in the fitting room at Sak's Fifth Avenue Men's Shop. Subsequently, John Eastwood found the wallet with several blank checks inside. He forged Mayer's name and cashed the checks against Mayer's account. Later that day, William Mayer reported the checks stolen. He signed a sworn affidavit to that effect. Is Mayer entitled to have his account recredited for the amount paid by the bank to John Eastwood? Yes! William Mayer, as owner of the checks, may recover from the bank which cashed the checks. The bank must then look to John Eastwood, the person who cashed the checks, if he can be found.

BANK DEPOSITS AND COLLECTIONS

Classification of Banks

Depository bank is the first bank the commercial paper is transferred to for collection.

Intermediary bank is the bank through which the commercial paper is transferred during the course of collection. They are usually large banks which maintain accounts with the Federal Reserve Bank in their district. Intermediary banks provide access for smaller banks to the Federal Reserve Bank check-clearing process by allowing smaller banks to maintain accounts with them for this purpose.

Collection Banks include the thirteen Federal Reserve Banks which handle commercial paper for collection.

Payor Bank is the bank on which payment is drawn. It may be the same as the depository bank.

EXAMPLE | Margaret Quinn draws a check on the St. Petersburg Savings Bank and mails it to her niece Mary Kathryn, who deposits the check in her account at the Staten Island Savings Bank. The check-clearing process begins. The Staten Island Savings Bank transfers the check to Citibank, with whom it maintains an account for collection. Citibank transfers the check to the New York Federal Reserve Bank, with whom it, in turn, maintains an account for collection purposes. The New York Federal Reserve Bank transfers the check to the Atlanta Federal Reserve Bank, which covers the state of Florida. The Atlanta Federal Reserve Bank transfers the check to the First National Bank of Florida, which maintains an account with the Atlanta Federal Reserve Bank for collection purposes. The First National Bank of Florida in Tampa transfers the check to the St. Petersburg Savings Bank, which maintains an account with the First National Bank of Florida for collection. The St. Petersburg Savings Bank finally returns the check to Margaret Quinn along with her other checks and monthly bank statement. What are the classifications of the respective banks? The Staten Island Savings Bank is the depository bank. Citibank and the First National Bank of Florida are intermediary banks. The New York and Atlanta Federal Reserve Banks are collection banks. The St. Petersburg Savings Bank is the payor bank.

Process of Posting

The process of posting is the usual procedure followed by a payor bank in determining whether to make payment and in recording payment.

The bank will

1. Verify the signature.
2. Check the drawer's account to determine whether sufficient funds are available.
3. Stamp the check "paid."
4. Make an entry to the drawer's account.

Warranties

The warranties made by the customer, collection banks, and the intermediary banks who obtain payment parallel the warranties made on presentment discussed earlier:

1. Good title
2. No knowledge of forgery
3. No knowledge of material alteration

A customer and any bank in the collection process which obtains payment and who qualifies as a holder in due course, do not make the warranties concerning knowledge of forgery and alteration.

Each customer and bank in the collection process that transfers the check, makes the same warranties as those made by a transferor of commercial paper:

1. Good title
2. All signatures are genuine
3. No knowledge of material alteration
4. There is no valid defense against him or her
5. No knowledge of any bankruptcy proceeding against the maker or drawer of the instrument

Bank's Right to Revoke

A depository bank has the right to revoke, charge back, or obtain a refund of any amount credited to the customer's account up until the time payment becomes final.

Final Payment

Payment becomes final when

1. The process of posting is completed
2. The payor bank has paid cash
3. The payor bank settled the instrument without reserving the right to revoke or

4. Provisionally settled the instrument and failed to revoke within the statutory period

Stop Payment Order

The payor bank must receive a stop payment order within a reasonable time for the bank to act on it. This means the order must be received before the bank has

1. Accepted or certified the check
2. Paid cash for the check
3. Settled the check without reserving its right to revoke
4. Completed the process of posting to the drawer's account

The effect of a stop payment order is to suspend the bank's duty to pay on a check or to charge the drawer's account for it. Oral stop payment orders are effective for fourteen days; written ones are effective for six months. If the bank pays on a check after receiving a stop payment order within a reasonable time, the bank will be liable only for the loss actually suffered by the drawer. If the check was negotiated to a holder in due course and then negligently paid by the bank in spite of a stop payment order, the holder in due course and the payor bank (which would be subrogated to the rights of a holder in due course) would prevail—that is, unless the drawer could set up a real defense to justify the stop payment order.

Payor Bank's Rights and Duties

The payor bank has the following rights:

1. The right to charge a customer's account for any check which is properly payable
2. The right to subrogation of the rights of a holder in due course or payee against the drawer; or the right to subrogation of a drawer's rights against the payee or other holder
3. The right to dishonor stale checks
4. The right to honor checks for ten days after the date a person becomes incompetent or dies unless notified to stop payment

The payor bank has a duty to act by midnight of the banking day on which it receives the check by paying the check, returning it, or sending notice of dishonor.

Mitchell Livestock Auction Co., Inc. v. Bryant State Bank et al. 65 S.D. 488, 275 N.W. 262 (1937)

Mitchell Livestock Auction Company received a check for over $1,500 from Claude Landergaard. It indorsed and deposited the check with the Mitchell National Bank. The Mitchell National Bank forwarded it to the First National Bank & Trust Company of Minneapolis, which indorsed the check and forwarded it to the Bryant State Bank, the payor bank. Bryant State Bank received the check on July 16, but did not give notice that it dishonored the check because of insufficient funds until July 23. The bank claims that the retention of a check without acting on it is not grounds, in and of itself, to require the bank to pay it without acceptance or certification.

The issue is whether the bank should be liable for payment as a result of its breach of duty to act promptly with regard to the check.

The court held, ". . . a drawee bank will be deemed to have accepted a check if it refuses within twenty-four hours after delivery . . ." to return it to the holder. ". . . The drawee has twenty-four hours within which to determine the status of the drawer's account and to make other investigation . . ." Judgment for Mitchell Livestock.

Drawer's Rights and Duties

A drawer has the following rights:

1. The right to damages for the bank's wrongful dishonor. This is a breach of contract action. The drawer's recourse includes consequential damages for arrest or prosecution for passing a bad check.
2. The right to stop payment.

The drawer has the duty to examine his or her bank statement and cancelled checks to discover and report unauthorized signatures and alterations.

After the bank statement is received by the drawer, the drawer must use reasonable care and promptness in discovering the forgery or alteration, and must notify the bank promptly. If the bank establishes that the drawer failed to comply with this requirement, then the drawer cannot assert the forgery or alteration if the bank has suffered a loss or if the drawer had possession of the bank statement and cancelled checks for fourteen days before the bank is notified. The drawer can assert the forgery or alteration regardless of the above if the bank was negligent in paying the check. Even if the bank is negligent, the drawer must report the forgery of his or her signature or alteration within one year, or the unauthorized indorsement of another within three years, for the defense to be valid. If the bank waives its defense against the drawer, it forfeits its claim against any collecting bank or prior transferor.

REVIEW QUESTIONS _____

1. Explain the banking deposit and collection process.
2. What are the payor bank's rights and duties?
3. What are the drawer's rights and duties?
4. Define presentment.
5. How does an agent properly sign for a principal in order for the agent to absolve himself or herself from all liability?
6. What is the contractual liability of the drawer, maker, drawee, indorser, surety, and accommodation indorser?

7. Who is liable when an impostor defrauds a person by inducing that person to send a check to the impostor payable to an individual being impersonated?

8. List and explain the warranties made on transfer and on presentment.

9. Martin deposited a sum of money in the Iowa National Bank for which he was given a certificate of deposit. Dean received the certificate thirty-two years later as a result of a series of transfers by indorsement, presented it for payment, and demanded a return of the principal plus interest from the date he received it. The bank argued the statute of limitations had lapsed. What result? Dean v. Iowa–Des Moines National Bank & Trust Co., 227 Iowa 1239, 290 N.W. 664 (1938).

10. In return for a delivery of furniture to Reimann Furniture Manufacturing Company, Rich L. Reimann and L. D. Reimann signed a promissory note agreeing to pay West Coast Lumber & Supply Company the full purchase price of the furniture. The note was signed Reimann Furniture Mfg. Co. by Rich L. Reimann and L. D. Reimann. The Reimanns argue that the debt was incurred by the corporation for which they were signing. Murphy contended that the Reimanns failed to sign in their representative capacities, therefore they are individually liable. Murphy received the note as the result of an assignment from West Coast Lumber & Supply after the note matured. Will Murphy's suit for payment on the note be successful? Murphy et al. v. Reimann Furniture Mfg. Co. et al., 183 Ore. 474, 193 P.2d 1000 (1948).

23

SECURED TRANSACTIONS

INTRODUCTION

Transactions involving consumers and businesses may be made on a cash or credit basis. No debt is incurred in a cash transaction because payment is made when performance is rendered. In a credit transaction, part or full payment is deferred until a later date. This creates a debt owed by the purchaser to the seller. The purchaser becomes known as a debtor and the seller becomes known as a creditor.

Credit transactions may be secured or unsecured. A secured credit transaction is one in which the creditor has a security interest in personal property belonging to the debtor. The personal property acts as collateral for the debt owed. The security interest, once attached and perfected, gives the creditor the right to sell the collateral if the debtor defaults, with the proceeds applied to the debt. A security agreement is generally signed by the debtor, thus evidencing the existence of a security interest in the collateral. An unsecured credit transaction is one in which no security interest exists; no collateral is offered to secure the debt owed. Consumers or businesses enter into unsecured credit transactions on the strength of the name, goodwill, and reliability of the debtor for prompt payment. Secured transactions are covered by Article 9 of the Uniform Commercial Code.

COLLATERAL

There are two general classifications of personal property which may serve as collateral: tangible (goods), and intangible (commercial paper, accounts, chattel mortgage, documents of title, and other general intangibles).

Tangible Personal Property

Tangible personal property refers to goods. Goods are defined as all personal property and fixtures which are movable at the time a security interest attaches. Fixtures are personal property which have been permanently attached to real property in such a way as to become a part of it. Fixtures include such things as cabinets, shelving, plumbing, oil and gas burners, hot water heaters, air conditioning units, chandeliers, and mirrors. Goods do not include money and intangible personal property.

Goods may be further subdivided into the following categories: consumer goods, equipment, farm products, and inventory.

Consumer goods are goods purchased for personal or household use. Examples of consumer goods are utensils, pots and pans, and furniture.

Equipment used in a business includes such things as machinery, trucks, office furniture, computers, and copiers.

Farm products include livestock, cattle, poultry, and their byproducts (meat, milk, cheese, eggs); and crops, such as wheat, corn, soybeans, rice, sugar, potatoes and the products made from them (corn oil, processed sugar).

Inventory consists of goods held for sale or lease and raw materials on hand which are used in the production of goods.

Intangible Personal Property

Intangible personal property consists of the following:

Chattel mortgages are a security interest held in particular goods to secure payment of a debt. The debt may or may not relate to the goods mortgaged. The word *chattel* refers to personal property including goods.

Accounts receivable are the right to payment for goods sold or leased, or for services rendered.

Negotiable instruments are checks, notes, and other forms of commercial paper.

Documents of title include bills of lading, warehouse receipts, and other documents which evidence that the person holding them is entitled to possession of the goods they cover.

Other intangible personal property include such things as patent rights, copyrights, and trademarks.

CREATION OF A SECURITY INTEREST

A security interest is created and attaches to the specified collateral when the following criteria are satisfied. First, either the collateral must be in the possession of the creditor or a security agreement must be signed by the debtor in which the collateral is described. If the collateral consists of crops or timber, then a legal description of the real estate on which the crops or timber are located must be included. Second, the creditor must have given valuable consideration for the security interest. Third, the debtor must have rights in the collateral. The creation of a security interest gives a creditor the right to sell the property upon the debtor's default in payment and to apply the proceeds to the debt.

PERFECTION OF A SECURITY INTEREST

When a security interest is created, it protects the creditor against the debtor alone. The creation of a security interest, in and of itself, does not protect a creditor against other secured creditors, general creditors represented by a trustee in bankruptcy, and good-faith purchasers. The security interest must be perfected.

There are three methods of perfecting a security interest.

Transfer of Collateral

A security interest is perfected when the debtor transfers possession of the collateral to the creditor.

EXAMPLE Joseph Rice pawns his wedding band and his gold watch at Christopher Strauss's Pawn Shop, for $350 in cash. Is Strauss's security interest in the wedding band and gold watch perfected? Yes! Strauss's security interest in the watch was created when he gave valuable consideration in the amount of $350, and when Rice transferred possession of the watch to Strauss. This also perfected the security interest.

Purchase-Money Security Interest

A security interest is automatically perfected when a purchase-money security interest is created. This rule applies only to the sale of consumer goods on credit, pursuant to a security agreement signed by the debtor. The purchase money is advanced in return for a security interest in the goods sold.

EXAMPLE Charles Lerner bought a $4,000 personal computer from William Lipton's Video Electronic store on credit. Lerner made a down payment of $500 and signed a security agreement pledging the computer as collateral for the $3,500 debt. Does Lipton have a security interest in the computer and is it perfected? Yes! This is a purchase-money security interest. The security interest was created and perfected pursuant to a signed security agreement in which possession of the computer was transferred to Lerner in return for his promise to repay the debt owed, with the computer serving as collateral.

Filing a Financing Statement

A security interest is perfected when a financing statement is filed. The financing statement must include the names and addresses of the debtor and creditor, and a statement describing the collateral. If the collateral is timber or crops, a description of the real estate on which they are located must be set forth as well. A copy of the security agreement may be used as long as the pertinent information is conveyed. The financing statement must be filed with the appropriate government official designated by state law. In most states, the designated official is the secretary of state or the county clerk when the collateral involves consumer goods, farm products, or farm equipment. The use of the secretary of state means that a state-wide filing system, which is centrally located, has been adopted. This system affords businesses which operate nationally or throughout the state with easy access to information concerning prospective customers who wish to borrow on credit. It would prove to be a burdensome task if they were relegated to contacting each county clerk throughout one or more states. However, where consumers, farmers, and other local businesses are concerned, it is more convenient to have the information filed with the county clerk. This is why some states require filing with the secretary of state except for local matters, in which case the financing statement is filed with the county clerk.

A financing statement, giving rise to a perfected security interest, is effective for five years, at which time a continuation statement may be filed. Otherwise the security interest will lapse. Once the financing statement is filed by the creditor, it puts all subsequent purchasers on constructive notice of the existence of a perfected security interest in the secured property which has been offered as collateral. This perfected security interest is a lien and others may purchase this secured property subject only to this lien. This means that a person who buys subject to a perfected security interest cannot qualify as a good-faith purchaser.

GOOD-FAITH PURCHASERS

A purchaser who buys goods in the regular course of business in good faith, for value, and without notice of a perfected security interest is given preference to the goods over a creditor with a perfected security interest.

EXAMPLE Theresa Mandrell buys a stereo for $700 cash from the World of Music, Inc. The World of Music is an outlet which sells stereo and musical equipment. The inventory carried by the World of Music is financed by the equipment manufacturers. They have a purchase money security interest which has been automatically perfected. Shortly thereafter, the World of Music defaults on the debts it owes to the equipment manufacturers. Can the manufacturer of the stereo sold to Theresa Mandrell reclaim it from her? No! Theresa is a good-faith purchaser who promised to pay valuable consideration for the stereo and who bought it without knowledge of the perfected security interest. She is entitled to the stereo as against the claims of the manufacturer for redress. The stereo manufacturer must look to the proceeds received by the World of Music from the sale of the stereo.

A good-faith purchaser who buys goods from a consumer who in turn bought the goods pursuant to a credit transaction in which the retailer has a purchase money security interest in the goods, is also given preference over the retailer regardless of the retailer's perfected security interest unless the retailer filed a financing statement.

EXAMPLE Frank MacNeil bought a chain saw for $369 on credit from Sears. He used the saw once to cut a number of tree branches which hung over his house. A week later, his neighbor, Ralph Pisano, offered to buy the saw from him for $300. Pisano wanted to cut wood for his fireplace. After the sale to Pisano, MacNeil stopped making payments on the saw to Sears. Sears tried to enforce its perfected security interest by suing Pisano for return of the saw. Sears never filed a financing statement because its security interest was automatically perfected on the creation of the purchase money security interest. Who has the paramount right to the saw? Ralph Pisano! He made a good-faith purchase of the saw, for valuable consideration, and without knowledge of Sears's perfected security interest. Sears was protected against the original buyer's other creditors, but not against a good-faith purchaser for value.

PRIORITIES

A perfected purchase money security interest in collateral other than inventory is given priority over conflicting security interests where the perfection of the purchase money security interest occurs at the time or within ten days after the debtor takes possession of the collateral. Perfection of a purchase money security interest occurs when a security agreement is signed by the debtor.

A perfected purchase money security interest in inventory is given priority over conflicting security interests in the inventory, and any cash proceeds received by the debtor on or before delivery to a buyer, provided the following criteria are satisfied. First, the security interest must be perfected when the debtor receives the inventory and, second, notice must be given to the holders of the conflicting security interests.

Priority among conflicting security interests in the same collateral is given to the person who first filed the financing statement or, otherwise, the person who first perfected the security interest. The latter may be accomplished by receiving possession of the collateral pursuant to a signed security agreement. Among conflicting security interests which remain unperfected, the first security interest created and attached to the specified collateral will be given priority.

The creditor having priority may use the collateral to satisfy the debt owed to him or her either by retaining the collateral, or selling it and keeping the proceeds. If the value of the collateral exceeds the amount owed, the creditor must return the proceeds to the debtor.

Matter of Ultra Precision Industries, Inc.
503 F.2d 414 (9th Cir. 1974)

National Acceptance Company brought a petition for review to contest the priority of claims made by others which were perfected subsequently.

National Acceptance Company of California loaned Ultra Precision Industries almost $700,000, which was secured by a chattel mortgage agreement referring to Ultra's equipment. The security interest was perfected by National when it filed a financing statement. Subsequent to National's obtaining a security interest in Ultra's equipment, Wolf Machinery Company sold two machines to Ultra pursuant to a purchase money security interest agreement and then assigned its rights to Community Bank. The bank's security interest was also perfected. Wolf held a security interest in a third machine it had sold to Ultra. Before Ultra purchased the equipment from Wolf, National had a perfected security interest in all equipment owned by Ultra. National contends that at the moment the three machines were delivered to Ultra, its perfected security interest attached.

The issue is on what date did the conflicting security interest arise and who has paramount right to the machines serving as collateral.

The court held, "It is manifest that Ultra was not a 'debtor' of Wolf and did not owe payment or other performance of the obligation secured unto Wolf until the moment of execution and delivery of the Security Interest Agreements . . ."

The court decided,

> We hold that Ultra became the purchase money security interest "debtor receiving possession of the collateral (the three respective machines)" at the instant of the execution and delivery of the Security Interest Agreements, respectively, and not before; and further, that since each of the Security Interest Agreements were timely perfected, the security interests of Wolf and Bank, respectively are each prior and superior to the conflicting security interest held by National. (Citation.)

Judgment for Wolf and Bank.

REVIEW QUESTIONS

1. Define secured transaction, collateral, security interest, debtor, and creditor.
2. How can a security interest be perfected?
3. In what order will priorities be accorded among conflicting security interests?
4. What are the rights of a good-faith purchaser as against a person holding a perfected security interest?
5. How is a security interest created?
6. List and explain the various types of collateral.
7. Plant Reclamation sold equipment to Amex-Protein Development Corporation before Amex filed for bankruptcy. Plant Reclamation refused to continue selling to Amex on an open account and requested a promissory note securing the debt owed with specific personal property, which was set forth in a financing statement filed by Plant Reclamation. The note said, "This note is secured by a Security Interest in subject personal property as per invoices." This referred to invoices of property recently sold to Amex. Was a security interest created? Matter of Amex-Protein Development Corporation, 504 F.2d 1056 (9th Cir. 1974).

24

BANKRUPTCY

INTRODUCTION

Bankruptcy is the relief afforded an honest debtor by discharging all of the debts he or she owes. A debtor is an individual, association, joint venture, partnership, or corporation that owes a debt to a creditor. A creditor is the person or entity to whom the debt is owed. A debt is an obligation owed by a debtor to a creditor.

The following is a discussion of the Federal Bankruptcy Reform Act of 1978 which has been the first major revision of the bankruptcy laws in forty years.

BANKRUPTCY REFORM ACT

Provisions

Chapter 1   General Provisions
Chapter 3   Case Administration
Chapter 5   Creditors, The Debtor and The Estate
Chapter 7   Liquidation
Chapter 9   Adjustment of Debts of a Municipality
Chapter 11 Reorganization
Chapter 13 Adjustment of Debts of an Individual with Regular Income

Chapters 1, 3, and 5 are general provisions which apply to all bankruptcy proceedings. Chapters 7, 9, 11, and 13 are the four types of bankruptcy proceedings. Chapter 7 is also known as straight or ordinary bankruptcy. It provides for the termination of the debtor's business through liquidation of its assets. Chapters 9, 11, and 13 are reorganization plans geared to keeping the debtor's business operational.

Chapter 9 will not be discussed in detail because it refers to the reorganization of a municipality.

Bankruptcy Courts

On April 1, 1984, a United States bankruptcy court was established in each of the ninety-eight judicial districts in which a district court was located. This plan originated in the Bankruptcy Reform Act of 1978. Appeals from the bankruptcy court may be heard by either a panel of three bankruptcy judges or by the district court. Previously, district courts held jurisdiction over bankruptcy cases. New judges appointed by the president will preside over the bankruptcy courts for a period of fourteen years. They will replace referees who were appointed for a six-year term to hear evidence in bankruptcy proceedings.

ADMINISTRATION OF A BANKRUPTCY PROCEEDING

Chapter 3 of the Federal Bankruptcy Reform Act deals with commencement of a bankruptcy proceeding, bankruptcy officers and their administrative powers, and the creditors' meetings. A bankruptcy proceeding may be commenced by filing a petition voluntarily or involuntarily.

Voluntary Petition

A voluntary petition may be filed under any chapter of the Bankruptcy Reform Act by any person who has accumulated debts which he or she is unable to pay. This person, known as a debtor, is seeking relief by asking in the petition that his or her debts be discharged. In addition to an individual, any association, partnership, joint venture, or corporation may file a voluntary petition for bankruptcy in the judicial district where it is incorporated or where its principal place of business is located. The following are prohibited from filing a voluntary petition and are relegated to proceeding under Chapter 7, Liquidation, or Chapter 11, Reorganization, through an involuntary petition:

Bank
Railroad
Insurance company
Municipal corporation
Savings and loan association

A voluntary petition must set forth the following information:

Names and addresses of all secured and unsecured creditors and the amount owed to each
Assets and property owned by the debtor
Material facts leading to bankruptcy
Exempt property claimed by the debtor

If the information set forth is determined to be accurate and the debtor has not filed for bankruptcy within the last six years, then the court will transform the petition into an order for relief in bankruptcy.

Involuntary Petitions

The creditor of a debtor who is not paying his or her debts may force the debtor into bankruptcy by filing an involuntary petition. The petition must be signed by three or more creditors whose claims collectively amount to at least $5,000 if the number of creditors total twelve or more. If there are less than twelve creditors, the petition need be signed only by one of the creditors who has a claim of $5,000 or more. A debtor can contest the petition, but it will be upheld if he or she is not paying the debts owed. An involuntary petition may be brought against any debtor except a farmer or nonprofit corporation.

Once a petition is voluntarily or involuntarily filed, the debtor is protected against any attempts made by creditors to collect a debt owed whether it be through a lawsuit, enforcing a judgment, or attacking the debtor's property. This is because the debtor is declared bankrupt by a court order and the bankruptcy court acquires jurisdiction over the debtor's assets.

Appointment of a Trustee

The court appoints an individual as trustee in all bankruptcy proceedings except for Chapter 7, where the trustee is selected by a vote of the creditors at their first meeting. However, in bankruptcy proceedings under Chapter 7, the court may appoint a receiver, who will act as a tempory trustee until one can be elected at the first meeting.

Duties of Trustees

A trustee has a duty to file a fidelity bond insuring the faithful performance of his or her duties. In a Chapter 7 proceeding, a trustee has a duty to take title to, and to sell and apportion the property of the debtor amongst the creditors according to the priority of their claims. The trustee takes title to property owned by the debtor on the date the petition was filed; property inherited within six months of filing the petition; property transferred to an unsecured creditor within ninety days preceding the date the petition was filed. Property transferred to a good-faith purchaser for value after the bankruptcy petition was filed will be upheld. Certain property owned by the bankrupt is exempt from the creditor's claims. In reorganization proceedings, the trustee has a duty to keep the debtor's business operational and to invest and distribute any income earned from the continued operation of the business.

First Meeting of the Creditors

The court will notify the creditors of the time and place of their first meeting. Prior to this, the creditors must each submit a claim stating the amount owed to them. The bankruptcy judge will not be present at this meeting; the court-appointed trustee or temporary receiver will preside. In Chapter 7 proceedings, the creditors will elect a trustee who will assume the duties of the temporary receiver. The debtor is required to attend the creditors' first meeting to have his or her debts discharged in bankruptcy. The debtor must respond to questions concerning the amount and location of his or her assets. The creditors will be trying to discern whether the debtor has concealed or fraudulently transferred any of the assets.

RIGHTS OF CREDITORS AND DEBTORS

Creditors' Claims

After the first meeting, all creditors must file proof of their claims. Claims will be allowed unless the debtor objects, at which time the court will hold a hearing to determine the validity of the debt. If a creditor was not informed of the bankruptcy proceedings because of an omission on the debtor's part, and therefore did not file proof of claim, that debt will not be discharged in bankruptcy, but will survive the proceedings. The debtor is responsible for providing an accurate list of all creditors in order to permit the court to give them proper notice.

Moureau v. Leaseamatic
542 F.2d 251 (5th Cir. 1976)

Leaseamatic appealed from the court order which discharged all of Moureau's debts because Moureau had purposely failed to notify the court of the debt he owed to Leaseamatic.

Moureau filed a voluntary petition of bankruptcy and in his schedule of creditors, he failed to disclose a debt owed to Leaseamatic. The court notified all of Moureau's creditors listed in the schedule. Leaseamatic repeatedly placed demands on Moureau which went unsatisfied. Leaseamatic learned of the bankruptcy proceeding just before the time for submitting claims expired, and therefore it never filed a proof of claim. The bankruptcy judge discharged all debts owed by Moureau. When Leaseamatic learned Moureau's debts had been discharged in bankruptcy, it appealed the bankruptcy judge's decision. Leaseamatic's argument was predicated on the fact that Moureau may not profit from his own fraud and concealment. It contended that its claim was not discharged because it had not received timely notice. Moureau argued that sufficient time remained during which Leaseamatic could have filed proof of claim.

The issue is whether the time limitation for filing proof of claims applies to a creditor who has not received timely notice of the bankruptcy proceeding.

The court held, ". . . the debtor must take great care in the scheduling of creditors. His failure to do so will make the unscheduled debt non-dischargeable . . ."

The court found in the present case,

> . . . notice of the discharge was provided two months after the fact. Furthermore, we cannot ignore Moureau's neglect to list the Leaseamatic debt in any of his schedules—despite its repeated demands for payment. . . . While these facts do not establish fraudulent intent, they do indicate Moureau's com-

plete disregard for the obligations imposed by statute. . . . We therefore hold that the debt was not discharged.

Judgment for Leaseamatic.

Nondischargeable Claims

EXAMPLE | Elliot Nicholson, who was forty years of age, lived in Darien, Connecticut, and worked for Christatos Shipping Company in Manhattan, where his salary was $60,000. One day, he got into a fight with Christatos's son over the son's apparent imcompetance and flattened the boy with a right hook. The son received a broken jaw and brought a successful suit against Nicholson for the intentional tort. Nicholson was given two weeks' notice that he was fired. During the two weeks time he embezzled more than $40,000 as an act of revenge. Although Nicholson and his wife were divorced, they were on a friendly basis. He informed his wife of his job loss and borrowed $3,500 from her under false pretenses, claiming he needed the money to start his own business. Nicholson stopped alimony payments to his wife, bought a toupee and a Ferrari and drove to the West Coast. He rented an apartment in San Francisco and enrolled as an art major in the University of California at Berkeley where he even took out a student loan. After failing to pay his taxes for three years, the IRS and his other creditors discovered his whereabouts. Nicholson immediately filed for voluntary bankruptcy, as he had squandered most of his money. He now claims all of his debts are discharged in the bankruptcy. Is he correct? No! The following debts are not dischargeable in bankruptcy:

Taxes

Alimony and child support payments

Property or money obtained under false pretenses

Intentional tort claims

Obligations incurred by students with regard to their education

Claims arising because of fraud, embezzlement, or breach of a fiduciary duty

Any claims which the debtor waives his or her right to discharge

Here Nicholson failed to pay his income taxes and alimony payments for the last three years, he obtained money from his wife under false pretenses, he committed an intentional tort against Christatos's son, he defaulted on his student loan, and embezzled $40,000 from Christatos Shipping Company. All of these debts will not be discharged, but will survive Nicholson's bankruptcy.

Priority Claims

There are two classes of creditors: secured and unsecured. A secured creditor is one who has a security interest in the debtor's property. The security interest acts as collateral and may be sold. The proceeds are used to satisfy the debt owed. If the proceeds from the sale of the security interest are insufficient to cover the secured creditor's claim, he or she has an unsecured claim for the amount unsatisfied and will share with the rest of the general unsecured creditors.

A secured creditor is assured of collecting the money owed to him or her out of a specific asset offered by the debtor as collateral. This is an advantage over unsecured creditors whose claims are paid out of the debtor's remaining assets, which may not be sufficient to completely satisfy the claims of all the creditors. That is why the unsecured creditors often collect only as much as twenty, thirty, or forty cents for every dollar owed to them.

EXAMPLE Larry Burke owns a Pontiac dealership in Portland, Oregon. One day, Thomas Rutherford entered the showroom and bought a new Firebird for $14,000. Rutherford paid $2,000 down and financed the remainder with General Motors Acceptance Corporation (GMAC). He signed an agreement with GMAC in which ownership was transferred to him while GMAC retained a security interest in the Firebird. Four months later, Rutherford had an accident with the car in which it sustained significant body damage. Rutherford could not afford to have the car repaired. In fact, his financial difficulties became so pressing that he filed a Chapter 7 liquidation proceeding. GMAC exercised its security interest by taking possession of the car. The amount remaining on the loan at the time of the default was $11,000. What priority will be given to GMAC's claim if we assume that the resale value of the Firebird is only $4,000 because of its condition? GMAC is a secured creditor up to $4,000 because it possesses a security interest in the car. This means the debt owed to GMAC may be partially satisfied by the sale of the Firebird. As to the other $7,000 owed, GMAC will become a general unsecured creditor of Rutherford.

An unsecured creditor is one to whom a debt is owed, but not secured by any specific property of the debtor. An unsecured creditor will be paid from the liquidation of the debtor's assets according to a priority schedule. The following list gives the order of payments made:

1. Bankruptcy administration expenses, including such things as court costs, attorney fees, trustee's compensation and expense, and appraisal fees.
2. Unsecured claims of a creditor arising between the time the petition was filed and the time a trustee was appointed. The creditor is referred to as a gap creditor.
3. Wages or commissions earned by employees within ninety days before the filing of a bankruptcy petition by their employer. The amount is limited to $2,000 per employee.
4. Unsecured claims relating to employee benefit plans made within 180 days before the filing of a bankruptcy petition. The amount is limited to $2,000 multiplied by the number of employees covered by the plan.
5. Unsecured claims for money paid to the debtor for goods, personal services, or rent, which were never delivered, performed, or provided. This amount is limited to $900 per claim.
6. Taxes owed to federal, state, and local governments which have occurred within three years prior to the filing for bankruptcy.
7. The amount remaining will be apportioned among all the general unsecured creditors. This includes any of the above unsecured priority claims to the extent that they are in excess of the stated limitations. If anything remains, it will be returned to the debtor.

EXAMPLE On June 1, George Larchmont filed a voluntary petition for a Chapter 7 liquidation proceeding for Larchmont Plumbing Supplies, Inc., located in Baton Rouge, Louisiana. A trustee was appointed one month later. Larchmont's assets totaled $75,000. The following claims were filed against the corporation: Baton Rouge Pipe Company, $15,000 claim, with the pipe that was delivered securing the entire debt; bankruptcy administration expenses, $5,000; $3,000 worth of plumbing, heating, and toilet fixtures purchased on June 15; wages earned by four employees for the previous two months, $1,500 per employee; unpaid claim by the employees' health insurance plan for $1,200; unpaid rent for the month of June, $800; unpaid state and federal income tax, $8,000; personal loans made to Larchmont Plumbing Supply, Inc., by George Larchmont ($15,000), Henry Gifford ($20,000), and Francis Rooney ($25,000). In which priority will the claims be paid?

Total Assets

Creditors' Claims			$75,000
1. Secured claims		$15,000	
2. Bankruptcy administration expenses		5,000	
3. Gap creditors		3,000	
4. Unpaid wages		6,000	
5. Unpaid employee health insurance		1,200	
6. Unpaid rent		800	
7. State and federal income taxes		8,000	
8. General unsecured creditors			
George Larchmont	$15,000	9,000	
Henry Gifford	20,000	12,000	
Francis Rooney	25,000	15,000	
Total debts discharged			$75,000

Since the general unsecured creditors' claims exceeded the amount of assets remaining for distribution after the priority classes had been satisfied, the three men will each receive sixty cents for every dollar of their claim.

Exempt Property

The Bankruptcy Reform Act allows a debtor to retain certain property which will be exempt from the creditor's claims. These exemptions may be restricted by state law:

House or burial plot up to $7,500

Motor vehicle up to $1,200

Household furnishings, goods, appliances, clothing, and the like, to $200

Jewelry up to $500

Any other property up to $400 plus the unused portion of the $7,500 exemption

Professional tools and books up to $750

Outstanding life insurance

Health aids prescribed

Social security, disability, and veterans benefits

Pension, profit sharing, and annuity payments

Unemployment compensation

Alimony and child support

Preferential Transfers

An important objective of the Bankruptcy Reform Act is to assure equal treatment for all creditors in the same class. To enforce this stipulation, the trustee in bankruptcy has been given the power to set aside all preferential transfers of money or property made by the debtor in favor of one or more of the creditors at the expense of the others. A preferential transfer is one in which a creditor receives an amount greater than his or her proportionate share would be, thereby reducing the proportionate shares of the other members of that class. Preferential transfers occur within ninety days before the filing of a bankruptcy petition unless the recipient of the preferential transfer had knowledge of the debtor's insolvency at the time the transfer was made. In these cases, any property transferred may be reclaimed for a period up to one year preceding the date when the bankruptcy petition was filed.

EXAMPLE James Maxwell is the owner of a self-service laundromat. The business is failing and Maxwell realizes that he may have to file a petition for bankruptcy. Maxwell's assets total $20,000. He has three creditors: Commonwealth Finance Company, $15,000; Crown Washers and Dryers, $10,000; and Carl Davenport, $10,000. Maxwell decides to satisfy the full amount of the debt owed to his close friend, Carl Davenport, five weeks before the petition is filed. This leaves only $10,000 to be split between Commonwealth and Crown, and their payment would be reduced to forty cents for every dollar of their claim. Can this transfer be voided? Yes! This is a preferential transfer in which one creditor is favored over the other. This preferential treatment causes the victimized creditors to suffer financial loss. Preferential transfers can be set aside as long as they occur within ninety days of when the bankruptcy petition is filed.

If a creditor receives payment from a debtor for the sale of goods or the performance of personal services in the ordinary course of business, the trustee can not recover the amount transferred. The fact that it occurred during the ordinary course of business makes the difference, because there was no preferential treatment. A trustee cannot recover the proceeds of the sale of collateral by a secured creditor because of the security interest held unless the proceeds exceed the secured creditor's claim. A good-faith purchaser who buys goods from an unsecured creditor who received them because of preferential treatment is entitled to retain the goods as against the trustee in bankruptcy.

EXAMPLE In the previous example, suppose Maxwell had paid Procter and Gamble $150 for a shipment of soap powder and detergents, and $275 to Morris Decker for repairs to the three washing machines. These payments were made four weeks before Maxwell filed for bankruptcy. Could these payments be set aside as preferential transfers? No! These payments occurred during the ordinary course of business. It was in the best interests of the business to maintain the machines and keep the laundromat operating with full supplies.

Fraudulent Conveyances

A fraudulent conveyance made by a debtor with the intent to conceal nonexempt property from the creditors and to delay or otherwise obstruct the bankruptcy proceedings is void and may be set aside by the trustee. This applies to fraudulent transfers made after the filing of the bankruptcy petition or up to one year prior to the filing of the petition. Some states have extended the period to up to five years before the petition was filed. A fraudulent conveyance differs from a preferential transfer. A fraudulent conveyance is made by the debtor for his or her own benefit. It deprives all creditors of any claim they may have with regard to certain property owned by the debtor. A preferential transfer is made by the debtor for the benefit of one or more of his or her creditors. It deprives the remaining creditors of any claim they may have had to the transferred property.

EXAMPLE Robert J. Milton has filed a voluntary petition for a Chapter 7 bankruptcy proceeding for the purpose of liquidating his personal assets and discharging his personal debts. Milton's personal assets total $85,000 including a new Chevrolet Corvette worth $22,000. His debts exceed his assets by $20,000. Milton does not want to part with the Corvette, so he sells it to his girlfriend, Joanne, for $10. The creditors demand the trustee set aside the transfer as a fraudulent conveyance. Does the trustee have the power to do this? Yes! Fraudulent conveyances made by the debtor with the intent to deprive creditors of his or her assets may be set aside by a trustee.

Acts of the Debtor Which Will Prevent Bankruptcy

A debtor's obligations will not be discharged where the debtor has committed any of the following acts:

Fraudulently conveyed property or concealed assets with intent to defraud creditors.

Adjudicated a bankrupt within the previous six years.

Destroyed, falsified, or otherwise concealed accounting records so as to impair an investigation into the financial condition of the business.

Secured credit through falsifying documents with respect to a person's own financial status or the status of his or her business.

There are three basic bankruptcy proceedings:

Liquidation
Business reorganization
Individual rehabilitation

LIQUIDATION PROCEEDING

This is the only bankruptcy proceeding in which the debtor's business will be terminated, with its assets liquidated and then distributed to the creditors in accordance with the priority of their claims. Liquidation proceedings are also referred to as straight or ordinary bankruptcy and are covered under Chapter 7 of the Bankruptcy Reform Act. All of the previous discussion applies to a liquidation proceeding under Chapter 7: the commencement of a bankruptcy proceeding through the filing of a voluntary or involuntary petition; the appointment of a temporary receiver; the first meeting of creditors with the election of a trustee; the duties of a trustee; exempt property; debts not discharged; priority distribution of claims; preferential transfers and fraudulent conveyances.

BUSINESS REORGANIZATION

Introduction

Business reorganization is governed by Chapter 11 of the Bankruptcy Reform Act. It provides an alternative to terminating and liquidating the debtor's business under a straight bankruptcy proceeding, and it may be initiated pursuant to either a voluntary or an involuntary petition. The main purpose of Chapter 11 is to formulate an effective plan for reorganization. After the court issues its order for relief in bankruptcy, it will appoint a committee composed of the seven unsecured creditors having the largest claims. The committee's duties include consulting with the trustee or debtor concerning the administration of the bankrupt's affairs; investigating the financial background of the debtor, especially concerning any preferential or fraudulent transfer of property; and participating in the drafting of the plan for reorganization. A trustee will be appointed only if the debtor acted in a fraudulent, dishonest, or negligent manner in conducting the business, or if the court determines the appointment is in the best interests of the creditor. A reorganization proceeding may be converted to a Chapter 7 liquidation proceeding by the court for cause, or by the debtor, unless a trustee is in possession of the assets of the business or the proceeding was begun pursuant to an involuntary petition.

Reorganization Plan

The plan for reorganization must be filed within four months after the order for relief in bankruptcy is granted. This is the debtor's exclusive right unless a trustee has been appointed. The court-appointed creditors committee, a trustee, or a creditor may propose a plan for reorganization after 120 days if the debtor has not presented a plan, or after 180 days if the debtor's timely presentation was not accepted by the creditors. A plan must be approved first by the court before it is made available to the creditors. A plan has been accepted if more than one-half of the creditors holding at least two-thirds of the value of all claims voted in favor of it. After the creditors have accepted the plan, the court must determine whether the plan is feasible, made in good faith, and fair and equitable with respect to each class of unsecured creditors. The latter requirement may be assessed by comparing what each creditor would have received under a Chapter 7 liquidation proceeding with what he or she will purportedly receive under the reorganization plan. A creditor's compensation under a Chapter 11 reorganization must be comparable; otherwise the plan will be disapproved for impairing the creditor's claim.

Successful adherence to the reorganization plan by making all payments revives the business and allows it to continue operations free of all debts.

Matter of Landmark at Plaza Park, Ltd.
7 B.R. 653 (D. N.J. 1980)

Landmark at Plaza Park, Ltd., owned a 200-unit garden apartment. City Federal held a first mortgage on the property for $2,250,000 at an interest rate of 9.5 percent. Landmark defaulted on its payments and City Federal took possession of the garden apartments and began to collect the rents. Landmark's debt to City Federal exceeded the value of the garden apartment complex. City Federal wanted to sell the complex and apply the proceeds to satisfy the debt owed to it.

Landmark filed for reorganization under Chapter 11 and proposed the following reorganization plan:

1. Possession of the apartment complex is to be redelivered to Landmark.
2. Landmark will pay City Federal 12.5 percent on the face value of the property beginning with the sixteenth month after the date the plan is approved through the thirty-sixth month.
3. City Federal will receive a note for $2,705,820, payable in three years in lieu of the interest at 12.5 percent for the first through fifteenth month plus interest on the unpaid interest.
4. City Federal's existing mortgage will secure the $2,705,820 note.

Landmark's plan of repayment at the end of three years is contingent upon its ability to secure refinancing for the first mortgage by the end of the three-year period.

City Federal rejected the plan, contending that its rights were impaired. The plan called for redelivery of possession of the apartment complex to Landmark. This amounts to a 100 percent loan with the interest for the first fifteen months deferred.

The main issue is whether the court should approve the plan. In reading the issue, the court must decide whether the debtor will be able to repay the loan and whether the interest rate provided reflects the risk undertaken by the secured creditor.

The court decided that 12.5 percent rate of interest was modest in comparison to the risk undertaken by City Federal. The rate of interest provided in the plan should correspond to the market rate of interest that would be charged based on the risks involved.

The court held, "It appears clear to the Court that the forced loan proposed by the debtor includes terms less favorable to City than would typically be found in the market and that any confirmable plan must compensate City for this deficiency . . ."

The court denied approval of the plan because it believed fulfillment of its proposals was highly unrealistic and would result either in further reorganization attempts or liquidation.

INDIVIDUAL REHABILITATION

Individuals may avoid having all of their assets liquidated under straight bankruptcy proceedings by rehabilitating themselves under Chapter 13. This proceeding must be filed voluntarily and is open to all individuals who have outstanding secured debts less than $350,000 and unsecured debts less than $160,000. This proceeding may be converted to a Chapter 7 liquidation proceeding by the court for cause or upon the debtor's request.

Rehabilitation Plan

The debtor must file a plan for rehabilitation. The court will appoint a trustee to monitor the administration of the plan. Under the plan, the debtor must agree to furnish all or part of his or her future income to the trustee for repayment of the creditor's claims; repay all creditors within three years according to the priority distribution schedule; and treat all members of a class equally.

Court Approval

The court will then determine whether the plan is made in good faith and is feasible, that is, capable of being carried out by the debtor; whether the unsecured creditors are assured of receiving at least an amount equivalent to what they would have received under a Chapter 7 liquidation proceeding; and whether the secured creditors are sufficiently protected by either having possession of the collateral or by being allowed to retain their security interests in property with a value equivalent to their claim.

Discharge of Debts

The debtor will be rehabilitated and his debts will be discharged when he or she has made all payments in accordance with the court-approved plans. This discharge is of greater scope than that granted by Chapter 7. The debtor may also be discharged after making part of the payments if the failure of the plan was not directly attributed to the debtor, and if each of the creditors received an amount at least equivalent to what they would have received under a Chapter 7 liquidation proceeding.

REVIEW QUESTIONS _____

1. Define bankruptcy, debtor, creditor, and debt.
2. When is a trustee appointed and what are the trustee's duties?
3. Explain the terms *preferential transfer* and *fraudulent conveyance*.

4. List the priority distribution of unsecured claims.
5. What claims are nondischargable?
6. List the property which will be classified as exempt.
7. Explain the three major types of bankruptcy proceedings.
8. Marshall sold his farm to a group of individuals who, in return, personally guaranteed to pay Marshall's debts, which amounted to $213,000. A promissory note of $300,000 was made payable to Marshall and his wife. Marshall transferred his interest in the note to his wife for one dollar. His creditors filed an involuntary petition to have Marshall declared bankrupt and to have the transfer set aside. What result? Marshall v. Showalter, 375 F.2d 529 (1967).
9. Smith and Gisevius obtained a judgment against Kohnke in January. In August, Kohnke filed a voluntary petition in bankruptcy and all his debts including any monetary judgments against him were discharged in November. Kohnke claimed that the court should cancel the Smith and Gisevius judgment because the bankruptcy law provides that all judgments rendered in the last twelve months preceding the discharge of the debtor's assets are no longer enforceable. Smith and Gisevius were not able to prove they still possessed a secured interest in the property. Will Smith and Gisevius be able to enforce the judgment? Kohnke v. Justice, 280 So.2d 665 (La.) 1973.
10. Johnson was traveling south on Highway 55 when his car was struck from behind by Perrett. Both cars traveled more than 300 feet after the point of impact and Johnson was thrown from his car and killed. A nearly empty bottle of vodka was found in Perrett's car. Subsequent tests proved that Perrett was drunk. A wrongful death action was brought by the widow of the deceased. She received a judgment for $23,000 which was to be enforced by garnishing Perrett's salary. A week later, Perrett filed a voluntary bankruptcy petition and raised the defense that his debts, including this judgment, were discharged in bankruptcy. What result? Perrett v. Johnson, 253 Miss. 209, 175 So.2d 497 (1965).

25

BAILMENTS

INTRODUCTION

A bailment is a temporary transfer of possession of personal property to another for a specific purpose with the understanding it will be returned upon the fulfillment of that purpose or at the owner's request. A bailor is the owner of the personal property. A bailee is the person to whom the personal property has been transferred. A bailee must exercise a certain degree of care toward the property while it is in his or her possession. The purpose for which bailments are made include: (1) loan of property; (2) delivery of property to have a service performed on it, such as cleaning, repairing, or remodeling; (3) delivery of property for storage or safekeeping until requested.

The key to determining whether a bailment exists is whether the owner has turned over possession or title of the personal property. Delivery of possession constitutes a bailment; delivery of title constitutes a sales contract. A sales contract is covered by Article 2 of the UCC; a bailment is not. A sales contract in excess of $500 must be in writing to satisfy the statute of frauds; a bailment contract need not be in writing. A bailment may be expressed orally or in writing, or it may be implied from the actions of the parties. It is wise to have a writing to evidence the transfer of possession, but it is not a legal requirement.

STANDARD OF CARE OWED BY A BAILEE

There are three types of bailments. Each type requires a different standard of care on the part of the bailee.

Benefit of the Bailee

When the bailor transfers possession of property to the bailee solely for the bailee's use and enjoyment, the bailee is held to a high standard of care towards the property and will be liable for the slightest negligence.

EXAMPLE | Hughes was attending his first black tie affair but did not own a tuxedo. He borrowed one from his friend Getty, and then purchased a pair of pure white sneakers to complete his outfit. While discussing the manufacture of his overgrown airplane, Hughes accidently dribbled tomato sauce on the tuxedo. When Hughes returned the tuxedo, Getty asked him to pay for the cleaning costs. Hughes strenuously objected. Was Hughes responsible? Yes! This is a bailment contract for the sole benefit of Hughes, the bailee.

Mutual Benefit of the Bailor and the Bailee

This is the most prevalent type of bailment. If a bailor transfers possession of property for the purpose of renting the property to the bailee, or having the bailee store the property, or perform a service on it in return for compensation, then the bailee must take reasonable care of the property. Should damage occur, the bailee would be liable if he or she could have been reasonably expected to have prevented the damage in question.

EXAMPLE | Hilton brings his Rolls-Royce to Doug Miller's service station for repairs. He leaves the car overnight. Miller has taken steps to guard against vandalism by having a sophisticated security system installed with an alarm that rings at a central station. Despite the protective device, vandals attack Miller's station during the night and strip Hilton's car. Hilton sues Miller for the damages. Is he entitled to collect? No! This is a bailment for the mutual benefit of both the bailor and the bailee. Hilton is deriving valuable consideration in the form of repairs to his car, while Miller is receiving payment for the work he performed. Miller is a bailee, not an insurer. He owes Hilton a duty to exercise reasonable care over the car and he will be liable for only ordinary negligence. Here, by taking the precaution to have a security system installed, Miller has satisfied his duty of reasonable care and he is not responsible for the damages to Hilton's car.

Benefit of the Bailor

If the bailee receives possession of the bailor's property and agrees to hold or store it without compensation, then the bailment is solely for the benefit of the bailor. The bailee owes a lower standard of care to the property and will be liable only if grossly negligent.

EXAMPLE | Two old friends, Rockefeller and Morgan, are vacationing on the Riviera. Rockefeller, deciding to go for a swim, gives his watch to Morgan and asks him to keep an eye on it. Morgan tells Rockefeller he will wrap it in a beach towel. When Rockefeller returns, he dries himself off and the two of them head back to the hotel. They suddenly realize the watch is gone. They search frantically, but to no avail. Rockefeller insists Morgan pay for the watch. Morgan says, "To hell with you!" Is Morgan responsible? No! Since this contract is for the sole benefit of Rockefeller, the bailor; Morgan, the bailee, has only a slight duty of care. Since both he and Rockefeller forgot about the watch, he is not liable. His actions were not grossly negligent.

A bailment for the mutual benefit of both the bailor and the bailee is a contract. A bailment solely for the benefit of the bailor or bailee is a gratuitous bailment because no consideration is received in return. Bailees will be liable for the loss or destruction of property resulting from accident, fire, or theft, only if it occurs through their negligence in failing to meet the appropriate standard of care. They are not insurers of property unless stipulated in the contract.

LIABILITY OF A BAILEE

A bailee is liable for failing to exercise the proper standard of care with regard to the safety of the bailed property. This liability may be limited to a certain value by contract. The bailor must be informed by conspicuous notice. Tickets given as an indication of ownership which attempt to limit or disclaim liability are not conspicuous; something more is required. The privilege of limiting liability does not extend to damages resulting from the unauthorized use of the bailed property by the bailee or one of his or her agents. In such a case, the bailee is liable for any loss regardless of the care exercised over the property.

SPECIAL TYPES OF BAILMENTS

Finders

A bailment will be implied when a person finds lost property. The finder is a bailee for the true owner. Since the bailment is created solely for the benefit of the true owner-bailor, the finder owes a lower standard of care to the property he or she found.

EXAMPLE J.P. Morgan had agreed to deliver 5,000 gold bars to the Rothchilds in London. He placed the gold aboard a brand new oceanliner called the *Titanic*. The *Titanic* embarked for London, but while crossing the icy Atlantic, it rammed the top of an iceberg and sank. A number of years later, deep-sea divers discovered the wreck and claimed its treasure. The Rothchilds sued the divers for return of the gold and produced the bill of lading for the gold. Are they entitled to recover it? Yes! A finder of lost property is entitled to it against all save the true owner. The divers actually became constructive bailees for the true owners, the Rothchilds, once they had taken possession of the gold.

Safe Deposit Boxes

A bank which maintains safe deposit boxes is liable for the contents of the box if it has been damaged, destroyed, or stolen through the negligence of the bank. This is true even though the contents of the box have not been declared, because the bank realizes that people keep valuable property in safe deposit boxes. Since the renting of a safe deposit box is a bailment for the mutual benefit of both the depositor (bailor) and the bank (bailee), the standard of care owed by the bank is a reasonable one—reasonable in light of the high caliber of security maintained over the safe deposit vault.

The ever-popular Mrs. McLean placed her Hope diamond in a safe deposit box at Mellon bank. Later that year, the notorious bank robber, Willie Sutton, robbed the bank's safe deposit vault. Mrs. McLean sued Mellon's bank for $2,000,000, the value of the diamond. Is she entitled to the full value? Yes, if she can prove ownership of the diamond, its value, and that it was inside her safe deposit box at the time of the theft, plus the fact that the bank was negligent in maintaining its security system.

Coat Checks

Establishments providing coat checks create a bailment where the customer relinquishes possession of the coat to the cloakroom attendant. The degree of care required of the establishment depends on whether a fee is charged. If a fee is charged, the bailment is for the mutual benefit of both the establishment and customer and reasonable care must be exercised. When a fee is not charged, a bailment is created for the sole benefit of the customer and a lower standard of care is owed by the establishment. If a person hangs his coat in an unattended cloakroom, no bailment is generally created. But courts have ruled to the contrary where a coat is hung in a closet set aside by a physician or a dentist in his or her reception room.

EXAMPLE Lady Astor was having dinner at the Copa with her husband. When she entered the nightclub, she checked her sable coat for a fee of two dollars. In return, she received a ticket disclaiming all liability. After a gala evening of wining and dining, she sought to reclaim her coat. The fur coat had slipped off the hanger because it was too heavy for it, and laid on the dusty floor where it was trampled on and a large hole was burned in it by a cigarette stub. Lady Astor sued the Copa for damages stemming from their negligence in handling her fur coat. The Copa asserts they have effectively disclaimed all liability. Will Lady Astor triumph? Yes! The coat check attendant acted negligently in placing such an expensive coat on a hanger which would not support it. Furthermore, tickets given as an indication of ownership cannot be used to disclaim liability for negligence.

Parking Lots

Parking lots which require car owners to leave their car keys with the attendant have created a bailment for the mutual benefit of the operator of the lot and the car owner. Once possession of the keys has been transferred, the parking lot, through its attendant, has the right to exercise dominion and control over the car. This gives rise to a bailment contract. In addition to being responsible for property left in the passenger compartment of the car, parking lots are generally responsible only for property ordinarily expected to be in the trunk of a car, unless the contents of the trunk have been made known to them.

Park-and-locks, where car owners park in a lot without transferring possession of the keys, do not create bailment contracts because the parking lot, through its attendant, is not exercising any control over the car. The car owner is being given permission merely to park in the lot, which is something less than a bailment. This permission guarantees the car owner that the operator of the lot will refrain from removing the car from the lot or otherwise causing it damage. If the damage is caused by someone other than the parking lot operator or one of his or her attendants, then the lot has no liability.

Rhodes v. Pioneer Parking Lot, Inc.
501 S.W.2d 569 (Tenn.) 1973

Rhodes sued Pioneer Parking Lot for damages to his automobile, which was stripped in their lot.

In October 1969, Rhodes entered Pioneer Parking Lot and after placing fifty cents in a meter received a ticket which stated:

NOTICE
THIS CONTRACT LIMITS OUR LIABILITY—
READ IT
WE RENT SPACE ONLY. No bailment is created and we are not responsible for loss of or damage to, car or contents. This ticket is sold subject to space being available and is not transferable.

After finding a space, Rhodes removed the keys from his car. When he returned later in the day, he found that the car had been vandalized.

The issue is whether the relationship between the parking lot and Rhodes is a bailment which would make the parking lot responsible for the damages because of failure to exercise reasonable care.

The court concluded that there was no bailment because Rhodes did not deliver the car into the custody of the parking lot. The parking lot, which is a park-and-lock, asserted no dominion and control over the car because Rhodes retained the keys. Judgment for Pioneer Parking Lot.

Parking lots which require the car owner to present a ticket to a guard for access to the lot are considered to have created a bailment contract even though the operator of the lot does not possess the keys to the car and therefore does not have control over it. It is a bailment because of the guard's power to exclude from the lot all but the car owners who pay.

EXAMPLE | Vanderbilt and Dupont were attending a Broadway musical called *If I Were a Rich Man*. Vanderbilt parked his car at a lot across the street from the theatre and gave the attendant the ignition key. Dupont parked a few blocks down in a park-and-lock on Tenth Avenue in order to save a few bucks. After they left the theatre, both men found that their cars had been vandalized. Both men sued the parking lot owners. Will either Vanderbilt or Dupont recover? Vanderbilt may recover for breach of the bailment contract, since the lot owner failed to exercise reasonable care in preventing vandals access to cars parked in the lot. Dupont will not recover because he received a mere license to park. No bailment contract was created between him and the park-and-lot owner.

Car Rental

In car rental situations, the bailment is for the mutual benefit of both parties. The person renting the car is the bailee and the owner of the car rental business is the bailor. The bailee has a duty to pay for all ordinary repair and maintenance expenses. This duty may be altered by a stipulation in the contract. The bailor's duty is limited only to extraordinary repairs which are not normally needed by a car of similiar condition, age, and mileage. If a third person is injured by the person renting the car (bailee), the bailee is responsible for those injuries as though he or she was the original owner. The owner of the rented car is not liable.

EXAMPLE

The Kennedys are inviting a few New York associates for an afternoon of tea, trimming sails, and touch-tackle on Cape Cod. They hire a Volkswagon mini-bus from Budget Rent-A-Car to transport their guests to Massachusetts. On Interstate 95, they experience a sudden stop in motion when a piece of glass punctures a tire. Since neither Kennedy nor his associates wishes to soil their hands with a laborer's task, they have the car towed off the expressway to the nearest service station, where the tire is repaired. The tow and repair bill comes to $54. Kennedy pays the sum and sues Budget for reimbursement. Is Kennedy entitled to it? No! A flat tire caused by glass is an ordinary expenditure which must be anticipated by the individual renting the car.

Hotels

Hotels are liable to their guests for the full value of property stolen or destroyed when it occurs because of the negligence of the hotel or its employees. A guest is a person who is staying at the hotel for a limited duration while traveling. Hotels may limit their liability when the guest's property is stolen or damaged without negligence on the hotel's part. This may be accomplished by providing a safe and posting conspicuous notices concerning its availability. For those items not placed in the safe, each state restricts recovery to a maximum amount, which is usually not very much. Hotels providing parking facilities become bailees only if they take possession of the keys to the guest's automobile.

EXAMPLE

Lady Diana Windmere and her husband, while vacationing in Monte Carlo, are staying at the Lucky "7". When they check in, they are informed by the desk clerk that all valuables should be placed in the hotel safe, otherwise liability will be limited to $500 for personal effects, as set forth by the state statute. A sign containing the same message is hanging in the lobby. Lady Diana places her tiara in the safe, but retains her diamond necklace and bracelet. While taking a dip in the pool, the hotel maid steals her necklace. Later that evening, her bracelet is stolen by the occupant of a suite down the hall. Lady Diana had carelessly left her door open when she went to dine in the hotel restaurant. Lady Diana sues the hotel for the full value of her stolen jewelry. Will she recover it? She will recover the value of the necklace because it was stolen by an employee of the hotel. Her award as to the stolen bracelet will be limited to $500 because it was not placed in the safe as she was notified.

Warehousemen

Warehousemen are people engaged in the business of storing goods in return for compensation. When warehousemen receive goods, they issue a warehouse receipt, which is a document of title. It entitles the holder to title and possession of the goods, it evidences the existence of a contract for storage, and sets forth the terms of the contract for storage. Warehouse receipts along with negotiation and transfer are governed by the UCC under Article 7.

Warehousemen may limit their liability by conspicuous notice. The limitation must be set forth in terms of units, or by weight. The person storing the goods must also be given the choice of paying a higher rate for unlimited liability. Although warehousemen are bailees, they are subject to extensive state and federal regulation in addition to Article 7 of the UCC.

EXAMPLE On Saturday, Willy Hearst stored 1.5 million copies of the Sunday edition of his newspaper, the *Journal American,* in a warehouse on Park Row. The contract provided for unlimited liability on the warehouseman's part. That evening a fire broke out, burning the contents of five warehouses on Park Row including the one where Hearst's newspapers were stored. Hearst sued the warehouseman for the value of his newspapers. Will the warehouseman have to pay even if he did not cause the fire? Yes! The unlimited liability provision is designated to cover those instances where the warehouseman is not at fault. If Hearst had not paid the additional cost for unlimited liability, would the result be different? Yes! Hearst would be entitled to recover only the amount per pound in the limited liability provision. If Hearst could prove that, even though the fire was not caused by the warehouseman, the installation of a sprinkler system would have minimized damages, would this change the result? Yes! This evidence would go to prove that the warehouseman did not exercise reasonable care in regard to the safety of the newspapers.

Common Carriers

Common carriers are transporters of goods and passengers who offer their services to the general public in return for compensation. They are a special type of bailee. On receipt of goods, they are held to an extraordinary standard of care, almost that of an insurer. Common carriers are responsible for all damages or injuries that occur, without regard to fault or negligence. Common carriers occupy a position of privilege and as such, hold a public trust. Furthermore, they must serve all who apply and they have an affirmative duty to provide reasonable services.

Common carriers issue a bill of lading for land or sea transportation or an air bill for transportation by air, when they accept goods from a shipper. The shipper may negotiate this bill to his or her purchaser. Bills of lading and air bills are documents of title evidencing the receipt of goods for shipment. The person holding the bill of lading (the purchaser of the goods) is entitled to title and possession of the goods on the presentation of the bill. Bills of lading and their negotiation and transfer are treated in Article 7 of the UCC.

Common carriers have a duty to deliver the goods listed in the bailment contract on time. Failure to adhere to this duty gives the shipper a cause of action for damages. Common carriers are extensively regulated by federal and state statutes, as well as

Article 7 of the UCC. They may limit their liability by contract in accordance with the governing statutes. Common carriers generally limit their liability for goods to a certain value per package. An additonal higher rate must be offered for those individuals who want unlimited liability for their packages.

EXAMPLE

The Shah of Iran sent 10,000 barrels of oil to Hunt by ship. When the ship passed through the Sargasso Sea in the Bermuda Triangle, it sank. The Shah's bailment contract with the shipping line provides that liability for each barrel shall be limited to $750. Each barrel is worth $1,000. What will the Shah recover? He will recover $750 per barrel. This is true as long as the limitation placed in the contract is in accordance with the appropriate federal statute governing common carriers and interstate shipments.

Greyhound Lines, Inc. v. K. C. Mah
216 Va. 401, 219 S.E.2d 842 (1975)

Mrs. Mah brought a lawsuit against Greyhound for the negligent loss of her baggage.

An agent of Greyhound informed Mrs. Mah that there was a "through bus" leaving New York which stopped in Radford, Virginia. She purchased a full-fare ticket and checked three pieces of baggage, for which she was given a claim check. The claim check stated: "BAGGAGE LIABILITY LIMITED TO $50.00 (SEE OVER)." The reverse side stated that Greyhound's liability was limited to $50 for all baggage checked unless a greater value was declared in writing at the time the baggage was checked. There were notices posted to this effect. Mrs. Mah stated that she did not read the printed matter on the ticket or see any of the signs posted. The supposed "through bus" stopped at Washington D.C., where she was transferred to another bus bound for Radford. When she presented her claim checks in Radford, her baggage could not be found. The value of the lost baggage exceeded $1,000.

The issue is whether Mrs. Mah is limited in her recovery to $50, the amount printed on the claim check. The court held that since Mrs. Mah was traveling across state lines, the Interstate Commerce Act applies. It permits common carriers to limit their liability for baggage lost due to their negligence if they issued a receipt (claim check) which contained the limitation of liability and if this notice of limitation was filed with the Interstate Commerce Commission. The court was satisfied that Greyhound met the criteria. They further held that under statute, a carrier cannot guarantee that a passenger's baggage will be shipped on the same bus. The carrier can transport the baggage on a preceding or following bus or by a different route altogether. Mrs. Mah was permitted to recover only $50 for her lost baggage. Judgment for Greyhound.

Although common carriers have a duty to serve the general public, they need not accept goods which are not within their capacity, not of the kind normally carried, improperly prepared, or dangerous to the health and safety of the passengers and crew aboard the carrier.

Although common carriers are not generally responsible for the loss, destruction, or damage to goods occasioned by an act of God, the public enemy, the negligence of the shipper, or the inherent nature of the goods, they can be held responsible if they are negligent in dealing with the conditions that result. The burden of proof remains on the carrier. It must prove it was not negligent.

An act of God is a force of nature that cannot be anticipated and provided against. If the force of nature unexpectedly destroys goods in the possession of the carrier, the carrier will be absolved from liability. Extreme weather conditions in places with no past records of such a predicament, earthquakes, and volcanic eruptions are examples.

The public enemy is not meant to refer to the FBI's most-wanted list, hijackers, or looters, but rather to enemy nations at war with the United States, pirates of the seven seas, and revolutionists seeking to overthrow the government.

A common carrier is not liable for any destruction or damage to the goods if they are packaged, labeled, or loaded in a negligent manner by the shipper. The carrier has a duty to follow the reasonable instructions of the shipper. If the goods are damaged as a result of the shipper's instructions, the carrier is not responsible.

A common carrier is held to a higher standard of care for perishable goods. However, a carrier will not be liable for the natural spoilage of perishable goods if they are shipped without delay. Concerning fruits and vegetables, it is not the carrier's responsibility to examine each piece to see how ripe it is and whether it may spoil during shipping; this is the shipper's obligation.

Connecting Carriers Where two or more carriers are required to make delivery, the initial carrier is liable even though the loss may be occasioned by a connecting carrier. The shipper may sue either or both carriers for damages. If the initial carrier is relegated to paying the damages, it has a right to be indemnified by the connecting carrier where the connecting carrier is at fault for causing the loss.

Passengers Common carries have a contractual obligation to take reasonable care of passengers while the passengers are on the carrier and when the passengers enter or leave the carrier. This reasonable care extends to protection of passengers from the negligence of the carrier's employees and from the other passengers. What is reasonable will vary depending on the age and health of the passenger. Since a cause of action against a common carrier is predicated on negligence, the three-year statute of limitation for negligence applies.

REVIEW QUESTIONS

1. Define bailment, bailor, bailee, warehouseman, and common carrier.
2. List and explain the various kinds of bailments.
3. What is the standard of care owed by a bailee in each of the three types of bailments?
4. Capezzaro was the victim of a robbery. The police arrested a suspect named Winfrey and found the money that had been stolen from Capezzaro in Winfrey's girdle. Subsequently, the indictments against Winfrey were dismissed and the

allegedly stolen money was returned to her by the police without notifying Capezzaro. Capezzaro sued the police for returning the money to Winfrey. He argued that his claim for the money did not lose its validity solely because the indictments against Winfrey were dismissed. What result? Capezzaro v. Winfrey, 153 N.J. Super. 267, 379 A.2d 493 (1977).

5. Suda delivered potatoes to F-M Potatoes for storage. Suda advised F-M that the potatoes were going to be used for potato chips. Therefore, a higher temperature was required to adjust the distribution of sugars to starches. F-M agreed to exercise control over the temperature setting. Months later, a sample of the potatoes was tested and it was discovered that the potatoes did not attain the proper color shade to be suitable for potential potato chips. As a result, Suda could not sell his potatoes anywhere. He sued F-M for breach of the bailment contract in not maintaining the correct temperature control. What result? F-M Potatoes, Inc. v. Suda, 259 N.W.2d 487 (N.D.) 1977.

6. Allen parked his car in Houserman's lot and left the keys to the ignition and trunk in the car. When Allen returned, he discovered that the golf clubs he stored in the trunk were missing. He sued Houserman for the value of the clubs. Houserman argued that he was not notified of the presence of the clubs by Allen nor were the clubs in plain view. Allen argued that this was a bailment situation where the bailee failed to exercise reasonable care for the bailed goods. What result? Allen v. Houserman, 250 A.2d 389 (Del.) 1969.

7. Stovall Tire and Marine contracted to repair Fowler's eighteen-foot boat. For Fowler's convenience, the repairs were to be made at Lake Lanier where he operated the boat. Stovall's chief engineer rented a slip where the boat was stored while being repaired. After two months, Fowler was notified that the boat sank during a severe storm. During the two months leading up to the storm, no repairs were made to the boat nor was the condition of the boat periodically checked. Fowler sued Stovall for the value of the boat, but Stovall asserted that the damages were caused by an act of God. Does Stovall's argument hold water? Stovall Tire & Marine, Inc. v. Fowler, 135 Ga. 26, 217 S.E.2d 367 (1975).

8. Walls was a registered guest at the Cosmopolitan Hotel. During one evening, he left his hotel room to have dinner. He had locked the room, leaving his wristwatch, valued at over $3,600, on a night table. When he returned the watch had been stolen. Upon examination of the door to his room, it was discovered that the lock had been severely damaged on a prior occasion and the repairs to the lock were made in a negligent manner, allowing access to the room without a key. The hotel argued that a state statute provided that valuable items must be left in the hotel safe; otherwise the hotel is not responsible even if negligent. What result? Walls v. Cosmopolitan Hotels, Inc., 13 Wash. App. 478, 534 P.2d 1373 (1975).

9. Katamay was standing on an elevated platform in Chicago waiting to board a train. When the train arrived, Katamay fell forward and injured herself because her high heels had become wedged in the wooden platform. She sued the carrier, Chicago Transit Authority, for failing to exercise the highest degree of care which is owed to a passenger boarding a train. The CTA argued that Katamay had not

come into contact with the train; therefore she was not in the act of boarding it and that they had no notice of the crack in the wooden platform. Is this argument correct? Katamay v. Chicago Transit Authority, 53 Ill. 2d 27, 289 N.E.2d 623 (1972).

10. The Waldorf Astoria provided a safe for valuables and requested its guests to store all jewelry in it. A guest at the hotel had a pair of gold cuff links stolen from his room and sued the hotel for failing to exercise the proper standard of care in regard to articles of ordinary wear worn by its guests. The Waldorf claimed the gold cuff links were jewelry, rather than items of ordinary wear, and refused to pay for the stolen cuff links. What result? Federal Insurance Co. v. Waldorf Astoria Hotel, 60 Misc.2d 996, 303 N.Y.S.2d 297 (1969).

26

INSURANCE

INTRODUCTION

Insurance is a contract in which the insurer agrees to indemnify the insured, or the designated beneficiary, if loss to property or injury or death of a person ensues. Insurance protects people against risk of loss. An insurance policy is a contract between the insurer and insured which sets forth the rights and responsibilities of each, including the limit of the insurer's liability and the premiums to be paid by the insured in consideration for the insurance. The insurer is an insurance company which agrees to be liable for any loss sustained by the insured up to the face value of the policy. The face value of an insurance policy is the insurer's limit of liability. The insured is any individual, family, partnership, or corporation that pays premiums in return for insurance coverage. Premiums are designated by an insurance company at a certain rate depending on the amount of insurance purchased by the insured.

An insurance company operates through its agents, specifically those individuals who convince people to buy insurance. These insurance agents are employees of the insurance company and are usually paid a salary, plus commissions based on a percentage of the face value of insurance policies they sell. An insurance broker is an independent contractor who is the agent of the insured, rather than an insurance company. An insurance broker services clients by attempting to place their insurance needs with any of a number of insurance companies. Brokers are compensated by charging their clients a fee for the services they render. Brokers may become agents for an insurance company if the company authorizes them to accept premiums on its behalf.

The law of contracts is applicable to insurance policies, since they are special contracts. The following contractual elements must be present for an insurance policy to be valid:

Purpose (lawful)
Agreement
Legal capacity
Act
Consideration
Executed in proper form

When people say they wish to take out an insurance policy, this is considered to be an offer. The insurance agent who suggested they do this is merely inviting them to make an offer. An agent is not usually empowered with the authority to accept an offer to contract for insurance. With the possible exception of fire and casualty insurance, the insurance policy must be approved by the home office of the insurance company. A question of fact may arise concerning the agent's apparent authority when a premium is paid and the agent has given the insured a binding receipt with the assurance that the policy is in effect.

A person buying insurance must have sufficient capacity to contract. An infant who purchases insurance can not abrogate the contract solely because of his or her age. Otherwise, an infant could purchase fire, automobile, health, or term life insurance and then request a return of the premiums upon reaching legal age. The result would be that no insurance company would insure the property, automobile, health, or life of an infant. This is an exception to the general rule because the benefit to an infant in being able to purchase insurance outweighs the underlying risks of incapacity.

LIFE INSURANCE

Life insurance is a third-party beneficiary contract in which the insurer agrees to pay the face value of the policy to a designated beneficiary on the death of the insured.

Insurable Interest

An insurable interest is required to insure the life of a person. In addition to the ability to insure one's own life, a spouse may insure the life of the other spouse, and a parent can insure the life of a child.

A person may also establish an insurable interest in the life of another based on blood, love and affection, employment, or on the fact that a debt is owed, if it can be shown that the person requesting the insurance will suffer a financial loss should the person he or she wishes to insure dies. In addition to this, the insured's consent must also be acquired. Before the insurance company will issue the policy, it will usually require the insured's signature consenting to the creation of the policy on his or her life. This applies to all of the above relationships except in the case of a young child who is not able to sign. In this case, the policy will be issued to the parent on the basis of his or her signature alone.

Elmore v. Life Insurance Co. of Virginia
187 S.C. 504, 198 S.E. 5 (1938)

Luther Elmore sued the Life Insurance Company of Virginia for breach of contract for nonpayment of the proceeds of a policy he took out on the life of his aunt, in which he was named as beneficiary.

The court stated the facts are as follows:

> The respondent [Luther Elmore] was solicited by the agent of the insurance company to take out a policy on his own life, but upon being told that the respondent was carrying all the insurance he wished to carry at that time, the agent suggested that he take out insurance upon some member of his family. It was then agreed that he would insure the life of his aunt, Mrs. Driggers. A reference to the testimony at this point will prove enlightening:

Q. How many aunts did you have at this time?

A. A good many, but she was the only aunt on my father's side.

Q. And that is the reason you picked her out?

A. No, Sir.

Q. Why did you pick her out?

A. Well, I got insurance on different ones.

Q. Just why did you pick out this particular one?

A. No particular one. I got insurance on my father-in-law and my brother-in-law.

> The application for the insurance was then given to the respondent [Luther Elmore] by the agent, who stated to him that it would be necessary only for Mrs. Driggers to sign the application in blank; that when it was returned the agent would himself fill in all the blank spaces.

Mrs. Drigger signed the application and the policy was issued without a medical examination. Four months later, she died of a chronic heart condition of which Luther Elmore was unaware.

The issue is whether Luther Elmore had an insurable interest in the life of his aunt.

The court held Luther Elmore had no insurable interest in the life of his aunt because he did not suffer any pecuniary loss by her death. The court decided Luther Elmore did not have any

> . . . reasonable expectation of benefit or advantage from the continuance of the life of the insured, and, as shown, the mere fact of relationship of aunt and nephew is not sufficient to create such insurable interest. There is no evidence in this case that Mrs. Driggers contributed anything to the support or maintenance of the respondent [Luther Elmore] . . .

The court ruled that the insurance company should refund all of the premiums paid by Luther Elmore toward this insurance policy. Judgment for Life Insurance Co. of Virginia.

Partnerships may insure the life of each of the partners up to the value of the partner's interest. The partnership will pay the proceeds of the policy to the heirs of the deceased partner in lieu of permanently dissolving the partnership and accounting for the deceased partner's share. Corporations may insure the life of their executives for the expected financial loss they will suffer if the executive dies. Creditors can insure debtors up to the amount of the debt owed. An insurable interest need only exist at the time the insurance is taken out.

EXAMPLE Richard and Gail Hyland were married when they were both twenty-five years of age. They each had taken out an insurance policy on the life of the other. Five years later, they were divorced. When Richard was forty years old, he died from cancer. Gail, as beneficiary, attempted to collect the proceeds of the policy, but the insurance company refused to pay her because she no longer had any insurable interest in her husband after the divorce. Has Gail any recourse? Yes! The insurer's contention is true, but insignificant. Gail is entitled to the proceeds as the named beneficiary because she had an insurable interest in her husband when the policy was taken out.

Types of Life Insurance

Ordinary Straight Life A fixed sum is payable on the death of the insured to the designated beneficiary; premiums must be paid for the entire life of the insured.

Limited Payment Life This is the same as the above except that premiums need only be paid for a specified period, such as fifteen, twenty, or twenty-five years.

Endowment Premiums are paid by the insured until he or she reaches a designated age, at which time the insurer will pay a lump sum to the insured. If the insured dies prematurely, the lump sum will be paid to the named beneficiary on the date of the insured's death.

Annuity One premium in the form of a lump sum is payed by the insured at the time the policy is taken out. In return, the insurance company promises to make periodic payments to the insured for either a fixed amount of time or until the insured dies. The amount of the periodic payments is usually fixed at the time the policy is taken out, but the insured may elect for the payments to fluctuate with prevailing interest rates, by choosing a variable annuity.

Term Insurance A fixed sum is payable to a covered beneficiary if the insured dies within the term covered by the insurance. Premiums must be paid for the duration of the term.

EXAMPLE Steven Conroy is a conversationalist. After two years of college, he decides to avoid the rigors of studying and applies to Metropolitan Life to become an insurance agent. Before he is hired, he is given a test which in part asks him to identify the following policies:

1. Johnny Rodgers takes out a $50,000 policy when he is thirty years of age, with monthly premiums payable until the date of his death. Johnny dies at age fifty-five. His wife Kathy will be entitled to $50,000, the face value of the policy, as long as his premiums have been paid up to date. What type of life insurance policy is this? Ordinary straight life insurance!

2. Assume the same facts, but Johnny Rodgers is only required to pay premiums for twenty years, until the age of fifty. What type of policy would this be? Limited payment life!

3. Alfred Gable is forty-five years old when he takes out a $75,000 insurance policy which requires him to pay premiums for twenty years, until he reaches the age of sixty-five, at which time a lump sum of $75,000 will be paid to him. If Gable dies at age sixty, his beneficiary will be entitled to the $75,000. What type of coverage is this? This is an endowment policy!

4. Clarence Silverman invests $160,000 with a life insurance company which, in turn, agrees to pay Silverman $1,500 per month for the rest of his life. Clarence is fifty-two years old. What type of insurance has Clarence purchased? Annuity!

5. Mark Richardson is twenty-five years old when he marries Michele. Two years later, they have their first child. Mark decides to take out a $40,000 policy on his life for ten years, with his wife Michele as the designated beneficiary. By the time this policy expires, Mark expects to take out one of the previously mentioned types of insurance. By then, Mark plans to be established and have sufficient income to afford one of the more expensive policies. But for now, Mark has a policy which pays his wife $40,000 if he dies within the next ten years and nothing if he lives beyond it. What type of insurance is this? Term insurance!

The policy issued by the company constitutes the entire agreement between the parties. Although the statute of frauds does not require a life insurance policy to be in writing because it is possible for the insured to die within one year, many states now require a life insurance policy to be in writing.

Standard Provisions

Incontestible clause provides that the validity of the policy may not be attacked because of material misrepresentations after two years from the issuance of the policy. The two-year period gives the insurer sufficient time to investigate the statements made by the insured.

Misstatement of age is not a material misrepresentation and the beneficiary may recover the amount of insurance the premiums would buy based on the correct age.

Change of beneficiary clause allows the owner of the policy to change the name of the beneficiary, usually upon written notice, at any time prior to the death of the insured. Although this provision is usually standard, if it was not included in the policy, the owner would have no right to change the beneficiary without the consent of the beneficiary.

Grace period of thirty days past the due date is allowed during which the policy owner may pay the premium. In most states, the insurer must send a written notice to this effect.

Nonforfeiture clause. If the premium is not paid by the end of the grace period, the owner of the policy has a choice to

1. Terminate the policy and accept the cash surrender value
2. Apply the premiums to purchase paid-up life insurance in a reduced amount
3. Apply the premiums to purchase term insurance
4. Apply for a loan against the cash value of the policy in an amount sufficient to pay the required premium

The cash surrender value is the amount of reserves built up in addition to the portion of the premium used to pay claims. Not all of the premium is used to pay life insurance claims. The extra amount is placed in a reserve fund. The amount in the reserve fund is known as the cash surrender value. It is this amount that will be paid to a policy owner who decides to terminate insurance coverage.

EXAMPLE | Douglas Grant purchases a $100,000 straight life insurance policy on his wife Carol, who was forty years of age at the time. After paying premiums for fifteen years, he defaults. Assume that: the annual premium is $2,000; the cash value of the policy is $35,000; twenty years of term insurance with a face amount of $100,000 could be purchased with the $30,000 of premiums paid; the premiums paid would also buy $70,000 worth of paid-up life insurance. What options are available to Douglas Grant? He may

1. Terminate the policy and accept the cash surrender value of $35,000
2. Apply the $30,000 in premiums to purchase $70,000 worth of paid-up life insurance
3. Apply the $30,000 in premiums to purchase twenty years of term insurance with a face value of $100,000
4. Apply for a $2,000 loan against the cash value of the policy to pay the annual premium and retain the present insurance coverage

FIRE INSURANCE

Fire insurance is a contract created for the purpose of indemnifying the insured for property loss caused by fire.

Substantial Economic Interest

The insured must have a substantial economic interest in the property to satisfy the insurable interest requirement. In addition to being able to insure one's own property, the following relationships give rise to an insurable interest in property:

Bailee

Tenant

Contractor

Buyer of goods

Shareholder of corporate property

Mortgagee

A bailee can insure goods incident to a bailment contract when they are in his or her possession. A tenant can insure the property rented for the duration of the lease. Usually, a landlord will maintain adequate insurance, but a tenant will be required to insure his or her own personal property. A contractor who is building a house on land owned by another may purchase insurance because he or she has a substantial economic interest in the house until it is completed. A buyer may insure goods once they have become identified to the contract of sale. Shareholders have an insurable interest in corporate property because the assets of the corporation are directly related to the value of the shareholder's stock. A lending institution or an individual mortgagee has a substantial economic interest in the mortgaged property and may acquire insurance coverage up to the balance remaining on the mortgage. The insured's substantial economic interest must exist at the time the insurance is purchased and at the time the loss occurs.

Liverpool & London & Globe Ins. Co., Ltd.
v. Bolling
176 Va. 182, 10 S.E.2d 518 (1940)

Anne Bolling brought a lawsuit againt an insurance company for breach of contract caused by their failure to pay the face value of an insurance policy which covered a building destroyed by fire. Henry Bolling owned a building in which his daughter-in-law, Anne, operated a business. Anne's business was the only means she had of supporting herself and her children. Anne was subsequently divorced from Henry's son Clarence. Henry decided to give Anne the building for as long as she wanted it without requiring rent. It was his intention to transfer ownership to Anne some time in the future. This is subtantiated by Anne's testimony:

> The first question Mr. Dennis [the insurance agent] asked was, who owned that business, and I told him I owned the merchandise, fixtures and everything in the building and he asked who owned the building and I told him my father-in-law, Henry Bolling, and he said that I couldn't insure a building that didn't belong to me, and I told him that Mr. Bolling said to use the building as if it were my own, and that Mr. Bolling said he intended to give it to me later, and he [the insurance agent] said that there was a little clause that could be added in the policy . . .

Anne Bolling contends the insurance company had knowledge of her economic interest in the building and the fact she did not own it when they approved and issued the policy.

The issue is whether Anne Bolling had a substantial economic interest in the building owned by her father-in-law.

The court held Anne was entitled to the face value of the policy because she relied on the business for her means of support and she would suffer a monetary loss as a result of the destruction of the building by fire. The court cited a ruling from another case,

> . . . (Citations) Any person who has any interest in the property, legal or equitable, or who stands in such a relation thereto that its destruction would entail pecuniary loss upon him, has an insurable interest to the extent of his interest therein, or of the loss to which he is subjected by the casualty . . .

Judgment for Bolling.

Coinsurance Provisions

Insurance coverage of 80 percent of the fair market value of the property must be maintained, otherwise the insured becomes a coinsurer. Coinsurers are liable for the proportion of the loss to the property for which they are underinsured.

EXAMPLE | Lance Kroll purchased a house for $60,000 and took out an insurance policy for the same value. Five years later, the house had appreciated in value to $100,000, but Kroll never increased his insurance. That same year, a fire partially destroyed his home. The insurance adjuster estimated the loss to be 50 percent or $50,000. What percent of the loss will Kroll recover from the insurance company? He will recover 75 percent or $37,500. Since Kroll did not have his house insured for 80 percent of its fair market value, he will be entitled to a percentage of $60,000 divided by $80,000 or 75 percent. This is the amount of insurance Kroll had, divided by the amount he was required to carry. Kroll becomes coinsurer for the other 25 percent of the loss or $12,500.

A person who intentionally ignites a fire on property he or she has insured will be barred from recovering the proceeds of the policy.

EXAMPLE | Milton Washburn owned a tenement in the Watts section of Los Angeles. The building was in a state of disrepair and all the tenants had vacated the building. Washburn attempted to sell the building, but was offered only a fraction of its insured value. Late one night, Washburn entered the buiding with a can of kerosene and ignited a fire. The buiding was consumed with flames and totally destroyed. Washburn notified the insurance company immediately and put in a claim to collect the proceeds. Some of Washburn's former tenants lived nearby; they had observed him entering the building shortly before the fire began. They informed the insurer of their observations. Will Washburn be able to collect the proceeds of the policy? No! The insurance company will refuse to pay on the strength of the witnesses' testimony that Washburn committed arson, a criminal offense. A person may not profit from his or her own criminal conduct.

LIABILITY INSURANCE

Liability insurance is acquired by businesses to protect them from lawsuits by people who are injured on their premises or through the negligence of employees acting within the scope of their employment. Businesses also need liability coverage in the following areas. Employers have workmen's compensation coverage for injuries sustained by employees on the job. Manufacturers carry product liability insurance to protect them from lawsuits arising from injuries caused by the use of their product. Common carriers utilize insurance to indemnify shippers whose goods are damaged or destroyed through the fault of the carrier. Insurance protects contractors by covering employees and subcontractors who are injured due to unsafe working conditions or the negligence of another worker. Landlords need liability coverage for injuries caused to their tenants through neglect in maintaining the habitability of the tenants' apartments or areas of common use such as hallways, sidewalks, and courtyards. Homeowners also need liability insurance to protect them from lawsuits brought by individuals injured on their premises; for example, guests, repairmen, deliverymen, and gas and electric meter readers. This protection is usually afforded in a homeowner's policy.

HOMEOWNER'S INSURANCE

A homeowner's policy provides comprehensive coverage incorporating standard fire insurance, liability insurance, and casualty insurance plus an assortment of riders to suit the needs of the individual homeowner.

CASUALTY INSURANCE

In most states, casualty insurance applies to accidental damage to property. This may include property of the insured that is damaged or stolen during a burglary or other civil commotion. It also includes the insured's real or personal property damaged by vandalism or malicious mischief. Personal property of the insured may also be covered while the insured is away from his or her principal place of residence, that is, while visiting, vacationing, or on a business trip.

Casualty insurance also encompasses the property of others which is accidentally damaged by the insured. Casualty insurance is usually included in a homeowner's policy, but may be acquired separately. In some states, casualty insurance applies to personal injury caused to the insured or others, but, for convenience, these areas are dealt with under health insurance, liability insurance, and automobile insurance.

HEALTH INSURANCE

Health insurance protects individuals who are in need of medical treatment. There are two types of coverage: hospital service and surgical-medical service. These services may be administered jointly, as when a patient is admitted to a hospital for surgery, or separately, as when a patient visits a physician at an office or clinic, for medical care. Coverage may be extended to home care services. Health insurance may be provided for an individual, family, or group. Group coverage is a plan purchased by an association, partnership, or corporation for its members and employees.

AUTOMOBILE INSURANCE

An automobile policy may cover either or both personal injury or property damage. Insurance for property damage may encompass collision insurance and/or fire and theft insurance. Collision insurance protects the value of the insured's car against resulting damage even if the damage was caused by the insured's negligence. A person who does not have collision insurance and was not at fault may still collect from the insurance company of the negligent driver by making a claim, or may collect from the negligent driver by suing him or her in court.

NO-FAULT AUTO INSURANCE

The significance of no-fault insurance is that medical payments may be paid out by insurance companies to their insured individuals without first determining which person is at fault. The insurance companies resolve this amongst themselves by apportioning the fault between the parties. Meanwhile, the insured's medical expenses are being paid. No-fault was also designed to relieve court calendar congestion by prohibiting an individual who is a "covered person" from suing in court for basic economic loss up to $50,000 (this amount may vary from state to state) unless a serious injury was sustained. Some form of no-fault insurance has been adopted in more than half of the states. This ensuing discussion is predicated on the laws of New York, which is representative of those states which have converted their automobile insurance laws to no-fault.

A "covered person" includes the owner, operator, or occupant of a vehicle which has proper no-fault insurance, as well as an injured pedestrian. Persons not covered include those individuals who are:

Stealing a car

Avoiding arrest

Committing a felony

Racing

Intentionally injuring themselves

Drunk or intoxicated

Basic economic loss encompasses

1. Treatment expenses: medical, surgical, dental, hospital, therapeutic, psychiatric, and ambulance
2. Loss of earnings up to $1,000 per month
3. Reasonable necessary expenses incident to treatment and recovery

A negligence suit is permitted under circumstances where no-fault insurance does not apply:

Serious injury or permanent disfigurement

Medical expenses exceed $500

Individual injured is not a "covered person"

Loss of earnings exceed $1,000 per month

Economic loss exceeds $50,000

Damage to property

An insured innocent victim who is injured as a result of an uninsured, unregistered, unidentified, or stolen vehicle, may recover from his or her own insurance company if the policy provides for uninsured motorist coverage. Many states require a mandatory provision to this effect. An insured innocent victim includes the person insured, his or her spouse, relatives while in the same household, and any other occupant who is in the vehicle with permission.

INSURER'S RIGHT OF SUBROGATION

Once an insurance company makes a payment to an insured for a loss suffered, it has a right of subrogation. This means the insurer takes the place of the insured and is entitled to whatever rights and remedies the insured has against the person who had caused the loss.

EXAMPLE | Sylvia Jordan is driving through an intersection when Clark Peterson runs a red light in his Lincoln and smashes into her Toyota. Sylvia sustains severe injuries and her car is totally ruined. The damages amount to $450,000. Clark Peterson is insured only to $300,000. Sylvia's insurance company pays her the additional $150,000 and then sues Peterson. Peterson claims the right to sue for personal injuries can only be brought by

Sylvia. Is his argument correct? No! Sylvia's insurance company guaranteed to pay Sylvia up to $1,000,000, the extent of her liability coverage. The $450,000 is a debt owed by Clark Peterson and his insurance company. Once Sylvia's insurance company pays her the $450,000, it acquires her rights and remedies by subrogation. Through the right of subrogation, it has recovered $300,000 from Peterson's insurance company. It may now sue Peterson for the other $150,000, because the accident was due solely to his fault.

REVIEW QUESTIONS

1. Define insurance, insurer, insured, and insurable interest.
2. What does the term *coinsurance* mean?
3. What are the various types of life insurance?
4. Describe the other major kinds of insurance.
5. What is no-fault insurance?
6. Who is a "covered person" under no-fault insurance?
7. Anderson bought property which was financed by Palmetto Trust Company. Palmetto assigned its mortgage to Metropolitan Life Insurance Company. Pursuant to the terms of the mortgage agreement, Anderson procured appropriate insurance coverage and transferred the policy to Metropolitan. Metropolitan then assigned the mortgage and insurance policy to Central Union Bank. The day after the assignment was completed, the property was destroyed by fire. New York Underwriters' Insurance Company, insurers of the property, disclaimed liability on the grounds an insurance policy cannot be assigned without the insurer's consent. The bank mortgagee contended this was an assignment of rights as security for the mortgage owed, not an assignment of the policy itself to a new owner with a potential increase in risk. What result? Central Union Bank v. New York Underwriters' Insurance Co., 52 F.2d 823 (4th Cir. 1931).
8. Minasian sued Aetna Life Insurance Company for breach of contract in failing to pay the proceeds of a policy on the life of his wife. He was named as beneficiary. His wife died of bullet wounds. He was convicted of manslaughter and sentenced to serve a period of from ten to twenty years. The law of the state prohibits a person from collecting insurance proceeds on the life of another when he or she is responsible for the death of the insured. Minasian claims that the revolver was discharged accidentally during a struggle and furthermore at that time he could not distinguish between right and wrong. If he can prove this will he be able to collect the proceeds? Minasian v. Aetna Life Insurance Co., 295 Mass. 1, 3 N.E.2d 17 (1936).
9. Gervant owned a building in Brooklyn which was partially damaged by fire. He had an insurance policy with New England Fire Insurance Company for $6,000. Both Gervant and the insurance company could not agree on the actual cash value of the building at the time of the fire. Thereafter, an individual was appointed by the court to appraise the property. This appraisal was grossly overstated and disregarded by the court. Gervant refused to acquire a new appraisal and demanded the face value of the policy. The insurer contended that

Gervant was underinsured and was therefore not entitled to the face value but only a percentage thereof as a coinsurer. What result? Gervant v. New England Fire Ins. Co., 306 N.Y. 393, 118 N.E.2d 574 (1954).

10. Braun's truck was damaged in a collision with a railroad train. The truck was insured by Illinois Automobile Insurance Exchange, but not for its full value. The insurance company paid Braun the proceeds of the policy. Braun then initiated a lawsuit against the railroad without informing the insurance company. The lawsuit against the railroad was subsequently settled for a fixed amount. This barred the insurance company from exercising their right of subrogation against the railroad for the amount they paid to Braun. They claimed that since Braun interfered with their right of subrogation, he should have to return the proceeds of the policy paid to him. What result? Illinois Automobile Ins. Exchange v. Braun, 280 Pa. 550, 124 A. 691 (1924).

27

SURETYSHIP

INTRODUCTION

Suretyship is a contract between a surety and a creditor in which the surety promises to be responsible for the debt of another. This provides security for the creditor in case the principal debtor defaults. Suretyship evolved because the lenders of money frequently looked for greater protection than was afforded by the mere promise of the borrower to repay the amount loaned. A surety is a person who guarantees payment to a creditor for another person's debt. The principal debtor is the person who borrowed money from the creditor or who had the direct responsibility to perform for the creditor. The creditor is the person to whom the debtor owes either money or performance, and to whom the surety will be liable if the debtor does not perform.

RULES OF SURETYSHIP

Suretyship is a contract; therefore the rules of contract laws are applicable. The elements of a contract must be satisfied for the suretyship to be valid:

Purpose (lawful)
Agreement
Legal capacity
Act
Consideration
Executed in proper form

Valuable consideration must be given by both the surety and the creditor. The consideration furnished by the surety is his or her guarantee to pay or perform the obligation owed by the principal debtor if the principal debtor defaults. The consideration given in return to the surety is the promise by the creditor to loan money, sell goods, or perform a service for the principal debtor.

A suretyship contract must be executed in proper form: in writing and signed by the surety to evidence the existence of his or her promise. This is a requirement of the statute of frauds. An oral contract to be liable for the debt of another is not enforceable. The reasoning behind the signed writing is to prevent fraud because it is unusual for people to guarantee to pay for the debts of others.

Many times there is a question as to whether the writing is a guarantee of payment or merely a recommendation of the debtor's ability to pay. To make a proper interpretation, the court will look to the relationship of the parties, the circumstances under which the writing is made, and the motivation of the potential surety for making the statement.

EXAMPLE | Christine Lambert is in the process of filling out a Streamline credit card application. She uses her Aunt May as a reference. Streamline Credit Company sends Aunt May a form requesting her to attest to her niece's ability to pay her debts. Aunt May signs the form and returns it. Subsequently, Christine purchases a fur jacket and other apparel costing $2,000, which she fails to pay. Streamline brings suit against Aunt May claiming she is a surety and the form she signed is a suretyship contract. Is Aunt May responsible for Christine's debts? No! Aunt May did not agree to be responsible for Christine's debts. She merely recommended Christine's ability to pay. A recommendation of ability to pay is an opinion, not a personal guaranty.

A surety who guarantees the debts of an infant or an insane person is liable even if they abrogate the contract. Only the infant or the insane person can raise their respective defenses because those defenses are personal to them. If the person were declared insane judicially, then the contract would be void and the surety would not be responsible. For more information on the different classifications of insane individuals, see Chapter 9, Legal Capacity.

A partner who retires from a partnership becomes a surety for all of the past debts of the partnership incurred before he or she gave notice of retirement.

Bankruptcy does not discharge the surety even though the creditor has accepted partial payment during the bankruptcy proceeding. Illegality will cancel a surety's obligation, as will an alteration of the written suretyship contract, unless it is negotiable and held by a holder in due course. See Chapter 21, Commercial Paper: Holder in Due Course, for a discussion of negotiable instruments and the rights of a holder in due course.

A surety contract may not be altered without the consent of the surety unless it is a mere act of leniency toward the principal debtor; a release of the debtor for part of the obligation owed; or an extension of the time to pay, as long as the extension does not materially alter or increase the surety's burden.

Death of a surety will not discharge his or her obligation to perform because a contract does not terminate on the death of one of the parties unless it is a personal service contract. The estate of the surety will be responsible for guaranteeing payment. This responsibility extends only to past debts, not future ones incurred after the surety's death. A surety would be liable for the future debts of a principal debtor only if he or she were a continuing surety and were alive when the debts were incurred.

LIABILITY OF A SURETY

The surety's liability must be secondary. Primary responsibility for payment of the debt must rest with the debtor. Only in the event the debtor does not pay or perform does the surety become liable. But, does the surety become liable at the moment that the debtor breaches the contract by failing to pay or perform? The answer depends on whether the surety is a guarantor of payment or a guarantor of collection. The terms *surety* and *guarantor* are now used interchangeably in contracts involving the sale of goods under the UCC.

A guarantor of collection is only responsible to the creditor after the creditor has taken legal action against the principal debtor to collect the amount owed. The effect of a judgment in favor of the creditor against the principal debtor is that it proves the creditor has a claim against the surety for that amount. The creditor must make a good-faith effort to enforce the judgment by collecting the amount owed from the assets of the principal debtor. Only if this proves fruitless may the creditor proceed against the surety. A guarantor of payment is responsible for the debt immediately on the principal debtor's default. The liability of the principal debtor and surety coincide. On the principal debtor's default, the creditor may recover from the surety just as if he or she were the prinicipal debtor.

EXAMPLE

Stewart Manchester III was seventeen years old when he passed his driver's test. He lived in Beverly Hills with his family. Stewart's parents took him to a Porsche dealership in town where the boy picked out a royal blue Sport Carrera for $42,000. Stewart agreed to be personally liable for payment. The dealer requested his parents to sign the contract for the sale of the car as sureties guaranteeing payment. The parents agreed. The dealer promised the car would be ready in six weeks. In the interim, Stewart was vacationing in Monte Carlo. One night while returning from a casino, Stewart, who was dressed in princely fashion, was mugged by a pauper who exchanged clothes with him and relieved him of $15,000 in cash. Stewart failed to make his first monthly payment on the car and was held in default. The Porsche dealer brought suit against his parents for the $42,000. Are they responsible? Yes, but only for the dealer's loss of profits, if the car is returned. The parents are guarantors of payment. They may be sued immediately on the default of the principal debtor. If Stewart's parents had signed as guarantors of collection, the Porsche dealer would have to sue Stewart first and obtain a judgment against him. Then the dealer would have to attempt to enforce the judgment. Only if this proved fruitless would the dealer be allowed to proceed against Stewart's parents. Could Stewart have abrogated the contract because of his infancy? Yes! In most states, a car is not considered a necessity, especially a Porsche Carrera. Would Stewart's parents be relieved of their responsibility as sureties? No! An infant's special right to rescind a contract is personal and applies only to him or her. Must the suretyship agreement be attached to the contract for the sale of the car? Yes! This is a retail installment contract and most states require this contract be attached to the suretyship agreement when the agreement is given to the surety.

The surety's promise must be made to the creditor. If it is made to the debtor, then an issue of indemnity arises and no writing is required. Indemnity is the reimbursement of money to the person to whom the money is owed. The validity of the promise will depend on whether the debtor has given valid consideration in return for the surety's promise.

EXAMPLE Dennis Calhoun is a young lad of nineteen. Dennis has frequently found himself in awkward financial situations, but has been able to extricate himself with the aid of his friend, Mr. Wolf. On two prior occasions, Wolf bailed Dennis out. Then Dennis approached Wolf with his plan to buy a house near the Prince William Forest in Virginia. Mr. Wolf congratulated Dennis and told him if he was unable to make payment at anytime that he, Mr. Wolf, would be responsible for the debt. Mr. Wolf sent Dennis a letter to this effect as well. Subsequently, Dennis defaulted on the mortgage payments. When the bank began forclosure proceedings, Dennis cried "Wolf" for the third time, but this time his friend did not respond. If Dennis presents the friend's letter to the bank will Mr. Wolf be liable as a surety? No! Mr. Wolf would only be responsible as a surety if his promise was made in writing to the creditor, that is, the bank. Here, Wolf's promise was made to Dennis, the principal debtor. Dennis is solely liable for the debt and since he can not make the payments the mortgage will be foreclosed and Dennis and the family will be evicted. Although Wolf has no responsibility toward the bank, he is liable to Dennis for indemnification if Dennis gave valuable consideration in return for Wolf's promise. Here, Dennis gave none so he will only be remembered as the boy who cried "Wolf" once too often.

A person's statement that he or she will be responsible for payment or that the debt should be charged to his or her account is one of primary accountability. The substitution of the surety for the debtor at the surety's request is a novation. A novation was previously discussed in Chapter 12, Rights of Third Parties. A novation releases the debtor from all responsibility with the result that primary liability falls upon the surety. The same reasoning applies where the surety's main purpose in guaranteeing the debt of another is to gain economic benefit. A primary promise serves the surety's own interests even though it involves the debt of another, while a secondary promise simply guarantees the debt of another. Written evidence is required only where the surety's promise is secondary.

EXAMPLE Martin Baxter is the managing partner in the law firm of Livingston, Maxwell & Baxter. The firm moved to new offices in the Seaport Plaza. Baxter gives a messenger a list and sends him to Milbank's Office Equipment and Supplies, Inc.. Baxter telephones Milbank, instructing him to charge whatever the messenger orders to the firm's account. The messenger orders all of the requested supplies plus a $650 IBM typewriter which he takes with him for parts unknown. When the firm is billed, Baxter refuses to pay for the typewriter, claiming the debt was incurred by the messenger and an oral suretyship contract is unenforceable. Is Baxter correct? No! Baxter's oral promise was a primary one in which he assumed direct responsibility for payment of the debt. Baxter should reread this chapter on Suretyship; he is lacking in legal knowlege.

To be positive that a surety's promise is secondary, certain criteria must be present. A surety's guarantee of payment must be made to a creditor for the benefit of a debtor. The performance of a surety must be conditioned on the principal debtor's nonperformance. The duty owed by the debtor will be forgiven upon payment by the surety. A new duty then arises in the principal debtor to indemnify the surety, but not in excess of what the surety paid.

The statute of limitations governing all suretyship contracts is six years. Even if the underlying contract between the principal debtor and the creditor is a contract for the sale of goods with a four-year statute of limitations, this will not alter the surety's liability, which is for six years.

RIGHTS OF A SURETY

A surety has the following rights:

Subrogation
Indemnification
Release

Subrogation

Once the surety has paid the creditor the full amount owed by the principal debtor, he or she steps into the shoes of the creditor and acquires all of the creditor's rights and remedies against the principal debtor. This transfer of rights and remedies from the creditor to the surety is called subrogation. It is the most important right a surety has.

EXAMPLE Nelson Douglas bought a baby grand piano from Baldwin United for $8,500. In the contract of sale, Baldwin United retained a surety interest in the piano for the unpaid balance until all installments were paid. Douglas bought the piano for his daughter Jennifer, who expressed interest in learning to play. Douglas's friend, Stuart Lippmann, signed as a surety. Subsequently, Jennifer's interest in the piano waned and so did her father's ability to pay. When Douglas defaulted on the piano payments, Lippmann paid the $8,500. Lippmann now seeks to enforce Baldwin United's security interest in the piano and gain possession of it. Will he be successful? Yes! After fulfilling his responsibilities as a surety, Lippmann is subrogated to the rights of Douglas's creditor, Baldwin United, and acquires all the rights and remedies it has through subrogation, including the security interest in the piano.

Indemnification

The surety's right to indemnification arises after he or she has paid the creditor the amount owed by the principal debtor. Indemnification entitles the surety to reimbursement for the money paid to the creditor or the performance rendered for the creditor by the surety.

EXAMPLE Chico Mendez takes out a $15,000 homeowner's loan from Household Finance to have aluminum siding placed on his house. His neighbor, Jose Sanchez, signs the loan as a surety. Subsequently, Mendez defaults on the loan and Sanchez is forced to pay the balance owed. What recourse does Sanchez have? He may seek indemnification by suing Mendez for reimbursement for the amount he paid out.

Release

Release is the forgiveness of a debt. If the creditor releases the principal debtor from all his or her obligations, then this will release the surety from his or her guarantee. The surety will lose his or her right to subrogation as a consequence of the exoneration of the principal debtor. A surety's liability is contingent upon his or her right to subrogation. If the surety loses the right to subrogation because of the creditor's act of exoneration, then the surety is no longer liable on the contract between the creditor and the principal debtor.

EXAMPLE Ralph Martel's Uncle Eddie owns an electronics store. Ralph purchases an expensive car stereo with speakers for $450. Uncle Eddie asks Ralph's friend, Chuck, to sign as a surety. After a few months, Uncle Eddie exonerates Ralph from all liability and sues Chuck for the $450. Is Chuck responsible? No! Uncle Eddie's exoneration of his nephew, Ralph, released Chuck from all liability as his surety. Chuck has lost his right to subrogation because of the release and it would be unfair to hold Chuck liable when he would have no remedies against Ralph.

Fox v. Kroeger
119 Tex. 511, 35 S.W.2d 679 (1931)

Levi State Bank & Trust Company of Victoria, Texas, loaned a sum of money to Mrs. C. M. Fox. Mrs. Fox, in turn, signed a promissory note for the amount of the loan, and J. H. Kroeger cosigned the note as a surety. Mrs. Fox died prior to the maturity of the note. Ben J. Fox was appointed executor of her estate. When the note matured, Kroeger paid it in full and requested the bank to assign the note to him. The bank did so. Kroeger then brought suit against the estate for payment of the note, asserting his right of subrogation. Ben J. Fox contended that the note could not be assigned to Kroeger; that Kroeger could only proceed on the theory of indemnification.

The issue is whether Kroeger, after making payment in full on Mrs. Fox's debt, is entitled to the assignment of the note under the remedy of subrogation or is restricted to the remedy of indemnification.

The court held,

> . . . where the surety pays the debt of the principal, he has his election to either pursue . . . the obligation implied by law in his favor for reimbursement by the principal [debtor]; or he can prosecute an action on the very debt itself, and in either event he stands in the shoes of the original creditor as to any securities and rights of priority. What we have already said applies with equal force to all debts whether represented by a negotiable instrument or not.

The court ruled,

> Kroeger was compelled to pay the note, and on doing so took an assignment thereof, and brings this action on the note itself. . . . the payment by the principal debtor or by the party accommodated discharges the instrument,

but payment by a party secondarily liable, other than the principal debtor or party accommodated, does not discharge or extinguish the debt . . .

Judgment for Kroeger.

CONTINUING SURETY

A continuous suretyship contract covers a course of dealings between a creditor and a principal debtor for a definite or indefinite period of time. The continuing surety guarantees the principal debtor's obligation to a specific creditor for a succession of credit transactions. Some states do not allow a continuing suretyship contract in a retail credit transaction where payments are to be made on an installment basis. Instead, a separate suretyship contract is required for each guarantee of payment by the surety. The suretyship contract must be affixed to the retail installment contract and a copy must be given to the surety. This apprises the surety of the extent to which he or she will be liable if the principal debtor defaults; otherwise the surety's liability would be unlimited. Death terminates a continung suretyship and the surety will be liable for only those obligations incurred by the principal debtor up to the surety's date of death.

EXAMPLE Daniel Rosenberg guarantees all payments of stock transactions entered into by his nephew, Jacob, for the calendar year. Rosenberg's guarantee is transformed into a signed writing and given to a representative of Shearson-American Express. Jacob makes the following purchases:

January 21	100 shares IBM
February 21	100 shares GM
March 21	100 shares AT&T

On March 3, Daniel Rosenberg dies. Jacob did not make payment on any of the listed stock transactions. Which transactions are Daniel Rosenberg's estate liable for? His estate is liable for only those transactions which occurred prior to Rosenberg's death, namely the purchase of IBM and GM. Although Daniel Rosenberg is a continuing surety and his liability under the suretyship contract is supposed to continue for the calendar year, his death cancels the suretyship contract with respect to all future transactions including the one for AT&T.

COSURETIES

Cosureties are two or more individuals who agree to be responsible for the obligations of the principal debtor. They are equally bound. The creditor may collect all or part of the entire debt from one cosurety. A cosurety who pays more than his or her proportionate share has the right of contribution against the other cosurety for reimbursement. If a creditor releases one cosurety, the other is limited to 50 percent of the debt.

| Mark Billingham and Chester Hayes are wealthy entrepreneurs. They both sign as sureties for a $2 million loan to Colossal Construction Corporation, a condominium development with an eighteen-hole golf course. Due to a rise in the interest rates, the condominium market falls off. Colossal has trouble selling the condominiums for a premium price and cannot pay off the $2 million balance remaining on the loan. The bank sues Billingham and collects the $2 million from him. Hayes has left the United States on a permanent vacation to Switzerland. Should he return, will Billingham have any recourse against him? Yes! As cosureties, both Billingham and Hayes were each liable for 50 percent of the corporation's unpaid debt. Since Billingham paid more than his share, he can recoup $1 million from Hayes by exercising his right of contribution.

United States Fidelity & Guaranty Co. v. Naylor
237 F. 314 (8th Cir. 1916)

Dickerson and Starrett organized the Toronto Bank in January. The county approved a bond given by United States Fidelity for $5,000 in February; and in March, approved a bond given by the firm of Bradey, Naylor, Thompson, Gilroy, and Haggatt, for $10,000. Both the bank and the firm were acting as sureties for Dickerson and Starrett. The firm paid only $2,530 whereas the county collected over $6,500 from United States Fidelity. United States Fidelity contended that it should be responsible for one-third of the bank's liability with the remaining two-thirds falling on the shoulders of the firm. Since United States Fidelity paid more than their one-third proportionate share as determined by their $5,000 bond, it should be entitled to be indemnified from the other cosureties for the amount in excess of the one-third share.

The issue is whether United States Fidelity is entitled to a right of contribution from its cosureties.

The court held,

Hence, where some of the cosureties for a common debt have been compensated, but not indemnified, for their suretyship, and others became cosureties for the accommodation of their principals, that fact is immaterial, and the compensated cosureties [United States Fidelity], who have paid more than their proportion of the common liability, are entitled to contribution from the accommodation cosureties. . . .

The court ruled, "Where there are several bonds securing the same debt, and the surety or sureties on one of these pays more than his proportion of the debt, the contribution between the sureties must be in proportion to the penalties of their respective bonds. (Citations.)" Judgment for United States Fidelity.

REVIEW QUESTIONS

1. What does the term *suretyship* mean?
2. Who are the three parties involved in a suretyship contract?
3. What is the difference between a primary promise and a secondary promise, and which one must be in writing?

4. Explain the two types of suretyship contracts: guarantor of payment and guarantor of collection.

5. What are the rights of a surety?

6. Define cosureties and state their rights and responsibilities.

7. What is a continuing surety and in what instances will his or her liability terminate?

8. Buckley agreed to perform masonary and carpentry work on a construction site for Brody & Sons, Inc. Buckley bought lumber from the Westbury Lumber Company, Inc., but failed to pay for it. Since more lumber was required to complete the work and Westbury Lumber refused to make further delivery, Ben Brody spoke to the officers of Westbury Lumber and personally guaranteed payment for what was delivered and for all future deliveries. Westbury Lumber sued Brody after Buckley defaulted. Brody contended that his promise to pay for the debt of another should have been in writing, and since it was not he raised the statute of frauds as a defense to a suit alleging he was a surety. What result? Westbury v. A. Brody & Sons, Inc., 257 N.Y. 97, 177 N.E. 385 (1931).

9. Wood delivered goods to Miller on the reliance of Dodge's oral promise to pay for the goods. Dodge denied ever making the promise and refused to pay for the goods delivered to Miller. Dodge claimed the promise would have to have been in writing and signed by him to satisfy the statute of frauds requirements. Will Wood be able to recover the value of the goods from Dodge? Wood v. Dodge, 23 S.D. 95, 120 N.W. 774 (1909).

10. Maxwell loaned money to Davis. Davis signed a promissory note which Smith and others signed as cosureties. Davis failed to repay the amount owed. The cosureties paid Maxwell. The cosureties brought an action against Davis, but he did not possess any property at the time. Nine years later when Davis purchased some real estate, Smith sought to exercise his right of subrogation based on the judgment Maxwell obtained against Davis. The issue concerns which statute of limitations would be applicable: the six-year statute of limitations which relates to the time in which a surety could sue the principal debtor for the amount paid on his or her account, or a ten-year statute of limitations which governs the time during which a judgment may be enforced. David, the principal debtor, argues that the shorter one applies and bars Smith from recovery. Smith argues that the latter statute applies and allows him to enforce a lien against Davis's real estate. What result? Smith v. Davis et al., 71 W.Va. 316, 76 S.E. 670 (1912).

28

REAL ESTATE TRANSACTIONS

INTRODUCTION

A real estate transaction is a special type of contract involving the sale of land. All the rules of contract law are applicable and should be consulted in the drafting of the contract. This refers especially to the statute of frauds which requires a contract for the sale of real estate be executed in proper form, that is, it must be in writing.

Real estate transactions involve the buying and selling of land for use or speculation, of a house for living and/or investment through rentals or price appreciation, or of a building for commercial use. The seller and purchaser may be individuals, partnerships, corporations, or any combination of these.

There are three major stages involved in buying and selling real estate:

1. Contacting a broker
2. Signing a contract
3. Closing title

CONTACTING A BROKER

The first step in selling or buying real estate is to find a buyer or a seller. Although this can be accomplished by the individual parties themselves—through word of mouth or posting a sign or advertising in local newspapers—the most utilized and accepted method is through the services of a broker.

Real estate brokers help create a market for real estate transactions by listing a variety of land, houses, or business offices for sale or rent. Brokers have the resources to market the product through advertising and telephone contact and have a continually updated file of prospective buyers. They attempt to screen prospective purchasers to assure that they have the ability to finance the transaction. Brokers are licensed with the state to list real estate for sale. They employ salespeople, who must be licensed to sell real estate and to act as the brokers' agents. Where the parties can not agree on a price, brokers act as mediators in negotiations between seller and purchaser and attempt to bring the parties together on an agreeable price.

For the rendering of these services, the broker is entitled to a commission based on a percentage of the sale. The commission is actually earned by a broker when he or she produces a purchaser who is ready, willing, and able to pay a price agreeable to the seller on the seller's terms. For the seller's protection, the brokerage agreement should be amended to reflect that the broker's commission is due and payable only after the closing of title, when the purchase price is paid and the deed is delivered to the buyer. This protects the seller from having to pay a commission in all cases except where the seller willfully breaches the contract.

Lane—The Real Estate Department Store, Inc. v. Lawlet Corp. et al.
28 N.Y.2d 36, 319 N.Y.S.2d 752 (1971)

The Real Estate Department Store sued to recover real estate brokerage commissions in connection with the sale of a parcel of real estate.

Louis Licht, the president of the Real Estate Department Store, was approached by Gerald Cunningham, who asked him to locate a garage suitable for his father-in-law's taxicab business. Licht contacted George Lunny who represented himself as the owner of a garage. Lunny advised Licht that he would sell the garage property for $830,000, and listed the garage with him. They agreed on a brokerage commission of $19,000 based on the standard rate set by the Real Estate Board of New York. Licht informed Lunny that he had a prospective purchaser. After negotiations, both Lunny and Cunningham agreed on a price of $800,000.

Thereafter, Lunny's attorney mailed a copy of the proposed brokerage agreement to Licht which provided for a commission of only $15,000. Licht advised Lunny's attorney that this was not acceptable because it did not reflect the commission agreed upon orally between Lunny and himself. This dispute was to be resolved at closing. However, the closing of title never took place because Lunny no longer possessed title to the garage property. Two months before, Lunny defaulted on mortgage payments owed to Lawlet Corporation and surrendered title to the premises by deed in lieu of foreclosure.

The issue here is whether Licht earned his brokerage commission and not whether Cunningham, the purchaser, has any cause of action.

The court held that a broker need only introduce evidence tending to prove that he or she produced a purchaser who was ready, willing, and able to buy based on the terms dictated by the seller. Since the brokerage agreement is a contract for personal services rather than a contract for the sale of real estate, it does not have to be in writing to fulfill the statute of frauds requirement.

The court further held that,

The broker's ultimate right to compensation has never been held to be dependent upon the performance of the realty contract or the receipt by the seller of the full price unless the brokerage agreement with the vendor specifically so conditioned payment. [The term *vendor* refers to the seller.]

The court reasoned,

The parties are, of course, free to provide otherwise by agreement. For example, they can condition the seller's liability on the closing of title, or require the broker to supply a buyer to purchase the property at a specified price 'with terms to be arranged'. In the former case the broker would not earn a commission if the deal were not consummated (Citations) and in the latter situation, there would be no commission if terms were not arranged. (Citations). It should be observed, however, that even where the broker and seller expressly provide that there shall be no right to a commission unless some condition is fulfilled, and the condition is not performed, the seller will nevertheless be liable if he is responsible for the failure to perform the condition. (Citations.)

Judgment for Lane—The Real Estate Department Store.

The seller pays the broker's commission unless the parties provide otherwise in the contract. The broker's commission can be as high as 8 percent for the sale of a house. The more expensive the land, house, or business property, the smaller the commission, because the broker's task of locating a purchaser remains the same.

EXAMPLE John Saber operates a brokerage office in Little Rock, Arkansas. During the week of February 5, Saber earned two commissions for brokerage services rendered. The first was an 8 percent commission on the sale of a one-family house for $100,000 ($8,000 commission). The second was a 2 percent commission on the sale of an office building for $1,000,000 ($20,000 commission).

The commission earned will be split between the broker and his or her agent, who brought about the sale. A commission of 50/50 is the usual arrangement. However, the more successful a salesperson is, the more likely this arrangement will be altered to 55/45, or 60/40 in favor of the salesperson. The reason for this is the broker's costs for each salesperson is basically fixed. These fixed costs include desk space, telephone use, mailings, advertisements, and overhead costs. The broker will spend this fixed amount regardless of the numbers of homes sold by a particular salesperson. A successful salesperson can use this as leverage in demanding a greater percentage of the commissions.

EXAMPLE In the previous example, Charles Boyer brought about the sale of the house, and Edward Morris, the sale of the office building. Boyer receives a 60/40 commission split and Morris receives a 55/45 split. How will the commissions be divided? The $8,000 commission for the sale of the home will be allocated $4,800 for Charles Boyer, salesman; and $3,200 for John Saber, broker. The $20,000 commission for the sale of the building will be proportioned $11,000 for Edward Morris, salesman; and $9,000 for John Saber, broker.

There are various agreements which a seller can enter into with a broker.

Open listing   The seller reserves the right to sell the property himself or contract to sell with other brokers. A broker who accepts an open listing will be entitled to a commission only if he or she brings about a sale.

Exclusive Agency   The seller reserves the right to sell the property himself but agrees not to contract with other brokers. A broker who accepts an exclusive agency will be entitled to a commission in all cases except where the seller brings about the sale.

Exclusive Right to Sell   The seller reserves no rights and the broker is entitled to a commission regardless of who brings about the sale.

It is important to read a brokerage agreement before signing it regardless of the broker's oral representations. If a person has difficulty understanding the language, he or she should consult an attorney, preferably one who will represent him or her at the signing of the contract and at the closing of the title.

EXAMPLE   Bob and Christine Evans sign an open listing brokerage agreement. William and Susan Harrison sign an exclusive right to sell agreement. Both couples succeed in selling their houses themselves. Will either couple be responsible for paying a commission? Yes! The Harrisons signed an exclusive right to sell agreement. They must pay the full commission even though they brought about the sale themselves. The Evans do not have to pay the broker to whom they gave an open listing a commission because in such an agreement, the sellers reserve the right to bring about the sale by themselves.

Multiple Listing   This is a service brokers can subscribe to in which all members pool their exclusive listings and agree to split the commission earned with the broker who brings about the sale. Brokers will usually place the property with a multiple listing service after they have first tried to earn the full commission by selling the house themselves.

EXAMPLE   Henry and Harriet Blackstone give a salesman named Todd Jarrett an exclusive right to sell their home. The brokerage agreement includes a provision allowing Jarrett's broker, Lakewood Real Estate, to place the house with a multiple listing service where the commission will be divided 60/40 in favor of the selling broker.

The house is eventually sold by Alexander Corbin, a salesman for Grasmere Realty. The commission on the sale is $10,000. Assuming that the respective salesmen-brokers commissions are split 50/50, how much will each party get? The selling broker, Grasmere Realty, will get $6,000 according to the multiple listing fee arrangement. Out of this, $3,000 will be paid to Alexander Corbin, the salesman who brought about the deal. The listing broker, Lakewood Real Estate, will get $4,000 from which $2,000 will be paid to Todd Jarrett, the listing salesman.

A broker will usually request an interested purchaser to sign a binder. A binder is a statement setting forth the amount the prospective purchaser wishes to offer and is often accompanied by a check for $100 or more. A binder amounts to a good-faith interest on the prospective purchaser's part. But an interested purchaser should be wary of signing a binder because, if it includes all of the contractual elements, it may constitute a contract.

SIGNING A CONTRACT

After a ready, willing, and able purchaser is found, the next step is to sign a contract which will set forth the rights and liabilities of both parties. Before a contract is signed, both parties should hire a lawyer to represent them at the signing of the contract and up until the closing of title. An attorney's fee generally ranges from .5 percent to 1 percent of the sales price. The reason a purchaser and seller hire an attorney is for advice on the contract and protection against fraud and other unfair consequences.

The contract must be in writing. The signing of the contract will give effect to the oral agreement of the parties. The contract must set forth the consideration given by each party and the respective parties must have the legal capacity to enter into the contract. A contract entered into by an infant is valid only during the period of infancy. It may be voided by the infant within a reasonable time after reaching majority. A real estate contract made by a non-judicially declared incompetent is voidable. This means the contract is valid unless the incompetent person chooses to void it. A judicially declared incompetent's contract is absolutely void. Sale of real estate by a partnership must be done in the partnership's name and the signature of any general partner will be valid. A contract entered into by a corporation must have stockholder approval to be valid. A nonprofit corporation's real estate contract may have to be court-approved prior to the signing of the contract.

The sale of real estate by a fiduciary possessing power of attorney, such as an executor, trustee, or agent, is valid only if the document giving them the authority to act for another is in writing, signed by the person delegating the authority, and acknowledged by a notary public. A fiduciary is a person who has been given the authority to act for another based on a relationship of trust and confidence.

When the contract for sale is drawn, the following provisions are incorporated into the contract. The contract is generally prepared by the seller's attorney, then forwarded to the purchaser's attorney for approval.

1. Preliminary Provisions   The first provision sets forth the date of the contract together with the names and addresses of the seller and purchaser.

> *DATE:* THIS AGREEMENT, MADE THE 17th DAY OF NOVEMBER, NINETEEN HUNDRED AND NINETY-NINE.
> *PARTIES:* BETWEEN JOHN JUDE MORAN residing at One Cameron Lake, Staten Island, New York HEREINAFTER DESCRIBED AS THE SELLER, AND RITA HOLOCHWOST residing at 271 Bay Ridge Boulevard, Brooklyn, New York, HEREINAFTER DESCRIBED AS THE PURCHASER.

2. Legal Description   The legal description of the property must be set forth to satisfy the writing requirement of the statute of frauds. The legal description includes street address, section, lot and block numbers, and the metes and bounds.

> *LEGAL DESCRIPTION:* WITNESSETH, THAT THE SELLER AGREES TO SELL AND CONVEY, AND THE PURCHASER AGREES TO PURCHASE, ALL THAT CERTAIN PLOT, PIECE OR PARCEL OF LAND, WITH THE BUILDINGS AND IMPROVEMENTS THEREON ERECTED, SITUATE,

LYING AND BEING IN THE [Here, denote the county, city, and state of location together with the address and the lot and block number or the metes and bounds of said property].

LOT AND BLOCK NUMBER OF EACH PARCEL OF LAND IS FILED ON A MAP IDENTIFYING SUCH PROPERTY WITH THE COUNTY CLERK'S OFFICE.

METES AND BOUNDS: RELATIONSHIP OF SAID PROPERTY TO THE CORNER OF AN INTERSECTION OF TWO STREETS.

3. Personal Property and Fixtures Certain personal property and fixtures become part of the structure of the house once they have been installed. These objects are generally conveyed with the house, but a description of each must be set forth in the contract.

> *Personal Property and Fixtures:* The sale of real estate includes all articles of personal property and fixtures listed below unless specifically excluded. Lighting, heating, plumbing, bathroom and kitchen fixtures and cabinets, stoves and refrigerators, dishwashers, washing and drying machines, storm doors and windows, awnings, shades, screens, mantels, mail boxes, tool sheds, and wall-to-wall carpeting. The sale of real estate does not include household furnishings.

4. Purchase Price The amount of the purchase price together with the method of payment must be denoted. On the signing of the contract a down payment will be made which the seller's attorney will hold in an escrow account. An escrow account is a special account set aside by an attorney from his own personal account for the purpose of safeguarding a client's funds until the proper disposition of those funds has been determined either by the parties themselves or by a court of law.

The amount remaining on any existing mortgages will be deducted from the purchase price if the mortgage is to be assumed by the purchaser. If not, the seller must be paid in full and the mortgage will be satisfied out of the proceeds from the sale. The amount of a purchase money mortgage to be held by the seller will also be deducted from the purchase price.

The balance remaining must be paid at closing by either an official check of a bank located within the state or a personal check which has been certified by a bank located within the state. Provision is made for a personal check and/or a small amount of cash to be used as payment generally not exceeding $1,000. This is because of the problems which will arise if the personal check bounces, and also because of the inconvenience of carrying a great deal of cash especially if the closing is after banking hours.

Purchase Price

The purchase price is:	120,000
It is payable as follows:	
Down payment on the signing of the contract	12,000
The unpaid principal remaining on any existing mortgages	None
Purchase money note and mortgage executed by the purchaser and given to the seller	28,000
Balance at closing	80,000

5. "Subject to" Provisions The premises are sold subject to

Zoning laws and other governmental regulations that effect the use and maintenance of the property

Encroachments by stoops, fences, and cellar steps, on any street or highway

Any facts an accurate survey may show provided they do not render title unmarketable

Utility easements such as telephone, gas, electric, fuel, water, and sewer lines. An easement is a right of way, the right to use the property of another for a limited use. A utility easement is a right to install and maintain utility lines on the property of another.

6. Title The seller's title to the premises must be verified to determine whether he or she has proper ownership in the land to convey to the purchaser. This is known as marketable title. A marketable title is required unless there is a clause requiring the seller to transfer an insurable title, one which must be approved and insured by a reputable title company. An insurable title may be something less than marketable title. This means a title search must be run to examine whether there is a proper chain of title leading up to the seller from the time the house was built. The records are kept on the clerk's office in the county in which the property is located.

The title search may be done by a lawyer, but more often than not, it is handled by either an abstract company or a title insurance company, which specialize in these matters. An abstract company will issue a title report from which the purchaser's attorney can satisfy himself or herself as to whether the seller has proper title. A title insurance company, upon satisfying themselves that the seller has good title, will grant a title insurance policy in return for a fee. This insures the purchaser against claims made by others questioning the validity of the purchaser's title. If the purchaser's title was successfully contested, the purchaser would be entitled to reimbursement for the value of the property at the time the sale was made.

Title insurance companies do not insure property where there is a question as to the validity of the seller's title. It would be a rare case based on a big mistake in the title search where they would have to pay out. A purchaser who bought property which has greatly appreciated would lose heavily if his or her title was proven to be invalid because the title insurance is limited to the value of the property when it was purchased. There is legislation in some states to increase the value of title insurance as a house appreciates in return for the payment of an additional premium.

The title conveyed by the seller to the purchaser must satisfy the requirements of a reputable title company in the state where the property is located. The title company must be willing to approve and insure the title conveyed. A reputable title company is usually insured by the state's board of title underwriters.

Creative Living, Inc. v. Steinhauser
78 Misc. 2d 29, 355 N.Y.S.2d 897 (1974), aff'd, 365 N.Y.S.2d 987 (1975)

Creative Living sued to rescind the contract for sale of real estate because insurable rather than marketable title was being conveyed.

Creative Living and Steinhauser entered into a contract for the sale of real estate for $80,000 with a down payment of $8,000 being made on the signing of the contract. The contract was prepared on a standard New York Boad of Title Underwriters form and provided that "the seller shall give and the purchaser shall accept a title such as City Title or, a Member of the New York Board of Title Underwriters, will approve and insure."

Prior to the date set for closing, Creative Living learned that a resolution affecting the property they contracted to purchase was passed approving a plan for the city of New York to condemn the property for inclusion in the South Bronx Neighborhood Development Plan. The title report furnished by City Title failed to disclose any pending condemnation proceeding. City Title, a member of the New York Board of Title Underwriters, was prepared to issue title insurance for Creative Living. The first issue is whether Steinhauser, the seller, was obligated to convey marketable title, not insurable title.

The court held, "It is up to the parties to a contract to agree to the kind of title to be conveyed. In the absence of agreement otherwise, a buyer is entitled to a marketable title." This need not be expressly agreed but arises by implication from the contract. However, by contracting for an insurable title, the parties have abrogated the general rule.

The court resolved that ". . . the defendant was ready, willing and able to deliver insurable title on the closing date and that is all the defendant was required to do."

The second issue concerns whether the Uniform Vendor and Purchaser Risk Act is applicable. This act provides that if neither legal title or possession of the premises has been transferred to the purchaser, the seller cannot enforce the contract if all or a material part of the premises is taken by eminent domain; meaning condemned for the City's use.

The court decided that "the key word in the aforesaid section is 'taken'. In order for the section to apply, the condemnation must be completed. The section does not cover a pending or preliminary condemnation (Citation)."

A condemnation occurring after the closing date will not relieve a purchaser from liability. The seller may sue the purchaser for damages arising from the breach of contract. Judgment for Steinhauser.

7. Deed The deed delivered may be a general warranty deed, a specific warranty deed, or a quitclaim deed.

In a *general warranty deed*, the seller guarantees that neither he or she nor anyone preceding him or her as owner of the property has done any act which would make the title unmarketable.

In a *specific warranty deed*, more popularly known as a bargain and sale deed, the seller guarantees that from the date of purchase, he or she has not done any act which would make the title unmarketable.

In a *quitclaim deed*, the seller only relinquishes whatever interest he or she had in the real estate by transferring that interest to the purchaser. There are no guarantees made even as to whether the seller had any interest. If title to property is held by three people and one of them wishes to buy out the other two, the other two may issue a quitclaim deed transferring their portion of ownership in the property.

8. Time and Place of Closing   The time and place for the closing of title must be stated. These terms may be altered thereafter by mutual agreement in writing or at the request of one party as long as the request for an extension of time is not unreasonable.

The closing of title usually takes place in the office of either the seller's attorney or the lending institution when a mortgage is involved.

9. Broker   The name of the broker is stated in the contract along with an indemnification clause protecting the seller against claims made by other brokerages who allegedly found and dealt with the purchaser.

Purchaser states that he or she has not had dealings with any broker other than the broker who brought about the sale and agrees to indemnify seller against any claims made by other brokers with whom he or she has had dealings in connection with the property. Seller agrees to pay the named broker the commission agreed on in the separate brokerage agreement.

10. Compliance with State and Municipal Orders   The seller must cure all outstanding violations against the premises including those issued by the health department, building department, fire department, department of housing, and department of labor conditions.

11. Adjustments   The following items must be apportioned between the seller and purchaser: real estate taxes, water and sewer taxes, fuel remaining on premises, and rents.

EXAMPLE   Howard Grimsley sold his two-family house in Westerleigh, to Martin Hennessey. The closing of title took place on July 15. At the time of closing there was a tenant occupying the second floor pursuant to a two-year written lease, paying a monthly rent of $600. There were 200 gallons of fuel left in the oil tank. The water and sewer bill was $120 for the fiscal year beginning July 1 and ending the following June 30. The real estate taxes, $2,400 per year, are assessed on a quarterly basis, using the same fiscal year as the water and sewer taxes. The seller has paid the annual water and sewer bill and the first quarterly real estate tax bill. What adjustments must the seller and purchaser make at closing?

Adjustments	Credit to Purchaser	Credit to Seller
Fuel 200 gal. @ $1.25/gal.		$250
Real estate taxes		$500
Water and sewer taxes		$115
Rent	$300	
Total	$300	$865
		$565 Adjustment added to the purchase price

12. Personal Judgments or Violations   The title report will usually disclose any personal judgments, or violations against the seller's name. If these offenses apply to the seller, then the judgments are a lien against the property and the seller must pay them to insure that his or her title is marketable. If they are not paid, there is a defect in title that renders it unmarketable and the title insurance company, if any, will not insure the transfer of title. If the violation or judgments found are against a person with the same name as the seller, but do not pertain to the seller, then the seller must sign an affidavit before a notary to this effect.

Seller shall deliver an affidavit detailing the violation and judgment found in the title report against his or her name along with a statement that the violation and judgment does not apply to him or her.

13. Transfer and Recording Taxes A real estate transfer tax must be paid by the seller at the closing of title. It is usually a percentage of the sale price, such as 1 percent. A recording tax may also be charged as a dollar amount such as $4 for every $1,000 of the purchase price. For example, on the sale of $120,000 house, the transfer tax would be $1,200 (1 percent of the purchase price) and the recording tax would be $480 ($4 for every $1,000 of the actual purchase price).

Seller agrees to deliver a certified check payable to the appropriate state, city, or county offices for the transfer and recording taxes in connection with the property to be transferred.

14. Limitation of Liability If unable to convey a marketable or insurable title, the seller usually will limit his or her liability to a refund of the purchaser's down payment together with the expenses incurred by the purchaser for the title search and survey charges.

The purchaser's liability is usually limited to the down payment made. The purchaser would be wise to include a provision conditioning the contract on the purchaser's obtaining a mortgage for a certain amount, within a certain time. This implies that the purchaser must make a good-faith effort to secure a mortgage commitment.

15. Condition of Property The purchaser has inspected the property and agrees to accept it "as is" subject to reasonable use and wear and tear between the time of inspection and the closing of title. A purchaser would be wise to inspect the premises the day before closing and include a provision that on the day of the closing, the roof should be free of leaks; and the plumbing, heating, and lighting should be in good working order. This warranty made by the seller does not continue after the closing of title. The purchaser should also insist on a provision allowing for an inspection for termites and carpenter ants within ten days to two weeks after the signing of the contract to determine infestation, if any. If termites or ants are present, they may be removed and the damage repaired at the option of the seller. If the seller does not choose to exterminate and repair the resulting defects, the purchaser can cancel the contract.

16. Incorporation of Prior Agreements When a single writing is intended to be the final expression of the parties' intentions, then all prior oral and written agreements must be incorporated in the writing in order to have effect. This provision is in accord with the parol evidence rule which prohibits the introduction into evidence of prior oral or written agreements to contradict the written contract.

17. Subsequent Changes Any changes made subsequent to the signing of this contract must be in writing and signed by the parties.

18. Signatures

In the presence of the following witnesses   <u>s/John Jude Moran</u>, seller
s/Michael Murray, witness
s/Theresa Scofield, witness   <u>s/Rita Holochwost</u>, buyer

The signatures must be acknowledged by a notary public.

STATE of _____, County of _____ ss:
On the ___ day of _____ 19 __, _____ per-
sonally came before me. This person I know as the individual described as the
seller or purchaser, who executed this contract in proper form, and acknowledged
that fact before me _____Signature of Notary
                                             Stamp of Authority

A promise regarding the allocation of risk of loss is not included in the standard contract of sale form, but rather is governed by the Uniform Vendor and Purchaser Risk Act which has been adopted by most state legislatures and then included in the state's own statutes. The Uniform Vendor and Purchaser Risk Act places the risk of loss, if the premises are destroyed by fire or other means, on the seller until either title or possession of the premises is transferred to the purchaser. At the time of the closing of title, or at the time possession is transferred if it happens prior to the closing of the title, the risk of loss passes to the purchaser. The purchaser should make provisions to have the real estate insured from the time he or she assumes the risk of loss.

CLOSING OF TITLE

This is the final step in a real estate transaction. In the interim between the signing of the contract and the closing of title, the purchaser will run a title search and try to secure financing by obtaining a mortgage from a bank or other lending institution. Upon the satisfactory completion of both of these tasks, the closing of title will take place.

The basic scenario at the closing of title is the delivery of the deed in which the seller transfers his or her title to the purchaser in return for payment of the balance owed on the purchase price. The seller must pay his or her attorney's fee, the broker's commission, the real estate transfer and recording taxes, any real estate taxes, water and sewer taxes, parking violations, or other judgments that remain unpaid. The contract will usually contain a provision that these encumbrances can be paid out of the proceeds of the sale. The purchaser must pay his or her attorney's fee, the title company fee, charges assessed in connection with the mortgage, and any adjustments to the purchase price in favor of the seller. The deed must state the date of the closing of title, the names of the parties, the legal description of the premises including the metes and bounds. It must be signed by the seller, and his or her signature must be acknowledged by a notary public. The deed will then be taken by either a representative of the title insurance company or by the purchaser's attorney to the clerk's office in the county in which the property is located to have the deed recorded. This gives notice to all other prospective purchasers that title to the property now belongs to the purchaser. Recording makes it official; the transfer of title is now on the records of the county clerk's office. The county clerk will then mail the deed back to the purchaser for safekeeping.

If a deed or any other interest in real estate is not recorded, it is practically worthless because a subsequent good-faith purchaser who records a deed with no knowledge of a prior unrecorded deed has paramount title to the land.

REVIEW QUESTIONS

1. Explain the steps in a real estate transaction.
2. Define broker, title, real estate contract, brokerage agreement, and closing of title.
3. What are the three types of brokerage agreements and explain the difference between each?
4. Why are all real estate transactions required to be in writing?
5. Explain how a commission is split between a broker and his or her salesperson.
6. Explain the types of deeds that can be conveyed.
7. How does the multiple listings service operate?
8. Stern, a broker, procured a purchaser named Pierce for property owned by Gepo Realty. On the day the contract of sale was entered into by Gepo Realty, Pierce, Stern, and Gepo Realty signed a written brokerage agreement which provided the commission was payable on the closing of title. Title was never closed because Gepo Realty as owner and seller refused to satisfy certain taxes and assessments which constituted liens against the property. Pierce, the purchaser, was able to recover his down payment because the seller breached the contract by impeding the conveyance of marketable title. But is Stern entitled to the brokerage commission regardless of the clause in the contract conditioning payment on the closing of title? Stern v. Gepo Realty Corporation, 289 N.Y. 274, 45 N.E.2d 440 (1942).
9. Parness entered into a contract to purchase real estate from Bobover Yeshiva Bnei Zion. A $3,000 down payment was made on the signing of the contract. The contract contained a provision conditioning payment upon the purchaser's obtaining all of the necessary permits to operate a funeral parlor on the premises. Parness sued Bobover for a return of the down payment, contending the condition precedent was never met. Bobover argued that the condition failed because Parness never applied for the permits after "they discovered that another funeral parlor was operating in the neighborhood." Bobover further alleges that the contract also contained a stipulated damages clause which provided that the purchaser who breaches the contract shall forfeit the down payment made against the purchase price. Will Parness be entitled to rescind the contract and recover the down payment or will the stipulated damage clause be given effect? Parness v. Bobover, N.Y.L.J., Dec. 8, 1976 (Sup.Ct. Nassau Cty.).
10. Boehm and Coon requested Leon Tanenbaum, a broker, to procure a tenant for a parcel of real estate that they wished to rent. Tanenbaum found an interested person named Mr. Ball. All of the parties met to negotiate the terms of the

lease. An oral agreement was reached which involved a lease of certain property for a designated number of years at a fixed rental. The parties shook hands and agreed to sign the written lease as soon as the attorneys had prepared it. All terms had been agreed upon; nothing was left open for negotiation. Thereafter, Boehm and Coon made an unreasonable demand concerning a provision they wanted to incorporate into the written lease which actually ran contrary to the applicable statute. When Mr. Ball refused to accede to the unreasonable demand, Boehm and Coon refused to sign the contract. Is Tanenbaum still entitled to his commission under the oral agreement he had with Boehm and Coon? Tanenbaum v. Boehm, 202 N.Y. 293, 95 N.E. 708 (1911).

29

FORMS OF OWNERSHIP AND MORTGAGES

FORMS OF OWNERSHIP

Individuals can own property in various forms:

      Tenancy in common
      Joint tenancy
      Tenancy by the entirety
      Community property
      Condominiums
      Cooperatives

Tenancy in Common

Tenancy in common is the concurrent ownership of real estate by two or more individuals with no right of survivorship and with each individual owning an undivided interest in the entire parcel of real estate. The significance behind the statement "no right of survivorship" means that when one of the tenants in common dies, that interest passes to his or her heirs by will or intestate succession; the heirs may not necessarily be the other tenants in common.

EXAMPLE | Marion Fletcher died, leaving a will devising her house in Des Moines, Iowa, to her three daughters, Christine, Francine, and Charlene, in equal shares. What form of ownership has been created and what are the rights of Francine? A tenancy in common has been created with each daughter owning a one-third individual interest in the house. This means that although Francine owns one-third of the real estate, the house or property cannot be divided to reflect her interest unless it is sold.

Joint Tenancy

Joint tenants have an undivided concurrent ownership in the entire parcel of real estate with a right of survivorship. This means that when one joint tenant dies, his or her share passes to the other joint tenant.

EXAMPLE | Marjorie Hamilton bought a house with her youngest son, Scott, as joint tenants with right of survivorship. The house was on the outskirts of Lincoln, Nebraska, on the shores of a beautiful lake. The purchase price of $150,000 was paid solely from Marjorie's funds. Three years later, she died. In her will, Marjorie requested that her assets, which consisted of the house and her savings of $50,000, be distributed equally among her three sons. Do the other two sons have any right of ownership to the house? No! As the survivor of a joint tenancy, Scott has exclusive ownership of the home. The three brothers will share the $50,000 equally.

Overheiser v. Lackey
207 N.Y. 229, 100 N.E. 738 (1913)

Hester Marsh died leaving a will which devised the real estate she owned in the following manner:

"I give and devise to my daughters Elaine Jane Marsh and Hester Marsh, jointly, the lot of ground with the dwelling house and improvements thereon situate in the City of New York and known as No. 15 Christopher Street."

Overheiser is an heir of the younger Hester Marsh. He has brought an action to partition the real estate so he may get his fair share. His suit rests upon the claim that Hester Marsh and Elaine Jane Marsh, both of whom were daughters of Hester Marsh were tenants in common. If this is the case, Overheiser will be successful because a tenant in common's share passes to his or her heirs. If however, the two daughters were joint tenants, Overheiser's suit would fail because Hester Marsh predeceased Elaine Jane Marsh. A joint tenant's share passes to the surviving tenant, rather than the deceased's heirs.

The issue is whether a joint tenancy or tenancy in common was created by the will.

The court held, "The rule of common law that a grant or devise to two or more persons without other words created a joint tenancy was abolished early in the history of this state . . ." This rule was replaced by the revised statutes which declared, "Every estate granted or devised to two or more persons, in their own right, shall be a tenancy in common, unless expressly declared to be joint tenancy. (Citations.)"

The court decided,

In view of the indications that the devise in question here was formulated by a layman who did not use the word "jointly" in its distinctively technical sense, we conclude that it is not a sufficiently express declaration of an intent to create a joint tenancy to negative the presumption established by our statute that a tenancy in common was intended.

Since the devise to the two daughters was a tenancy in common, Overheiser inherited a portion of Hester Marsh's one-half share in the real estate and his request for a partition was granted. Judgment for Overheiser.

Tenancy by the Entirety

Tenants by the entirety is a special form of joint tenancy reserved to a husband and wife. This tenancy may be terminated by divorce or by the mutual agreement of the husband and wife; whereas a joint tenancy can be terminated by one joint tenant.

EXAMPLE | Patricia and John O'Brien are newlyweds who purchase a house in Elizabethton, Tennessee, as tenants by the entirety. The purchase price of the house is paid exclusively with John's funds. Five years later, John dies in a car accident. The house is valued at $75,000 and John's total assets amount to $100,000. His will leaves one-half of his estate to his wife, Patricia, and the other half to his parents. Is Patricia entitled to exclusive ownership of the house? Yes! She is the surviving member of a tenancy by the entirety. The entire interest in the house of the deceased spouse passes to the survivor.

Community Property

Community property may be defined as property acquired by a husband and wife during their marriage. It does not include property acquired by gift or inheritance. Each spouse owns an undivided one-half interest in the community property regardless of who earned or acquired it. Community property laws have been adopted in several western states. Most of these states provide that the surviving spouse will receive one-half of the community property with the remainder passed according to the deceased spouse's will or the laws of intestacy. If the husband and wife become divorced, each will receive one-half of the community property. Most other states provide for equitable distribution when divorce occurs, which divides property between the spouses according to need.

Condominiums

There are two other special forms of ownership, known as a condominium and a cooperative. These may be purchased by an individual, a corporation, a partnership, or by two or more individuals in any of the tenancies previously described.

The owner of a condominium acquires individual ownership in an apartment unit and becomes a tenant in common, along with the rest of the apartment owners, in the common property. The common property includes the land on which the apartments are built, the apartments, roofs, corridors, lobbies, stairways, elevators, fire escapes, basements, gardens, recreational facilities, parking and storage areas, and the like. In a cooperative, this property is owned by the corporation.

Cooperatives

A cooperative is formed by the establishment of a corporation which owns title to the real estate on which the cooperative apartments are built. Each purchaser becomes a shareholder in the corporation and therefore owns only personal property in the form of stock certificates, not real property. A shareholder in the cooperative is entitled to lease an apartment owned by the cooperative corporation as long as he or she owns the shares. Each purchaser-shareholder is actually a tenant of the corporation. The number of shares allocated to each tenant must bear a reasonable relationship to the rental value of the apartment occupied.

Condominium owners can usually sell, lease, assign, or sublet the apartment without any restrictions; whereas a shareholder in a cooperative must obtain the written consent of the corporation. Both condominium and cooperative purchasers must pay their proportionate share of the maintenance costs attributed to the common property.

MORTGAGES

A mortgage is a contract securing payment of a debt, called a loan, through the creation of an interest for the lender in the property purchased. A mortgage creates a debtor-creditor relationship. The mortgagor is the one who is mortgaging his or her property by giving an interest in the property to the lender in consideration of a loan. The mortgagee is the one who is holding the mortgage by giving the loan in consideration for an interest in the borrower's property. The mortgagee's interest in the property is a qualified or dormant one which develops into a viable right of ownership only upon foreclosure. Foreclosure is the satisfaction of the mortgage debt through the judicial sale of the real estate pledged as collateral. A judicial sale is the sale of property to achieve a fair and reasonable price with judicial supervision. It arises upon the mortgagor's default in payment. A mortgage note accompanies the mortgage and serves as a promissory note evidencing the debt. A parcel of real estate may be subjected to several mortgages; however, the entire first mortgage has preference over the second mortgage, with the second having preference over the third, and so on. The preference is created by the order in which the mortgages are recorded against the particular property.

EXAMPLE Charles Russell owns a one-family house in Madison, Wisconsin. The National Bank of Wisconsin holds the first mortgage on Russell's house for $50,000. Herman Wise, the previous owner, holds a purchase money mortgage, which is second in preference, for $60,000. Charlie's cousin, Frederick, loaned Charles $25,000 to help finance an addition to the house in return for receiving a third mortgage. Charles Russell defaults on all of his mortgage payments and files for bankruptcy. The three mortgages are foreclosed and the house is sold at a judicial sale for $90,000. Assuming Charles has no other debts, how will the proceeds from the judicial sale be distributed? The bank will be entitled to the face value of its mortgage, $50,000. Herman Wise, the previous owner, will be entitled to collect the remaining $40,000 as holder of the second mortgage. Since he is not paid in full, he becomes a general creditor in regard to the other assets owned by Charles Russell. The mortgage held by Charles's cousin, Frederick, will go unsatisfied because the proceeds of the sale were insufficient to satisfy the third mortgage. Frederick will become a general creditor for $25,000. If the proceeds of the judicial sale exceed the mortgage owed, the remainder must be returned to the owner.

Recording the Mortgage

A mortgage must be recorded to insure that the mortgagee's lien against the real estate is given priority against all subsequent mortgagees. Recording puts these subsequent mortgagees on notice that a prior mortgage exists to which their claim must be subordinated. If a mortgage is not recorded, it is practically worthless.

EXAMPLE   In the previous example, assume the bank's mortgage was granted subsequent to the mortgages given by the previous owner and Charles's cousin, Frederick. Assume further that the bank's mortgage was recorded where the other two mortgages were not. Would the bank have preference to the proceeds of the foreclosure sale? Yes! The bank would have preference because it was the first and only one to have its mortgage recorded. This presupposes that the bank acted without knowledge of the other two unrecorded mortgages.

Types of Mortgages

There are various kinds of mortgages. A blanket mortgage covers all of the property of the debtor. A special mortgage covers a particular parcel of real estate. There may be more than one mortgage. A purchase-money mortgage arises when the former owner takes back a mortgage as security for the unpaid balance of the purchase price. A balloon mortgage requires periodic payments with a substantial final payment becoming due (ballooning) at a stated time.

EXAMPLE   Christopher Newman buys a house in Shaker Heights, an affluent suburb of Cleveland, with a mortgage of $140,000 providing $8,000 yearly payments with final payment of $60,000 ballooning after ten years.

Burnett v. Wright
135 N.Y. 543, 32 N.E. 253 (1892)

Burnett brought an action to foreclose on mortgaged property owned by Wright.

Burnett loaned money to Wright for the purpose of financing the purchase of real estate. In return, Wright executed a mortgage for the amount of the loan to Burnett. The mortgage set forth the amount of the mortgage; was signed by Wright and duly acknowledged; and was recorded in the county clerk's office. The mortgage contained a provision which stated that when the entire principal of the mortgage had been paid together with timely interest payments at designated intervals, the mortgage would be satisfied and thereafter would be null and void. In this provision, a space was left blank for inclusion of the amount of the mortgage. Wright contended ". . . the mortgage was defective; that the defect consisted in the omission to insert in writing in the blank the amount of the debt that was to be secured by it. . . ."

The issue is whether the omission of a material term in the mortgage will render it defective where the term is stated elsewhere in the mortgage and can be verified through parol evidence.

The court ruled,

The instrument upon which she [Burnett] relies must be read and construed in its entirety. Omissions and ambiguities in one part may be supplied or explained by references to other parts, if the necessary data can there be found for that purpose. The sum stated in the defeasance clause (satisfaction clause) is intended to be the amount of the debt to be secured by the mortgage which is but another form of expressing the consideration of the grant. The indefiniteness, therefore, occasioned by the failure of the parties to fill up the blank in this paragraph of the (mortgage) deed, may be removed and the sum intended to be secured ascertained by a reference to the consideration clause in the instrument; for generally the consideration named in a mortgage is the amount of the debt secured by it. (Citations.)

The court decided, ". . . the introduction of the mortgage would be sufficient in the first instance to establish the existence and amount of the mortgage debt . . ." Judgment for Burnett.

REVIEW QUESTIONS

1. List and explain the various forms of ownership.
2. Define condominium and cooperative.
3. What is the difference between the two?
4. Define mortgage, mortgage note, mortgagor, and mortgagee.
5. List and explain the different kinds of mortgages.
6. How is priority determined if there is more than one mortgage?
7. Nelson Hopkins and his wife conveyed a plot of land in Buffalo to Cornelius Day and Hannah Day. Hannah died after Cornelius. Hannah's administrator, Ellen Bertles, entered into a contract to sell the real estate to James Nunan. Nunan, thereafter, refused to close title claiming Ellen Bertles could transfer only a one-half share in the real estate because Cornelius and Hannah were tenants in common. Is Nunan's argument viable? Bertles v. Nunan, 92 N.Y. 152 (1883).

30

LANDLORD
AND TENANT

INTRODUCTION

A landlord and tenant relationship is a contractual one in which both parties are bound by a lease. A lease is a contract which sets forth the rights and duties of both parties as well as the terms on which the parties agree. An oral lease is enforceable unless its duration exceeds one year, in which case a written lease signed by both parties is required by the statute of frauds. A landlord is the owner of the premises who is granting the lease. A tenant is the person to whom possession of the premises is given in return for payment of rent.

TYPES OF TENANCIES

There are four basic tenancies:

Tenancy for years
Tenancy at will
Periodic tenancy
Tenancy at sufferance

Tenancy for Years

A tenancy for years is one created for a definite time, usually by a written lease. No notice of termination need be given because the lease automatically expires at the end of the term. The lease may then be renewed if the landlord and tenant so desire. The landlord has the option of increasing the rent as much as he or she wishes unless the apartment is rent-controlled or rent-stabilized. This means the local municipality regulates the amount by which the rent of an apartment may be increased.

On February 1, Joseph Patterson signs a written lease permitting him to occupy a storefront on Duncan Avenue in Jersey City for the purpose of opening a candy store. The term of the lease is for two years with the rental fixed at $900 per month. What type of tenancy has been created? A tenancy for years has been created which will expire in two years, on January 31.

Tenancy at Will

After the lease expires, quite often a tenant will remain in possession of the premises with the landlord's permission. This is a tenancy at will which means either party may terminate the tenancy when he or she wishes by giving adequate notice.

EXAMPLE As the two-year lease is coming to an end, Patterson is making arrangements to move to the nearby Hudson County mall where he expects a greater volume of business. However, he cannot take possession of the premises at the Mall until February 10. The owner of the storefront allows Patterson to remain in possession until February 10, for a daily rental fee of $50. Patterson agrees. What type of tenancy is this? This is a tenancy at will which will expire on February 10.

Periodic Tenancy

If the tenant pays rent for a certain time period, such as one month, and the landlord accepts it, then a periodic tenancy has been created. This tenancy will continue for the duration of the period. Adequate notice of termination must be given, which is usually construed to be the length of a period.

EXAMPLE Suppose Patterson's arrangements for occupying space at the Mall falls through and the storefront owner allows Patterson to say on a month-to-month basis with the monthly rental fee set at $950. What type of tenancy would be created? A periodic tenancy with a duration of one month has been created. This periodic tenancy is renewable each time the rent check is offered by the tenant and accepted by the landlord. Either party could terminate the tenancy by giving one month's notice, the equivalent of one period of the tenancy.

Tenancy at Sufferance

A tenant at sufferance is one who wrongfully stays on beyond the duration of the tenancy without the landlord's permission. He or she may be treated as a trespasser and evicted. A tenant at sufferance may also be sued for the rent during the period he or she wrongfully held over.

EXAMPLE Assume that after Patterson's lease falls through with the Mall, he asks the storefront owner if he may occupy the premises on a month-to-month basis, but the owner refuses. Patterson then wrongfully remains on beyond February 10, in defiance of the owner's refusal to allow him to continue as a tenant. What recourse does the owner have? This is a tenancy at sufferance. The owner may treat Patterson as a trespasser and start eviction proceedings. The owner may also recover the rent for the duration of the holdover period.

LANDLORD'S DUTIES

A landlord has the following duties:

Duty to deliver possession
Warranty of habitability
Duty to insure tenant's right to the use and quiet enjoyment of the premises
Duty to make repairs

Duty to Deliver Possession

A landlord has a duty to deliver possession of the premises on the date on which the tenancy is to begin. This means the landlord must oust any holdover tenants. A landlord may disclaim liability for failure to deliver possession because of a holdover tenant by incorporating a provision to this effect in the lease. This disclaimer will be conclusive as long as the landlord has taken every step necessary to oust the holdover. The new tenant may take possession when the holdover tenant is removed, or may cancel the lease for failure to deliver timely possession. In either event, the new tenant may not look to the landlord for damages caused by the breach where the disclaimer provision is agreed to by both parties.

EXAMPLE | Wayne and Theresa Scott rent a four-room apartment from James Sutter, pursuant to a written lease, for two years. The tenancy commences on May 1. They hire a moving van and make arrangements to leave their former apartment. On April 30, Sutter learns that the tenants in possession have no intention of moving out. He promptly notifies the Scotts and hires an attorney to start an eviction proceeding against the holdover tenants. The Scotts lose the deposit they gave the moving company. Furthermore, they are forced to put their furniture in storage and stay at a motel. The holdover tenants are ousted on May 21, three weeks into the Scotts' tenancy. The Scotts take possession on May 22 and then sue Sutter for the damages caused by his failure to deliver possession. A disclaimer provision was incorporated into the lease. Will the Scotts be successful? No! Sutter has effectively disclaimed his liability. Upon ousting the holdover tenants, he must make the apartment available to the Scotts, which he did. If Sutter sues the Scotts for the rent for the full month of May, will he collect it? Certainly not! He is precluded from collecting it because he failed to deliver possession. Since the tenancy has begun on May 22, will it continue for two years until May 21? No! The term of the tenancy has not been changed because possession was delayed. The tenancy will continue for two years, expiring on April 30.

Landlord's Warranty of Habitability

A landlord has a duty to guarantee that the premises are habitable. This means the premises must be in a condition fit for human occupancy; that is, clean, safe, and sanitary. Local housing codes have set forth minimum standards by which habitability is judged. Separate standards apply to conditions within an apartment as well as to areas of common use where the landlord has retained control.

Minimum standards requiring the landlord's compliance within an apartment include adequate kitchen and bathroom facilities, lighting and ventilation, and temperature settings for the purpose of providing hot water and heat. The landlord must also comply with the criteria set forth for the maintenance of areas of common use. The minimum criteria include such things as maintaining sidewalks free from ice, snow, and deep cracks; roofs free from leaks; lighting in hallways and lobbies; elevators in working order.

EXAMPLE | Carol and Denise Rodgers are twin sisters who are attending Georgetown University where they hope to become registered nurses. They rent a five-room apartment from Harriet Fallon for $400 a month. A provision of the lease requires two months' rent as security along with the payment of the first month's rent on the taking of possession. Carol and Denise pay Harriet $1,200 and take possession. After they have moved in, they discover the oven portion of the stove does not function. When they open the kitchen cabinets, they find roaches. Denise hurries into the bathroom to get the roach spray, but she is turned back by the stench caused by the back up in the toilet. The girls gather their possessions and move out. Harriet Fallon refuses to return their $1,200. They sue her, claiming she breached the implied warranty of habitability. Will they be successful? Yes! The apartment was not clean or sanitary and the kitchen appliances and bathroom facilities were not in proper working order. Harriet Fallon failed in her duty to see that the minimum standards of habitability were met.

A landlord has a further duty to disclose any condition dangerous to the tenant of which the landlord has actual knowledge, or even a belief that such a condition exists unknown to the tenant. Many states also require the landlord take the added precaution to protect tenants from criminal conduct by properly securing the house or building with adequate locks, burglar alarms, or security patrol and by providing adequate lighting on the outside of the building for tenants walking to and from the entrance.

EXAMPLE | It was around midnight when Grace Appelton was returning home after dinner with friends. As she walked through the dimly lit lobby and turned toward the elevator, she caught her foot in a crack. She tripped and fell, severely injuring her left knee. She managed to hobble into the elevator only to encounter three muggers who had gained entrance to the building through a malfunction of the locking device. They grabbed her purse, knocked her to the ground, and beat her. When she regained consciousness, she found herself in a hospital bed. That afternoon, her cousin, a lawyer, visited her. She asked him whether she could sue the landlord for the injuries she sustained. What should his reply be? Yes! The landlord is responsible for the injuries to her knee because of his failure to uphold his duty to maintain the areas of common use by providing adequate lighting in the lobby. He is also responsible for the other harm she sustained as a result of the mugging because he did not provide proper security for the premises by maintaining the locking devices.

Landlord's Duty to Insure Tenant's Right to the Use and Quiet Enjoyment of the Premises

This is an important provision in which the landlord makes the following guarantees: he or she has title to the premises; the tenant has the right to absolute possession for the duration of the tenancy; the use and quiet possession of the premises will not be disturbed by either the landlord or other objectionable tenants; the tenant will not be evicted without just cause, that is, a violation of a major provision of the lease.

EXAMPLE | Edgar and Edith Brandt are an elderly couple who retire to bed after the "Merv Griffin Show." They have been living at the Cresthaven Apartments for twenty-eight years. Recently, Gary Howser rented the apartment next door. He works a 4 P.M. to 12 A.M. shift as a security guard at a midtown office building. When he arrives home, he plays his favorite hard rock albums with the stereo turned up high. To make matters worse, he vocalizes along with the lead singers. Edgar has asked Gary on several occasions to lower the volume, but Gary's only reply is "Bug off!" Is the landlord responsible for turning Gary down? Yes! Each tenant has a duty to respect the use and quiet enjoyment of the premises by the other tenants. Since Gary Howser does not respect this duty, the landlord has an obligation to enforce the Brandts' rights by informing Howser of his duty not to disturb other tenants. If Howser does not abide by this warning, then the landlord has a further obligation to remove Howser from the premises.

Colonial Court Apartments, Inc. v. Kern
282 Minn. 533, 163 N.W.2d 770 (1968)

Colonial Court Apartments sued Kern for abandoning her apartment, requesting that she be liable for the remaining rental payment.

Irene Kern rented an apartment in Colonial Court for a period of one year beginning January 1. A young coupled rented directly above her apartment. They constantly were hosting wild parties, operating heavy appliances during the night, and using foul language. Irene Kern notified the landlord in January and early February that her quiet enjoyment of the premises was constantly being disturbed by the young couple. The landlord notified the couple that their lease was terminated the last day in February, but then permitted then to stay on through the young wife's pregnancy. The baby was born the beginning of May. Shortly thereafter, the young couple notified the landlord of their intent to move out on June 1. The landlord replied they would be responsible for the rent for the full month of June because they had not given the required one month's notice to cancel a periodic, month-to-month tenancy.

On June 16, after repeated annoyances by the young couple, Irene Kern vacated the premises claiming constructive eviction in that the landlord failed in his duty to uphold her right to the use and quiet enjoyment of the premises. Colonial Court Apartments claimed Irene Kern had an obligation to make the rental payment for the duration of the tenancy and that they had taken reasonable steps to insure her right to the quiet enjoyment of her apartment.

The issue is whether repeated disturbances amounted to constructive eviction which precluded Irene Kern's right to quietly enjoy the premises.

The court ruled in favor of Irene Kern, stating the enjoyment of her apartment was interfered with to such a degree by the other tenants that it amounted to constructive eviction and justified her abandonment. The obligation to pay rent is contingent upon the landlord's guarantee of habitability and the right of the tenant to the use and quite enjoyment of the premises. If either of these guarantees is not upheld by the landlord, it amounts to constructive eviction and the tenant's obligation to remain in the premises and pay rent lapses. Judgment for Kern.

Landlord's Duty to Make Repairs

A landlord generally has no duty to make repairs and will not be liable for injuries due to a defective condition unless:

1. The repairs are of the kind required to maintain the habitability of the individual apartments and the areas of common use
2. A major repair is needed involving a structural defect
3. The defect-causing injury resulted from the intentional concealment on the part of the landlord
4. The landlord has agreed to make the repairs
5. The landlord voluntarily undertakes to make the repairs even though he or she has not expressly agreed to do so
6. The injury is caused by the inherently dangerous work of an independent contractor

EXAMPLE | Anna Morgan lives in a two-family house owned by Stanley Cooper. Anna invites her friend, Martha Reilly, to visit her for coffee and cake. After conversing for a while, Martha asks to use the bathroom. On entering, she slips on a puddle caused by a leak in the sink's drain pipe. As a result of her fall, her right arm is broken. Martha does not wish to sue her friend, Anna, but decides instead to sue the landlord, Stanley Cooper. Is he liable? No! The responsibility for cleaning the puddle caused by a leak in a bathroom sink pipe rests with the tenant. Anna alone is liable for Martha's injury.

Altz v. Lieberson
233 N.Y. 16, 134 N.E. 703 (1922)

Altz sued Lieberson for injuries she sustained due to a structural defect in the premises.

Altz rented an apartment from Lieberson. During the term of her tenancy, the ceiling in her apartment began to crack, with pieces of plaster falling down. She notified the landlord of this dangerous condition, but he neglected to make the appropriate repairs. Subsequently, Altz was injured when a piece of plaster fell from the ceiling and struck her on the head. Lieberson claimed that he owed no duty to the tenant to make the repair.

The issue is whether the landlord is liable for the injuries sustained by the tenant as a result of a defective condition in the premises.

Although the landlord is not usually liable for ordinary repairs, he or she is liable for structural repairs, including the ceiling of the premises, especially where the structural defect affects the habitability of the premises. The dangerous condition caused by the plaster cracking and falling made the apartment unsafe, in other words, not suitable for habitation.

Where the landlord has knowledge of the dangerous condition and it is caused by a structural defect, and/or it affects the habitability of the premises, and does not make timely repairs, the landlord will be liable for any injuries sustained as a result of the defective condition. Judgment for Altz.

TENANT'S DUTIES

A tenant must comply with the following duties:

Duty to make ordinary repairs
Duty to refrain from disturbing other tenants
Duty to pay rent and to give a security deposit

Duty to Make Ordinary Repairs

A tenant has a duty to make all repairs necessary for the general upkeep of the apartment. The tenant will be liable for injuries caused by a neglect of this duty, as was seen in the previous example, unless this injury occurs in one of those instances where the landlord is responsible.

Duty to Refrain from Disturbing Other Tenants

A tenant has a duty to refrain from disturbing others and to refrain from altering the premises or otherwise causing any material or substantial change that results in permanent damage.

EXAMPLE | Randolph Martin rented the second floor of his two-story house to Laurence Wexton. During the six months that he remained in the premises, Wexton nailed a dart board to the living room wall and proceeded to make countless dart holes in the wall. He painted the kitchen fire-engine red and the bedrooms purple, removed the kitchen cabinets, rolled up the wall-to-wall carpeting, and scuffed the parquet floors. Randolph Martin brought an eviction proceeding for disturbance. Upon inspecting the apartment, Martin was horrified at its condition. He amended his complaint to include a cause of action for damages to the apartment. Will he be successful with both causes of action? Yes! Wexton will be evicted for failing to refrain from disturbing the landlord who lived beneath him. Furthermore, Wexton materially altered the nature of the premises without the landlord's permission; he will be liable for these alterations.

Duty to Pay Rent and to Give a Security Deposit

The tenant has a duty to pay rent and to give a security deposit in accordance with the provisions of the lease. The duty to pay rent is conditioned upon the premises being habitable and upon the tenant's being able to enjoy quietly the use of the premises.

EXAMPLE | Carl and Sarah Lewis rented an apartment for $600 a month from Andrew Clark, the owner of Carlisle Manor. During the month of February, the oil burner broke down, forcing Carl and Sarah to vacate their apartment and move in with her sister. Clark took his time in seeing to it that the burner was repaired and heat was restored. It was two weeks before the Lewises were able to move back into their apartment. On the first of March they gave Clark a check for $300. He sued them for the other $300. Is he entitled to it? No! The Lewises' duty to pay rent was conditioned upon the apartment being habitable. Since the apartment was not suitable for living in, the Lewises had every right to withhold the equivalent portion from the next month's rent. Some states will even permit the tenants to withhold the rent, pool it, and apply it to having the condition remedied.

The landlord is obliged to keep the security deposit in a separate interest-bearing account in most states. If there are no damages, the landlord must return the security deposit in full together with the interest earned. The tenant's duty to leave a security deposit with the landlord is designed to protect the landlord from tenants who abandon the premises, refuse to pay rent, or materially alter the condition of the premises.

The security deposit will be applied to these losses. If the losses exceed the security deposit, then the landlord will have a cause of action, a right to sue for the remaining damages. The tenant who breaks the lease becomes liable for the rent payments throughout the remaining portion of the tenancy. In most states, the landlord has a duty to mitigate damages by trying to rerent the vacant apartment.

EXAMPLE
Upon graduating from college, Thomas Abernathy decides to leave his family and go out on his own. He rents a three-room apartment from Robert Decker for $400 a month, pursuant to an oral lease. After three months, Thomas realizes that times are difficult and that it is no fun doing his own laundry, cooking, and cleaning. He returns home to his family, vacating the apartment and breaking the lease. It takes Decker three months to rerent the apartment and the best rental price the new tenants can afford is $350 a month. What will Decker be able to recover from Thomas Abernathy? $1,500! When Thomas broke the lease, the remaining rental payments became due. Robert Decker had a duty to mitigate damages, to keep them low by rerenting the apartment. Decker is entitled to recover the rent for the three months the apartment was vacant ($1,200), plus $300 (the difference in the original rental price of $400 and the rerental price of $350 for the six remaining months on Thomas's lease). If Thomas had left a two-months' security deposit of $800, this would be applied to the amount owed.

ASSIGNMENT AND SUBLETTING

A lease is a contract. All contracts are assignable unless (1) a clause in the contract forbids assignment; (2) the assignment will materially alter the provisions of the lease; or (3) the risk to the landlord will be greatly increased should the assignment be made. A clause is usually incorporated in most leases prohibiting assignments without the landlord's consent. In leases involving commercial buildings and private homes, the landlord can arbitrarily withhold consent as long as consent is not withheld because of a discrimination that violates the Fourteenth Amendment. In leases involving multiple dwellings—that is, four or more apartment units—the landlord cannot arbitrarily withhold consent. In an assignment of a lease, the assignee pays the rent directly to the landlord.

EXAMPLE | Donna Cartwright is establishing a career for herself as an operations manager for IBM in San Diego. She has been living in a garden apartment for four years now, and has recently renewed her lease, in writing, for an additional two-year period. Suddenly, she is offered a promotion to assistant vice-president in charge of operations. The promotion involves relocating to San Francisco. She places an ad in the *San Diego Tribune* to assign the apartment. Alison Macauley responds. Both parties sign a contract in which Donna assigns Alison her right to the use, possession, and quiet enjoyment of the premises and her duty to pay the monthly rent. Three months later, Alison vacates the apartment for parts unknown. The owner of the apartment complex sues Donna for the unpaid rent. Is she responsible? Yes! An assignor remains liable to the landlord if the assignee fails to perform the assignment. Donna can then sue Alison for indemnification, if she can find her, because it was actually Alison who breached the contract. If Donna had requested that Alison pay her the rent, this would be an example of subletting.

Subletting occurs when the tenant rents either part or all of the premises to a third party in return for payment of rent. The third party's rental payments are made directly to the original tenant. In the previous example, if Donna had requested Alison to make the rental payment directly to her, this would be an example of subletting, where a new landlord and tenant relationship has actually been created with the original tenant being the landlord and the third party the subtenant. In both an assignment of a lease and the subletting of the premises, the original tenant remains liable for the rent. Refer to Chapter 12, Rights of Third Parties, for more information.

EXAMPLE | Martin Halloran is the president of Heart to Heart Medical Supplies, Inc. He rented a large warehouse which he planned to use for the manufacture and storage of medical supplies. Subsequently, he found the warehouse was much too large for his needs. He decided to rent out one-quarter of the space to another manufacturing concern, which would pay him a monthly rental. The owner of the premises consented. What type of arrangement would this be called? Subletting! Halloran has sublet a portion of the premises to a third party who, as a subtenant, has a duty to pay Halloran the monthly rental.

TERMINATION OF A TENANCY

A tenancy most often terminates when the duration of the tenancy comes to an end. A tenancy may also end prior to the expiration of the tenancy by mutual agreement, abandonment, constructive eviction, or eviction.

Abandonment

A tenant who abandons property immediately becomes liable for all of the remaining rental payments. The landlord has a duty to mitigate these damages by attempting to rerent the premises. Refer to the example concerning Thomas Abernathy.

Constructive Eviction

The tenant may abandon the premises, and be justified in so doing, if the premises become uninhabitable through no fault or negligence of the tenant. Constructive eviction results when there is loss of heat and hot water; uninhabitability of the premises which may have been caused by fire; deterioration of structural supports; rat infestation; other tenants who disrupt the quiet enjoyment of the premises against whom the landlord has not commenced eviction proceedings; etc. In the prior examples concerning Edgar and Edith Brandt and the hard rock fanatic, and Carl and Sarah Lewis and the broken oil burner, if these conditions affecting the quiet enjoyment and habitability of the premises were not promptly remedied by the landlord, both of these couples could permanently abandon the premises, refuse to pay the rent, and claim the conditions in the premises caused them to leave. This is constructive eviction.

Eviction

An eviction proceeding may be brought by a landlord against a tenant for the tenant's failure to pay rent or failure to abide by the provisions set forth in the lease. Common lease provisions prohibit the tenant from making any structural changes; installing a clothes washer, dryer or dishwasher; harboring pets; inviting third parties to live in the apartment; and assigning or subletting the apartment without the consent of the landlord. It is important for a tenant to read a lease thoroughly before assenting to it. If a tenant wants to do something which the lease prohibits, such as keep a pet, then either the lease provision could be changed or the landlord's consent should be obtained in writing.

REVIEW QUESTIONS

1. Define the following terms: landlord, tenant, lease.
2. What are the various types of tenancies?
3. List and explain the duties of a landlord.
4. List and explain the duties of a tenant.
5. What is the difference between assignment and subletting and when are they permitted?
6. Under what conditions can a tenancy be terminated?
7. For what duration of tenancy is an oral lease effective?
8. Florence Trentacost was an elderly woman. One afternoon, when returning to her apartment, she was mugged in a hallway of the apartment complex. She suffered severe injuries and sued the landlord for recourse. Florence claimed there was no lock on the front door and, in failing to provide one, the landlord violated his warranty of habitability. Furthermore, the apartment complex was located in a high-crime area and unsavory characters had been seen lurking in the corridors on prior occasions. Will Florence be successful? Trentacost v. Brussel, 164 N.J. Super. 9, 395 A.2d 540 (1978).

9. The Harrises own a legal two-family house in Brooklyn, New York. They are renting it to three families, which is illegal. Mrs. Corbin, one of those tenants, occupies the basement apartment on a month-to-month basis for $75 per month including utilities. The Department of Buildings issues a violation ordering the Harrises to restore the house to a lawful two-family dwelling. However, when the Harrises attempted to evict Mrs. Corbin, the court ruled in her favor because she had not caused the violation. She then decided to cease paying the rent because the apartment was judged illegal. Meanwhile, the Harrises were providing her with utilities free of charge. Should the Harrises be forced to continue to provide her with free space and all utilities or should they be allowed to cure the violation by evicting Mrs. Corbin thereby restoring the premises to a legal two-family dwelling? Corbin v. Harris, 92 Misc. 2d 480, 400 N.Y.S.2d 309 (1977).

10. On June 21, Steefel rented three floors of an eight-story building owned by Rothschild, pursuant to a written lease, for a term of six months beginning on September 1. After Steefel took possession and placed fixtures and inventory on the premises, which he intended to use as a men's clothing store, he learned that the municipal authorities had declared the building to be unsafe and in danger of collapse. Steefel, upon learning of the condition of the building, promptly vacated, claiming the building was not habitable. Steefel sued for the return of the rental payments made and for damages to his inventory and fixtures caused by the landlord's breach of duty. He also alleged that Rothschild had rented the building with knowledge of the dangerous condition caused by the defect in the building's structure. Rothschild retorted that he had learned of the defect in July, after the lease had been signed. Will Rothschild's argument absolve him from liability? Steefel v. Rothschild, 179 N.Y. 273, 72 N.E. 112 (1904).

31

WILLS AND TRUSTS

WILLS

A will is a declaration which states the intention of the testator or testatrix concerning:

Distribution of his or her property

Administration of his or her estate

Disposition of his or her remains

The testator or testatrix is the person who is making the will. That person will decide what relatives, friends, or charities will be the beneficiaries of the estate. An estate consists of all the property owned by a person at the time of death. The decedent's estate must be administered by a person designated by the testator or testatrix in his or her will. That person is known as the executor or executrix. If a person should die intestate (without a will), the court will appoint a public administrator to handle the decedent's estate. There is a fee set by statute which must be paid to the executor or public administrator for services rendered.

REASONS FOR MAKING A WILL

In the United States, we have certain guaranteed freedoms. One is the right to distribute our property on our death as we choose, and the right to designate who will carry out our wishes. To take advantage of this freedom, we have to draft a legal document known as a will.

Where there's a will, there's a way to leave the property to the people one wishes to have it. Where there's no will, the decedent's property will be distributed according to the laws of intestacy, which require that the property be given to the spouse or closest blood relatives. Without a will, there's no way for property to be given to a good friend or charitable institution.

Mary and Darren Blackburn had been married for forty-seven years when suddenly Darren had a heart attack and died. Mary's will, drafted fourteen years before Darren's death, provided that all her property should pass to Darren; if he should predecease her, the property should be given to her mother. Mary's mother had been in a nursing home for the past five years. At the christening of her grandniece, Mary met an attorney, named Mark Younger and informed him of her current situation. He advised her to draft a new will immediately, for as it now stands, her estate would pass to her mother, and then be subject to the claims of the nursing home. Mary agreed, stipulating that she wanted to leave her niece $150,000, but did not know how to leave the rest. Mark Younger reminded her of the possible consequences of her indecision. Mary replied that she would get in touch with him after she made up her mind. Two weeks later, Mary suffered a stroke and died. The niece contested the probate of the will by offering the testimony of witnesses who stated that Mary wanted to leave her niece $150,000. Will the niece be successful? Unfortunately, no! This example signifies the importance of making a new will when the old will no longer represents the person's desires.

FORMAL REQUIREMENTS

The will must comply with the laws of the state in which it is drafted and it must be drafted in the state in which the person making the will is domiciled. A person may have residences in many states, but only one domicile. A person's domicile is the state in which the permanent home is located and from which he or she votes.

The will must be in writing and signed at the end either by the testator or by his or her agent in the presence and at the direction of the testator. If an agent signs for the testator, that agent must sign his or her own name as well (Rita Connolly by John Burns). In drawing the will, the testator must declare and sign or acknowledge the signature as his or her own in the presence of at least two witnesses (some states require three). The witnesses also must sign the will at the direction and in the presence of the testator attesting to the testator's signature and competency. If the witness is an interested party—one who is to receive property through the will— the will remains valid, but the witness is apt to lose his or her share unless there is another witness who signs. This is to prevent fraud. Otherwise there would be nothing to keep two individuals from conspiring to influence a weak-minded person to draft a will leaving them the bulk of his or her estate with them signing as witnesses. However, if the witness is a spouse, child, or other close relative who would be entitled to receive an intestate share if the will was declared invalid, then that witness will be entitled to the lesser of either the share provided in the will or the intestate share.

An eighty-seven-year-old spinster named Catherine Washington was befriended by a young writer named Thomas Fairfax. He lived adjacent to Catherine and took care of her shopping needs, her gardening, and assisted her in her financial affairs. Catherine had promised Thomas on several occasions that he would receive a sizable portion of her estate. She informed him that she had two younger sisters who lived in Connecticut, but because she had not heard from them for several years, she wanted to exclude them from her will. When Thomas offered to accompany her to a lawyer's office, she asked him the price of drafting a will. Thomas advised her it would cost about $100. She gave him a staunch look and said, "I will make my own will." Catherine drafted the will, leaving the bulk of her estate to Thomas, and signed it at the end. She had her one other trusted friend attest the genuineness of her signature and her capacity. When Catherine dies, will Thomas be entitled to her fortune? No! The will is not valid because it did not comply with the formal requirements mandating the attestation of at least two witnesses. Catherine's estate will pass intestate. This means that her two sisters, who are her closest heirs, will inherit her fortune. If Thomas signed as a witness to the will would this change matters? Yes and no! The will would be valid, but Thomas would forfeit his share. If Thomas was a blood relation as well as a witness would he be entitled to a share? Maybe! Thomas would be entitled to the lesser of the share under the will or his intestate share, if any. For Thomas to receive an intestate share, he would have to be the closest blood relative of the decedent.

TESTAMENTARY CAPACITY

The testator must have the capacity to understand and appreciate the nature and extent of his or her property, the persons who are the natural objects of his or her bounty, and the disposition which he or she is making in regard to such persons and property.

The testator must be eighteen years of age or older in most states, and of sound mind. However an insane person may make a will during a lucid interval.

If a person making a will lacks this testamentary capacity or does not make the will freely of his or her own initiative, the will may be challenged and rendered invalid.

EXAMPLE

Millie Frankhart lived the better part of her life with her niece, Loretta, who attended to her needs. In her will, Millie left her entire estate to Loretta. After Loretta's marriage, Millie moved to Florida and lived with some friends. During that time she became senile. While in the presence of a doctor and a nurse, Millie signed a will leaving her entire estate to her friends, forgetful of her previous will and of her niece, Loretta. Loretta contested the validity of the new will on the grounds of senility. Will she be successful? Yes! Millie lacked the testamentary capacity to make a valid will because she did not know the heirs who were the natural objects of her bounty. Millie's estate will pass to her niece in accordance with the laws of intestacy.

CLASSIFICATIONS OF INDIVIDUALS AND PROPERTY

1. *Testator* is the person disposing of his or her property by will. A woman who makes a will is referred to as a testatrix.
2. *Executor* is the representative of the decedent who handles the administration and disposition of the estate. A woman who is appointed as a representative is known as an executrix.

3. *Administrator* is a representative appointed by the court for a person who dies intestate, without a will.

4. *Guardian* is a representative appointed to look after the decedent's children. A guardian is appointed by the testator through a will, or by the court in cases where the decedent had died intestate or where the will failed to appoint a guardian for minor children.

5. *Conservator* is the representative of a judicially declared incompetent, appointed by the court to administer the estate of the incompetent while he or she is still alive.

6. *Issue* are the legitimate children of a decedent, including those conceived before but born alive after the decedent's death.

7. *Adopted children* are treated as natural children for the purpose of inheriting.

8. *One-half blood relations*—step-brothers and step-sisters—are treated as equal full-blood relatives for the purpose of inheriting.

9. *Illegitimate children* inherit from the mother and the maternal grandparents and great-grandparents. They inherit from the father only if he is acknowledged through an order of paternity or if he makes a specific bequest in his will. A father may inherit from an illegitimate child only by an order of affiliation.

10. *Devise* is a disposition of real property through a will.

11. *Devisee* is the recipient of the disposition of real property through a will.

12. *Bequest* is the disposition of personal property (such as money, jewelry, silver) through a will.

13. *Legatee* is the recipient of the disposition of personal property through a will.

14. *Distributee* is an heir who is entitled to share in the estate of a decedent who died with or without a will.

15. *Residuary clause* in a will determines to whom the remainder of the decedent's real and personal property shall be given after specific devises and bequests have been made. Without a residuary clause, the property remaining would pass according to the laws of intestacy. An example of a residuary clause is set forth in the sample will.

16. *Intestate* refers to a person who dies with no will and whose property will be distributed in accordance with the laws of the state in which he or she has died.

SAMPLE WILL

THE LAST WILL AND TESTAMENT
OF
JAMES BOND

I, JAMES BOND, residing at the headquarters of Her Majesty's Secret Service, being of sound and disposing mind and memory, do make, publish, and declare the following as for and to be my Last Will and Testament.

FIRST: I hereby revoke any and all Wills and Codicils by me at any time heretofore made.

SECOND: I direct the payment of all my just debts, funeral and testamentary expenses as soon after my decease as may be practicable.

THIRD: I give and bequeath my Astor Martin to GOLDFINGER with my best wishes for his being able to fit inside the car.

FOURTH: I give and bequeath my top hat to ODD JOB to replace the one he lost in Fort Knox.

FIFTH: I give and bequeath a golden wedding band to MISS MONEYPENNY because she had always wanted to be Mrs. James Bond.

SIXTH: I give and bequeath to ERNST BLOFELD my white kitten, Pussy Galore, to replace his cat that died.

SEVENTH: I give and bequeath $2,000 to JAWS for the purpose of buying a new set of dentures.

EIGHTH: I give and devise and bequeath all the rest, residue, and remainder of my estate, both real and personal, of whatsoever kind or nature and wheresoever the same may be situate, of which I may die seized and possessed, or be entitled to at the time of my death, in equal shares to my two sons of my late wife, 008 and 009.

NINTH: I hereby nominate, constitute, and appoint my good friend, FELIX LICHTER, to be executor of my Last Will and Testament, and I direct that no bond or other security shall be required of him in any jurisdiction in which he may seek to qualify.

TENTH: I direct that any and all estate, inheritance, legacy, succession, or other death taxes payable in respect of my estate, or any devise, legacy, or distribution under this, my Will, or levied by reason of my death, including but not limited to those levied on proceeds of policies of insurance on my life, whether or not the property, transfer, or proceeds with respect to which said taxes are levied pass by virtue of my Will or outside my Will, shall be paid out of my residuary estate as administration expenses, and said taxes shall not be apportioned.

IN WITNESS WHEREOF, I have hereunto subscribed my name and affixed my seal this 17th day of November in the year of our Lord, One Thousand Nine Hundred and Eighty-Eight.

James Bond (L.S.)

WITNESSES:

      "M"

      "Q"

The foregoing instrument was on this 17th day of November, 1988, subscribed by JAMES BOND, the Testator therein. In the presence of each of us, said Testator, did, in advance of signing said instrument, declare to us that he had read the same; that he understood it and that it expressed his wishes and purposes; and said Testator did immediately subsequent to making said subscription, declare and publish the instrument so subscribed by him to be his Last Will and Testament, whereupon we, at his request, in his presence and in the presence of each other, did on the same day hereunto subscribe our names as witnesses thereto.

REVOCATION OF A WILL

A will may be revoked by the drafting of a new will which contains a provision that all prior wills are hereby revoked. A will may also be revoked by physical destruction or by a writing manifesting the testator's intention of revocation. Divorce or annulment revokes any distribution of property to the spouse. The spouse is treated as though he or she predeceased the testator. Marriage has the effect of entitling the surviving spouse to exercise the right to elect against the will and take the statutory share. In most states, the statutory share is one-half if there are no children and one-third if there are. A child who is born or adopted after the parent has made his or her last will, is entitled to the intestate share if there are no other children. If there are other children, then the after-born or after-adoped child shall be entitled to a proportionate share of what the other children received. If the other children receive nothing, then the after-born child will receive nothing.

PROBATE

Before a decedent's property can be distributed in accordance with the will, the will must be probated. Probate is the procedure for proving the will to be valid and genuine and that it manifests the testator's true intent. The probate or surrogate court located in the state where the decedent died has jurisdiction over the decedent's will and estate. The disposition of real estate located in a state other then the state where the decedent died will be governed by the laws of the state where the real estate is located. No state has the power to make a decision regarding ownership of real estate in another state.

The original will must be filed with the court along with an affidavit of sub-scribing witnesses and a probate petition which sets forth the testator's heirs, and any person named in the will as either an executor or beneficiary who is not an heir. Notice of probate must be sent to the parties named in the probate petition to advise them the decedent has died and that the will has been admitted to probate. An heir who is not named in the will, or a person named in the will who is not satisfied with the bequest or devise he or she received, may contest the validity of the will at a hearing.

Once the will has been approved by the surrogate or probate judge, letters will be issued to the executor or executrix giving that person the authority to administer the estate and dispose of the property according to the directions in the will.

INTESTATE DISTRIBUTION

The estate of a person who dies with no will is governed by the intestacy laws of the state where the decedent died. The laws of intestacy are based on spouse and blood relationship. The following is a description of the priority distribution of a typical state's laws of intestacy.

1. Surviving spouse and child
   a. Spouse gets one-half
   b. Child gets one-half
2. Surviving spouse and children
   a. Spouse gets one-third
   b. Children split two-thirds
3. Surviving spouse and parents, no children
   a. Spouse gets one-half
   b. Parents get one-half
4. Surviving spouse, no children or parents
   a. Spouse gets whole
5. One or more children, no surviving spouse
   a. Child or children get whole
6. Parent(s), no surviving spouse or children
   a. Parent(s) get whole
7. Brothers and sisters or their children
   a. Brothers and sisters or their children (cousins) split whole

EXAMPLE Jonathan Goodman, who lives on Park Avenue, has two sons who now live in Arizona. Jonathan's wife had passed away five years ago, and now he gets only letters from his boys with best wishes, but no invitations to visit. Jonathan's grandnephew, William, lives nearby with his mother. William often visits Jonathan, bringing him books and magazines. Jonathan enjoys telling William stories about the family and showing him the family heirlooms. Jonathan often tells William, "When I die all of these antiques will be yours." Eventually, Jonathan dies, but without a will. What happens to the family treasures? Jonathan's estate will pass intestate to his two sons, who may dispose of the family heirlooms as they please. Jonathan could have avoided this by drafting a will leaving his treasures to William.

RIGHT OF ELECTION

A surviving spouse cannot be disinherited. The statutory right of election provides against this by allowing the surviving spouse to elect against the will for a one-third share of the estate if there are children, or a one-half share if there are no children. For the purpose of determining the spouse's right of election, all testamentary substitutes are included in the estate; testamentary substitutes include real or personal property held jointly by the decedent and someone other than the surviving spouse, including joint bank accounts, gifts made to others with knowledge of impending death, and trusts established with others named as beneficiary.

EXAMPLE Jim Spencer, a corporate executive, has found the attributes of charm, passion, and intelligence in his administrative assistant, Lisa, that he feels are lacking in his wife Alice. In his will, Jim leaves one-half of his estate to his three children and the other half to Lisa. Will his attempt to disinherit his wife be successful? No! Alice may exercise her statutory right of election against the will and receive a one-third share of Jim's estate. What remains will be divided equally among Jim's three children and Lisa.

While a testator cannot totally disinherit a spouse, a testator can create a trust in an amount equal to or greater than the surviving spouse's right of election with the income from this trust payable to the surviving spouse for life and with the principal paid to a beneficiary designated by the testator on the surviving spouse's death. In this way, the surviving spouse does not have the free use of the entire trust principal, but only the income from it for his or her life. This trust cannot be terminated prior to the surviving spouse's death nor be invaded by or for anyone else. This trust must pay out all the income to the surviving spouse. If any one of these contingencies is violated, the surviving spouse is entitled to the principal of the trust outright.

CONTESTING A WILL

A will may be contested by an heir or any other person who is named in either the last will or a prior will on the grounds of

Lack of capacity
Improper execution
Undue influence
Fraud

Lack of Capacity

The burden of proving capacity is on the proponents of the will. They must prove the testator was of legal age and sane at the time of the signing of the will. The sanity requirement is usually sworn to by the subscribing witnesses who must attest truthfully with no motive to lie.

Improper Execution

A contest because of improper execution arises when it is alleged one of the formal requirements has not been adhered to. The person contesting the validity of the will has the burden of proving this.

Undue Influence

The question of undue influence hinges upon whether the mind of the testator was dominated to the extent that no testamentary intent existed. Evidence may be presented concerning the susceptibility of the testator, the opportunity of the accused to unduly influence the testator, and the accused's motive for doing so. The burden of proving undue influence rests with the person contesting the estate.

Wingrove v. Wingrove
L.R.11 Prob. Div. 81 (1885)

Charles Wingrove had frequented a house of ill repute on several occasions for the purpose of engaging in a meretricious relationship with a harlot. The coy and attractive little harlot had caught Charles's fancy and he began to be seen publicly in her company. In his will, he decided to exclude his relatives in favor of the harlot with regard to the assets comprising his estate. As fate would have it, young Charles passed from this earth with his whole estate bequeathed to the little harlot. His relatives protested vehemently, contesting the validity of the will by arguing that the harlot had unduly influenced Charles into leaving his estate to her.

The issue is whether the harlot's persuasiveness amounted to undue influence which would render the will invalid.

The court decided,

> A young man may be caught in the toils of a harlot, who makes use of her influence to induce him to make a will in her favor, to the exclusion of his relatives. It is unfortunately quite natural that a man so entangled should yield to that influence and confer large bounties on the person with whom he has been brought into such relation; yet, the law does not attempt to guard against those contingencies. . . . To be undue influence in the eye of the law there must be—to sum it up in a word—coercion. . . . If, therefore, the act is shown to be the result of the wish and will of the testator at the time, then, however it has been brought about—for we are not dealing with a case of fraud—though you may condemn . . . any person who has endeavored to persuade, and has succeeded in persuading, the testator to adopt the view—still it is not undue influence.

Judgment for the Estate of Wingrove and the harlot.

Fraud

A will is not valid if the testator was the victim of a deception which led him or her to disinherit an heir. The heir is entitled to his or her intestate share. The following case illustrates this principle.

Estate of Holmes
98 Colo. 360, 56 P.2d 1333 (1936)

Samuel Holmes died, leaving a will naming his nieces, Daisy M. Holmes and Florence Holmes Soule, as beneficiaries. Daisy filed a probate petition stating under oath that she and Florence were the decedent's only heirs, even though she knew the decedent had a sister, W. H. Huber. The will was admitted to probate, but no notice of probate was ever given to the decedent's sister. When she discoverd the decedent's death, Mrs. Huber contested the will on the grounds of fraudulent representations by Daisy. Daisy had written to Samuel Holmes advising him that his sister had died, whereupon Samuel Holmes made a will devising and bequeathing all of his property to his two nieces, Daisy and Florence. He informed the witnesses before signing the will that, were his sister still living, he would have remembered her in his will.

The issue is whether the will should be declared invalid due to the decedent's mistaken belief that his sister was dead. The court ruled,

> . . . The fact that he was mistaken in that regard would not, of itself, avoid the will. If however, the mistaken belief was caused by false representations

knowingly made by Miss Holmes and Mrs. Soule with the fraudulent purpose of inducing Holmes to make his will in their favor, to the exclusion of his sister, and he so made the will in reliance upon such representations, the will would be void as to both.

Judgment for decedent's sister, Mrs. Huber.

TRUSTS

A trust is the legal title to real or personal property held by one party for the benefit of another. The person creating the trust is called the creator; the person for whom it is created is known as the beneficiary; and the person who has been entrusted by the creator with the legal title to the trust funds until the designated time for payment to the beneficiary is referred to as the trustee. A trust involves a fiduciary relationship in which the trustee must administer the trust property in good faith, as a reasonably prudent person would.

TYPES OF TRUSTS

A trust may be created during the life of the creator through an *inter vivos*, or living, trust, or may be created on the death of the creator through a will. The latter is known as a testamentary trust. A living trust may have a provision incorporated in it giving the creator the right to revoke the trust and reclaim the principal. If the creator does not reserve this right, the trust is irrevocable unless it is a Totten trust.

A Totten trust is a special trust consisting of a bank account opened in one's own name for the benefit of another, with retention and control of the passbook remaining with the creator. Any funds on deposit on the date of the decedent's death will automatically pass to the named beneficiary. The creator is also the trustee and he or she may revoke the trust at any time by withdrawing the funds from the bank account.

PURPOSE OF TRUSTS

The purposes for which trusts may be created are varied. Some are set up to provide for the support and education of a child. In this case, money or other property may be held in trust for a child until he or she reaches an age of financial responsibility that will be predetermined by the creator. Trusts may also be created for the purpose of providing for a relative or friend who is not capable of managing his or her financial affairs. In this way, the beneficiary is assured of receiving a fixed income without the need to manage or otherwise be accountable for the money. The creator is thus assured that the principal of the trust will not be squandered.

EXAMPLE Paul Murrow died leaving his house to his twenty-six-year-old mildly retarded son, Michael. Paul also left a $300,000 trust fund managed by First Federal Trust Company as trustee, with the income from the trust payable to Michael for his support and maintenance. Was Paul wise to set up a trust fund for Michael? Yes! Paul knew Michael lacked the mental capacity to invest the $300,000 prudently. Since Michael can handle his ordinary affairs, he will have an ample source of regular income to pay his normal everyday expenses.

A person may create a scholarship trust fund where the income from the principal of the trust will be used to pay for the tuition of promising students. Many universities, societies, and clubs have funds designated for this purpose. Trusts may also be created for other educational, religious, or charitable purposes. If, for some reason, circumstances change and make it impracticable to carry out the purpose of the trust concerning dispositions of a religious, educational, or charitable nature, the court may invoke the *cy pres* doctrine. This allows the court to alter the purpose or beneficiary of the trust in order that the trust does not fail. This is to accomplish the creator's purpose in a feasible manner.

EXAMPLE   Mildred Kettering, who had no heirs, died leaving her entire estate in trust for the St. Thomas More Church in Boston. Shortly after her death, a fire destroyed the church. The Archdiocese of Boston decided to refrain from building a new church and merged this parish with the neighboring one. What will become of Mildred's trust fund? The court may invoke the *cy pres* doctrine and alter the specific purpose of the trust to best serve Mildred's intentions. The trust fund will most likely be given to the Archdiocese of Boston to use for the neighboring parish or as it otherwise sees fit.

REVIEW QUESTIONS _____

1. Define the following terms: will, estate, testator, executor, administrator, guardian, conservator, issue, devise, devisee, bequest, legatee, intestate, distributee, and probate.
2. What are the rights of adopted childen, one-half blood relations, illegitimate children, and after-born children?
3. Why should a person make a will?
4. What are the formal requirements which must be adhered to in drafting a will?
5. How will a decedent's estate be distributed if he or she dies without making a will?
6. When may a spouse exercise his or her right of election?
7. On what grounds may a will be contested?
8. Define trusts and state the purposes for which they may be used.
9. Is the following handwritten will valid?

    To whom it may concern:
    I—Edwin Durand Bamberger bequeath all my property both Real Estate and personal to my wife Lillian Dorothy Bamberger. To her also and alone I bequeath

all my life insurance of whatever kind. She is to serve as sole executrix without bond.

Witness James M. Northcott
Witness Blanche P. McKinnie.

Bamberger v. Barbour, 335 Ill. 458, 167 N.E. 122 (1929).

10. Miss Ella Wendel, a relative of the Astors and Roosevelts, died leaving a will and an extremely sizable estate. Over sixteen hundred claimants, personally or through their attorneys, have appeared and alleged they are within the class of distributees. One woman, Rosa Dew Stansbury, established that she was related to Ella Wendel by the fifth degree as the child of Ella Wendel's granduncle, Carville S. Stansbury. How will the court determine which, if any, of the sixteen hundred alleged distributees have the right to share in Ella Wendel's estate? Matter of Wendel, 143 Misc. 480, 257 N.Y.S. 87 (Surr. Ct. N.Y. Cty. 1932).

32

AGENCY: CREATION AND DUTIES

INTRODUCTION

Agency is a contractual relationship, involving an agent and a principal, in which the agent is given the authority to represent the principal in dealings with third parties. The most common example is an employer-employee relationship wherein an agent (employee) is given the power by a principal (employer) to act on his or her behalf. An agent may be an employee, an independent contractor, or a professional agent. A principal is a person who employs an agent to act on his or her behalf.

A principal (employer) has full control over his or her employee. The employee must complete the work assigned by following the instructions of the principal. An independent contractor and a professional agent are individuals hired by a principal to perform a specific task. The principal has no control over the methods used by the independent contractor or professional agent. The following are among those who act independent of a principal: independent contractors (electricians, carpenters, plumbers, television repairmen, and automobile mechanics); and professional agents (lawyers, physicians, accountants, securities brokers, insurance brokers, real estate brokers, and investment advisors). These special agents may also employ others in their field who will be bound to them as employees.

A principal may be disclosed, partially disclosed, or undisclosed. An agent acting for a disclosed principal will make that fact known to the third parties with whom he or she is dealing. When an agent represents an undisclosed principal, the agent will pretend to act for himself or herself, thus assuring the individual principal that his or her identity will remain anonymous.

EXAMPLE | Exxon Corporation has good reason to believe there is oil shale embedded in the side of a mountain on the outskirts of Glenwood Springs, Colorado. The tract of land they are interested in is owned by Homer Lampson. Exxon feels that if they approach Lampson, he will raise his price in the belief that Exxon knows something that he doesn't. Instead, Exxon sends an employee, Wendel Tyson, to negotiate a contract of sale with Lampson in Tyson's own name. Tyson will then transfer the land to Exxon at a later date. What type of relationship has been created between Exxon and Wendel Tyson? An agency has been created with Tyson acting as an agent for Exxon, an undisclosed principal. If Tyson represented to Homer Lampson that he was purchasing the land on behalf of Exxon, Exxon's status would be that of a disclosed principal.

All of the requirements of contract law are applicable to the creation of an agency. Both a principal and an agent must have the capacity to contract.

An infant may act through an agent, but will not be liable for the reasonable value of the agent's services or any contracts entered into by the agent unless they involve necessities or come under one of the other exceptions to the defense of infancy, such as hiring an employment agency. This is because contracts entered into by an infant are voidable at his or her discretion.

The agency contracts of insane people are voidable by the insane individual unless he or she has been adjudicated as an incompetent in which case the agency contract would be void.

Partnerships enter into contracts through the individual partners who are both agents and principals of the partnership. Corporations also act through officers and other designated employees who are agents of the corporation.

An agency contract may be created expressly, through a writing or a verbal conversation, or impliedly, through the actions of the parties. However, if an agent's duties involve entering into a contract on behalf of the principal which is required to be in writing under the statute of frauds, then the agency contract must also be in writing.

EXAMPLE | In the previous example, Exxon's agency relationship with Wendel Tyson must have been evidenced by a signed writing because it involved the purchase of real estate.

TYPES OF AUTHORITY

Actual Authority

The scope of an agent's authority is usually determined by the principal. Actual authority is the express authority conveyed by the principal to the agent. It also includes the implied authority to do whatever is reasonably necessary to complete the task. This implied authority also gives the agent power to act in an emergency.

EXAMPLE | Charlie Mason is a garage mechanic at the Seagate Service Station. His actual authority is limited to servicing automobiles. He has no authority to enter into contracts with customers for his services. He has no authority to decide on which cars he will work. One day while the gas attendant is out to lunch, a customer pulls up to the gas pump.

Does Charlie Mason have the authority to service the customer? Yes! Inherent in the authority delegated to Charlie is the implied authority to perform those routine tasks necessary for the continuation of the business when the other mechanics or gas attendants are out to lunch or otherwise occupied. If a boy threw a brick through the office window, and it had to be repaired before closing, Charlie would have the authority to board up the window or have a glazier replace the glass if the service station manager could not be notified.

Apparent Authority

Apparent authority is the authority the agent professes to have which induces a reasonable person to believe in the agent. The reliance on apparent authority must be justifiable.

EXAMPLE | In the previous example, suppose Charlie is alone at the service station, finishing a tune-up on a Monte Carlo, when Arthur Moriarity drives up in his Rolls-Royce. He informs Charlie that there is a rumbling sound in the engine. Charlie inspects the engine and informs Arthur Moriarity that the valves are worn and need to be reseated. Moriarity agrees to leave the car overnight. The next morning Charlie has completed the valve job, but the engine's rumbling has become worse. When Arthur calls for the Rolls-Royce, he threatens to sue the service station for negligence in its attempted repair of his car. Can the service station raise the defense that Charlie Mason acted without authority? No! Although Charlie did not possess the actual authority to bind the Seagate Service Station to a contract, he appeared to have the authority in entering into the contract of repair. Arthur Moriarity was justified because a reasonable person would believe a garage mechanic would possess the authority to decide whether a car could be repaired at the service station for which he or she worked.

Watteau v. Fenwick
1 Q. B. 346 (1893)

Watteau sued Fenwick for breach of contract in refusing to pay for cigars contracted for by Fenwick's agent, Humble.

Humble was the proprietor of a beerhouse called the Victoria Hotel. He transferred the business to Fenwick, but stayed on as the manager. His actual authority was limited to the purchase of bottled ales and mineral water. Humble entered into a contract to purchase cigars from Watteau. Watteau believed Humble was still the proprietor because the liquor license was taken out in his name and his name was inscribed over the entrance. When Fenwick learned of the contract, he refused to ratify Humble's contract for cigars, claiming Humble acted without authority. Watteau sued Fenwick for the price of the cigars when he learned of Fenwick's identity.

The issue is whether Fenwick, an undisclosed principal, is bound by the unauthorized acts of his agent, Humble.

The court decided that Humble had the apparent authority to contract on the principal's behalf because Fenwick put Humble in the position of manager and allowed Humble's name to remain over the door. These facts alone would lead a distributor into justifiably believing that Humble was either the owner of the tavern or that, as an agent, Humble possessed the authority to contract to purchase supplies.

The court held, ". . . once it is established that the defendant [Fenwick] was the real principal, the ordinary doctrine as to principal and agent applies—that the principal is liable for all the acts of the agent which are within the authority usually confided to an agent of that character . . ." Judgment for Watteau.

AGENT'S DUTIES

Duty of Loyalty

The relationship between principal and agent is a fiduciary one, based on trust and confidence. Inherent in this relationship is the agent's duty of loyalty. An agent has a duty to disclose all pertinent information he or she learns of that will affect the principal, the principal's business, or the task at hand. An agent must not take advantage of the principal's prospective business opportunities or enter into contracts on behalf of the principal for personal aggrandizement without the principal's knowledge. An agent may not work for two principals who have competing interests.

EXAMPLE Peter Stapelton works as a sales clerk and mechanic in South Shore Auto Parts and Repair Shop. One day Stapelton is approached by Malcohm Ripkin, owner of Ripkin's Limousine Service, who informs him he would like South Shore to maintain his fleet of seventeen limousines. Stapelton takes Ripkin's card, but instead of passing it along to the owners of South Shore, he decides to negotiate with Ripkin on his own behalf. Stapelton reasons that if he can get the contract for the maintenance of the seventeen limousines, it would enable him to establish his own auto repair station. Stapelton enters into a personal service contract with Ripkin and then contracts with South Shore Auto Parts to purchase all of the supplies he needs at wholesale prices. Six months later, South Shore learns of Stapelton's disloyalty. What recourse do they have? South Shore may sue Stapelton for breach of contract because he violated his duty of loyalty in failing to disclose Ripkin's offer and in taking advantage of South Shore's business opportunity. Stapelton also contracted on behalf of South Shore for his own benefit without informing them of what he was doing. Stapelton will be liable to South Shore for consequential damages—that is, the loss of profits they sustained as a result of losing Ripkin's limousine contract and the loss of profits they suffered because of Stapelton's unauthorized contracts made on behalf of South Shore with himself at wholesale prices. South Shore will be able to recover the difference between the wholesale price and the retail price. They may also fire Stapelton for his disloyal actions.

Duty to Act in Good Faith

An agent has an obligation to perform all duties in good faith. He or she must carry out the task assigned by using reasonable skill and care. The agent has a further duty to follow the principal's instructions and not to exceed the authority delegated to him or her.

EXAMPLE Vito Torrino worked in a Burger King Restaurant for three years. During his employment, he felt that the manager was continually mistreating him by using abusive language, assigning him hours which purposely conflicted with his class studies, and making him perform janitorial services which were not included in his job description. When an opening arose at a nearby McDonald's on a late shift, Torrino accepted the position, but he retained his regular job with Burger King. During the manager's absence one busy Saturday afternoon, Torrino neglected his routine duties and took charge of the cash register. He proceeded to give away three Whoppers free with every purchase of a small soda. He informed the customers that it was an anniversary celebration. Torrino's intent was to repay the Burger King manager for his unkindness by causing him to lose profits. What recourse does the Burger King manager have against Torrino? Torrino violated his duty of loyalty to Burger King by working for a competing principal, McDonald's, and by purposely causing Burger King to lose profits. Torrino refused to obey instructions to perform his delegated duties. He exceeded his authority through the authorization of a free offer. If Torrino was displeased with his job, he should have left to find another position rather than allowing his resentment to build up for three years. In all respects, Torrino violated his duty to act in good faith.

City of East Grand Forks v. Steele et al.
121 Minn. 296, 141 N.W. 181 (1913)

The City of East Grand Forks, Minnesota, hired Steele and his companions, who represented themselves to be expert accountants. The city asked the accountants to verify their books and records for two successive years. The accountants made the investigation and audit and falsely reported each year that the city's books were accurate. Following the publication of the reports, the city clerk embezzled almost $2,000 in the first year and over $5,000 in the second year. The state examiner subsequently discovered the accountant's error and the city clerk's embezzlement.

The city sued the accountants for breach of their contractual duty to exercise reasonable care in conducting the audit. The city demanded reimbursement from the accountants for the fees paid to them as well as the amounts embezzled by the city clerk.

The issue is whether the accountants failed to fulfill their duty to act in good faith by neglecting to exercise reasonable care in their audit investigation, and, if so, whether the city clerk's embezzlement is a direct result of their breach of duty.

The court held,

> The full contract price having been paid in the belief, induced by the defendants' report, that such report disclosed fully and accurately the condition of the city's accounts, the city is entitled to recover back the amounts so paid, upon proving that, through the incompetence or the negligence of the defendants, the report was in substance false and misleading.

The court decided, "The defendants failed to discover these defalcations, by reason of incompetence and negligence."

The city clerk's embezzlement was too remote to be considered a direct result of the accountants' failure to act in good faith. The court stated,

> Such losses are neither the natural nor the proximate consequences of the failure of defendants to make a proper audit. Neither are any facts shown

from which it may be inferred that a loss from either of these causes was or ought to have been contemplated, when the contract was made, as likely to result from a breach of duty on the part of the defendants.

Judgment for the city of East Grand Forks as to reimbursement for the accountants' fees paid. Judgment for Steele et al., with respect to the accountants' liability for the embezzled funds.

Duty to Account

An agent has a duty to account for all compensations received, including kickbacks. Upon the principal's request, an agent must make a full disclosure, known as an accounting, of all receipts and expenditures. The agent must not commingle funds, but rather keep the principal's funds in an account separate from his or her own. Furthermore, an agent must not use the principal's funds for his or her own purposes.

EXAMPLE | Murray Stockman is a securities broker at a branch office of Pearlman & Associates, located in Silver City, New Mexico. Each of Stockman's clients signed an agreement appointing him as their agent to buy and sell securities. Stockman would often borrow from individual's accounts in order to further his own investment opportunities. He did this without informing either the client or the company. He would later repay the amount borrowed. Since Silver City is not a large city, many clients make deposits in cash. Stockman would stamp the deposit slip, but then deposit the cash in his own account expecting to repay it at a later date. Finally, Stockman has a bad streak of luck and is unable to repay the money before the monthly statements are sent out. The clients sue Pearlman & Associates, and Murray Stockman, for conversion of the funds in their accounts. What recourse does Pearlman & Associates have against Stockman? They may sue Stockman for breach of contract and for reimbursement of any of the clients' losses. Stockman breached his duty of loyalty, his duty to act in good faith, and his duty to fully disclose all deposits he received. He commingled clients' funds with his own for the purpose of furthering his own investment schemes.

PRINCIPAL'S DUTIES

Duty to Compensate

A principal has the duty to compensate the agent for the work performed. An agent will be entitled to the amount agreed upon in the contract; otherwise he or she will be entitled to the reasonable value of the services rendered. A principal must also reimburse an agent for the expenses incurred by the agent during the course of conducting the principal's business. For tax purposes, a principal has a duty to keep a record of the compensation earned by an agent and the reimbursements made for expenditures.

Duty to Maintain Safe Working Conditions

The maintenance of safe working conditions is another obligation placed on the principal. Any tools or equipment furnished the agent must be in proper working order; otherwise the principal may be liable for the harm resulting to an agent.

Dolores Wright, an agent of the Green Bay Housing Authority, is in charge of tenant complaints regarding lack of heat and hot water. She is a part-time employee who works only during the winter months. Dolores Wright's office is in a three-story building, located in the downtown section and owned by the city. In February, the building's oil burner malfunctioned. Dolores Wright made numerous calls to her superiors, but no action was taken. When Dolores called the oil company, they said the burner needed to be replaced. It was not replaced. Of her own volition, Dolores bought and paid for a heater, insulated her office, and continued to work through the month of February. At that time, she became ill with pneumonia and was hospitalized. Since she was a part-time employee, the city did not pay for her medical plan. She thereupon sued the city for her medical bills, loss of compensation while she was hospitalized, and the expenses she incurred in attempting to make the office habitable during the month of February. Is she entitled to be reimbursed? Yes! The city is liable for her medical expenses because it failed to provide her with a safe and healthy working environment. She is entitled to compensation for the time she lost from work because it was directly caused by the city's negligence. She is also entitled to reimbursement for the expenses she incurred in attempting to create a healthy environment in the office.

REVIEW QUESTIONS

1. Define agency, principal, and agent.
2. What is the difference between express and implied actual authority? Give an example of each.
3. What is apparent authority? Give an example.
4. Define the agent's duty of loyalty and give an example of a breach of that duty.
5. Define the agent's duty to act in good faith and give an example of a breach of that duty.
6. Define the agent's duty to account and give an example of a breach of that duty.
7. What are the two main duties a principal must fulfill?
8. Conkey requested Bond to act as his agent in procuring stock of the Oswego River Starch Company. Bond sold Conkey his own stock in Oswego River Starch Company at a price which exceeded its value. Bond represented that he purchased the stock from third parties, which was untrue. Conkey sued to have the sale of the stock rescinded and to get restitution in the amount paid to Bond. Under what theory will Conkey triumph? Conkey v. Bond, 36 N.Y. 427 (1867).
9. Howard, an actress, contracted to perform for Daly at his theater in New York from September 15 through the following July 1 at an agreed-upon salary. This contract was entered into on April 20. Before she was required to act for Daly, he cancelled the contract and refused to pay her the promised salary. Has Daly, as a principal, breached his duty to compensate Howard? Howard v. Daly, 61 N.Y. 362 (1875).
10. Sierra Pacific purchased a large tract of timberland. They contacted Carter, a real estate broker, and requested him to find a ready, willing, and able buyer for ten acres of nontimberland which was included in the large tract of land they purchased. Carter represented the value of the land to be $85,000. Thereafter,

he sold the land to his daughter and son-in-law for $85,000, while retaining the agreed-upon commission of $5,000. Sierra Pacific sued Carter for (1) breach of his duty of loyalty as its agent in failing to disclose his dual representation and the fact that the purchasers were his relatives, and (2) for breach of his duty to act in good faith by misrepresenting the value of the property. Has Carter breached both of his duties? Sierra Pacific Industries v. Carter, 104 Cal. App. 3d 579, 163 Cal. Rptr. 764 (1980).

33

AGENCY: LIABILITY AND TERMINATION

LIABILITY OF AGENTS

Agents will be liable for breach of contract if they fail to uphold their duties, including duty of loyalty, duty to act in good faith, and duty to account for all receipts and expenses. An agent will be liable for all unauthorized acts or misrepresentations made to third parties in the principal's name.

An agent's liability extends to situations where the agent contracts with a third party on behalf of a nonexistent principal, or where the agent contracts in his or her own name on behalf of a principal who does exist. To protect themselves against personal liability, agents should always sign the principal's name and then their own name as agent. Of course, when an agent represents an undisclosed principal, the agent will have to contract in his or her own name to protect the identity of the principal. In this case, the agent would be personally liable.

An agent will be personally liable to a third party when he or she acts without actual or apparent authority, except in an emergency. A principal will be liable to a third party for an agent's acts during an emergency if the agent's acts were reasonable, even though the agent may have acted without authority.

EXAMPLE Robert McMillen lists farm land he owns north of Cheyenne, Wyoming, with Tumbleweed Real Estate, and gives them an exclusive agency. After four months of attempting to locate a buyer, they learn that an interstate highway will proceed north from Denver and Cheyenne through McMillen's farm land, thus enhancing the purchase price. Tumbleweed contracts with McMillen to purchase the farm land for Dexter Brady, supposedly an out-of-state principal who has given Tumbleweed power of attorney to act on his behalf. Tumbleweed is actually purchasing the land for itself. Brady is a fictitious principal who does not exist. McMillen is happy with the purchase price until he learns about the interstate highway plan. He sues Tumbleweed Real Estate and Dexter Brady only to discover Brady is nonexistent. What recourse does McMillen have against Tumbleweed? Tumbleweed can be compelled to return the farm land to McMillen even though there were no other ready, willing, and able buyers. Tumbleweed attempted to defraud McMillen by purportedly acting for a principal who did not exist, while they were actually buying the land for themselves.

Assume that there was no interstate highway plan and that Dexter Brady actually existed and gave Tumbleweed authority to act for him. Suppose Tumbleweed contracted with McMillen in their own name and Brady later reneged on the purchase, would Tumbleweed be liable on the contract for the sale of McMillen's farmland? Yes! An agent who signs in his or her own name is personally liable to a third party unless the principal admits he or she is liable by approving the agent's acts. Although Tumbleweed may be liable to McMillen, they may sue Brady for breach of his agency contract with them.

LIABILITY OF PRINCIPALS

Contractual Liability

A disclosed principal is bound by his or her agent's contract with a third party where the agent acted with actual authority, either express or implied, or with apparent authority. A disclosed principal is not liable for the unauthorized acts of an agent unless he or she ratifies them.

When a contract is made on behalf of an undisclosed principal, the third party may elect to hold either the principal or the agent responsible. The agent is responsible because he or she is contracting in his or her own name for an undisclosed principal. The undisclosed principal will become liable only when his or her identity is disclosed.

EXAMPLE | Clifford Branch and James Alworth were both attending an auction at Sothebys in London. Branch was representing the Ford Foundation as he had done on numerous occasions in the past. Alworth was representing a man named Vanderbilt, an undisclosed principal. During the auction, Branch was declared the highest bidder on paintings by Paul Cezanne and Henri Matisse for $850,000 and $700,000, respectively. Alworth was successful with his $1,450,000 bid for a Van Gogh. Both Branch and Alworth signed a contract agreeing to deliver the purchase price within two weeks, at which time the painting would be transferred. Branch signed "Ford Foundation by Clifford Branch, Agent." Alworth signed his own name. If the Ford Foundation claimed that Branch exceeded his authority by paying a sum greater than the agreed-upon $500,000 for each painting, would this be a good defense to a suit by Sothebys? No! Branch had actual authority to pay up to $500,000 and apparent authority beyond that, since he had acted for the Ford Foundation on prior occasions. The Ford Foundation must pay for the painting. Their sole recourse lies against Branch for exceeding his actual authority. If Vanderbilt refuses to pay for the Van Gogh, will Alworth be liable? Yes! Sothebys may sue Alworth because he signed the contract in his own name. The prudent move for Alworth would have been to disclose Vanderbilt's identity and produce the agency contract with Vanderbilt. Sothebys may then proceed against either Alworth or Vanderbilt, but most likely will choose the deepest pocket to assure themselves of collecting payment. If Alworth paid for the painting, would he have any recourse against Vanderbilt? Yes! Alworth would be entitled to sue Vanderbilt for indemnification of the loss Alworth suffered because of Vanderbilt's breach of duty.

A principal is not liable for the unauthorized acts of an agent in cases where the third party has a duty to inquire about the agent's actual authority when that authority is not apparent. A third party who takes it for granted that the agent possesses the authority to contract and is not justified in so relying, will have no recourse against the principal, but will be restricted to recovering from the agent alone.

Wen Kroy Realty Co. v. Public National Bank & Trust Co.
260 N.Y. 84, 183 N.E. 73 (1932)

Wen Kroy Realty Company sued Public National Bank & Trust Company for permitting Moses Silverman to negotiate a check and convert the funds to his own use when they could have easily verified Silverman's authority to act.

Moses Silverman was the president of both the Wen Kroy Realty Company and the Silfo Amusement Company. Silverman indorsed a check made out to Wen Kroy Realty by placing his signature on the back of the check as president and then requesting his son to sign as secretary, a position which the son did not hold. Silverman then deposited the check in the account of Silfo Amusement Company. After it had cleared and the funds were credited to the account, Silverman withdrew the amount of the check and appropriated the same to his own use. Wen Kroy Realty argues that the bylaws of the corporation gave only the treasurer the power to deposit and transfer corporate funds. The treasurer's signature, alone, is on file with the bank. The bank contends that inherent in the managerial duties of a corporate president is the power to deposit and withdraw corporate funds.

The issue is whether Silverman possessed apparent authority to deposit, withdraw, and convert corporate funds for his own use.

The court held that Silverman's act of conversion was unauthorized and that the bank was not justified in relying on his position as president of the corporation in permitting him to convert the funds for his own use. This is true because the bank had the means to verify Silverman's authority by checking the signature cards. This would have shown the treasurer as the only one with the authority to deposit or withdraw corporate funds.

The court stated,

> It is true that "the principal is often bound by the act of his agent in excess or abuse of his actual authority but this is only true between the principal and third persons, who believing and having a right to believe that the agent was acting within and not exceeding his authority, would sustain loss if the act was not considered that of the principal." (Citations.)

Here, the bank had no right to believe that Silverman was acting within his authority because a third party may not rely on an agent's apparent authority when he or she possesses the means to verify that agent's actual authority. Judgment for Wen Kroy.

Tort Liability

A principal is liable for the torts committed by his or her agent if the tort is committed within the scope of employment—that is, if it is related to the business at hand. Principals may contract for liability insurance to minimize their risk and to avoid paying for the damages out of the profits of the business.

EXAMPLE

Luis Manulto is a construction worker who was hired by Valenti Construction Company. Currently, Luis is working on the forty-fourth floor of an office building in downtown Houston. Manulto has his toolbox at his feet, but when someone calls him abruptly, he accidentally knocks it off the beam. The toolbox falls onto a pedestrian walkway that was covered by a heavy plastic grating. Linda Anderson, who was walking through the passageway at the time, is severely injured. Who is liable for her injuries? Linda may sue both Luis Manulto (agent) and Valenti Construction Company (principal). Manulto acted negligently in knocking over the toolbox. Valenti Construction Company is liable for Manulto's negligence because it occurred during his scope of employment; the accident related directly to the business at hand.

Suppose at lunch time, Manulto stops in across the street to drown his sorrows and a patron comments, "I saw the whole episode, and it was a real stupid thing you did." Manulto, angered by the patron's comments, punches him in the face causing the patron to suffer a fractured nose and a concussion. Is the principal liable for Manulto's acts? No! Valenti Construction Company is not liable for Manulto's tort of assault and battery because it did not occur within the scope of employment—the tort was not related to the business at hand. Manulto will be solely liable.

Home Telephone & Electric Co. v. Branton
7 S.W.2d 627 (Tex.) 1928

W. A. Branton sued Home Telephone for injuries sustained as a result of an assault and battery committed by Paul Beardon, an agent of Home Telephone.

Home Telephone & Electric erected a telephone pole, guy wire, and anchor on property belonging to W. A. Branton without his permission. Branton contacted Paul Beardon, the local manager for Home Telephone, on several occasions, and asked him to remove the telephone equipment. Beardon repeatedly assured Branton that he would, but never did. Subsequently, the two met on the street. An argument ensued during which Branton called Beardon a liar. Beardon punched Branton, causing him to sustain injuries.

The issue is whether Home Telephone is responsible for the injuries Branton suffered. This issue will turn on whether Beardon committed the tort of assault and battery during his scope of employment.

The court held,

The rule of *respondeat superior* applies, and renders a master liable to a third person assaulted by a servant of the master while acting within the scope of the servant's employment. The rule arises out of the relation of superior and subordinate, and must necessarily be coextensive with that relation and ceases when the relation ceases. Whenever the very nature of the employment expressly or impliedly authorizes the servant to use force, and in the exercise of that authority he negligently or willfully uses more force than is necessary to further his master's business and thereby injures a third person, the master is clearly liable. On the other hand, where the act of the servant is not in the furtherance of the master's business, or for the accomplishment of the object for which he is employed, but is performed as resentment of insults, or in the furtherance of personal animosities of the servant, the master is not liable. (Citations.)

Here, Beardon's actions were not within his scope of employment; that is, they were not related to the business at hand. The court reasoned,

Beardon was not engaged in the erection of the telephone pole upon appellee's [Branton's] land, nor in the removal thereof when the assault occurred. The assault, in and of itself, was not necessarily linked to, and did not have the effect either of continuing the alleged trespass or removing it from the appellee's land. While the erection of the telephone pole was the remote cause of the difficulty, it was too remote to connect the appellee with it.

Judgment for Home Telephone.

A principal is also liable for the fraud or misrepresentations committed by an agent where the principal has placed the agent in a position which leads people to believe that the agent has the apparent authority to make certain actual representations.

EXAMPLE Keith Stewart, a representative of Super Duper Vacuum Company, calls on Thelma Williams at her house. At first, Thelma is reluctant to make a purchase, but Stewart convinces her when he makes the false representation that this household vacuum cleaner will also clean basements and garages, with the purchase of certain attachments. He does this intentionally to get the sale. Thelma purchases the vacuum cleaner as well as the attachments. When her husband comes home, she gives him a demonstration in the living room, where the vacuum cleaner works perfectly. Then using the attachments, Thelma's husband attempts to clean the garage floor. The machine breaks down. Thelma and her husband sue Super Duper Vacuum Company and Keith Stewart for fraud. Super Duper never instructed Stewart to make false statements of fact and never advertised its vacuum cleaner for anything more than household use. Who will be responsible for the fraud? Both Super Duper and Keith Stewart. Super Duper is liable for its agent's fraudulent representations because it placed Stewart in a position where people would reasonably believe that he had the authority to make such a statement. Super Duper may seek indemnification from Stewart because of his breach of duty of loyalty. Stewart breached the duty by exceeding his authority through the making of statements which were false and unauthorized.

Ratification of an Agent's Unauthorized Acts

Ratification is the approval or sanction given by the principal to the unauthorized acts of an agent. The principal may ratify the unauthorized contracts made by the agent as well as the torts committed by the agent. The following requirements are necessary for ratification:

1. Agent acts in excess of or without authority
2. Principal is made aware of all important facts
3. Principal ratifies entire act, not part of it
4. Ratification must be made in the same manner as the authority given to the agent

Ratification may be implied when a principal fails to condemn an agent's acts within a reasonable time after the principal acquires knowledge of all of the important facts. Once the principal ratifies the agent's contractual acts and the third party is notified, a contract exists between the principal and the third party which the principal is now legally obligated to perform. When notice is conveyed to a third party that the principal assumes all responsibilities for an agent's torts, the principal will be liable for the injuries sustained by that third party.

EXAMPLE Christopher Evans is a salesclerk in Montclair's Electronics Store. Evans is greeted one morning by an enthusiastic salesman offering to sell the store two hundred videotapes on consignment. Evans believes the sale of video movies will greatly enhance the store's business, especially the sale of its video players and recorders. Evans signs the contract on behalf of Montclair even though he has no authority to do so. When apprised of Evans's actions, Montclair believes it to be a smart move and notifies the salesman of his approval. If Montclair changes his mind and claims Evans's acts were not authorized, who will be responsible, Evans or Montclair? Evans was originally liable for breaching his duty of loyalty by exceeding the authority given to him. But, once Montclair ratified Evans's actions, Evans is no longer liable. Montclair will be solely liable to the third party—the videotape distributor. Would it be the same if Evans advised Montclair of his unauthorized act and Montclair said nothing? Yes! Ratification may be implied by silence, if the principal fails to disaffirm responsibility for the agent's acts after learning all the facts. Would Montclair be liable to the videotape distributor if he immediately notified them that he would not assume liability for Evans's unauthorized acts? It would depend on whether it was the usual practice in the trade for a salesclerk to order new merchandise. If so, Montclair would be liable because Evans acted with apparent authority. If it was not the usual practice, then the salesman should have known that a salesclerk does not possess the authority to contract with a new concern and the owner should have been consulted.

LIABILITY OF THIRD PARTIES

A third party is liable only to the principal, whether the principal is disclosed, partially disclosed, or undisclosed. A third party is not liable to an agent unless the agent signs the contract in his or her own name.

EXAMPLE In the prior example concerning the Sothebys art auction, if Sothebys refused to sell the painting to Alworth after Alworth's bid had been accepted and a contract had been signed by Alworth and Sothebys, then either Alworth or Vanderbilt, the undisclosed principal, could enforce the contract. Alworth has the right to enforce the contract against Sothebys even though he is an agent, because he signed the contract in his own name. The fact that he is personally liable on the contract also gives him the right to enforce it.

TERMINATION OF AN AGENCY

An agency relationship may terminate in the following ways:

Fulfillment of purpose
Unfulfilled condition
Mutual agreement
Revocation of authority
Operation of law

Fulfillment of Purpose

The authority of an agent hired for a specific term of employment, as in an employee-employer relationship, will terminate upon the expiration of that term. An agency relationship created for the fulfillment of a specific purpose will terminate when that purpose is completed.

EXAMPLE Jonathan Murrow, a lawyer, was engaged by Marvelous Mini-Bikes, Inc., to represent it in several product liability suits. Murrow hired Timothy Hines, a paralegal, to assist him by researching the numerous cases in point and writing a legal memorandum of the principles of law applicable to the issues presented. Hines was hired for two years, by which time Murrow figured the suits would be settled. What is the status of the agency relationships created and when will they terminate? Jonathan Murrow is a special agent hired by Marvelous Mini-Bikes, and is free to use his own methods to handle the case. This agency will terminate when all of the product liability suits against Marvelous Mini-Bikes have been settled. Timothy Hines is an employee of Jonathan Murrow. Hines must follow Murrow's instructions with regard to the work he undertakes. This agency relationship will expire at the end of the two-year term of employment.

Unfulfilled Condition

The creation of an agency relationship may be conditioned on the happening of an event. If the condition precedent fails, the agency will not be created. An agency may also be created with its continued existence dependent on the fulfillment of a condition subsequent. If this condition should fail, the agency will be terminated.

EXAMPLE George Larsen applied to Chevrolet for a franchise in order to open a dealership. Confident that his request would be approved, Larsen called Kenneth Washburn and asked him to be a sales agent for the new dealership if the franchise was approved. If the franchise is approved, the condition precedent has been met and an agency relationship has been created between Larsen and Washburn. If not, there will be no agency relationship. Suppose the franchise is approved and Larsen hires Washburn on the condition that Washburn sell seventy cars each year. During the first two years of his employment, Washburn meets his quota, but in the third year he sells only fifty-seven cars and is dismissed. Has he any recourse? No! Washburn's agency terminated because he failed to continue to meet the required condition.

Mutual Agreement

An agency contract can be terminated, like any other contract, by the mutual agreement of the parties. This termination is valid even if the contract had called for a longer term of employment.

Revocation of Authority

An agent's authority may be revoked if the duration of the contract is indefinite or if no time limit has been specified. The principal may also revoke an agent's authority for cause where the agent has breached one of the duties owed. The agent must be notified that his or her authority is revoked. If the agency contract was in writing, then the revocation must also be in writing. Under other circumstances, it may be oral. This notice is effective when the agent receives it.

Notice of termination by revocation or mutual agreement must also be communicated to third persons who have dealt with the principal through the agent. Otherwise, the principal will be liable to third persons who contract with the agent. The principal's liability is based on the agent's apparent authority to act based on prior dealings which the third party is justified in believing. Third parties who have dealt with the agent on prior occasions must be sent actual notice of termination. This becomes effective when the third party receives it. For all other third parties, the principal's duty to notify may be satisfied by publishing a statement regarding termination of the agent's authority in a newspaper.

EXAMPLE | Irving Kaufman was the managing agent for the Barons, a singing group that performed at clubs and weddings. When it came time to renew his contract, Kaufman demanded that his commission be increased from 10 percent to 15 percent of the band's gross earnings. The Barons informed him they would consider his request, but subsequently informed him that they would not accede to his request, and terminated his agency. Infuriated by their reply, Kaufman, who was in the process of negotiating with several clubs for bookings, informed each of the clubs that the Barons would perform on the dates requested for $250 less than their usual price. Kaufman said, "They're glad to get the work." The Barons were familiar with these particular clubs, but never informed them of the termination of Kaufman's employment. Are they bound to perform at the clubs for the lower fee? Yes! The Barons, as principals, have a duty to inform the clubs of Kaufman's termination. Otherwise, as in the case here, the clubs are justified in relying on Kaufman's apparent authority because they have dealt with the Barons through him on past occasions.

Operation of Law

An agency may terminate by operation of law in the following ways:

Bankruptcy of the principal or the agent will terminate the agent's authority in financial transactions

Insanity or death of either the principal or the agent

Destruction or loss of the subject matter, if the agency was created for a purpose related to that subject matter

Enactment of a new law which makes it illegal for the agent to exercise his or her authority

EXAMPLE | Billy Watts is a salesman for Atomizer, which manufactures a sophisticated gas boiler predicated on principles of atomic energy. The boiler has been installed in many residential houses since its inception two years ago. Suddenly, a number of fires occur in houses that have an Atomizer boiler. The fires are caused by explosions within the boiler itself. The Consumer Product Safety Commission and the Federal Trade Commission pass regulations prohibiting the sale of gas boilers manufactured by Atomizer. What effect do these regulations have on Billy Watts's position with Atomizer? The agency relationship between Billy Watts and Atomizer is terminated due to the enactment of a law which prohibits the sale of Atomizer's boiler, which is what Watts is employed to do.

REVIEW QUESTIONS

1. When is an agent personally liable?
2. Under what circumstances will a principal be liable for an agent's torts?
3. What are the requirements for ratification?
4. When will an undisclosed principal be liable for his or her agent's acts?
5. Can a principal ratify a contract even though he or she is silent?
6. In what way can an agency relationship be terminated?
7. List the four ways an agency can be dissolved by operation of law.
8. Baker entered into an agency contract with two separate real estate brokers, Wheeler and Fairchild, giving each of them authority to sell property he owned. He did not advise either one of them of the other's agency. Eventually Wheeler produced a ready, willing, and able buyer who entered into a contract with Baker. At a later date, Fairchild procured a prospective purchaser unaware that the real estate had already been sold by Wheeler. In a suit for a commission, will Fairchild be successful because he did not have notice of any revocation of his agency? Ahern v. Baker, 34 Minn. 98, 24 N.W. 341 (1885).
9. Lenheim managed a store for his brother and acted as his brother's purchasing agent. A fire consumed the store in July. After this date, Lenheim's agency was terminated by his brother. Claflin contracted with Lenheim in November and December, unaware that the agency had been terminated. In a suit by Claflin for the unpaid price, will Lenheim's brother be responsible for the goods sold to Lenheim even though the agency was terminated? Claflin v. Lenheim, 66 N.Y. 301 (1876).
10. Shoenthal was hired as manager of a clothing store operated by Ruth Shops, Inc. The letter confirming this employment was signed by Aaron Bernstein, an agent of Ruth Shops. Subsequently, Shoenthal was fired without just cause. He

sued Bernstein personally. Although Bernstein signed his name without designating his agency, the letter was written on Ruth Shops stationery. The issue is whether Bernstein is personally liable or whether Shoenthal clearly understood that Bernstein was acting as an agent for Ruth Shops. What result? Shoenthal v. Bernstein, 276 App. Div. 200, 93 N.Y.S.2d 187 (1949).

34

PARTNERSHIPS: FORMATION AND DUTIES

INTRODUCTION

A partnership is a voluntary association of two or more persons who

1. act for each other as agents
2. are involved in a fiduciary relationship (one of trust and confidence)
3. operate a business, trade, or profession for profit
4. share in the profits and the losses of the partnership as well as the partnership property by express or implied agreement.

Simply stated, a partnership is a voluntary association of two or more persons established for profit. Partnerships are governed by the Uniform Partnership Act, which has been adopted in every state except Georgia, Mississippi, Louisiana, and the District of Columbia. A partner is an individual who voluntarily enters into an agreement with one or more individuals to operate a business and to share the resulting profits or losses. A partner is an agent of the partnership. This means that he or she has the right to act on behalf of the partnership. The relationship between the partners is based on principles of agency involving a fiduciary relationship—one of trust and confidence.

Since a partnership is created by contract and in fact is a special kind of a contract, all the rules of contract law apply and all the elements of a contract must be met, including the requirement of capacity. An infant may be a partner. However, since the infant is entering into a partnership, which is a form of business contract, he or she will be liable as a partner, but only up to his or her capital contribution. In the legal sense, the term *person* also includes corporations and other partnerships. A corporation may become a partner in those states where permission has been granted by statutory authority; otherwise corporations lack the requisite capacity. Partnerships may become partners with other partnerships if all of the partners of both partnerships agree. Sharing of profits is evidence of a partnership.

PARTNERSHIP COMPARED TO OTHER LEGAL ENTITIES

A partnership must be distinguished from other legal entities formed for profit, such as corporations, associations, or joint ventures. A partnership may be created without legal formalities, whereas a corporation must be formed with state approval by the filing of a certificate of incorporation. A partnership is not a legal entity for tax purposes. As a result, it may have favorable tax consequences for those persons who would prefer their share of the profits to be taxed as individual income. In certain instances, partnerships may act with greater expediency, since they do not require stockholder approval for action. Partners are personally liable for all the debts of a partnership, whereas stockholders' liability is limited to their investment in the corporation. Partners' unlimited liability may lead to greater borrowing power because they can pledge their individual assets, in addition to those of the partnership, as collateral in consideration for the loan. A partnership's existence is limited to the life of each of the partners, or to their desire to remain voluntarily associated. A corporation's existence is perpetual.

A joint venture is organized for a specific purpose and continues in existence until the purpose is completed, at which time it terminates. A joint venture may be considered a special form of partnership, since all the rules of partnership law apply. Religious, fraternal, charitable, and labor associations are not partnerships because they are not created for the purpose of profit. These organizations include the Knights of Columbus, Masons, Elks, Moose, Kiwanis, Covenant House, Brotherhood of Teamsters, the AFL-CIO, the United Federation of Teachers, and the United Auto Workers.

Ash v. Guie
97 Pa. 493 (1881)

Ash sued the individual members of a Masonic lodge, claiming they were personally liable for the cost of constructing the lodge.

The members of a Masonic lodge wanted to have a temple built for their meetings and affairs. They contracted with Ash to do the construction work. When it was completed, the Masonic lodge did not pay Ash the contract price. Ash sued all of the members of the lodge individually, claiming they were liable as partners. The Masons claim that their club was organized for charitable and social reasons.

The issue is whether the Masonic lodge has the characteristics of a partnership and whether the individual members are responsible for the breach of contract.

The court held that voluntary associations like this Masonic lodge are not partnerships because they are not organized for profit, but rather for charitable and social purposes. The court stated,

Here there is no evidence to warrant an inference that when a person joined the lodge he bound himself as a partner in the business of purchasing real estate and erecting buildings, or as a partner so that other members could borrow money on his credit. The proof fails to show that the officers or a committee, or any number of the members, had a right to contract debts for the building of a temple, which would be valid against every member from the mere fact that he was a member of the lodge.

A voluntary association organized for religious, charitable, benevolent, or social purposes, although not a partnership, can enter into contracts based on the theory of agency where the club is the principal and its officers are its agents. The authority of the officers to act must be set forth in the club's constitution and the action to be taken by the officers must be ratified by the individual members.

In the present case, the court decided,

. . . those who engaged in the enterprise are liable for the debts they contracted, and all are included in such liability who assented to the undertaking or subsequently ratified it. Those who participated in the erection of the building by voting for and advising it, are bound the same as the committee who had it in charge. And so with reference to borrowing money. A member who subsequently approved the erection or borrowing could be held on the ground of ratification of the agents' acts.

Judgment for Guie (Masonic Lodge) on issue of whether the club constituted a partnership. Judgment for Ash on liability of members who voted in favor of the construction contract.

ORGANIZATION OF A PARTNERSHIP

A partnership is a special contract which does not have to be in writing under the statute of frauds unless the partnership is organized for the purpose of selling real estate or otherwise comes under one of the provisions of the statute of frauds. A partnership may be created orally, by implication through the actions of the parties; but most often it is created in writing. A writing is important for the protection of the individual partners in that it evidences the existence of the partnership and sets forth the rights and duties of the partners. This writing is the partnership agreement, which is often referred to as the articles of partnership.

The partnership may choose a name that is either real or fictitious as long as it does not deceive or otherwise mislead the general public. The partnership may use the name of one of the partners, as well. Usually, one of the following is added to the partnership name to distinguish it from a corporation or sole proprietorship: Company, Co., Associates, or Firm.

A partnership must file a certificate of partnership with the county clerk in the county where the partnership intends to have its principal place of business. This rule applies to all partnerships except law firms. The articles of partnership sets forth the rights and duties of each partner.

RIGHTS AND DUTIES OF PARTNERS

A partner has the following basic rights and duties in a partnership:

Make capital contributions
Share in the partnership property
Participate in management
Share in the profits
Duty of loyalty

Capital Contributions

Each partner's share in the profits is determined by the value of his or her contribution. This contribution may be in the form of money, real estate, fixtures, goods, or services.

EXAMPLE Bruno Santino, Casper McCord, and Frederick Weinberger open a nightclub on Bourbon Street, New Orleans, called The Blues Alley, and advertised as the jazziest club on Bourbon Street. The start-up costs for the rental and renovation of the premises, the advertisement, and hiring of Big Al Hirt for their opening night run to $60,000. The club will be open six nights a week for a total of thirty hours a week. The articles of partnership call for the three partners to divide all profits equally. Bruno is required to contribute $25,000 and work one night a week. Casper must contribute $20,000 and work two nights a week and Frederick must contribute $15,000 and work the remaining three nights.

Partnership Property

All property, both real and personal, that is held in the partnership name, bought with partnership funds, or used in the partnership business is presumed to be an asset of the partnership. This presumption can be rebutted, since property held by a partner individually can be loaned or otherwise used in the business. The assets of the partnership are held by the partners as tenants in partnership. Each partner has an equal right to use the partnership assets, but only in connection with the partnership business. If one partner dies, the remaining partners have the right of survivorship to all property held by the partnership. The heirs of the deceased partner have no right to the assets of the partnership, but they must be paid the proportionate value of the assets representing the decedent's interest in the partnership. The heirs are third-party beneficiaries to the partnership agreement.

EXAMPLE If Bruno Santino dies, his heirs have no right to any of the assets of the Blues Alley Nightclub. However, Casper McCord and Frederick Weinberger must pay the heirs the value of Bruno's interest in the partnership on his date of death. If the net assets of the club on Bruno's date of death were determined to be $195,000, Bruno's heirs would be entitled to $65,000. This represents Bruno's one-third share. If Casper and Frederick do not have the $65,000 in cash to pay the heirs, because the nightclub itself represents most of the assets, they may be forced to take out a loan or to liquidate the partnership assets by selling the nightclub. As an alternative, surviving partners might be able to work out an agreement with the heirs to reimburse them for the deceased partner's proportionate share over a period of time, with interest. The prudent thing for partners to do when setting up a partnership is to take out a life insurance policy on each partner in an amount equivalent to their interest in the partnership and pay the premiums from the partnership's assets. The face value of the policy can be increased as the value of the partners' interests grow.

Participate in Management

The articles of partnership delineate the officers and the responsibilities of each. It also stipulates the voting power of each partner. If there is no stipulation, then voting power is considered equal. The articles also specify whether matters must be decided by a simple majority, a two-thirds majority, or by unanimous vote. Routine matters might be decided by a majority vote, whereas special or important matters might require a unanimous vote. Also, the number of partners that must be present to establish a quorum must be set forth in the partnership agreement.

EXAMPLE

In the articles of partnership of the Blues Alley Nightclub, all decisions concerning advertisement or change in the profit-sharing structure require unanimity on the part of all three partners. Frederick Weinberger is designated as president and is in charge of all accounting and record keeping. Casper McCord is the partner in charge of hiring and firing of all personnel. Bruno Santino is in charge of decor, maintenance of premises including the stage and bar, and the ordering of all food and liquor.

Since each partner is an agent of the partnership, he or she has the power to act on behalf of the partnership in such matters as making contracts for employment, for the sale of goods, for the purchase or sale of real estate, and for the rendering of personal services. A partner does not have to have written authority to bind the partnership, even if the contract is required to be in writing, because a partner is both a principal and an agent of the partnership and the articles of partnership will have to be in writing.

EXAMPLE

Marvin Cantuckee and Lee Derby are both licensed brokers. They enter into a partnership to form Cantuckee Derby Real Estate Company. The company attempts to sell houses for individuals by advertising the property, and to aid prospective purchasers in their search for a suitable house. Must these articles of partnership be in writing to satisfy the statute of frauds? No! This business is devoted to personal services, not to the purchase and sale of real estate. If they decided to speculate in real estate, then the articles of partnership would have to be in writing. Would each of the partners need written authority as well? No! Each partner is both a principal and agent of the partnership.

Share in the Profits

The articles of partnership dictate the percentage of the profits that each partner will receive based on the capital contributions made and the services rendered by each partner. Partners shall be liable for the losses of the partnership to the same extent as they share in the profits. If there is no agreement as to profit sharing, then the profits and, impliedly, the losses, shall be divided equally among the partners regardless of the capital contribution made or the time devoted to the partnership business.

EXAMPLE | The Blues Alley partnership agreement provides that all members will share profits and losses equally. The first year the Blues Alley is in the red for $15,000. The second year they turn a profit of $27,000. The partners vote unanimously that Frederick Weinberger should be the full-time manager of the club in return for a 40 percent share in the profits, with Bruno Santino and Casper McCord each receiving 30 percent. In the third year, their profit is $72,000, partly due to the fact that the Super Bowl was played in New Orleans. How much will each of the partners receive? In the first year, each of the partners will be responsible for $5,000 of the loss. In the second year, each partner will receive $9,000 profit. In the third year, Frederick will receive $28,800—40 percent of the profits—while Bruno and Casper each receive $21,600—30 percent of the profits.

The partnership agreement may also provide for salaries to compensate the partners for their individual services, although normally each partner's compensation is determined through profit sharing.

EXAMPLE | The partnership agreement of the Blues Alley is once again amended by unanimous consent. This time it restores equal profit sharing among all three partners, but provides Frederick Weinberger with a salary of $25,000. In the fourth year, the Blues Alley earns $145,000. How much will each partner receive? Frederick Weinberger will be entitled to a salary of $25,000 plus $40,000—an equal share in the remaining $120,000. Bruno Santino and Casper McCord will each receive $40,000.

A partner has the contractual right to assign his or her share in the profits to a third person. For more information on assignments consult Chapter 12, Rights of Third Parties.

All partners have the right to inspect the bookkeeping and accounting records of the partnership to assure themselves that they are receiving a fair distribution of the profits in accordance with the percentages set forth in the articles of partnership.

Duty of Loyalty

A partner as an agent of the partnership must comply with an agent's duty of loyalty and duty to act in good faith. Inherent in these duties are the following: duty to avoid self-dealing; duty not to compete; duty to exercise reasonable business judgment; duty not to exceed authority.

Duty to Avoid Self-Dealing Each partner has a duty of loyalty to the partnership. This means that each partner must act in good faith with regard to all transactions entered into on behalf of the partnership. A partner may buy from or sell to the partnership, but must avoid self-dealing—entering into contracts with the partnership solely for personal benefit. To avoid self-dealing, all pertinent information relating to the purchase or sale should be disclosed to the other partners.

EXAMPLE | Albert Lancaster is one of four partners in Mariner's Harbor Seafood Restaurant. In addition to its dining room, the restaurant has an adjacent facility which sells fresh fish. Mariner's Harbor Seafood contracts to buy huge quantities of fish at rock bottom prices. Lancaster takes advantage of this by secretly ordering additional amounts of fish through the partnership at the same wholesale prices and selling it to the public through the Swordfish Store, which he operates with his brother. Since the Swordfish Store has obtained the fish at such a low price, it is able to compete effectively. The other three partners eventually discover Lancaster's scheme. Have they any recourse against him? Yes! Lancaster is guilty of self-dealing. He has violated his duty of loyalty to the partnership. The partnership may sue him for any loss of profits it has suffered as a result of his breach of duty.

Duty Not to Compete   It is inherent in a partner's duty of loyalty to refrain from engaging in any business which will compete or otherwise affect the partnership in a detrimental manner. This includes a partner's taking advantage of the partnership's business opportunities for his or her own use or profit. A partner has a duty to inform the other partners of all material relating to new business or the operation of the partnership. If a partner is guilty of self-dealing, competing with the partnership, or usurping the partnership's business opportunities, the partner must account for all profits earned at the partnership's expense.

EXAMPLE   Artie Mandel is a partner in Douglas Roofing Company. One day the partnership receives a phone call from Martin Goldstein, who owns five apartment buildings. He asks Artie to inspect the roofs on the five buildings, Artie does so. He finds several major leaks and some structural defects and offers to do the repair work for a price of $60,000. Goldstein agrees. Artie hires five other roofers to help him, and over the course of a summer, working during his free time and on weekends, he completes the contract to Goldstein's satisfaction. The other partners in Douglas Roofing Company learn of the roofing contract after Goldstein has paid Artie the $60,000. Has Douglas Roofing Company any recourse against Artie? Yes! Artie has breached his duty of loyalty to Douglas Roofing Company by taking advantage of the partnership's business opportunity. Artie must account for the profits that Douglas Roofing Company would have earned if it had been allowed to do the work.

Meinhard v. Salmon
249 N.Y. 458, 164 N.E. 545 (1928)

Meinhard sued Salmon for breach of his duty of loyalty in taking advantage of the partnership's opportunity for his own benefit.

Salmon was in the process of negotiating a twenty-year lease with Louisa M. Gerry for the rental of the Hotel Bristol on Forty-second Street and Fifth Avenue in New York when he employed the financial backing of Meinhard to complete the deal. A partnership was formed with Meinhard contributing one-half of the funds required to reconstruct, manage, and operate the hotel. Meinhard was to share in 40 percent of the profits for the first five years and 50 percent for the remaining fifteen years, at which time the lease would expire.

Before the lease expired, Elbridge T. Gerry, the heir of Louisa M. Gerry and now owner of the Hotel Bristol, entered into a long-term lease with a corporation called Midpoint Realty, which was owned by Salmon. Salmon did not advise Meinhard of the new leasing arrangement until after the lease had been signed. Meinhard sued Salmon to make him hold one-half of the lease in trust for him.

The issue is whether Salmon breached his duty of loyalty to Meinhard by taking advantage of the partnership's opportunity for his own benefit.

The court held "one partner may not appropriate to his own use a renewal of a lease, though its term is to begin at the expiration of the partnership. (Citations.)" The problem with Salmon's conduct is he excluded Meinhard ". . . from any chance to enjoy the opportunity for benefit that had come to him alone by virtue of his agency. This chance, if nothing more, he was under a duty to concede. The price of its denial is an extension of the trust at the option and for the benefit of the one whom he excluded." Judgment for Meinhard.

Duty to Exercise Reasonable Business Judgment A partner's duty to act in good faith means that the partner must exercise reasonable care in representing the partnership and in making business judgments on its behalf. However, a partner will not be liable for honest mistakes resulting from his or her judgments if they were reasonable in light of the surrounding circumstances.

EXAMPLE Mark Randall is the managing partner in the accounting firm of Charles, Stanwick, and Mitchell. One day, Randall receives a call from the vice-president of the Raleigh Textile Manufacturing Corporation, who asks Randall if his firm can prepare the appropriate financial statements for inclusion in their annual report. The vice-president explains that over the past year, the corporation has acquired a smaller corporation with huge assets in raw materials. Randall knows that his accounting firm does not specialize in mergers and acquisitions, but decides to accept the offer of Raleigh Textile, figuring a new account of that size would improve his position in the firm. Subsequently, through Randall's inexperience, a faulty financial statement is made. Raleigh Textile is later audited and the government files a lawsuit against it for issuing a false annual accounting report. After paying several fines and penalties, and suffering a loss to its reputation, Raleigh Textile sues Randall's acccounting firm for malpractice. Is the accounting firm liable? Yes! Has the firm any recourse against Randall? Yes! He failed to use reasonable care in accepting work which the firm did not have the experience to handle. This is more than an honest business mistake, since he acted out of self-interest.

Duty Not to Exceed Authority The articles of partnership spell out the managerial responsibilities of each partner. A partner has an obligation not to exceed the authority granted to him or her by the articles of partnership. If a partner exceeds that authority or fails to exercise reasonable judgment in transacting partnership business, the partner is negligent and will be liable for the consequential damages.

EXAMPLE In the prior example of the Blues Alley partnership, it was agreed that all matters of employment required a unanimous vote before entering into a contract. Casper McCord had a few too many drinks one night while enjoying the company of Mandy LaRose. He offered her a lucrative contract to sing at the Blues Alley for three weeks. In the opinion of McCord's partners, Mandy was a bomb. As a result, the Blues Alley suffered a decline in business. The other partners brought a lawsuit to make McCord account for the loss of profits. Is McCord liable? Yes! McCord exceeded the authority given to him under the Blues Alley's articles of partnership. He will be liable as long as his partners express their discontent with his actions and do not ratify the contract.

1. Define partnership.

2. What is the difference between a partnership and the following: corporation, joint venture, and association or club?

3. What are the rights of the individual partners?

4. What are the obligations owed by a partner under his or her duty of loyalty to the partnership?

5. Dr. Witlin was one of forty-five physicians who formed a partnership for the purpose of opening a medical center which they would operate together. After Dr. Witlin died, the surviving partners offered his widow $65,000, which they claimed represented the book value of Dr. Witlin's interest in the partnership. The partnership agreement stated that the determination of the deceased partner's interest should represent its corresponding fair market value. Dr. Witlin's widow claimed that the partnership was in the process of negotiating a sale of the medical center which would place the value of her deceased husband's interest at almost triple the amount offered to her. The widow sued the partnership for the fair market value of her husband's interest, alleging a breach of the partnership duty to act in good faith. The partnership claims she is precluded from maintaining the lawsuit because she had already accepted the partnership's offer. What result? Estate of Witlin, 83 Cal. App. 3d 167, 147 Cal. Rptr. 723 (1978).

6. Lindsey and Stranahan were copartners in a business called J. K. Lindsey & Co. Lindsey managed the business and did more than his share of the work. Lindsey claimed he should be awarded a salary for the reasonable value of the services he rendered. No provision about a salary was made in the partnership agreement. Is Lindsey entitled to a salary in addition to his right to share in the profits earned from the partnership business? Lindsey v. Stranahan, 129 Pa. 635, 18 A. 524 (1889).

7. Berger, Eichler, and Reese drafted, acknowledged, and filed a certificate of incorporation of the Kumaron Co., Inc. Berger contends that Eichler fraudulently induced him to sell his shares in the corporation, shares which Eichler subsequently purchased under the pretense that the partnership was losing money. Berger further asserts that Eichler induced the sale by concealing the fact that he was negotiating with Du Pont for the sale to them of patent rights, and the manufacturing plant. Berger alleges that the corporation is a mere shell and that a partnership actually exists. He brought a lawsuit demanding an accounting of the profits realized on the sale of assets of their business. Eichler claims Berger cannot be a stockholder and then seek a partnership remedy. What result? Berger v. Eichler, 211 App. Div. 479, 207 N.Y.S. 147 (1924).

8. Williams and Pedersen were copartners in a logging business. The partnership agreement did not specify the division of profits between them. Pedersen claimed Williams was away from the logging camp much of the time and that because of these absences, the burden of operating the logging business fell upon him.

Pedersen further claimed that he should receive a greater share of the profits because of the added responsibility forced on him. Williams claimed that since the partnership agreement was silent, both he and Pedersen must divide the profits equally. What result? Williams v. Pedersen, 47 Wash. 472, 92 P. 287 (1907).

9. Latta, Kilbourn, and Osborn were partners in a real estate brokerage. Their partnership agreement stated the purpose of their partnership was to negotiate the sale and purchase of real estate for other individuals. There was no mention in the partnership agreement of giving the partners authority to buy or sell real estate in the partnership's name. On several occasions, the partners purchased property in their individual names. On one occasion, Latta speculated by purchasing real estate with a third party named Stearns. The joint venture was very successful and huge profits were realized. Kilbourn and Osborn sued Latta, claiming that Latta acted without informing them of the speculation and in doing so, he directly competed with the partnership and should account to it for the profits he realized at the partnership's expense. What result? Latta v. Kilbourn, 150 U.S. 524, 14 S.Ct. 201 (1893).

10. Katz and Brewington entered into a partnership wherein Katz contributed capital and services and Brewington contributed only his services. Katz kept the books and accounting records of the business and refused to let Brewington see them. Brewington wanted to know whether the partnership was making any profits, but Katz would not give him this information. Brewington brought a lawsuit requesting enforcement of his right to participate in the management of the partnership, to inspect the partnership's books and records, and to be informed of all pertinent information regarding the partnership. Will his request be granted? Katz v. Brewington, 71 Md. 79, 20 A. 139 (1889).

35

PARTNERSHIPS: DISSOLUTION AND LIABILITIES

LIABILITY OF PARTNERS

Generally

A partnership is liable for the actions of its partners and it will be primarily responsible for the contracts entered into by them. This is because a partner is both a principal and an agent of the partnership. The partners are also jointly and individually liable for the debts incurred by the partnership.

A partnership and the individual partners will be liable for any crime or tort committed by any one of the partners while he or she was engaging in partnership business. However, the partnership and the individual partners are not liable for any debts incurred or crimes or torts committed by a partner outside the scope of the partnership business.

Partners take a risk that one of the other partners may bind the partnership to a contract that may place unlimited liability on the partnership and on themselves as individuals. There is a definite risk when entering into a partnership—that an individual's personal assets may be sold to cover the debts of the partnership. Individuals should be very careful with whom they are entering into a partnership for this very reason. Many individuals take the risk because of their trust and confidence in their partners.

EXAMPLE | Henry Moore, Thomas Colbert, and Richard Clyne are partners in a securities firm called Bull and Bear Investment Company. Henry Moore embezzles $500,000 of investor deposits for speculative trading. He loses a sizable portion of the funds he had embezzled. When the investors find out, they sue the partnership to recover their lost funds. Is the partnership liable? Yes! The partnership is liable for Moore's conversion because it occurred while Moore was engaging in partnership business. If the partnership is unable to repay all of its investors, would the other partners be personally liable? Yes! Thomas Colbert and Richard Clyne are responsible for the tort committed by Henry Moore. They have the right to recoup any monies paid out from Moore because the damages were caused by him. Suppose Thomas Colbert became so upset that he went to a nearby pub for a few drinks and started a fight with another patron wherein Colbert brutalized the other patron. Would the victim of Colbert's assault and battery be able to sue the partnership? No! The fight occurred outside the scope of the partnership's business.

A partnership may be sued in its own name. The summons must contain the name of the partnership and service may be made by personally serving any one of the partners. In order for the partners to be personally liable, they must be named in the summons and each one of them must be personally served.

EXAMPLE

Caesar Brothers company operated a health spa which employed "specialists" to give massages. This service helped to entice members of established health spas to join Caesar's Health Spas. Eventually, the competing health spas offered the same attraction. As a result, the Caesar Brothers' business dwindled and they were forced to close down. They did not return the current membership fees paid. The remaining members of the Caesar Brothers Health Spa sued collectively to get a return of their membership fees.

The summons named Caesar Brothers Company and individually named Tiberius and Augustus, but not Julius. Only Augustus was personally served. The partnership's debts greatly outweight the partnership's assets. After the assets are sold and the proceeds are paid to the members, only Augustus will be personally liable because he was the only partner named on the summons and personally served. Tiberius was named but not served; and Julius was neither named nor served. It would be a violation of their constitutional rights to hold them personally liable if proper notice was not given to them.

If only one of the partners is personally accountable and must pay, his or her recourse lies in the right to contribution from the other partners for their proportionate share of the profits as dictated by the articles of partnership. If the articles of partnership are silent on this matter, the partners' share in the profits and losses will be equal. If this were the case in the previous example, Augustus may look to Tiberius and Julius each for one-third of what he paid out.

A judgment against a partnership must be enforced against the assets of the partnership first, and only when they are depleted are the partner's individual assets subject to the claims of the partnership's creditors.

EXAMPLE

In the previous example about the health spa, assume the debts of the partnership were $350,000 and the assets of the partnership totaled $200,000. The $200,000 would be applied to the debt, leaving the partners jointly liable for the remaining $150,000. Each partner would be liable for $50,000, but the entire $150,000 may be collected from one partner, Augustus. Augustus would then have the right to sue Tiberius and Julius for $50,000 each.

Ham and Gilmore formed a partnership to operate a clothing business. They borrowed $675 from Ham's wife, Sarah. Subsequently Gilmore moved elsewhere, leaving the entire assets of the partnership to Ham.

Ham caused a notice of dissolution to be published in the *Syracuse Daily Standard*. The notice stated, "all the assets are in the hands of the undersigned, and he will settle all accounts with the firm and debts against it." When Sarah Ham requested her husband repay the principal of the loan with interest, he refused in spite of his publication to the contrary. Sarah Ham sued the partnership and Gilmore and her husband individually. This suit was brought seventeen years after the partnership was dissolved. This action was timely because the partnership accounts were never settled. She was awarded over $1,500, which was paid by Gilmore four years later. Gilmore then commenced an action against Ham for his right of contribution for one-half of the debt paid. Gilmore also alleges that Ham conspired with his wife to enable her to get a judgment against the partnership which he (Gilmore) was forced to pay.

The issue is whether Gilmore may maintain an action for contribution or whether the six-year statute of limitations bars such an action.

The court held,

> In the present case all the assets of the concern were left with the defendant, [Ham] and he apparently undertook to pay the debt—close up the business. He has not yet completed his undertaking. Having the assets, it was his duty to apply them to the payment of the debt. He held them in trust for that purpose and they were in amount sufficient. This trust was apparently never repudiated until the commencement of the action by Mrs. Ham. Upon this basis it may be said with some force that the statute is not available to defendant [Ham] as a defense, so far, at least, as the claim of plaintiff [Gilmore] upon the judgment is concerned. Ham was not entitled to be excused from paying his fair share of the debt by raising the statute of limitations as a defense to Gilmore's suit; thus profiting from his own fraud.

> The rule is well settled that if a partnership has been dissolved and the partnership accounts adjusted, and one partner is afterwards obliged to pay an outstanding claim not provided for, he may maintain an action . . . against his copartner for the proportion of it which the latter ought to pay by reason of his joint liability.

Judgment for Gilmore.

Incoming Partner

An incoming partner is not personally responsible for the past debts of the partnership. However, the capital contribution of an incoming partner will be subject to the claims of past debts because once the contribution is made, it becomes an asset of the partnership.

EXAMPLE | George Mason and Paul McGregor are partners in a candy manufacturing company called Sugar Daddy and Associates. In November, Clifford Marshall also becomes a partner in Sugar Daddy. His capital contribution to the company is $20,000. Sugar Daddy is supposed to deliver fourteen tons of candy by the last week in November for sale during the Christmas season. Due to a malfunction in their machinery, they are prevented from doing so. They are sued by several candy distributors and retailers. The damages sustained outweigh the partnership assets. What is the extent of Clifford Marshall's liability? As an incoming partner, he will lose his capital contribution, but will not be personally liable because the contract was made before he became a partner.

Retiring Partners

A retiring partner is liable for present debts as a surety, but not for future debts, as long as notice of his or her retirement was conveyed and actually received by the customers of the partnership. New customers are not entitled to notice because they would not be relying on the retiring partner's presence in the partnership out of past experience.

EXAMPLE | Murray Bloomfeld, Myron Cheninski, and Abe Cohen are partners in Williamsburg Furriers Company. They sell and store expensive furs. After thirty-five years in the business, Cohen decides to retire. Notice is given to all of their regular customers. One night the storage room of the Williamsburg Furriers is vandalized and fifteen fur coats are stolen, ten of which were stored before Cohen retired. The owners of the furs sue Williamsburg Furriers. If the partnership assets are insufficient to meet the damages sustained by the fur owners, will Cohen be personally liable? Yes, but only for the storage contracts entered into while he was a partner. Cohen will not be personally liable for the other five stolen fur coats because he was no longer a partner when owners of these fur coats entered into storage contracts with the partnership and notice of his retirement was properly conveyed.

DISSOLUTION

A partnership's existence is not perpetual like that of a corporation. Rather, it may be dissolved due to a number of factors:

Bankruptcy
Agreement
Death
Withdrawal
Illegality
Lack of capacity

Bankruptcy

Personal insolvency of a partner will not dissolve a partnership. But if the insolvent partner files for bankruptcy, that may dissolve the partnership because inherent in extending credit to a partnership is the guarantee that each of the partners will be individually liable. If one partner is bankrupt then this guarantee no longer exists.

EXAMPLE Clarence McGregor and Peter Kinsella open a video store in a shopping mall in Olympia, Washington. Their immediate expenses include the first month's rent plus two months' rent as security, and the purchase of over two hundred films for inventory with credit extended for only thirty days. After thirty days, the store has sold only fourteen tapes and rented only another twenty-six. The partners agree to bear the losses equally. Meanwhile, McGregor, in the expectation of immediate profits, bought several "puts" stock options which become valuable if the particular stock declines in value. The stock options were purchased on margin just before a bull raid. To buy on margin, a portion of the price is paid and the rest is borrowed from the brokerage company. A person might buy on margin if he or she expected an immediate fluctuation in price. During the stock market rally, McGregor received a margin call from his broker. When he could not come up with the required payment, he filed for bankruptcy. What will happen to his video partnership with Kinsella? It will dissolve by operation of law. Kinsella will become personally liable for all of the partnership's debts and may either continue the video business as sole proprietor or he may discontinue operating the business completely.

Agreement

A partnership may be voluntarily dissolved at any point by the mutual agreement of all partners. Even at the outset, the partners can stipulate in the partnership agreement that the partnership will continue for a definite duration or until the happening of a contingency, at which time the partnership will end. The partners can override the partnership agreement by mutually agreeing to extend the partnership beyond the stipulated duration or to end it beforehand.

EXAMPLE Cynthia Stafford, an English scholar, and Gina Sabatini, a mathematics scholar, form a partnership at the start of their college careers to perform tutorial services in their respective specialties. In their partnership agreement, they stipulate that all profits should be divided equally and that the purpose of the partnership was to defray tuition expenses. Four years later, Cynthia and Gina realize they are very successful at tutoring. By mutual agreement, they decide to open an educational institution for tutoring and to extend the partnership beyond the date in their original agreement. Is this valid? Yes! Cynthia and Gina can amend or override the original partnership agreement and extend the partnership beyond the expiration date. If they chose not to extend the partnership, when would it end? It would automatically dissolve on the last date of their college studies.

Death

Death of a partner terminates the partnership; however, the remaining partners can carry on the business by forming a new partnership, a corporation, or, if there is only one partner left, by continuing the business as a sole proprietorship.

EXAMPLE Samuel Rose, Matthew Green, and Irving Klein form the Diamonds Are Forever Company. After several years of successful operations, Irving Klein dies. The partnership, when it began, had taken out a life insurance policy on Klein tantamount to his interest in Diamonds Are Forever, with the proceeds payable to his heirs. The day after his death, Samuel Rosen and Matthew Green agree to from a new partnership under the same name, to continue the business. Must the assets of the partnership be liquidated? No! If a partnership is dissolved, the remaining partners may form a new partnership but can continue the business with no interruption.

Withdrawal

Any partner may withdraw from the partnership upon giving the other partners sufficient notice of that intent. Every partner must be apprised of the partner's withdrawal; otherwise the withdrawing partner will be liable, along with the rest of the partners, for any contract entered into or other action engaged in, by a partner who acted without notice.

EXAMPLE | Jennifer Williams, Tina Vitucci, and Bridgette Donat form Waves and Curls, a beauty salon. The three women work together for a number of years. One day during lunch, Jennifer informs Tina that she is leaving the business. Tina saddened, returns to work alone. The next morning, Bridgette opens the salon without notice of Jennifer's departure and orders a series of supplies for the next two months. Subsequently, Bridgette and Tina are forced to cancel the order because they cannot afford to continue operating the salon without Jennifer's assistance. Meanwhile, later that day while giving a permanent to a customer with very fine hair, Tina inadvertently leaves the woman under the dryer too long, and the woman's hair falls out. The irate customer proceeds to call her lawyer. In separate lawsuits brought by the injured customer and the supplier, is Jennifer personally liable as a partner for the ensuing damages, if the partnership's assets are insufficient to satisfy the damages incurred? Jennifer would be personally liable to the supplier because when Bridgette entered into the contract, she did so on behalf of all three partners. She had no notice of Jennifer's withdrawal at the time. Although all partners are generally liable for a tort committed by another partner within the scope of the business, Jennifer is not liable because she gave notice to Tina that she was withdrawing from the partnership.

The partnership agreement may provide a buy-out provision allowing the remaining partners to buy out the withdrawing or retiring partners without dissolving the partnership. A partner may also be forced to withdraw from the partnership because of a breach of the duty of loyalty. A breach of the duty of loyalty may occur where a partner is guilty of self-dealing, has taken advantage of a partnership business opportunity, did not exercise reasonable care in making business judgments, or exceeded the authority given to him or her by the articles of partnership.

EXAMPLE | Edward Morgan, a wealthy entrepreneur, had a great idea: to open a McDonald's franchise on the Long Island Expressway, known as the world's largest parking lot. Unwilling to take the risk alone, Edward Morgan asked two former business associates to operate the franchise with him as partners. The idea proved a great success. Morgan then opened several other franchises by himself along the expressway. Two of the franchises were so close to the one owned by the partnership that the partnership's profits declined severely. Do Morgan's partners have any recourse against him? Yes! They may bring a lawsuit compelling dissolution of the partnership because of Morgan's improper conduct. He has breached his duty of loyalty to the partnership by competing directly against it. He may also be guilty of fraud by intentionally deceiving his partners into taking a major risk and then undermining them for his own benefit. Morgan must account for the loss of profits sustained by the partnership. After dissolution, the other partners may create a new partnership and continue the business without interruption.

Illegality

If a partnership is formed illegally or with an unlawful purpose in mind, or if it is operating legally, but a change in the law renders the business of the partnership unlawful, then the partnership must either comply with the legal requirements of formation, change its type of business, or dissolve the partnership.

EXAMPLE Stanley Kramer and Simon Osborn are partners in Pelts & Felts Company, distributors of baby seal pelts in the northwestern United States. A law is passed prohibiting the sale of baby seal pelts in the United States. What effect does this new law have on the partnership? Pelts & Felts must either change the nature of their business by shipping other types of furs, or dissolve the partnership and liquidate its assets.

Lack of Capacity

A partnership may be dissolved where it is shown that one of the partners no longer possesses the mental capabilities to perform adequately his or her managerial responsibilities.

EXAMPLE Sylvester Claremont and Oscar Kolb are partners in the law firm of Reynolds, Shutt, and Kingman. Claremont is eighty-five years old and oftens runs around the law firm trying to pinch the young secretaries. He also invites clients to lunch, then fails to show up. Kolb is a thirty-four-year-old bachelor, who has become an alcoholic. He has failed to show up for work every other Monday and on the other days, often comes in to work with a hangover. The quality of his work has suffered and his condition sometimes prevents him from making court appearances. The law firm decides to dissolve the partnership because of the incapacity of these two individuals. Can the other members of the firm continue their work without interruption? Yes! The partnership is dissolved because of the senility of Claremont and the inebriated condition of Kolb. A new partnership may be formed by all of the original partners except these two. There is no need to liquidate the partnership, but the capital contribution of Claremont and Kolb must be returned to them. The law firm may continue business without interruption.

WINDING UP

A partnership which is being dissolved may be immediately recreated in the form of a new partnership, and business may be continued without the need for liquidating the partnership's assets. However, if there are no plans by the remaining partners to form a new partnership, or if they cannot afford to buy out a partner who has withdrawn, or pay off a deceased partner's heirs, then the partnership must be dissolved. During the period of winding up, the partnership may continue to operate, as such, only for the following purposes: completing unfinished business; liquidating the assets of the partnership; accounting for all claims made against it.

Peterson v. Eppler et al.
67 N.Y.S.2d 498 (1946)

Peterson brought a lawsuit for the dissolution and winding up of the accounting firm with which he was associated because he was not paid in accordance with the agreement he had with the partnership.

Peterson was a junior partner. His pay was in the form of a fixed monthly salary in addition to a percentage of the net profits earned from the partnership's practice. The agreement between Peterson and the firm provided that as a junior partner, Peterson was to have no further right to share in the partnership property or profits, and that he was to have no right whatsoever to participate in management of the firm's affairs except for those duties occasionally delegated by the "capital partners." The accounting firm alleged that no partnership was created by the agreement.

The issue is whether the agreement between Peterson and the accounting firm constitutes a partnership agreement or a contract of employment.

The court held that the agreement was nothing more than a contract of employment. A partnership is composed of individuals who have co-ownership in the partnership property. Peterson was not a co-owner of the business. He was limited to receiving a salary and a share in the profits from one aspect of the partnership's business. Peterson was restricted from participating in the management of the firm, an integral right of a partner.

The fact that Peterson was referred to as a "junior partner" does not create a partnership. The court held,

> Although the fact that parties to an agreement may refer to their relationship as one of partnership is a circumstance entitled to great weight, it is by no means conclusive. The parties cannot by using the word "partnership" create such a relationship when the contract between them clearly provides that there was to be no community of interest in the business as such and no right to participate in the management of the business. (Citations.)

Peterson is not entitled to a dissolution of the partnership and an accounting of its assets. His remedy for nonpayment is to sue for compensatory damages. Judgment for the partnership of Eppler et al.

DISTRIBUTION OF ASSETS ACCORDING TO PRIORITY

The following priorities exist in the distributions of the partnership's assets. First, the creditors of the partnership are entitled to payment, then the creditors of the individual partners. With regard to the assets of the individual partners, the individual's creditors have preference over the partnership's creditors. Next, the partners' claims will be satisfied if there are assets left. Loans made by a partner to the partnership will be refunded first. Second, the capital contributed by each partner will be returned. If the partnership's assets are insufficient, then each partner will be entitled to a proportionate share of his or her capital contribution. Finally, whatever remains will be distributed to the partners in accordance with their right to share in the profits of the partnership.

EXAMPLE | 1. Nathan Campbell, Benjamin Davis, and Dwight Curtis are partners in the Green Giant Company, publishers of the *Farmer's Weekly*. Due to the recent decline in agriculture, sales of the *Farmer's Weekly* have plummeted. The three partners declare by mutual agreement that the partnership should be dissolved. The total assets of the partnership are $450,000. The debts owed to the general creditors of the partnership amount to $120,000. Nathan Campbell loaned the partnership $30,000 and contributed $70,000 to capital. Benjamin Davis contributed $120,000 to capital and Dwight Curtis contributed $50,000. The partnership agreement provided that the partners would share equally in all profits and losses. How will the partnership's assets be distributed?

Total assets		$450,000
Claims of creditors	$120,000	120,000
		$330,000
Loans		
Nathan Campbell	$ 30,000	30,000
Capital contributions		$300,000
Nathan Campbell	$ 70,000	
Benjamin Davis	120,000	
Dwight Curtis	50,000	
Total capital contributions		240,000
		$ 60,000
Profit sharing		
Nathan Campbell, one-third share	$20,000	
Benjamin Davis, one-third share	20,000	
Dwight Curtis, one-third share	20,000	
Total profit sharing		60,000
		—0—

EXAMPLE | 2. Assume that the monetary value of the partnership's assets after liquidation totaled $270,000. In what priority would the assets be distributed?

Total assets		$270,000
Claims of creditors	$120,000	120,000
		$150,000
Loans		
Nathan Campbell	$30,000	30,000
		$120,000

	Capital Contribution	Amount Distributed from Partnership Assets	Equal Share in Losses	Amount Owed to Partner for Capital Contribution
Nathan Campbell	$70,000	$35,000	$40,000	− $5,000
Benjamin Davis	120,000	60,000	40,000	20,000
Dwight Curtis	50,000	25,000	40,000	− 15,000

The amount remaining from the partnership's assets totaled $120,000 which is one-half the total capital contributions made by the partners. Since the partnership agreement provides that each partner share equally in what remains, then each partner is entitled to one-half of his original capital contribution from the partnership. This depletes the partnership's assets, but it does not relieve the individual partner from personal liability for the debts that remain. Capital contributions become debts of the partnership when they are not repaid, and the individual partners become proportionately liable for these debts. Since the partnership agreement provides that all the partners are equally responsible for all losses or debts, each partner is responsible for one-third of the unpaid capital contributions that remain. Since Benjamin Davis's capital contribution exceeds his proportionate liability by $20,000, the other two partners must reimburse him based on their proportionate liability. Davis must get $5,000 reimbursement from Nathan Campbell and $15,000 reimbursement from Dwight Curtis.

EXAMPLE

3. Assume the following: total assets of the partnership are $255,000; total debts are $330,000; no loans were made by any of the partners; the capital contribution of each partner was the same; each partner shares equally in all profits and losses; Nathan Campbell has $45,000 in personal assets and $30,000 in liabilities; Benjamin Davis has $10,000 in personal assets and no liabilities; and Dwight Curtis has $60,000 in personal assets and $10,000 in liabilities. What is the priority of distribution?

Total assets		$255,000
Claim of creditors $330,000		330,000
		− $75,000
Partner's liability		
Nathan Campbell	− $25,000	
Benjamin Davis	− 25,000	
Dwight Curtis	− 25,000	
Total liabilities of partners		− $75,000
		—0—

Partner's Individual Assets

Nathan Campbell		
Assets	$45,000	
Creditors' claims	30,000	
Total assets available to offset partnership debts		$15,000
Total proportionate share of partnership debt		25,000
		− $10,000
Benjamin Davis		
Assets	$10,000	
Creditors' claims	—0—	
Total assets available to offset partnership debts		$10,000
Total proportionate share of partnership debt		25,000
		− $15,000
Dwight Curtis		
Assets	$60,000	
Creditors' claims	10,000	
Total assets available to offset partnership debts		$50,000
Total proportionate share of partnership debt		25,000
		$25,000

Since all partners are jointly and severally liable for the partnership's debts, and since $25,000 of partnership debts remain unpaid, the creditors may sue Dwight Curtis for that amount because he is the only partner who is still solvent. He must pay the $25,000 and then look to the other two partners for his right of contribution—$10,000 from Nathan Campbell and $15,000 from Benjamin Davis. Both of these partners are currently insolvent. Curtis's claim against them will be satisfied if and when they become solvent. If either or both of the two insolvent partners files for bankruptcy, Curtis's claims will go unsatisfied because a person's debts are discharged in bankruptcy and bankruptcy is a defense to a suit for breach of contract or right of contribution.

REVIEW QUESTIONS

1. What are the liabilities of an incoming and retiring partner?
2. In what ways can a partnership be dissolved?
3. What is a buy-out agreement?
4. What claims have priority in the distribution of the partnership's assets?
5. Barclay and Barrie were partners in the manufacture and sale of goods. Barrie subsequently suffered a stroke and was stricken with paralysis. This prevented him from fulfilling his duties in the business. Barclay commenced an action for dissolution of the partnership by reason of the fact that his copartner had become incapacitated so as to prevent him from continuing in his duties concerning the management and operations of the partnership. Barrie contested the request for dissolution, arguing that his incapacity was not an incurable and perpetual disability. But Barclay contended that the disability was more than temporary and the recovery is remote. What result? Barclay v. Barrie, 209 N.Y. 40, 102 N.E. 602 (1913).
6. Woofruff and Robinson were partners in a firm which they terminated pursuant to articles of dissolution signed by both parties. The articles of dissolution ordered the liquidation of the partnership's assets. Six months later, Robinson entered into a contract to purchase supplies from Hart and Youngs, under the partnership's name, for almost $1,500. Woodruff had no knowledge of the contract. The issue is whether Robinson had the power to bind Woodruff to a contract in the partnership name after the partnership has been dissolved. What result? Hart v. Woodruff, 24 N.Y. 510 (1881).
7. Bowen was engaged in the business of importing and selling fancy goods. He formed a partnership with Nichols under which it was agreed that Bowen's assets would be transferred to the partnership. Bowen represented to Nichols that the partnership was to assume Bowen's liabilities, but that his assets would exceed his liabilities by at least $30,000. This amount would become his capital contribution. As it turned out, Bowen's assets barely exceeded the debts that the partnership assumed. Since Bowen's assets and liabilities were transferred to the partnership, is Nichols, as an incoming partner, liable for the debts? Could Nichols have claimed that he was defrauded and dissolve the partnership because of Bowen's false representations? If Nichols continues as a partner, does he

forfeit his right to dissolve the partnership on the basis of fraud? Arnold v. Nichols, 64 N.Y. 117 (1876).

8. Cameron and Haun sold building materials and lumber to the partnership formed by La Porte and Voelxen for an amount in excess of $7,000. Subsequently, Voelxen withdrew from the partnership and it was dissolved. La Porte continued to run the business on his own. Cameron and Haun agreed to extend the time for payment of the unpaid debts. Voelxen claimed that La Porte, by taking over the business assumed all of the partnership's obligations. Voelxen also asserted that Cameron and Haun released him from his responsibilities for the debt by extending the time for reimbursement after the partnership had been dissolved. Cameron and Haun claim they had no knowledge of the dissolution until after they had extended the time for reimbursement and that Voelxen never transferred his interest in the partnership property, consisting of building materials and lumber, to La Porte. What result? Cameron & Haun v. La Porte, 216 App. Div. 579, 215 N.Y.S. 543 (1926).

9. Horn's Crane Service supplied materials and services to a partnership comprised of Prior, Cook, and Piper, pursuant to a written contract. The partnership failed to pay for the materials and services when billed. Horn's Crane Service sued Prior and Cook individually for breach of contract. They claim a creditor cannot sue a partner individually until all of the partnership's assets are depleted. Here, the partnership was not dissolved or insolvent. What result? Horn's Crane Service v. Prior, 182 Neb. 94, 152 N.W.2d 421 (1967).

10. Respass and Sharp were partners in crime. They were bookies who accepted wagers on horse races. On Sharp's death, almost $5,000 remained in his personal bank account that was attributed to their partnership. Respass sued Sharp's estate for his half share of the profits. The estate refused to account to Respass for half of the money in the bank account. Has Respass any recourse? Central Trust & Safe Co. v. Respass, 112 Ky. 606, 66 S.W. 421 (1902).

36

LIMITED PARTNERSHIPS

INTRODUCTION

Up to this point, we have been speaking about a partnership formed by general partners. This is called a general partnership. A general partnership is an individual who actively participates in the management and operation of the partnership and who has unlimited liability for the debts of the partnership. A general partner may also be required to make a capital contribution. The other form of partnership is called a limited partnership.

A limited partnership consists of one or more general partners and one or more limited partners. The general partners, as was just explained, actively manage the partnership and have unlimited liability for the debts incurred by the partnership. The limited partners make capital contributions; are liable for the partnership debts, but only up to the amount of their capital contribution; and do not in any way participate in the management of the partnership. Individuals, corporations, or other partnerships become limited partners for investment purposes. If they surmise that a business has potential for expansion and success, but the business is lacking adequate funds, they may form a limited partnership to provide the business with the funding. In return, the limited partner will receive a fixed rate of return on the capital he or she contributed.

A limited partnership must be formed in accordance with state statutes. Every state but Delaware, Louisiana, and the District of Columbia have adopted the Uniform Limited Partnership Act. There is also a Revised Uniform Limited Partnership Act which has modified the original act and which was undertaken for the purpose of replacing the original act.

LIMITED PARTNERSHIP CERTIFICATE

A certificate attesting to the formation of a limited partnership must be signed and sworn to in writing. The certificate should set forth:

1. The name of the limited partnership
2. The type of business the partnership plans to engage in
3. The duration of the partnership
4. The name and address of each partner with his or her title of general or limited partner specifically designated
5. The capital contribution of each limited and general partner
6. The percentage of the profits each general partner will receive
7. The rate of return a limited partner will receive on his or her capital contribution and the method by which it will be made
8. The right of the limited partner to assign his rights and/or duties to a third person

The name of the limited partnership must not contain the name of a limited partner, otherwise that limited partner may be liable as a general partner.

RIGHTS OF A LIMITED PARTNER

Limited partners shall have the right to limited liability up to their capital contribution as long as they do not take an active part in the management or operations of the partnership.

A limited partner shall have the same rights as a general partner in regard to the following:

1. Inspecting the books and accounting records of the partnership
2. Being informed of all pertinent information affecting the partnership
3. Seeking a court order dissolving the partnership and winding up its assets

A limited partner shall also have the right to a return of his or her original contribution to capital

1. When the partnership is dissolved
2. On the date specified in the limited partnership certificate
3. On six months notice in writing if no provision exists for (1) and (2). This notice must be given to all of the partners.

DISSOLUTION

On dissolution of a limited partnership, the following priority of claims will be adhered to in the distribution of the partnership's assets:

1. Creditors' claims
2. Limited partners' claims
   a. Return on capital contributed
   b. Capital contribution
3. General partners' claims
   a. Loans
   b. Profit sharing
   c. Capital contribution

The limited partner's claims are subordinate to the claims of other creditors, but are given preference over all the claims of the general partners.

EXAMPLE

Jose Rodriguez, Manuel Ortiz, and Juan Rivera form a limited partnership for the sale of used cars. Rodriguez and Ortiz each contribute $10,000 and agree to be responsible for the management and operations of the business. Juan Rivera contributes $50,000 as a limited partner. A certificate of limited partnership is signed and sworn in writing to this effect. The certificate sets forth the annual rate of return guaranteed Juan Rivera: 15 percent of his capital contribution—$7,500—to be paid every year on June 30. Rodriguez and Ortiz will split the remaining profits equally. On June 30 of the following year, Rodriguez and Ortiz inform Rivera that the partnership is operating at a loss and they cannot afford to pay him at this time. Rivera brings a lawsuit seeking a dissolution of the partnership by court order and an accounting of the financial operations of the partnership. The accounting produces the following results: partnership assets, $137,500; partnership liabilities, $70,000. How will the distribution of assets be made?

Total assets		$137,500
Creditors' claims 70,000		70,000
Total creditors' claims		$67,500
Limited partners' claims		
Juan Rivera		
Return on capital contributed $7,500		
Capital contribution $50,000		
Claim of limited partner		$57,500
		$10,000
General partners' claims		
Jose Rodriguez		
Loans –0–		
Capital contribution $5,000		
(50% of remainder)		
Profit sharing –0–		
Manuel Ortiz		
Loans –0–		
Capital contribution $5,000		
(one-half of amount contributed)		
Profit sharing –0–		
Total claims of general partners		$10,000
		–0–

1. What is a limited partnership?
2. What information must be contained in the limited partnership certificate?
3. What are the rights and liabilities of a limited partner?
4. What is the priority in the distribution of assets upon the dissolution of a limited partnership?

37

CORPORATE FORMATION

INTRODUCTION

A corporation is a legal entity, organized for profit, with limited liability in accordance with state law. Capital stock is issued by a corporation to raise money and to determine ownership of corporate assets. Shareholders are the individuals who purchase the capital stock of a corporation and who own the corporation. Shareholders are not principals or agents; they do not have the power to bind the corporation in any way. Their liability is limited to their investment in the capital stock of the corporation. The board of directors is elected by the shareholders. The board is responsible for managing the corporation for the shareholders. The board of directors appoints officers to manage the day-to-day activities of the corporation. The officers of the corporation include the president, vice-president, secretary, and treasurer.

FORMATION

A corporation is formed when individuals agree to invest in the proposed corporation by purchasing stock subscriptions from promoters. Promoters issue a prospectus to persuade investors to become owners in the proposed corporation. A prospectus is a statement, made by the promoters of a corporation, that invites the public to purchase stock subscriptions. A stock subscription is a contract, entered into by the promoters and subscribers, wherein subscribers agree to pay a certain amount of money per share in return for a designated number of shares in the corporation when the proposed corporation has become legally incorporated. At that point, the stock subscriptions become shares of capital stock and the subscribers become shareholders.

CERTIFICATE OF INCORPORATION

The formation of a corporation requires legal formalities. A certificate of incorporation must be filed with the secretary of state in the state of incorporation. A certificate of incorporation is a document which gives rise to corporate status when filed with the secretary of state along with the filing fee. In addition, yearly fees must be paid by corporations to the state for the privilege of doing business. This certificate is conclusive evidence, when filed and approved, that all conditions precedent have been met and a corporation is formed. The person filing the certificate of incorporation is an incorporator. The following is an explanation of each provision contained within the certificate of incorporation. This will be followed by a sample certificate of incorporation.

Corporate Name

The name must be cleared with the secretary of state to ascertain whether it is suffficiently different so as not to defraud or confuse anyone. It must include one of the following: Inc., Incorporated, Corp., Corporation, Ltd., Limited, Co., Company (as long as it is not written "_____ and Company," which would tend to indicate a partnership).

Purpose for its Formation

The purpose must be lawful. Since the corporation will be restricted to the purposes set forth, this provision should be sufficiently broad and flexible to include all the areas in which the corporation may wish to become involved.

Location of Corporate Offices

The corporation must have an office where the secretary of state in the state may contact it. In most states, the corporate headquarters may be located outside the state. The promoters may choose to incorporate in a particular state, even though they do not intend to do business there, because of certain tax advantages or the lack of restrictions.

Capital Stock

The aggregate number of shares which the corporation shall have the authority to issue must be set forth, as well as the class of stock, common or preferred, and its par value. The capital stock of the corporation may either be fixed at a certain value (par value) below which it may never fall, or it may have no designated minimum amount (no par value).

Share Transfer Restrictions

Shareholders may be restricted from freely transferring shares, especially in a closely held corporation. Restrictions regarding shareholders' freedom to transfer shares must be placed on the stock certificate. Article 8 of the UCC provides that good-faith purchasers who acquire a stock certificate are not bound by transfer restrictions that do not appear on the face of the certificate.

Designation of the Secretary of State as Agent

The secretary of the state in which incorporation takes place must be designated as the corporation's agent upon whom service of process may be made. Service of process refers to the serving of a summons and complaint on the corporation.

Directors

The number of directors must be set forth, along with the quorum and voting requirements for approval of transactions confronting the board of directors at their meetings.

Shareholders

The quorum and voting requirements of shareholders must be delineated in order that the shareholders can conduct a proper meeting.

Dividends

An accounting of earned surplus with possible distribution to shareholders shall be made at regular intervals.

Establishment of an Accounting Period

The corporation must select a fiscal or calendar tax year to account for income received.

Requirements of an Incorporator

An incorporator must be a human being eighteen years of age or older.

CERTIFICATE OF INCORPORATION OF PRACTICAL BUSINESS LAW, INC.

Under the Business Corporation Law of the State, the undersigned, for the purpose of forming a corporation pursuant to the Business Corporation Law of the State certify:

Section 1. The name of the corporation shall be Practical Business Law, Incorporated.

Section 2. The purposes for which it is to be formed are: to publish a college textbook for students and to do everything necessary, suitable, or proper for the accomplishment of any of these purposes or of any objective incidental to or connected with any of these purposes.

Section 3. The offices of the corporation shall be located at 271 Tennis Court, in Fun City, County of Kings, in the state.

Section 4. The aggregate number of shares which shall be authorized and which the corporation shall have the authority to issue is Two Thousand (2,000) shares at no par value, all of one class which shall be designated as common stock.

Section 5. The shareholders shall not transfer, sell, assign, pledge, or otherwise dispose of their shares of the stock of the corporation without first obtaining the written consent of the other shareholders to the sale or disposition, or without first offering to sell the shares to the corporation at a value to be determined by an arbitrator to be selected by the American Arbitration Association. The offer shall be in writing and shall be open for a period of 30 days. If the corporation fails to accept the offer within that period, a second offer, also in writing, shall then be made to sell the shares on similar terms, to the other shareholders, first on a pro rata basis, then individually. This offer shall also remain open for a period of 30 days following the expiration of the offer to the corporation. If the offer is not accepted either by the corporation or the other shareholders, the shares shall thereafter be freely transferable.

Section 6. Upon the death or retirement of any shareholder, the remaining shareholders shall purchase and the estate of the decedent shall sell all the decedent's shares in the corporation, now owned or hereafter acquired, and, in the case of the shareholder's retirement, the remaining shareholders shall purchase and the retiring shareholder shall sell all his shares in the corporation, now owned or hereafter acquired. The value of the shares purchased shall be determined according to the terms of Section 5, stated above.

Section 7. The Secretary of State of the State is designated as the agent of the corporation upon whom process in any action or proceeding against it may be served. The address, to which the Secretary of State shall mail a copy of process in any action or proceeding against the corporation which may be served upon him or her, is 271 Tennis Court, Fun City.

Section 8. There shall be nine directors of the corporation. A two-thirds vote by the quorum of the board of directors shall be necessary to approve a transaction being considered. A quorum shall consist of the chairman of the board plus five other directors. The position of the chairman of the board shall be held by the same person occupying the position of the president of the corporation.

Section 9. The presence, in person or by proxy, of a majority of the holders of common stock of this corporation shall be necessary in order to constitute a quorum for the transaction of any business at any meeting of the shareholders of the corporation. The affirmative vote of a majority of the shareholders of the common stock of the corporation shall be necessary for the transaction of the following items of business:

The removal of any director and the filling of any vacancy on the board, however created.

The fixing, if any, of the compensation and the duties and any changes therein, of any director.

Any merger or consolidation of the corporation with any other corporation, domestic or foreign, and any contract which in effect constitutes a merger or consolidation.

Any guaranty not in the furtherance of the corporate purposes.

Any amendment of the bylaws of the corporation.

Any amendment or change in the certificate of incorporation of the corporation.

Section 10. The earned surplus of the corporation shall be determined quarterly by the corporation's regular accountant, in accordance with generally accepted accounting principles on a basis consistent with that normally used in determining a corporation's earned surplus, and the board of directors shall determine, by a two-thirds vote of the quorum, the amount of said earned surplus that shall be distributed, provided that the corporation is not then insolvent or would not thereby be made insolvent.

Section 11. The accounting period which the corporation intends to establish as its first fiscal year for reporting of the franchise tax is July 1, to the following June 30.

Section 12. The incorporator is a natural person over the age of 18.

In witness whereof, the undersigned have signed this Certificate of Incorporation on May 1,

_____

_____

_____

BYLAWS

Bylaws are the rules by which the corporation agrees to govern itself. The bylaws may be adopted either by the board of directors or by the shareholders. This will be determined by the law of the state in which the business is incorporated. The following is a sample set of bylaws, including the important articles and provisions necessary to organize and operate the corporation.

BYLAWS OF PRACTICAL BUSINESS LAW, INC.
ORGANIZED UNDER
THE BUSINESS CORPORATION LAW

ARTICLE I
SHAREHOLDERS MEETING

Annual Meeting

Section 1. Annual meeting of the shareholders for the election of directors and for the transaction of such other business as may properly come before such meeting shall be held on the second Tuesday of May each year, if not a legal holiday, or if a legal holiday then on the next succeeding business day not a legal holiday at such hour as may be fixed by the board of directors.

Special Meeting

Section 2. A special meeting of the shareholders may be called at any time by the president or the board of directors, to be held at such time as he or they shall fix in the call. Upon the written request of the holders of not less than 10 percent of all the shares issued and outstanding and entitled to vote at the particular meeting, the secretary shall call a special meeting of the shareholders, to be held at such time as the secretary shall fix, not less than 10 nor more than 30 days after the receipt of the request. The request shall state the purpose or purposes of the meeting and shall be delivered to the secretary. Only such business may be transacted at a special meeting as is related to the purpose or purposes set forth in the notice thereof.

Location of Meetings

Section 3. Meetings of the shareholders shall be held at the offices of the corporation.

Voting Allotment

Section 4. At each meeting of the shareholders, each shareholder entitled to vote at such meeting shall be entitled to vote one vote for each share of stock outstanding in his name on the records of the corporation and he or she shall vote his or her shares in person or by proxy.

Proxy Entitlement

Section 5. Except as otherwise provided by the law, the presence at the shareholders meeting, in person or by proxy, of the holders of record of a majority of the shares of stock issued and outstanding, and entitled to vote thereat, shall be necessary to constitute a quorum for the transaction of business and the election of directors. A proxy is the written authorization giving one person the power to vote or otherwise act for another.

Written Notice of Meetings

Section 6. Written notice of the date, time, and place of each annual or special meeting of the shareholders shall be given by the president or secretary personally or by mail to each shareholder of record entitled to vote at such meeting, or who by reason of any action proposed at such meeting would be entitled to receive payment for his or her shares pursuant to the provisions of the business corporation law, not less than 10 or more than 50 days before the meeting. Notice of each special meeting shall also indicate that it is being issued by or at the direction of the person calling the meeting and shall state the purpose or purposes for which the meeting is called. Notices, if mailed, shall be directed to each shareholder at his or her address as it appears on the stock records of the corporation or, if he or she shall have filed with the secretary a written request that notices be mailed to some other address, at the address so designated.

Designation of Presiding Official

Section 7. Each meeting of the shareholders shall be presided over by the president or, if he shall not be present, by a person chosen by the shareholders at the meeting. The secretary of the corporation shall act as the secretary of each meeting or, if he shall not be present, by a person chosen by the shareholders at the meeting. The secretary shall keep the minutes of the proceedings of the meeting and shall cause the same to be recorded in the books provided for that purpose.

Shareholder Action Without Meeting

Section 8. Any action required or permitted to be taken by vote at any meeting of the shareholders may be taken without a meeting if written consent, setting forth the action so taken, is signed by the holders of all the issued and outstanding shares entitled to vote thereon.

ARTICLE II
DIRECTORS

Management of Affairs and Business

Section 1. The property affairs and business of the corporation shall be managed by the board of directors. In addition to the powers and authorities expressly conferred on it by these bylaws, the board of directors may exercise all such powers of the corporation and do all such lawful acts and things as are not by law, by the certificate of incorporation, or by these bylaws, directed or required to be exercised or done by the shareholders.

Number of Directors

Section 2. There shall be nine directors of the corporation. Any change in this number must be made pursuant to a majority vote of the shareholders.

Term of Office

Section 3. Each director shall serve a term of one year and each director's term shall be automatically extended for another term unless he or she is removed, for cause, by a majority vote of the shareholders.

Vacancies

Section 4. If any vacancy shall occur in the board of directors by reason of death, resignation, removal, increase in the number of directors, or otherwise, such vacancy shall be filled by the majority vote of all of the shareholders entitled to vote their shares.

First Meeting

Section 5. The first meeting of each newly elected board of directors shall be held for organization, for the election of officers, and for the transaction of such other business as may properly come before the meeting, as soon as practicable after each annual election of directors, at the time and place, within the state, specified in a notice, given as hereinafter provided for notice of special meetings, or specified in a written waiver of notice. Such first meeting may be held, however, without notice immediately following the annual meeting of shareholders at the place at which the annual meeting was held.

Regular Meetings

Section 6. Regular meetings of the board of directors shall be held on the first Tuesday of every month, if not a legal holiday, or if a legal holiday, then on the next succeeding business day not a legal holiday, at such hour as fixed by the board of directors. All such meetings shall be held at the corporation's offices.

Special Meetings

Section 7. Special meetings of the board of directors may be called by the president or secretary on the written request of one director. Special meetings shall be held at such time as shall be determined by the president. The place of such meeting shall be the corporation's offices.

Written Notice of Meetings

Section 8. Notice of the time and place of all meetings of the board of directors shall be mailed to each director, addressed to him or her at his or her address as it appears on the records of the corporation, at least three days before the day on which the meeting is to be held, or sent to him or her at such place by telegraph, radio, or cable, or telephoned or delivered to him personally, not later than three days before the day on which the meeting is to be held. Notice of any meeting need not be given to any director who submits a signed waiver of notice, whether before or after the meeting, or who attends the meeting without protesting, prior thereto or at its commencement, the lack of notice to him or her.

Quorum and Voting Requirements

Section 9. At all meetings of the board of directors, the presence in person of the chairman of the board plus five other directors shall constitute a quorum for the transaction of business, and, except as otherwise provided by law, the certificate of incorporation, the shareholders agreement, or by these bylaws, if a quorum shall be present, the act of a two-thirds vote of the quorum shall be the act of the board of directors.

ARTICLE III
OFFICERS

Officer-Held Positions

Section 1. The officers of the corporation shall be a president, a secretary, and a treasurer.

Election and Term

Section 2. Each officer specifically designated shall be elected by a two-thirds vote of the quorum of the board of directors. The officers shall serve a term of three years and their terms will be automatically renewed for another three-year term unless they are removed for cause by a two-thirds vote of the quorum of the board of directors.

Supplementary Officers

Section 3. The board of directors, by a two-thirds vote, may from time to time elect other officers, each of whom shall have such authority and perform such duties as the board of directors may from time to time determine and shall be subject to removal at the pleasure of the board of directors.

Vacancies

Section 4. Any vacancy occurring in any office may be filled by a two-thirds vote of the quorum of the board of directors.

Official Capacity of the President

Section 5. The president shall be the chief executive officer of the corporation and, subject to the control of the board of directors, shall exercise general supervision over the property, affairs, and business of the corporation. He or she shall call and preside at meetings of the shareholders and of the board of directors. He or she shall, unless otherwise provided by the board of directors, be an ex-officio member of the executive committee and call and preside at meetings thereof. He or she shall, in general, perform all duties and have all powers incident to the office of president and shall perform such other duties as from time to time may be assigned to him or her by these bylaws or by the board of directors.

Duties of the Secretary

Section 6. The secretary shall act as secretary at, and keep the minutes of, meetings of the shareholders and of the board of directors and cause the same to be recorded in books provided for that purpose. He or she shall, in general, perform all duties and have all powers incident to the office of secretary and shall perform such other duties and have such other powers as may from time to time be assigned to him or her by these bylaws, by the board of directors, or by the president. He or she shall have custody of the seal of the corporation and shall have authority to cause such seal to be affixed to, or impressed or otherwise reproduced upon, all documents the execution and delivery of which have been duly authorized.

Responsibilities of the Treasurer

Section 7. The treasurer shall have custody of the corporate funds and securities and shall keep full and accurate accounts of receipts and disbursements in books belonging to the corporation. He or she shall cause all monies and other valuable effects to be deposited in the name and to the credit of the corporation in such depositories as may be designated by the board of directors. He or she shall cause the funds of the corporation to be disbursed when such disbursements have been duly authorized, taking proper vouchers for such disbursements, and shall render to the president and the board of directors, whenever requested, an account of all his or her transactions as treasurer and of the financial condition of the corporation. He or she shall, in general, perform all duties and have all powers incident to the office of treasurer and shall perform such other duties and have such other powers as may from time to time be assigned to him or her by these bylaws, by the president, or by the board of directors.

ARTICLE IV
CAPITAL STOCK

Certification

Section 1. Certificates of stock, certifying the number of shares owned, shall be issued to each shareholder in such form not inconsistent with the certificate of incorporation as shall be approved by the board of directors. Such certificates of stock shall be numbered and registered in the order in which they are issued and shall be signed by the president and by the secretary; provided, however, that where such certificates are signed by a transfer agent or transfer clerk acting on behalf of the corporation and a registrar, the signatures of the president and the secretary may be facsimile. In case any officer or officers, who shall have signed or whose facsimile signature shall have been used on any such certificate or certificates, shall cease to be such officer or officers of the corporation, whether because of death, resignation or otherwise, before such certificates shall have been delivered by the corporation, such certificate or certificates may nevertheless be adopted by the corporation and be issued and delivered as though the person or persons whose facsimile signature shall have been used thereon, had not ceased to be such officer or officers of the corporation.

Transfer of Shares

Section 2. Transfers of shares shall be made only upon the books of the corporation by the holder, in person, and on the surrender of the certificate or certificates of such shares.

Lost, Stolen, or Destroyed Shares

Section 3. No certificate for shares of the capital stock of the corporation shall be issued in place of any certificate alleged to have been lost, stolen, or destroyed, except by order of the board of directors and on delivery to the corporation of a bond of indemnity in an amount satisfactory to the board of directors executed by the person to whom the stock should be issued and also by an approved surety company, against any claim upon or in respect of such lost, stolen, or destroyed certificate. Proper legal evidence of such loss, theft, or destruction shall be produced to the board of directors, if required. The board of directors, in its discretion, may refuse to issue such new certificate save upon the order of some court having jurisdiction in such matters.

ARTICLE V
SEAL

Description of the Seal

Section 1. The seal of the corporation shall bear the corporation name, the year of its incorporation, and the words, "Corporate Seal."

ARTICLE VI
WAIVER

Waiver of Notice

Section 1. Whenever any notice whatsoever is required to be given by statute or under the provisions of the certificate of incorporation, the bylaws, or the shareholders agreement, a waiver thereof in writing, signed by the person or persons entitled to such notice, whether before or after the time stated herein, shall be deemed equivalent thereto.

ARTICLE VII
FISCAL YEAR

Establishment of the Corporate Fiscal Year

Section 1. The fiscal year of the corporation shall begin on July 1, and end on the following June 30.

ARTICLE VIII
DIVIDENDS

Authorization and Distribution

Section 1. The board of directors shall have the power to authorize and distribute dividends on a quarterly basis by the affirmative vote of two-thirds of the directors.

ARTICLE IX
NEGOTIABLE INSTRUMENTS
Signature Requirements

Section 1. The signatures of the president and/or the treasurer are necessary to negotiate any financial instrument on behalf of the corporation.

ARTICLE X
CORPORATE OFFICES
Location

Section 1. The corporate offices shall be located at 271 Tennis Court in Fun City.

ARTICLE XI
AMENDMENTS

Bylaw Amendments by Shareholder Vote

Section 1. The shareholders, by the affirmative vote of two-thirds of the shareholders of the corporation, shall have the power to make, alter, amend, or repeal any and all of the bylaws.

ARTICLE XII
AUTHORITY

Authoritative Effect of Bylaws

Section 1. The preceding Articles shall be followed if not superseded by the certificate of incorporation.

FIRST MEETING OF THE BOARD OF DIRECTORS

The first meeting of the board of directors will be called after the certificate of incorporation has been filed and approved by the secretary of the state in which the incorporation takes place. The purpose of the board of directors' first meeting is to get the business under way. Officers will be elected, bank accounts established, and corporate documents, such as the certificate of incorporation, bylaws, and specimen shares of stock, will be ratified. The following is a sample of the minutes of a board of directors' first meeting.

MINUTES OF THE FIRST MEETING OF THE BOARD OF DIRECTORS OF PRACTICAL BUSINESS LAW. INC. HELD ON MAY 1

The first meeting of the board of directors of Practical Business Law, Inc., was held at 10:00 A.M. at the offices of the corporation. The following directors, constituting a quorum, were present:

Donald Vanderveer
Julia Michelson
Scott Meyers
Clifford Gardener
Joann Werner
Priscilla Peterson
Dennis O'Brien
Anthony Morano
Nancy Hamilton

Waiver of notice of the meeting of directors: We, the undersigned, being all of the directors of Practical Business Law, Inc., hereby severally waive notice of the time and place of the first meeting of the board of directors of said corporation and hereby consent that it be held at 271 Tennis Court, Fun City, at 10:00 A.M. on May 1, for the purpose of electing officers and for such other business as may come before said meeting.

Dated May 1 All Sign _____

RESOLUTIONS

Election of Officers

Resolved: Donald Vanderveer has been elected president of the corporation, at an annual salary of $125,000. He will assume his duties immediately and is to take over for the temporary chairman of this meeting. Clifford Gardener has been elected secretary of the corporation, at an annual salary of $75,000 and is to assume his duties immediately and to take over for the temporary secretary of this meeting. Julia Michelson has been elected treasurer of the corporation, at an annual salary of $75,000 and is to assume her duties immediately.

Ratification of Documents

Resolved: The following have been ratified and agreed to by the board:

1. Certificate of incorporation, attached hereto
2. Bylaws of the corporation, attached hereto
3. Specimen shares of stock, attached hereto
4. Corporate seal, affixed hereto

Establishment of Bank Accounts

Resolved: Bank accounts are to be started at the Chase Manhattan Bank, 1 Chase Plaza, New York, New York. The president and/or treasurer shall sign all corporate obligations with said Bank.

Proposal for Distribution of Stock

Resolved: A written proposal is to be prepared by the newly elected secretary for the distribution of the stock certificates. The secretary is to have this proposal prepared and ready for review at the first regular meeting of the board so that the shares can be issued.

Designation of Tax Filing Status

Resolved: That the corporation agrees to be treated as a subchapter S corporation for the purposes of filing its tax returns. The secretary shall prepare the necessary papers for this election and have them ready for the first regular meeting of the board.

Motion to Adjourn

Resolved: A motion to adjourn the meeting until the next scheduled meeting was approved and the board adjourned.

Dated: May 1 _____

Clifford Gardener, Secretary

CORPORATE CHARACTERISTICS

A corporation has the following characteristics:

Legally capable of suing and being sued in its corporate name and contracting in its corporate name

Organized for profit

Legal entity which possesses the rights of a person under many federal and state laws

Limited liability up to the value of the investment made in capital stock. This is often the main reason for incorporating because partners and sole proprietors are personally liable

Inherent tax advantages

Perpetual duration, unlike a partnership which may be dissolved for a variety of reasons

Ownership evidenced by stock which is freely transferable unless properly restricted

Powers of management invested in a board of directors

PIERCING THE CORPORATE VEIL

The law encourages individuals to limit their liability through incorporating. A shareholder will be liable only up to the amount of his or her investment. The corporate veil will be pierced only where the corporate form is used to perpetrate fraudulent, illegal activities. In these instances, the shareholders will be personally liable for all debts incurred or injuries caused by the corporation. The corporate veil will not be pierced solely because the corporation is 100 percent owned by one shareholder or by a parent corporation with the same board of directors.

Walkovszky v. Carlton
18 N.Y.2d 414, 276 N.Y.S.2d 585,
223 N.E.2d 6 (1966)

Walkovszky sued Carlton individually for injuries he sustained from a taxicab owned by a corporation of which Carlton is the principal stockholder.

Walkovszky was injured by a taxicab owned by the Seon Cab Corporation. Seon was one of ten corporations owned by Carlton. The assets of each corporation were composed of two taxicabs. The minimum amount of liability insurance, $10,000, was taken out on each taxicab. Carlton had set up the ten different corporations to limit his liability and to keep insurance payments low. Walkovszky argued that his recovery should not be limited to $10,000 plus the value of the two taxicabs, but rather that the corporate veil should be pierced to subject Carlton to personal liability. Walkovszky argued further that none of the corporations had a separate existence of its own.

The issue is whether Carlton was conducting business in his individual capacity and using the corporate form to defraud the public.

The court held that operating a fleet of taxicabs from several separate corporations is no different from operating them from one corporation as far as Carlton's personal liability is concerned. The fact that Carlton maintained minimum insurance and otherwise limited his liability through the corporate form is not tantamount to fraud.

If Carlton were found to be personally liable, thousands of taxicab owners who operate their business through corporate forms would be affected. It remains for the legislature to increase the minimum liability coverage for corporate-owned vehicles. Judgment for Carlton.

TYPES OF CORPORATIONS

Public Corporations

Public corporations include municipalities formed by cities, towns, or villages; and government corporations such as the post office and the Federal Deposit Insurance Corporation (FDIC).

Private Corporations

Private corporations encompass all other corporations that are organized for profit and owned by the general public, such as IBM, GM, and AT&T.

Nonprofit Corporations

Nonprofit corporations usually consist of religious, social, athletic, and educational societies or clubs organized for the benefit of the community. Any monies earned by a nonprofit corporation must be used exclusively for community purposes; it may not be distributed to its members. Examples include churches, synagogues, libraries, YMCAs, Elks, Moose and Kiwanis clubs, private schools, colleges, and universities.

Closely Held Corporations

Closely held corporations are those owned by a number of shareholders, often family members or relatives. There are usually share transfer limitations denoted in the certificate of incorporation as well as on the face of each stock certificate which restrict the shareholders from transferring their stock to anyone outside the corporation. This is how a corporation remains closely held.

Professional Corporations

Professional corporations allow individuals who practice the professions such as law, medicine, and accounting to incorporate their professional practices to reap tax advantages outside the scope of a partnership or individual proprietorship.

Subchapter S Corporations

Subchapter S corporations are small business corporations that, for income tax purposes, are treated as partnerships while still retaining the other characteristics of a corporation especially that of limited liability. In a Subchapter S corporation, all income earned will be allocated among the various shareholders by agreement. The shareholders, in turn, will be taxed on that income as individuals. This avoids double taxation which most corporations are faced with: first, corporations must pay corporate income tax; second, individual shareholders must pay personal income tax on their portion of that same corporate income, which they received in the form of dividends.

Domestic Corporations

Domestic corporations are those which are incorporated in the state.

Foreign Corporations

Foreign corporations are those incorporated in a state other than in the one they are doing business. For example, Practical Business Law, Inc., was incorporated in New York, but also does business in New Jersey and Connecticut. Practical Business Law is a domestic corporation in New York and a foreign corporation in New Jersey and Connecticut. Corporations incorporated in other countries, such as British Petroleum and Mitsubishi, are referred to as international corporations.

FRANCHISES

Introduction

A franchise is a license given by the owner of a trade name (the franchisor) to another (the franchisee) in return for a fee which allows the recipient to operate a business under the trade name. Inherent in this would be the stipulation that the products used in the business by the franchisee must be purchased from the franchisor. There may be other restrictions which are set forth in the franchise agreement.

The benefit to the franchisee, the person who is purchasing the franchise, is the opportunity to operate an independent business while still being affiliated with a much larger organization that will guarantee the supply of products and the advertising. Examples of areas where franchises flourish are car dealerships, gas stations, car rentals, ice cream shops, fast food establishments and distributorships for soft drinks.

Franchise Agreement

Franchise operations have grown remarkably over the last few decades, but laws regarding franchises have not kept pace. Currently, fifteen states have laws designed to deal specifically with franchises, while the other states rely on principles of contract law, agency, employment, independent contractors, and antitrust laws. Problems encountered by franchises are novel in many situations and call for the adoption of specific laws designed to deal with the difficulties.

Many franchisees have been defrauded because pertinent information had not been disclosed to them at the start. The Federal Trade Commission requires franchisors to disclose certain information to prospective franchisees, such as the name and address of the franchisor; the franchisor's financial statements for the last five years; a detailed description of the franchise offered, along with a copy of the franchise agreement which sets forth the restrictions and stipulations the franchisee must abide by; the royalties which must be paid to the franchisor, the amount, and how they are to be calculated.

A typical franchise agreement will set forth the name of the franchisor and the franchisee; the duration for which the franchise will be granted; the type of business authorized by the granting of the franchise; the royalty payments for the use of the trade name; a restrictive covenant stating the franchisee may only use the products marketed by the franchisor or distribute them in a certain area (the latter may have antitrust considerations); the stipulation that the franchisee must comply with the franchisor's standards of service, which must be set forth in detail as either part of the franchise agreement or in a separate manual; a clause requiring the franchisee to maintain liability insurance; and a provision allowing the franchisor to inspect the books and records of the franchisee to determine their accuracy with regard to the royalty payments made.

The franchisor may in no way dictate the price to be charged for the products sold by the franchisee, otherwise this would be price fixing in violation of the federal Sherman Antitrust Act as well as state antitrust laws. The franchisor may, however, suggest an appropriate price. This is what is often referred to as the manufacturer's suggested retail price.

REVIEW QUESTIONS

1. Define the following terms: corporation, capital stock, shareholder, board of directors, prospectus, promoter, stock subscriptions, incorporator, and franchise.
2. How is a corporation formed?
3. State the function of a certificate of incorporation and list what must be included in it.
4. State the purpose of bylaws and explain their main provisions.
5. What happens at the first meeting of the board of directors?
6. List the various types of corporations.
7. What are the various characteristics of a corporation?
8. What is the difference between a domestic and a foreign corporation? Give an example.
9. What is the main advantage of a Subchapter S corporation?
10. Why would a person or several people incorporate a business rather than form a partnership?

38

CORPORATE MANAGEMENT

CORPORATE POWERS

A corporation is a legal person. It has the powers that a natural person has to accomplish the purpose for which it was formed, usually, to earn a profit in a particular business. These powers include:

Contract in its own name, establish employee benefit plans, and make and alter bylaws

Lend or borrow money and make political or charitable contributions in its own name

Act as a partner in a joint venture or a partnership

Mortgage and/or hold title to real estate in its own name

Sue and be sued in its own name

The actions of a corporation must not exceed these powers or any other powers set forth in the certificate of incorporation or they will be *ultra vires* acts, acts that exceed corporate powers.

ULTRA VIRES DOCTRINE

If the *ultra vires* act has not begun, or has begun but has not yet been completed, a shareholder of the corporation or the attorney general of the state of incorporation may prevent the act from being performed through a request for an injunction. The court will grant the injunction if it feels that the result would be fair and equitable. By the court's discretion, a party suffering financial loss because of the injunction may recover damages from the corporation, or vice versa; but loss of profits is not recoverable. Rather, the shareholder's remedy lies against the officers or directors responsible for the proscribed act. This may be brought through a derivative suit, to be discussed later in this chapter. If the corporation illegally exceeded its powers, the attorney general may commence a proceeding to have the corporation dissolved.

The doctrine of *ultra vires* has been restricted to a great extent because most certificates of incorporation provide for very broad corporate purposes and extensive corporate powers.

Temple Lumber Co. v. Miller
169 S.W.2d 256 (Tex.) 1943

A. Miller sued Temple Lumber Company for breach of contract in using defective materials in the construction of a house for which Miller paid.

Temple Lumber Company was incorporated for the following purposes: "manufacturing lumber and the purchase and sale of material used in such business and doing all things necessary and incident to such lumber business." Miller entered into a contract with Temple Lumber in which Temple Lumber was to build a house for Miller by providing the necessary materials and labor.

After the house was completed and Temple Lumber was paid, Miller discovered defective materials had been used in the construction. He sued Temple Lumber for breach of contract. The shareholders on behalf of the corporation argued that its acts were *ultra vires* in that the corporation was not formed for the purpose of building houses; therefore the contract is not enforceable.

The issue is whether Temple Lumber's act in building Miller's house was *ultra vires*.

The court held,

> . . . the trend seems to be that even though the charter provisions [of the certificate of incorporation] do not, in so many words, authorize an act, the corporation may bind itself to do many things, when they are not against public policy and are not forbidden by law. There is a clear distinction between acts which are void because of legal inhibitions, and those which are not prohibited but are those which are not enumerated in the purpose clause of the charter.

The court ruled, "We think that if the act is not prohibited by law or public policy, and it inures to the direct benefit of the corporation, and is executed, it is not, strictly speaking, ultra vires . . ." Judgment for Temple Lumber.

POWERS OF DIRECTORS

The board of directors has certain powers through which it administers corporate affairs. A few of the more important powers include:

Responsibility for approving merger, acquisition, or consolidation by resolution

Election and removal of officers

Declaration of dividends

Creation, alteration, amendment, or repeal of bylaws

Determination of the price to be paid for newly issued shares

Sale, lease, or exchange of corporate assets

POWERS OF OFFICERS

Individuals are elected by the board of directors to fill the officer positions of the corporation dictated by the bylaws. These positions usually include president, vice-president(s), secretary, and treasurer. Officers manage the day-to-day business of the corporation and are agents of the corporation. Their term of office is often regulated by contract. The board of directors has the power to remove officers with or without cause. If an officer who is under contract is removed without cause, he or she may sue the corporation for breach of contract. The powers of the respective officers of the corporation are contained in the bylaws.

President

The president shall be the chief executive officer of the corporation and, subject to the control of the board of directors, shall exercise general supervision over the property, affairs, and business of the corporation. He or she shall call and preside at meetings of the shareholders and of the board of directors. He or she shall, unless otherwise provided by the board of directors, be an ex-officio member of the executive committee and call and preside at meetings thereof. He or she shall, in general, perform all duties and have all powers incident to the office of president and shall perform such other duties as from time to time may be assigned to him or her by the bylaws or by the board of directors.

Vice-President

The vice-president shall have the respective powers and duties of the president in the event the president is unable to fulfill his or her role.

Secretary

The secretary shall act as secretary at, and keep the minutes of, meetings of the shareholders and of the board of directors and cause the same to be recorded in books provided for that purpose. He or she shall, in general, perform all duties and have all powers incident to the office of secretary and shall perform such other duties and have such other powers as may from time to time be assigned to him or her by the bylaws, by the board of directors, or by the president. He or she shall have custody of the seal of the corporation and shall have authority to cause such seal to be affixed to, or impressed or otherwise reproduced upon, all documents the execution and delivery of which, on behalf of the corporation, shall have been duly authorized.

Treasurer

The treasurer shall have custody of the corporate funds and securities and shall keep full and accurate accounts of receipts and disbursements in books belonging to the corporation. He or she shall cause all monies and other valuable effects to be deposited in the name and to the credit of the corporation in such depositories as may be designated by the board of directors. He or she shall cause the funds of the corporation to be disbursed when such disbursements have been duly authorized, taking proper vouchers for such disbursements, and shall render to the president and the board of directors, whenever requested, an account of all his or her transactions as treasurer and of the financial condition of the corporation. He or she shall, in general, perform all duties and have all powers incident to the office of treasurer and shall perform such other duties and have such other powers as may from time to time be assigned to him or her by the bylaws, by the president, or by the board of directors.

DUTIES OF DIRECTORS AND OFFICERS

Fiduciary Duties

Fiduciary duties are those which grow out of a relationship of trust and confidence.

1. Duty of loyalty
2. Duty to act in good faith

    Officers and directors have an obligation to refrain from

    Misappropriation of corporate funds
    Oppression of minority shareholders
    Taking advantage of corporate opportunity for one's own personal use
    Trading with the use of inside information
    Creating a conflict of interest with the corporation

Managerial Duties

Managerial duties include:

1. Duty not to exceed authority; an officer or director who exceeds his or her authority will be absolutely liable only if negligent
2. Duty to exercise due care; an officer or director who fails to exercise due care in the management of corporate funds will be liable for any loss that occurs if he or she is negligent

BUSINESS JUDGMENT RULE

Officers and directors are not insurers of corporate investments or transactions. The business judgment rule renders management immune from responsibility and ratifies transactions where they are within the powers of the corporation, within the authority of management, and in compliance with the managerial and fiduciary duties just set forth.

Simon v. Socony-Vacuum Oil Co., Inc., et al.
179 Misc. 202, 38 N.Y.S.2d 270 (1942)

A shareholders' derivative suit was brought by Simon on behalf of the shareholders of Socony-Vacuum Oil Company (now known as Mobil) against the corporation and its directors for breach of duty.

Socony participated in a large buying program, along with other major oil companies, in which they purchased oil from several midwestern oil refiners at a preferred price in return for loaning the refiners money. This led to an unlawful combination and conspiracy to fix prices in violation of the Sherman Antitrust Act. Socony's actions were judged to be in restraint of trade and a fine was imposed. The shareholders are suing to recover the amount of the fine from the directors for breach of their duty to exercise sound business judgment.

The issue is whether the business judgment rule protects the directors from being personally liable for their mistake in judgment.

The court held,

> It is elementary that directors owe a corporation the duty to exercise reasonable care in managing its affairs; that is, the same degree of care which a business man of ordinary prudence generally exercises in the management of his own affairs. If the directors fail to use such care, they are liable to the corporation. However, if the directors act in good faith and exercise reasonable care in the performance of their duties, they are not liable for mistakes and errors of judgment, either of law or fact. (Citations.)

The court applied these principles to the present case, ". . . it would seem that defendants did not fail in their duty of reasonable care. At most, they made an honest and reasonable mistake or error of judgment."

The court decided,

> . . . In short, the directors must have known when they made the loans that they were ultra vires and illegal. Obviously, no such knowledge can be imputed to the defendants when they, in behalf of the defendant corporation, entered the buying programs which were later held to be in violation of law.

Judgment for Socony and its directors.

SHAREHOLDERS' RIGHTS

Shareholders have the right to:

Transfer shares by sale, gift, or exchange

Ratify corporate acts by shareholder resolution

Amend bylaws; this right coexists in the board of directors

Vote in person or through proxies

Inspect the books and records of the corporation, including accounting records, bylaws, minutes of the shareholders' and board of directors' meetings, contracts, tax returns and property owned

Limited liability up to the amount of their investment

Maintain their percentage of ownership when new shares are issued by exercising their preemptive right to purchase a proportionate share of the new stock; preemptive rights do not apply to the issuance of original shares

Approve amendments to the certificate of incorporation

Preserve the corporation by removing directors for cause, with court review, where they violate their managerial and/or fiduciary duties

Dividends, although the declaration and the amount is discretionary with the board of directors

SHAREHOLDERS' DERIVATIVE ACTION

Shareholders may bring a derivative action against the officers and directors or other shareholders of the corporation, either on their own behalf or on behalf of the corporation. Suits on behalf of the corporation are brought to recover damages sustained by the corporation from those directors or officers breaching a managerial or fiduciary duty; to recover improperly paid dividends; to recover from third parties who perpetuated a wrong on the corporation, whether in contract or in tort; to compel payment of lawfully declared dividends which were withheld or otherwise not paid. Derivative suits on behalf of the shareholders are initiated to enforce their right of inspection; to protect their preemptive rights to maintain their percentage of ownership in the corporation; to enforce their right to vote; to enjoin directors before they exceed their authority or commit an *ultra vires* act; to recover from insiders trading without proper disclosure; to compel corporate dissolution.

In small business corporations, shareholders often draft agreements to protect their rights.

Wilkes v. Springside Nursing Home, Inc.
370 Mass. 842, 353 N.E.2d 657 (1976)

Wilkes brought a shareholder derivative suit on his own behalf for breach of fiduciary duties owed to him by the three other shareholders.

The Springside Nursing Home was incorporated by Wilkes and three other individuals, all being equal shareholders. Wilkes had a falling-out with Quinn, one of the other shareholders. As a result, Wilkes was not reelected as a director or officer, his salary was discontinued, and no dividends were declared. Wilkes sued the corporation and its three directors for breach of their fiduciary duties of loyalty and good faith to him.

The issue is whether the majority can demonstrate a legitimate business purpose for discontinuing Wilkes as an officer and director.

The court held,

When an asserted business purpose for their action is advanced by the majority, however, we think it is open to minority stockholders to demonstrate that the same legitimate objective could have been achieved through an alternative course of action less harmful to the minority's interest. If called on to settle a dispute, our courts must weigh the legitimate business purpose, if any, against the practicability of a less harmful alternative.

The court concluded, " . . . the action of the majority stockholder here was a designed 'freeze out' for which no legitimate business purpose has been suggested. . . ." Judgment for Wilkes.

REVIEW QUESTIONS

1. Name the powers that a corporation, the board of directors, and the respective officers possess.
2. What is the *ultra vires* doctrine?
3. When will the corporate veil be pierced?
4. Explain the business judgment rule.
5. List the various rights of shareholders.
6. What are the fiduciary and managerial duties of directors and officers?
7. Michael P. Grace II was a life member (director) of Grace Institute. He commenced several frivolous lawsuits against the Institute. The Institute, in defending each suit, incurred court costs, bad publicity, and attorneys' fees. The Institute removed Michael P. Grace II. He argued that the charter (certificate of incorporation) creating the Grace Institute had no provision for removal of directors. The Institute claims removal of a director who is a detriment to the corporation is an inherent power. What result? Grace v. Grace Institute, 19 N.Y.2d 307, 279 N.Y.S.2d 721, 226 N.E.2d 531 (1967).
8. Most of the original shares of stock issued by Ross Transport, Inc., were divided among the original investors in the corporation. The remaining shares were to be sold to investors among the general public. Instead, two of the directors of Ross Transport sold the remaining shares to themselves and members of their family. The shareholders brought a derivative suit, claiming this is a violation of their preemptive rights. Is this argument correct? Ross Transport, Inc., et al. v. Crothers et al., 185 Md. 573, 45 A.2d 267 (1946).
9. Morad, Thompson, and Coupounas operated Bio-Lab, Inc. One of Bio-Lab's main purposes was to open another office. The cost for an additional office was $44,000. Bio-Lab would have had that amount if the corporation had not declared an exorbitant dividend of $20,000. This precluded Bio-Lab from opening the new office. Morad and Thompson used their dividend payments to open a competing office called Med-Lab. Coupounas brought a derivative suit on behalf of Bio-Lab against Morad and Thompson for breach of their fiduciary duties of loyalty and good faith in taking advantage of corporate opportunity for their own benefit. Coupounas requested that the profits earned by Med-Lab be transferred to Bio-Lab. What result? Morad v. Coupounas, 361 So.2d 6 (Ala.) 1978.
10. Riffe was an officer in the Wilshire Oil Company. He engaged in a business which directly competed with Wilshire. Wilshire sued Riffe for the profits he

earned from the competing business and for the return of the compensation he received from Wilshire during the time he was engaged in the competing business. Riffe argued that Wilshire earned a profit during the period in which he served a competing business and therefore, he should be entitled to compensation for his services. What result? Wilshire Oil Co. of Texas v. Riffe, 406 F.2d 1061 (10th Cir. 1969).

39

CORPORATE FINANCE

INTRODUCTION

A corporation is usually formed through the issuance of stock. Investors in the corporation pay a certain price for each share of stock. This price is initially set by the board of directors. The certificate of incorporation may provide for a price below which the shares cannot be sold. This is referred to as par value as it is arbitrarily set by the board of directors, usually at a low price. Shares may also be issued without par value. This means there is no minimum price at which the shares may be sold. Whether stock has par value or no par value does not effect the market price people pay. This confuses many investors who do not understand why par value is not related to market value or who confuse par value with book value. The market value of corporate stock may change daily. The shares of large corporations are usually sold to the public on an exchange. Exchanges provide a convenient medium for buying and selling stock and for determining the most accurate, up-to-the-minute market price of stock based on what the buyers in their latest transactions were willing to pay. The two types of stock issued are common stock and preferred stock.

COMMON STOCK

Common stock is the kind of stock issued by a corporation which gives the shareholder the right to vote without other special rights and privileges. Ownership in a corporation is determined by a percentage based on the number of shares owned by a stockholder in relation to the total number of shares issued.

EXAMPLE | Douglas Wright, a multimillionaire, purchased 4,000,000 shares in the Hughes Tool Corporation. There are 80,000,000 shares outstanding. What percentage of ownership does Douglas Wright have in Hughes Tool? He has 5 percent.

In large corporations, 1 or 2 percent of the shares owned may be sufficient to exercise some control over the corporation. This is because the shares can be voted as a block, whereas many other shareholders do not exercise their right to vote.

If the corporation should become insolvent and be forced to declare bankruptcy, owners of common stock are liable only up to the amount of their investment.

Dividends are the share in the profits of the corporation paid out to the stockholders. The remaining portion of the corporation's profits are reinvested in the business. Dividends are generally declared on a quarterly basis at the discretion of the board of directors. Dividends may be suspended when a corporation has lost money or when the corporation intends to use its profits for a capital investment such as a new factory or office building. In any case the declaration of dividends may not be arbitrarily withheld.

EXAMPLE | General Public Utilities (GPU) operates Three Mile Island Nuclear Plant. It has regularly paid dividends for a number of years. One historic but tragic day, the reactor develops a leak causing radioactive liquids to spill out into the plant. The plant is shut down for several years, causing a severe financial loss for GPU. Dividends are suspended indefinitely by the board of directors. Do the shareholders of GPU have any recourse against the corporation for the suspension of dividends? No, unless the shareholders could bring a derivative suit, which they did, for the loss in the value of their shares of stock.

**Dodge v. Ford Motor Co.
204 Mich. 459, 170 N.W. 668 (1919)**

The Dodge brothers brought a shareholders' derivative suit to compel the directors of Ford Motor Company to declare a dividend.

The Ford Motor Company was incorporated in 1903. In the ensuing years, its business of manufacturing and selling automobiles began to expand. The capital stock of the company was $2 million—20,000 shares with a par value of $100. The Dodge brothers owned 2,000 shares, 10 percent of the corporation. The regular dividend was equivalent to a 60 percent return on the capital stock. In addition, special dividends were declared on eleven occasions between 1911 and 1915. Henry Ford, president and one of the directors of the corporation, stated that no further special dividends were going to be paid; rather the capital surplus would be reinvested into the corporation. "My ambition," said Mr. Ford, "is to employ still more men to spread the benefits of this industrial system to the greatest possible number, to help them build up their lives and their homes. To do this we are putting the greatest share of our profits back in the business." In 1916, Ford Motor Company had assets of more than $132 million, a capital surplus of almost $112 million, and cash on hand of nearly $54 million.

The issue is whether the resolution to suspend special dividends indefinitely is an arbitrary and capricious action on part of the board of directors. The court held,

> A business corporation is organized and carried on primarily for the profit of the stockholders. The powers of the directors are to be employed for that end.
>
> When plaintiffs [Dodge brothers] made their complaint and demand for further dividends, the Ford Motor Company had concluded its most prosperous year of business. A refusal to declare and pay further dividends appears to be not an exercise of discretion on the part of the directors, but an arbitrary refusal to do what the circumstances required to be done.

Judgment for the Dodge brothers.

PREFERRED STOCK

Preferred stock is a type of corporate stock which enjoys preferences over common stock in the distribution of dividends, and in the distribution of assets if and when the corporation is liquidated. These privileges make preferred stock more attractive to investors seeking security in their investment and their return. Preferred stock dividends may be paid cumulatively or noncumulatively. If dividends have been suspended for any length of time, past dividends owed to preferred shareholders must be paid entirely before any dividends may be paid to common shareholders. This is called cumulative payments. The preferred shareholder is in effect a creditor of the corporation for the amount of the omitted dividend payments. Noncumulative payment means preferred shareholders do not have to be reimbursed for suspended dividend payments. The dividend payments are usually fixed at a percentage of par value.

EXAMPLE | AT&T issues a preferred class of stock called AT&T 3.00. This means the yearly dividend payment is $3.00 per share. Assume the market value of AT&T stock is $25; then the $3.00 dividend would represent an 8 percent dividend. Dividend payments are expressed in their yearly amount, although they are usually paid on a quarterly basis. Here AT&T would pay $.75 per share per quarter.

Preferred stockholders do not have the right to vote. The right to vote is the exclusive privilege of common stockholders.

Preferred stock does not fluctuate in price as much as common stock. This stability minimizes the risk of loss, and also minimizes the opportunity for gain, as compared to common stock. This characteristic, coupled with the lack of voting rights, act as a trade-off for priority in dividend payments and security in stock value. Preferred stock may contain a provision allowing the corporation to call in the stock at a price above par value. Preferred stock may also be convertible; this means it can be converted to common stock at the shareholder's option.

In re Olympic National Liquidation
Agencies, Inc.
74 Wash. 2d 1, 442 P.2d 246 (1968)

The common stockholders brought an action, questioning the distribution of corporate assets to preferred stockholders on the dissolution of the corporation.

Olympic National Agencies issued 2,000 shares of preferred stock ($50 par value) and 2,000 shares of common stock (no par value). Three years later, the corporation declared a ten-for-one stock split. The number of shares increased tenfold to 20,000 shares of preferred stock and 20,000 shares of common stock. The capitalization of preferred stock remained constant at $100,000 (20,000 shares multiplied by $50 per share) but the par value was reduced to $5 ($100,000 divided by 20,000 shares). A 7 percent dividend was paid each year on the preferred stock for thirty years, until the shareholders passed a resolution calling for dissolution. On liquidation of the corporate assets, the preferred stockholders were paid $5 per share; and the remainder was split between the two groups.

The common stockholders allege that after the preferred stockholders received a return of their capital, they had no further rights to the assets of the corporation. This is because of the preference given to them upon liquidation.

The issue is whether preferred shareholders are entitled only to a return of their capital investment upon liquidation of corporate assets.

The court concluded,

> We hold that, under facts such as in the instant case, here one class of stock is afforded a stated preference as to assets on liquidation, and the articles of incorporation are silent as to any further participation, the clear implication is that the rights of the preferred stock are exhausted once the preference has been satisfied. (Citations.)

Judgment for the common stockholders.

BONDS

When a corporation needs additional financing to expand its business via the purchase of new equipment, real estate, office buildings, factories, or the hiring of additional employees, it may raise money by issuing debt instruments known as bonds. Bonds are long-term debt instruments (ten years or more) as compared to a note, which is usually for a shorter duration, such as two or three years. A bond is a debt owed to a bondholder. The debt may be secured by the assets of the corporation or simply by its goodwill. The bondholder advances the corporation money in return for a fixed rate of interest payable at designated intervals (quarterly or semiannually). A bondholder is a creditor of the corporation and as such, has preference to the corporate assets over both preferred and common shareholders. A bond indenture is a contract between the corporation (borrower) and the bondholder (lender) which provides for: payments to be made to the bondholder at designated intervals; collateral to secure the amount owed, usually through the pledge of property or other assets; call provisions which give the corporation the right to call the bond in before the date of maturity by making payment of the principal owed. The effect of this provision is to cut short the number of intervals during which interest will be paid. A bond indenture also provides: protective covenants to restrict corporate financial action concerning payment of dividends and maintenance of a stipulated level of working capital, for the bondholders' protection; a sinking fund provision which requires the corporation to retire a portion of the bond each year in order to reduce outstanding debt and diminish the possibility of bankruptcy. This last provision is optional, but if included in the indenture, it is compulsory.

Terminology

Face value is the maturity value, the amount paid at the time the bond matures, on its expiration date.

Coupon rate is the annual rate of interest payable to the bondholder.

Market value is the present value of the bond, determined according to current interest rates. A bond may sell for more (premium) or less (discount) than its face value.

Yield to maturity is the current rate of return on the bond. This is determined by dividing the coupon rate by the current market value.

EXAMPLE | IBM issued a thirty-year, 12 percent bond. On January 15, Patricia Clarke purchases a $10,000 bond at 98, the purchase price being $9,800. On March 1, the bond is selling for 105. Have interest rates risen or fallen since January 15? They have fallen. Did Patricia buy the bond at a premium or a discount? A discount! On March 1, is it selling at a premium or discount? Premium! What is the coupon rate, face value, and yield to maturity on the respective dates? The coupon rate is 12 percent; the face value of Patricia's bond is $10,000. The respective yields to maturity (determined by dividing coupon rate of 12 percent by the market values of 98 and 105) are 12.24 percent on January 15, and 11.43 percent on March 1.

Classifications

Method of Interest Repayment   Bonds may be classified according to their method of interest repayment. Coupon bonds are in bearer form, which means that anyone in possession of the bonds is entitled to interest by detaching the coupons and presenting them for payment. Registered bonds are registered in the owner's name and transferable only through endorsement. Most bonds are registered because they are generally held by financial institutions such as banks and brokerage houses rather than by the owner, and to prevent theft.

Redeemable Stipulation   Bonds may be classified by the method in which they may be redeemed. These bonds are known as

1. Callable bonds
2. Convertible bonds

Callable bonds may be redeemed prior to the date of maturity. The right of a corporation to call a bond in is provided on the face of the bond. The corporation may exercise the right if interest rates are lower. For example, a 30 year 15% bond may be called in after 25 years if the interst rate is now 10%. It can be replaced by a new 10% bond which would save 5% in interest repayments.

Convertible bonds may be converted into common stock at the option of the bondholder. The number of shares exchanged for each bond will be denoted on the face of the bond. A bondholder could take advantage of this if the value of the common stock exceeds the value of the bond.

Security Pledged   Bonds may be classified according to the security pledged for the bond. The following are the major types:

Closed-end mortgage bonds are secured by real estate and prevent further issuance of debt of the same priority against the designated property.

Open-end mortgage bonds are secured by real estate, and allow the issuance of debt of the same priority against the designated property.

Chattel mortgage bonds are secured by personal property, such as equipment and inventory.

Debentures are secured only by the name and goodwill of the corporation. These bonds are only issued by corporations with excellent credit ratings. Debentures may contain a negative pledge clause stating that no new debt will be issued with preference over the debentures unless they are given equal security. Individuals holding debentures are general unsecured creditors as opposed to individuals holding real estate mortgage bonds or chattel mortgage bonds, who are secured creditors. The reason people buy debentures is because of the belief that the corporation, such as IBM, AT&T, or GM, will never go bankrupt.

Subordinated debentures are the same as debentures except that the bondholders are subordinated to other general unsecured creditors of the corporation.

REVIEW QUESTIONS _____

1. Define common stock, preferred stock, and bonds.
2. What are the various classifications of bonds?
3. Explain the difference between common stock and preferred stock.
4. What is cumulative preferred stock?
5. Define bondholder, indenture, and debenture.
6. Define face value, coupon rate, market value, and yield to maturity, as they refer to bonds.
7. The directors of Stanton Oil authorized dividend payments to the shareholders while the company was insolvent. The shareholders were not apprised of this when they received and accepted the dividends. The court-appointed receiver of corporate assets sued the shareholders for a return of the improperly declared dividends. Must the shareholders repay the dividends? Wood v. City National Bank, 24 F.2d 661 (2d Cir. 1928).

40

CORPORATE ANTITRUST LEGISLATION

INTRODUCTION

Our capitalistic system was formed with a reliance on competition. It is the purpose of the antitrust laws to maintain free, open, and continuing competition. This is to guarantee fair competition, safe working conditions for employees, equal employment opportunities, clean air and water, consumer safety, merchantable products fit for the use for which they are intended, and the like. Administrative agencies have been established by the federal government as well as by state and local governments, to insure that businesses are acting in compliance with these guarantees. Some of the better-known administrative agencies are the Federal Trade Commission (FTC), Internal Revenue Service (IRS), Interstate Commerce Commission (ICC), Environmental Protection Agency (EPA), Consumer Product Safety Commission (CPSC), and Food and Drug Administration (FDA). This chapter is devoted to the regulation of business through the antitrust laws.

ANTITRUST LAWS

Freedom to contract is a well-established principle of contract law. The United States Constitution, in Article I, Section 10, prohibits any state from passing a law impairing the obligation of contracts. Although freedom to contract is a fundamental right in our country, it is not absolute. Contracts which unreasonably restrain trade are illegal and unenforceable.

In the late 1800s, trusts developed in which a limited number of trustees were to hold all the stock of the company and its subsidiaries for the benefit of its stockholders. Trusts were created to monopolize particular industries. The most powerful of these trusts were the Standard Oil Company, the American Tobacco Company, and the American Sugar Refining Company, all of which controlled over 75 percent of their industry's business.

Public outcry against monopolies soon became widespread. This led to a series of congressional acts which were intended to break the power of monopolies, where they unreasonably restrained trade, and to maintain free competition.

SHERMAN ANTITRUST ACT

The Sherman Antitrust Act declared every business combination, whether a trust or another form which restricts competition, to be illegal and punishable by fine and/or imprisonment. The Sherman Antitrust Act also prohibited businesses or individuals from monopolizing an industry to the exclusion of others. Although passed in 1890, this act was not implemented by the courts to any great degree for the next twenty years. In 1911, the United States Supreme Court ruled that Standard Oil would have to be broken up. This was the most famous antitrust case until the recent divestiture of American Telephone & Telegraph (AT&T).

The Standard Oil Co. of New Jersey
v. United States
221 U.S. 1, 31 S. Ct., 502 (1911)

The United States brought an antitrust action against the Standard Oil Company of New Jersey for restraining trade and monopolizing the oil industry.

In 1870, John D. Rockefeller and his partners reorganized their oil refining firm as the Standard Oil Company of Ohio. It soon became the world's largest oil refiner. In 1882, Standard Oil set up a trust for the centralized control of Standard Oil and its subsidiaries. In 1892, the Ohio Supreme Court broke up the Standard Oil Trust into twenty companies. Rockefeller replaced the trust with a holding company called the Standard Oil Company of New Jersey. Its purpose was to hold the stock of all the Standard Oil subsidiaries, thus giving Rockefeller control of the subsidiaries through one company.

In 1911, the government brought an antitrust action alleging Rockefeller and his partners conspired to restrict competition in petroleum products and to monopolize the industry. The government argued that Rockefeller and his partners accomplished this through the organization of the Standard Oil Company of New Jersey.

The issues are whether the Standard Oil Company of New Jersey, and Rockefeller and his partners, were in violation of the Sherman Antitrust Act in that they restrained trade in petroleum products and monopolized the petroleum industry; and whether an injunction should be granted enjoining the company from engaging in any further action in violation of the Sherman Antitrust Act; and whether the company should be dissolved by divesting itself of the shares of stock it holds in its subsidiaries.

The court found Standard Oil to be in violation of the Sherman Antitrust Act because it restricted competition and monopolized its industry. This was the result of transferring the stock of all the subsidiaries to Standard Oil of New Jersey with the intent to use this company to dominate the oil industry. The court ordered the company to dissolve by divesting itself of all shares held in every Standard Oil subsidiary and to refrain from engaging in any future combination in violation of the Sherman Antitrust Act. Judgment for the United States.

CLAYTON ACT

The Clayton Act was passed in 1914 to strengthen the Sherman Antitrust Act. The Clayton Act prohibits the following actions where they tend to restrict competition and/or create a monopoly: exclusive dealing contracts which preclude purchasers from contracting with more than one seller; interlocking directorates where one or more directors of one corporation also serve as directors for another in a competitive or otherwise related business; acquisition by one corporation of stock in another corporation in a competitive or otherwise related field.

EXAMPLE | Thomas Andrews operates an electronics retail outlet which sells personal computers. Sixty percent of Andrews' sales are IBM computers. IBM informs Andrews that they wish to enter into an exclusive dealing contract with him in which he must promise to sell only IBM products in return for their promise to fulfill his needs. Andrews refuses at first, but then consents when IBM informs him they will stop all shipments to him if he does not sign the contract. Is this contract legal? No! It violates the Clayton Act in that it amounts to an exclusive dealing contract restricting other computer manufacturers from competing and causing Andrews to suffer a loss of profits he might have realized from the sales of other computers.

EXAMPLE | John D. Rockefeller, Henry Flagler, and Samuel Andrews serve as directors on the boards of Standard Oil of New Jersey (Exxon), Standard Oil of New York (Socony-Mobil), Standard Oil of Ohio (Sohio), and Standard Oil of California (Socal). Is it legal for Rockefeller and his partners to serve on the boards of these corporations? No! Interlocking directorates in corporations in a competitive field or industry are in violation of the Clayton Act.

ROBINSON-PATMAN ACT

The Robinson-Patman Act prohibits price discrimination in any commodity shipped through interstate commerce. The use of special discounts, rebates, or kickbacks by a corporation with a large market share of a product to influence another to sell, buy, ship, or use its product to the exclusion of its competitors is proscribed. Despite the act, it is becoming extremely difficult for small-town merchants to compete with the large nationwide chains, if only because the large nationwide chains are given bulk discounts (what many would consider a form of price discrimination).

EXAMPLE | Paul T. Simonsen and his partners purchased 900 of the 2,000 outstanding shares in South Improvement Company, which gave them control of the corporation. South Improvement Company contracted with three different railroads (New York Central, Erie, and Pennsylvania) wherein it was agreed that South Improvement Company would apportion shipments of oil from Simonsen Oil among the railroads, in return for a 45 percent rebate of shipping charges. In addition, it was agreed the railroads would pay a penalty to Simonsen Oil for every shipment made for one of Simonsen Oil's competitors. What recourse do the other oil refiners and other railroads have against Simonsen Oil and the three railroads? They can request that an injunction be granted to preclude Simonsen Oil and the railroads from restricting competition through price fixing. They may also sue for damages caused by the illegal contract in restraint of trade.

It is illegal for competitors in an industry to contract to set minimum prices or to raise prices across the board because this is an unreasonable restriction of fair competition that causes consumers and businesses to suffer losses.

EXAMPLE In Northumberland, New Hampshire, there are four gas stations: Shell, Gulf, Texaco, and Atlantic Richfield (Arco). The average price for no-lead gasoline in Northumberland has been $1.25. The proprietors of the Shell, Gulf, and Texaco gas stations enter into a contract to lower no-lead to $1.15 for three months for the purpose of driving their Arco competitor out of business. At that time prices will be gradually raised to $1.40. What recourse do the Arco proprietor and the citizens of Northumberland have against the proprietors of Shell, Gulf, and Texaco? They can bring an action claiming the three proprietors violated the Robinson-Patman Act in that they conspired to fix prices to restrict competition. Both the Arco proprietor and the citizens of Northumberland can recover damages for the losses they suffered due to the price-fixing arrangement.

The Great Atlantic & Pacific Tea Company v. FTC
440 U.S. 69, 99 S.Ct. 925 (1979)

The Federal Trade Commission (FTC) brought a suit against the Great Atlantic & Pacific Tea Company (A&P) alleging it violated the Robinson-Patman Act by accepting an illegal price discount.

A&P sold milk in the Chicago area under the name of Borden, the dairy supplying the milk. A&P realized it could cut costs by selling milk under its own label. A&P entered into negotiations with Borden, which agreed to deliver the milk at a discount amounting to $410,000 less than A&P had been paying previously. A&P was not satisfied with the offer and contacted other dairies. Bowman Dairy, a competitor of Borden, agreed to deliver the milk at an even greater discount. Borden had just invested over $5 million in a new dairy plant and was left in the predicament of not knowing whether to rebid. Borden decided to double its previous discount to $820,000. A&P accepted Borden's offer. The FTC brought an action when it learned of the agreement, claiming it restrained free trade.

The issue is whether A&P violated the Robinson-Patman Act by requesting Borden to give illegal price discounts.

The court said, ". . . we hold that a buyer who has done no more than accept the lower of two prices competitively offered does not violate . . . [the Robinson-Patman Act] provided the seller has a meeting competition defense." Meeting competition defense means the seller had readjusted its bid to meet or surpass a competitive bid. Here, Borden had met and exceeded the discount offered by its competitor, Bowman Dairy. Therefore, since Borden is not liable for restricting competition under the Robinson-Patman Act, A&P, who did nothing more than accept Borden's offer, is also not liable. Judgment for A&P.

FEDERAL TRADE COMMISSION

The Federal Trade Commission (FTC) is an administrative agency created in 1914 as part of an antitrust program along with the Clayton Act. The FTC is composed of five individuals appointed by the president with the advice and consent of the Senate. The purpose of the FTC is to prevent deceptive or otherwise unfair methods of competition in commerce. This includes administering the Sherman, Clayton, and Robinson-Patman antitrust laws. To carry out its duties, the FTC is entrusted with investigative powers. Upon discovering the practice of unfair competition, the FTC will hold a hearing to determine the truth of the allegations, after which the five-member board will render a decision. If they find the corporation guilty of unfair competition, they will issue a cease and desist order, the equivalent of an injunction. If the order is not complied with, the FTC may have its order affirmed by the District of Columbia (D.C.) Circuit Court of Appeals, to give the order judicial effect. Corporations wishing to contest the decision made by the FTC board may bring an appeal in the D.C. Circuit Court of Appeals. The court of appeals will usually affirm the FTC's decision unless it is arbitrary and capricious and bears no relation to the facts presented.

The majority of cease and desist orders declared by the FTC relate to false advertising, mislabeling, deceptive packaging, violation of trademarks through passing off an imitation as the original product, and commercial bribery through illegal kickbacks, discounts, and rebates.

EXAMPLE Francis Clark and Albert Gifford manufacture jeans of an inferior quality and pass them off as those made by the top designers by attaching various brand labels to them. They sell the jeans at a competitive price and are making huge profits. When several of the top designers find out, they notify the FTC which holds a hearing to determine the validity of their allegations. What remedies are available against Clark and Gifford? The FTC may issue a cease and desist order preventing them from engaging in the further practice of unfair competition. The top designers may sue Clark and Gifford in tort for violation of their trademarks and recoup profits they lost when consumers bought the imitation thinking it was the original. The designers may also recover damages caused by Clark and Gifford's selling of inferior merchandise under their brand names.

REVIEW QUESTIONS

1. Define a trust.
2. What is the function of the FTC?
3. Explain the significance of the Sherman Antitrust Act.
4. When it was originally enacted, was the Sherman Antitrust Act an effective tool for combating combinations formed to restrict competition and monopolize trade?
5. Explain the significance of the Clayton Act.

6. What was the purpose of the Robinson-Patman Act?

7. Explain the procedure undertaken by the FTC when a corporation is alleged to have used unfair methods of competition to restrain trade.

8. What remedy is available to the FTC and those injured by the unfair methods of competition?

9. Procter & Gamble Company was interested in gaining access to the liquid bleach market, which was dominated by Clorox with an 80 percent share. After careful research, Procter & Gamble decided it was more practical to merge with Clorox rather than to introduce a competitive brand. The FTC inquired into the merger alleging that the merger would substantially reduce competition in the liquid bleach industry since Procter & Gamble's advertising resources would strengthen Clorox's grip on the market and restrict competition because of the futility of competing with Procter & Gamble. The FTC claimed competition would be restored to the liquid bleach industry if Procter & Gamble introduced its own product. The FTC ordered Procter & Gamble to divest itself of Clorox. Procter & Gamble appealed. What result? FTC v. Procter & Gamble Co., 386 U.S. 568, 87 S.Ct. 1224 (1967).

10. Two successful grocery chains in Los Angeles, Von's Grocery Company and Shopping Bag Food Stores, merged to become the second largest grocery chain in the area. The number of small grocery companies in the Los Angeles area had been rapidly diminishing in recent years and continued to do so after the merger. The FTC claimed that the merger of the two corporations substantially lessened competition in the grocery business in violation of the Clayton Act. The FTC argued that the number of small chains was declining to the extent that the grocery business would soon be dominated by a few giant corporations. Should Von's Grocery Company be ordered to divest itself of the stock and assets of Shopping Bag Food Stores? United States v. Von's Grocery Co., 384 U.S. 270, 86 S.Ct. 1478 (1966).

INDEXES

SUBJECT INDEX

CASE INDEX